THE DEFINITIVE
BOB DYLAN
SONGBOOK

THE DEFINITIVE
BOB DYLAN
SONGBOOK

Amsco Publications
New York/London/Paris/Sydney/Copenhagen/Madrid/Berlin/Tokyo

Front cover photography:
Richard Noble
Back cover photography: left column
1. Morgan Renard 2. Sony Photo Archives 3. Sony Photo Archives
4. Unknown 5. Morgan Renard
Back cover photography: right column
1. Randee St. Nicholas 2. Mark Seliger 3. Morgan Renard
4. Joel Bernstein 5. Ken Regan
Spine photography:
Ken Regan

Project editors: Don Giller and Ed Lozano

The Publishers would like to extend a special thanks to
Jeff Rosen and Diane Lapson
for their help in the publication of this book.

Published 2001 by Amsco Publications,
A Division of Music Sales Corporation, New York

Order No. AM 961565
US International Standard Book Number: 0.8256.1774.X
UK International Standard Book Number: 0.7119.7509.7

Exclusive Distributors:
Music Sales Corporation
257 Park Avenue South, New York, NY 10010 USA
Music Sales Limited
8/9 Frith Street, London W1D 3JB England
Music Sales Pty. Limited
120 Rothschild Street, Rosebery, Sydney, NSW 2018, Australia

Printed in the United States of America by
Vicks Lithograph and Printing Corporation

CONTENTS

10,000 Men 8
2 X 2 10
4th Time Around 16
Abandoned Love 18
Absolutely Sweet Marie 13
Ain't Gonna Grieve 20
Alberta #1 23
Alberta #2 24
All Along the Watchtower 26
All I Really Want to Do 28
All the Tired Horses 22
Apple Suckling Tree 30
Are You Ready? 32
Arthur McBride 38
As I Went Out One Morning 40
Baby, I'm in the Mood for You 42
Baby, Stop Crying 44
Ballad in Plain D 50
Ballad of a Thin Man..................................52
The Ballad of Frankie Lee and Judas Priest 56
Ballad of Hollis Brown................................58
Belle Isle..35
Billy 60
Black Crow Blues..62
Black Diamond Bay......................................64
Blackjack Davey..66
Blood in My Eyes..68
Blowin' in the Wind 70
Bob Dylan's 115th Dream 47
Bob Dylan's Blues 55
Bob Dylan's Dream 72
Boots of Spanish Leather 74
Born in Time 79
Broke Down Engine 82
Brownsville Girl..76
Buckets of Rain 84
Can't Wait 86
Canadee-i-o 88
Cat's in the Well 90
Catfish 96
Changing of the Guards................................98
Chimes of Freedom 102
Clean-Cut Kid 108
Clothes Line 114
Cold Irons Bound 116
Corrina, Corrina 120
Country Pie 122
Covenant Woman 124
Dark Eyes 128
Day of the Locusts 130

Dead Man, Dead Man..................................93
Dear Landord 134
Death Is Not the End 136
The Death of Emmett Till 142
Delia 101
Desolation Row 144
Diamond Joe 146
Dignity 148
Dirge 154
Dirt Road Blues..156
Disease of Conceit 158
Do Right to Me, Baby 162
Don't Fall Apart on Me Tonight................164
Don't Think Twice, It's All Right 168
Don't Ya Tell Henry 170
Down Along the Cove 172
Down in the Flood 174
Down the Highway 176
Drifter's Escape 178
Driftin' Too Far from Shore 180
Emotionally Yours 182
Eternal Circle..184
Every Grain of Sand..................................186
Everything Is Broken 105
Farewell 192
Farewell Angelina......................................194
Father of Night 196
Foot of Pride 198
Forever Young 111
Frankie and Albert....................................202
Froggie Went A-Courtin' 204
From a Buick 6 206
Gates of Eden 208
George Jackson 210
Get Your Rocks Off! 212
Girl of the North Country........................119
God Knows 214
Goin' to Acapulco 220
Going, Going, Gone 222
Golden Loom 224
Gonna Change My Way of Thinking 226
Got My Mind Made Up 228
Gotta Serve Somebody................................234
The Groom's Still Waiting at the Altar......236
Guess I'm Doin' Fine 242
Gypsy Lou 244
Had a Dream About You, Baby 246
Handy Dandy 248
A Hard Rain's A-Gonna Fall 252
Hard Times 254

Hazel 139
Heart of Mine 151
Hero Blues 256
Highlands 189
Highway 61 Revisited 258
Honey, Just Allow Me One More Chance 201
Hurricane...260
I am a Lonesome Hobo 264
I and I 266
I Believe in You 268
I Don't Believe You 272
I Dreamed I Saw St. Augustine 274
I Pity the Poor Immigrant 276
I Shall Be Free 278
I Shall Be Released..............................280
I Threw It All Away 217
I Wanna Be Your Lover 282
I Want You..284
I'd Hate to Be You on That Dreadful Day 288
I'd Have You Anytime 290
I'll Be Your Baby Tonight......................292
I'll Keep It with Mine 294
I'll Remember You 296
Idiot Wind..298
If Dogs Run Free 302
If Not for You 231
If You See Her, Say Hello......................304
In Search of Little Sadie 239
In the Garden 306
In the Summertime 312
Is Your Love in Vain? 314
Isis 316
It Ain't Me Babe..................................318
It Takes a Lot to Laugh, It Takes a Train to Cry......263
It's All Over Now, Baby Blue 324
It's Alright, Ma (I'm Only Bleeding) 326
Jack-A-Roe...330
Jim Jones 332
Joey 336
John Brown 342
John Wesley Harding 287
Jokerman 344
Just Like a Woman...............................348
Just Like Tom Thumb's Blues.................350
Knockin' on Heaven's Door 301
Lay Down Your Weary Tune 352
Lay Lady Lay 309
Lenny Bruce 354
Leopard-Skin Pillbox Hat 356
Let Me Die in My Footsteps 358
License to Kill 360
Like a Rolling Stone.............................362
Lily, Rosemary and the Jack of Hearts 321
Little Maggie 368
Little Sadie...370
Living the Blues 372
Lo and Behold! 374
Lone Pilgrim 329

The Lonesome Death of Hattie Carroll 376
Long Ago, Far Away 382
Long Time Gone 384
Long-Distance Operator 386
Love Henry 335
Love Minus Zero/No Limit 388
Love Sick 390
Maggie's Farm 396
Make You Feel My Love 398
Mama, You Been on My Mind 400
Man Gave Names to All the Animals..................402
The Man in Me 406
Man in the Long Black Coat 339
Man of Peace 408
Masters of War....................................410
Maybe Someday...................................412
Meet Me in the Morning........................414
Million Dollar Bash 416
Million Miles 418
Minstrel Boy 424
Mixed Up Confusion 347
Money Blues 426
Most Likely You Go Your Way and I'll Go Mine....428
Most of the Time 430
Motorpsycho Nightmare 434
Mozambique 436
Mr. Tambourine Man 438
My Back Pages 444
Neighborhood Bully 446
Never Gonna Be the Same Again..................448
Never Say Goodbye 450
New Morning 452
New Pony 458
No Time to Think 460
Nobody 'Cept You................................466
North Country Blues.............................472
Not Dark Yet 474
Nothing Was Delivered 476
Obviously Five Believers 478
Odds and Ends 480
Oh, Sister..482
On a Night Like This 484
On the Road Again 486
One More Cup of Coffee (Valley Below) 488
One More Night 490
One More Weekend...............................365
One of Us Must Know (Sooner or Later) 492
One Too Many Mornings 494
Only a Hobo 496
Only a Pawn in Their Game 498
Open the Door, Homer 500
Outlaw Blues 502
Oxford Town 504
Paths of Victory 506
Peggy Day 508
Percy's Song 510
Playboys and Playgirls 512
Please, Mrs. Henry...............................514

Pledging My Time 516
Political World 518
Positively 4th Street 522
Precious Angel 524
Precious Memories...528
Pressing On 530
Property of Jesus 534
Queen Jane Approximately 538
Quinn the Eskimo (The Mighty Quinn)..................540
Quit Your Lowdown Ways....................................542
Ragged & Dirty...544
Rainy Day Women #12 & 35 546
Restless Farewell..548
Ring Them Bells 550
Rita May 554
Rocks and Gravel..556
Romance in Durango...558
Sad-Eyed Lady of the Lowlands 564
Sara 570
Saved 572
Saving Grace 576
Seeing the Real You at Last 582
Señor (Tales of Yankee Power).............................379
Series of Dreams 584
Seven Curses 588
Seven Days...393
She Belongs to Me 590
She's Your Lover Now 592
Shelter from the Storm 421
Shenandoah 596
Shooting Star 441
Shot of Love 602
Sign on the Window 455
Silent Weekend 608
Silvio 463
Simple Twist of Fate...605
Sittin' on Top of the World 610
Slow Train 612
Solid Rock 618
Something There Is About You 615
Song to Woody 622
Spanish Harlem Incident 624
Stack A Lee 626
Standing in the Doorway.......................................628
Step It Up and Go 630
Stuck Inside of Mobile
   with the Memphis Blues Again 632
Subterranean Homesick Blues 638
Sweetheart Like You 635
T.V. Talkin' Song 640
Talkin' World War III Blues....................................642
Tangled Up in Blue 644
Tears of Rage 650
Tell Me That It Isn't True.......................................652
Tell Me, Momma..647
Temporary Like Achilles 654
Things Have Changed 656
This Wheel's on Fire 662

Three Angels 664
Tight Connection to My Heart
   (Has Anybody Seen My Love) 659
'Til I Fell in Love with You 666
Time Passes Slowly...469
The Times They Are A-Changin' 668
To Be Alone with You 670
To Ramona 672
Tombstone Blues 674
Tomorrow Is a Long Time 533
Tonight I'll Be Staying Here with You 677
Too Much of Nothing 537
Tough Mama 680
Trouble 682
True Love Tends to Forget 561
Trust Yourself..685
Tryin' to Get to Heaven 688
Two Soldiers 692
Ugliest Girl in the World 694
Unbelievable 697
Under the Red Sky 702
Under Your Spell 706
Union Sundown...709
Up to Me...712
Visions of Johanna 714
Walkin' Down the Line 718
Wallflower 720
Walls of Red Wing...722
Wanted Man 724
Watching the River Flow 567
Watered-Down Love 726
We Better Talk This Over 729
Wedding Song 732
Went to See the Gypsy...579
What Can I Do for You? 734
What Good Am I? 599
What Was It You Wanted? 738
Whatcha Gonna Do 742
When He Returns 744
When I Paint My Masterpiece 750
When the Night Comes Falling from the Sky 747
When the Ship Comes In 752
When You Gonna Wake Up 754
Where Are You Tonight? 758
Where Teardrops Fall 762
Who Killed Davey Moore? 764
The Wicked Messenger 766
Wiggle Wiggle 786
Winterlude..768
With God on Our Side 770
World Gone Wrong..772
Yea! Heavy and a Bottle of Bread.........................774
You Ain't Going Nowhere 776
You Angel You 778
You're a Big Girl Now 780
You're Gonna Make Me Lonesome When You Go..782
You're Gonna Quit Me 784

10,000 Men

Words and Music by Bob Dylan

Additional lyrics

3. Ten thousand men on the move,
   Ten thousand men on the move,
   None of them doing nothin' that your mama wouldn't disapprove.

4. Ten thousand men digging for silver and gold,
   Ten thousand men digging for silver and gold,
   All clean shaven, all coming in from the cold.

5. Hey! Who could your lover be?
   Hey! Who could your lover be?
   Let me eat off his head so you can really see!

6. Ten thousand women all dressed in white,
   Ten thousand women all dressed in white,
   Standin' at my window wishing me goodnight.

7. Ten thousand men looking so lean and frail,
   Ten thousand men looking so lean and frail,
   Each one of 'em got seven wives, each one of 'em just out of jail.

8. Ten thousand women all sweepin' my room,
   Ten thousand women all sweepin' my room,
   Spilling my buttermilk, sweeping it up will a broom.

9. Ooh, baby, thank you for my tea!
   Baby, thank you for my tea!
   It's so sweet of you to be so nice to me.

2 x 2

Words and Music by Bob Dylan

11

Additional lyrics

Bridge #2:
How many tomorrows have they given away?
How many compared to yesterday?
How many more without any reward?
How many more can they afford?

Two by two, they stepped into the ark,
Two by two, they step in the dark.
Three by three, they're turning the key,
Four by four, they turn it some more,

One by one, they follow the sun,
Two by two, to another rendezvous.

Absolutely Sweet Marie

Words and Music by Bob Dylan

4th Time Around

Words and Music by Bob Dylan

Abandoned Love

Words and Music by Bob Dylan

Additional lyrics

2. My patron saint is a-fighting with a ghost
   He's always off somewhere when I need him most.
   The Spanish moon is rising on the hill
   But my heart is a-tellin' me I love ya still.

3. I come back to the town from the flaming moon
   I see you in the streets, I begin to swoon.
   I love to see you dress before the mirror
   Won't you let me in your room one time 'fore I finally disappear?

4. Everybody's wearing a disguise
   To hide what they've got left behind their eyes.
   But me, I can't cover what I am
   Wherever the children go I'll follow them.

5. I march in the parade of liberty
   But as long as I love you I'm not free.
   How long must I suffer such abuse
   Won't you let me see you smile one time before I turn you loose?

6. I've given up the game, I've got to leave,
   The pot of gold is only make-believe.
   The treasure can't be found by men who search
   Whose gods are dead and whose queens are in the church.

7. We sat in an empty theater and we kissed,
   I asked ya please to cross me off-a your list.
   My head tells me it's time to make a change
   But my heart is telling me I love ya but you're strange.

8. One more time at midnight, near the wall
   Take off your heavy make-up and your shawl.
   Won't you descend from the throne, from where you sit?
   Let me feel your love one more time before I abandon it.

Ain't Gonna Grieve

Words and Music by Bob Dylan

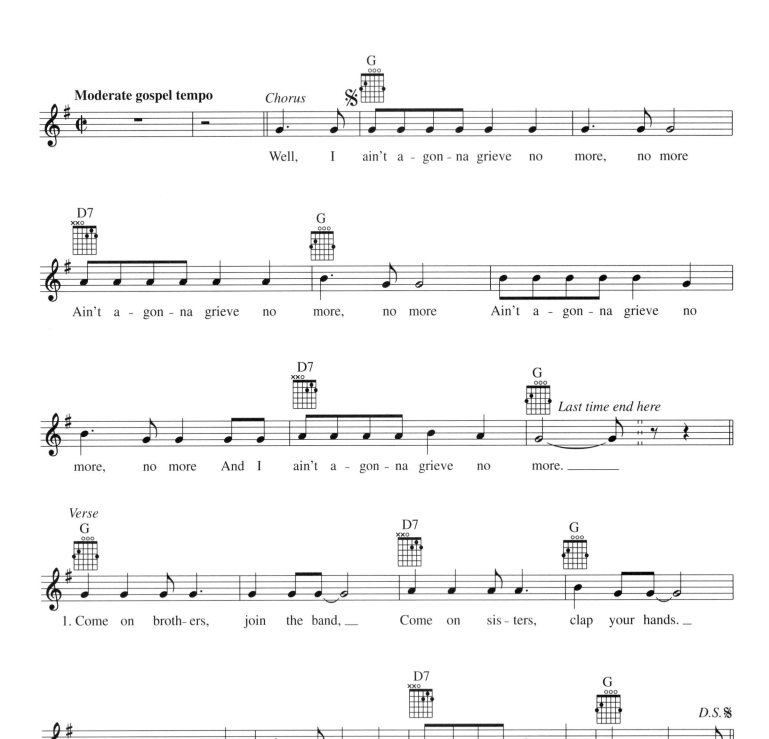

Additional lyrics

2. Brown and blue and white and black,
   All one color on the one-way track.
   We got this far and ain't a-goin' back
   And ain't a-gonna grieve no more.

   Chorus

3. We're gonna notify your next of kin,
   You're gonna raise the roof until the house falls in.
   If you get knocked down get up again,
   We ain't a-gonna grieve no more.

   Chorus

4. We'll sing this song all night long,
   Sing it to my baby from midnight on.
   She'll sing it to you when I'm dead and gone,
   Ain't a-gonna grieve no more.

   Chorus

All the Tired Horses

Words and Music by Bob Dylan

Moderately

No chord

All the tired hors - es in the sun, ___ How'm I s'posed to get an - y

rid - in' done. ___ Hmm _____

C Am Em

All the tired hors - es in the sun, ___ How'm I s'posed to get an - y

G C Am Em G

rid - in' done. ___ Hmm _____

C Am Em

All the tired hors - es in the sun, ___ How'm I s'posed to get an - y

G C Am Em G

repeat six times & fade

rid - in' done. ___ Hmm _____

Alberta #1

Words and Music by Bob Dylan

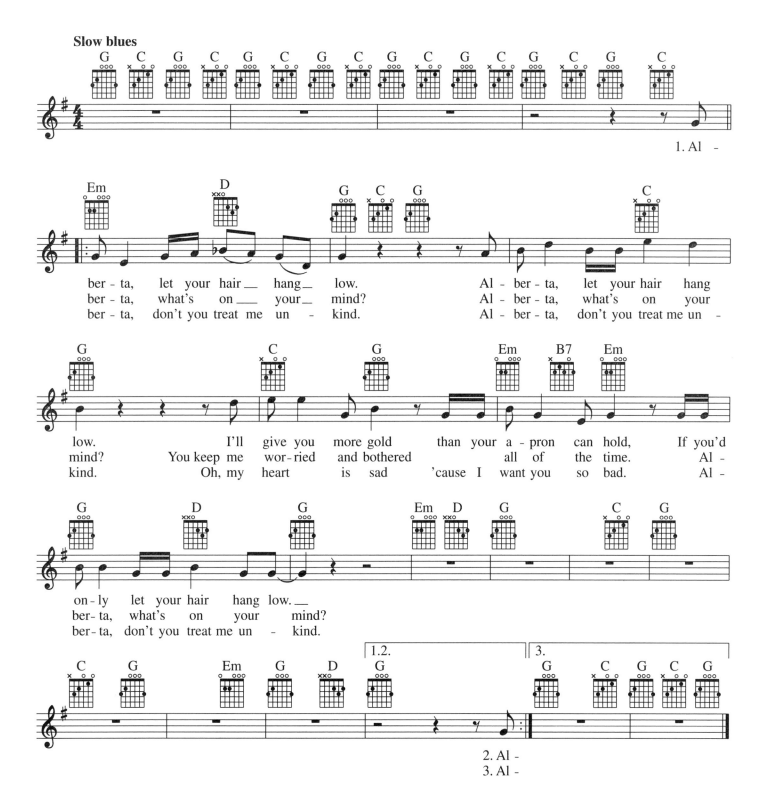

Slow blues

1. Al -

ber - ta, let your hair __ hang __ low.
ber - ta, what's on __ your __ mind?
ber - ta, don't you treat me un - kind.

Al - ber - ta, let your hair hang
Al - ber - ta, what's on your
Al - ber - ta, don't you treat me un -

low. I'll give you more gold than your a - pron can hold, If you'd
mind? You keep me wor - ried and bothered all of the time. Al -
kind. Oh, my heart is sad 'cause I want you so bad. Al -

on - ly let your hair hang low. __
ber - ta, what's on your mind?
ber - ta, don't you treat me un - kind.

1.2. 3.

2. Al -
3. Al -

Alberta #2

Words and Music by Bob Dylan

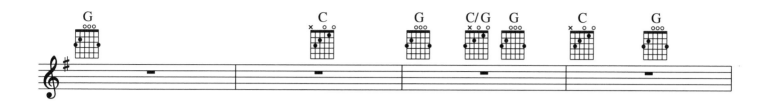

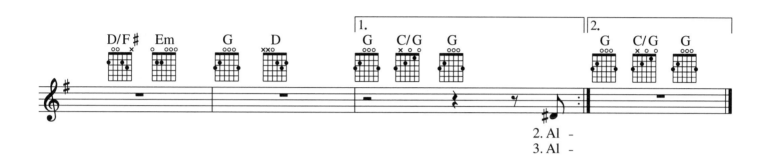

2. Al -
3. Al -

All Along the Watchtower

Words and Music by Bob Dylan

All I Really Want to Do

Words and Music by Bob Dylan

Additional lyrics

3. I ain't lookin' to block you up
   Shock or knock or lock you up,
   Analyze you, categorize you,
   Finalize you or advertise you.
   All I really want to do
   Is, baby, be friends with you.

4. I don't want to straight-face you,
   Race or chase you, track or trace you,
   Or disgrace you or displace you,
   Or define you or confine you.
   All I really want to do
   Is, baby, be friends with you.

5. I don't want to meet your kin,
   Make you spin or do you in,
   Or select you or dissect you,
   Or inspect you or reject you.
   All I really want to do
   Is, baby, be friends with you.

6. I don't want to fake you out,
   Take or shake or forsake you out,
   I ain't lookin' for you to feel like me,
   See like me or be like me.
   All I really want to do
   Is, baby, be friends with you.

Apple Suckling Tree

Words and Music by Bob Dylan

Moderately

Old man sail-in' in a din-ghy boat __ Down there __

__ Old man down __ is bait-in' a hook On there __

__ Gon-na pull man down __ on a suck-ling hook __ Gon-na

pull man in - to the suck-ling brook __ Oh yeah!

to Coda

Now, he's un-der-neath __ that ap-ple suck-ling tree __ Oh

yeah! Un-der that ap - ple suck-ling tree __ Oh

yeah! That's un - der - neath __ that tree There's gon - na

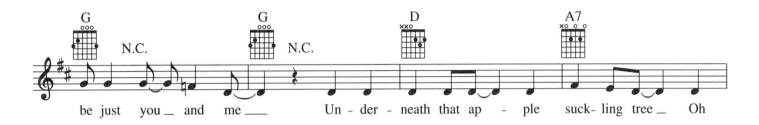

be just you __ and me ___ Un - der - neath that ap   - ple suck- ling tree __ Oh

yeah! I Now,

Additional lyrics

3. I push him back and I stand in line
   Oh yeah!
   Then I hush my Sadie and stand in line
   Oh yeah!
   Then I hush my Sadie and stand in line
   I get on board in two-eyed time
   Oh yeah!

4. Under that apple suckling tree
   Oh yeah!
   Under that apple suckling tree
   Oh yeah!
   Underneath that tree
   There's just gonna be you and me
   Underneath that apple suckling tree
   Oh yeah!

5. Now, who's on the table, who's to tell me?
   Oh yeah!
   Who's on the table, who's to tell me?
   Oh yeah!
   Who should I tell, oh, who should I tell?
   The forty-nine of you like bats out of hell
   Oh underneath that old apple suckling tree

Are You Ready?

Words and Music by Bob Dylan

am I read-y?   Am I

read-y,   am I read-y?

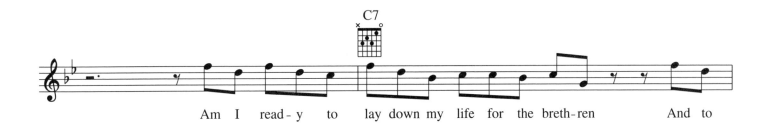

Am I read-y to   lay down my life for the breth-ren   And to

take up my cross?___   Have I sur-ren-dered___ to the will of God   Or am I

still   act-ing like the boss? ___   Am I   read-y,

hope I'm   read-y.   5. Are you

repeat & fade

Additional lyrics

3. When destruction cometh swiftly
   And there's no time to say a fare-thee-well,
   Have you decided whether you want to be
   In heaven or in hell?

   Are you ready, are you ready?

4. Have you got some unfinished business?
   Is there something holding you back?
   Are you thinking for yourself
   Or are you following the pack?

   Are you ready, hope you're ready.
   Are you ready?

5. Are you ready for the judgment?
   Are you ready for that terrible swift sword?
   Are you ready for Armageddon?
   Are you ready for the day of the Lord?

   Are you ready, I hope you're ready.

Belle Isle

New Music by Bob Dylan

beau - ty, "Fair maid - en where do you be - long? Are you

from heav - en de - scend - ed, A - bid - ing in Cu - pid's fair throne?" "Young

man, I will tell you a se - cret. It's true I'm a maid that is

poor And to part from my vows and my prom - ise, That's

more than my heart can en - dure." "There - fore, I re - main at my

ser - vice, And go through all my hard - ship and toil, And

wait for the lad that has left me All a - lone on the banks of Belle Isle."

Arthur McBride

Words and Music Arranged by Bob Dylan

Moderate waltz (in one)

1. Oh, me and my cous- in, one Ar- thur Mc- Bride, As we went a- wal- kin' down by the sea- side, Mark now what fol- lowed and what did _____ be- tide, For it be- in' on Christ- mas morn- in'. _____ Now, for re- cre- a- tion we went on a tramp, And we met Ser- geant Nap- per and Cor- p'ral ___ Vamp, And a

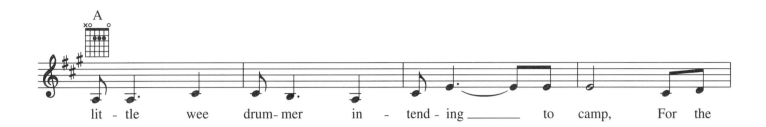

lit - tle   wee   drum- mer   in - tend - ing _____ to   camp,   For   the

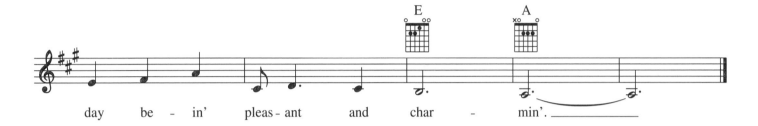

day   be - in'   pleas - ant   and   char - min'. _____

Additional lyrics

2. "Good morning, good morning," the Sergeant he cried,
   "And the same to you, gentlemen," we did reply,
   Intending no harm but meant to pass by,
   For it bein' on Christmas mornin'.
   "But," says he, "My fine fellows, if you will enlist,
   Ten guineas in gold I'll stick in your fist,
   And a crown in the bargain for to kick up the dust,
   And drink the king's health in the morning.

3. "For a soldier, he leads a very fine life,
   And he always is blessed with a charming young wife,
   And he pays all his debts without sorrow or strife,
   And he always lives pleasant and charmin'.
   And a soldier, he always is decent and clean,
   In the finest of clothing he's constantly seen,
   While other poor fellows go dirty and mean,
   And sup on thin gruel in the morning."

Instrumental

4. "But," says Arthur, "I wouldn't be proud of your clothes,
   For you've only the lend of them, as I suppose,
   But you dare not change them one night, for you know
   If you do, you'll be flogged in the morning.
   And although that we're single and free,
   We take great delight in our own company.
   We have no desire strange places to see,
   Although that your offers are charming.

5. "And we have no desire to take your advance,
   All hazards and dangers we barter on chance,
   For you'd have no scruples for to send us to France,
   Where we would get shot without warning."
   "Oh no," says the Sergeant, "I'll have no such chat,
   And neither will I take it from snappy young brats,
   For if you insult me with one other word,
   I'll cut off your heads in the morning."

6. And Arthur and I, we soon drew our hogs,
   And we scarce gave them time to draw their own blades
   When a trusty shillelagh came over their head
   And bid them take that as fair warning.
   And their old rusty rapiers that hung by their sides,
   We flung them as far as we could in the tide.
   "Now take them up, devils!" cried Arthur McBride,
   "And temper their edge in the mornin'!"

7. And the little wee drummer, we flattened his bow,
   And we made a football of his rowdy-dow-dow,
   Threw it in the tide for to rock and to roll,
   And bade it a tedious returning.
   And we havin' no money, paid them off in cracks.
   We paid no respect to their two bloody backs,
   And we lathered them there like a pair of wet sacks,
   And left them for dead in the morning.

8. And so, to conclude and to finish disputes,
   We obligingly asked if they wanted recruits,
   For we were the lads who would give them hard clouts
   And bid them look sharp in the mornin'.

Instrumental

9. Oh, me and my cousin, one Arthur McBride,
   As we went a-walkin' down by the seaside,
   Mark now what followed and what did betide,
   For it bein' on Christmas mornin'.

As I Went Out One Morning

Words and Music by Bob Dylan

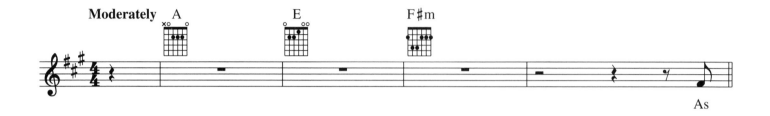

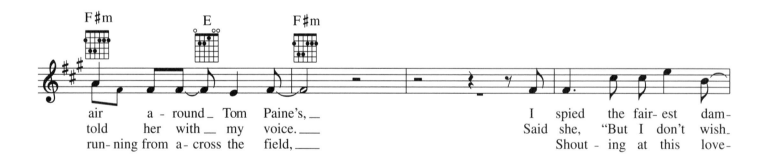

I went out ___ one morn - ing ___ To breathe the
part from me ___ this mo - ment," _____ I
Just then ___ Tom Paine, ___ him - self, ___ Came

air a - round_ Tom Paine's, ___ I spied the fair - est dam-
told her with ___ my voice. ___ Said she, "But I don't wish_
run - ning from a - cross the field, ___ Shout - ing at this love-

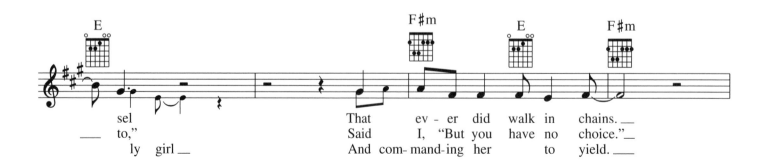

sel That ev - er did walk in chains. ___
___ to," Said I, "But you have no choice." ___
ly girl ___ And com - mand - ing her to yield. ___

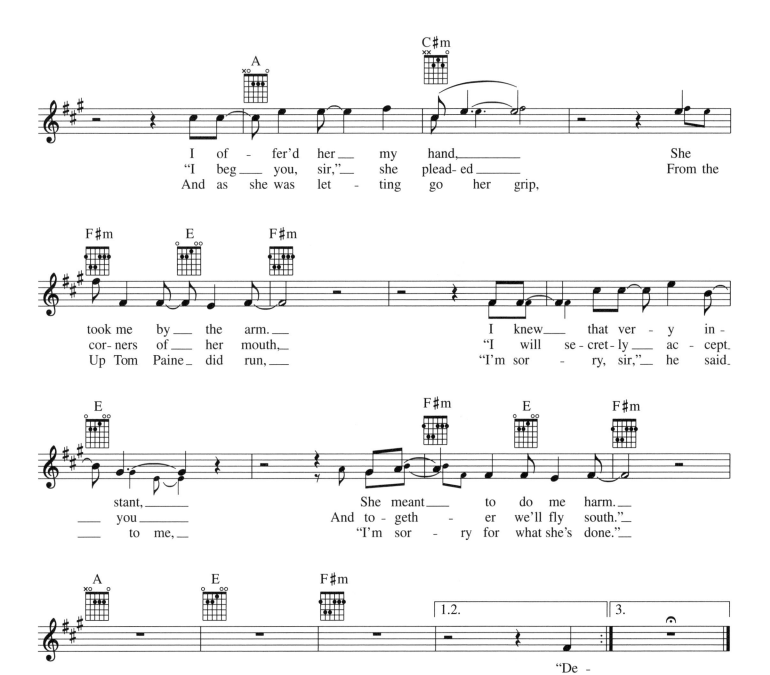

I of - fer'd her ___ my hand,_____ She
"I beg ___ you, sir,"__ she plead- ed _____ From the
And as she was let - ting go her grip,

took me by ___ the arm. ___ I knew___ that ver - y in -
cor - ners of ___ her mouth,__ "I will se - cret- ly ___ ac - cept_
Up Tom Paine_ did run, ___ "I'm sor - ry, sir,"__ he said_

stant,_____ She meant___ to do me harm. __
___ you_____ And to - geth - er we'll fly south."__
___ to me, __ "I'm sor - ry for what she's done."__

"De -

Baby, I'm in the Mood for You

Words and Music by Bob Dylan

Additional lyrics

2. Sometimes I'm in the mood, Lord, I had my overflowin' fill
   Sometimes I'm in the mood, I'm gonna make out my final will
   Sometimes I'm in the mood, I'm gonna head for the walkin' hill
   But then again, but then again, I said oh, I said oh, I said
   Oh babe, I'm in the mood for you.

3. Sometimes I'm in the mood, I wanna lay right down and die
   Sometimes I'm in the mood, I wanna climb up to the sky
   Sometimes I'm in the mood, I'm gonna laugh until I cry
   But then again, I said again, I said again, I said
   Oh babe, I'm in the mood for you.

4. Sometimes I'm in the mood, I'm gonna sleep in my pony's stall
   Sometimes I'm in the mood, I ain't gonna do nothin' at all
   Sometimes I'm in the mood, I wanna fly like a cannon ball
   But then again, but then again, I said oh, I said oh, I said
   Oh babe, I'm in the mood for you.

5. Sometimes I'm in the mood, I wanna back up against the wall
   Sometimes I'm in the mood, I wanna run till I have to crawl
   Sometimes I'm in the mood, I ain't gonna do nothin' at all
   But then again, but then again, I said oh, I said oh, I said
   Oh babe, I'm in the mood for you.

6. Sometimes I'm in the mood, I wanna change my house around
   Sometimes I'm in the mood, I'm gonna make a change in this here town
   Sometimes I'm in the mood, I'm gonna change the world around
   But then again, but then again, I said oh, I said oh, I said
   Oh babe, I'm in the mood for you.

Baby, Stop Crying

Words and Music by Bob Dylan

Slowly

Verse

1. You been down to the bot-tom with a bad man, babe, But you're_ back where you be-long._

Go get me my pis-tol, babe,

Chorus

Hon-ey, I can't tell _ right from wrong. Ba-by, please stop

cry-ing, stop cry-ing, stop cry-ing Ba-by, please stop cry-ing,

stop cry-ing, stop cry-ing Ba-by, please stop cry-ing.

You know, I know, the sun will al-ways shine So ba-by,

please stop cry-ing 'cause it's tear - ing up my __ mind. __

1.-3.

4.

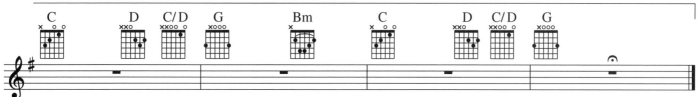

Additional lyrics

2. Go down to the river, babe,
   Honey, I will meet you there.
   Go down to the river, babe,
   Honey, I will pay your fare.

   Chorus

3. If you're looking for assistance, babe,
   Or if you just want some company
   Or if you just want a friend you can talk to,
   Honey, come and see about me.

   Chorus

4. You been hurt so many times
   And I know what you're thinking of.
   Well, I don't have to be no doctor, babe,
   To see that you're madly in love.

   Chorus

Bob Dylan's 115th Dream

Words and Music by Bob Dylan

48

Additional lyrics

2. "I think I'll call it America"
   I said as we hit land
   I took a deep breath
   I fell down, I could not stand
   Captain Arab he started
   Writing up some deeds
   He said, "Let's set up a fort
   And start buying the place with beads"
   Just then this cop comes down the street
   Crazy as a loon
   He throw us all in jail
   For carryin' harpoons

3. Ah me I busted out
   Don't even ask me how
   I went to get some help
   I walked by a Guernsey cow
   Who directed me down
   To the Bowery slums
   Where people carried signs around
   Saying, "Ban the bums"
   I jumped right into line
   Sayin', "I hope that I'm not late"
   When I realized I hadn't eaten
   For five days straight

4. I went into a restaurant
   Lookin' for the cook
   I told them I was the editor
   Of a famous etiquette book
   The waitress he was handsome
   He wore a powder blue cape
   I ordered some suzette, I said
   "Could you please make that crepe"
   Just then the whole kitchen exploded
   From boilin' fat
   Food was flying everywhere
   And I left without my hat

5. Now, I didn't mean to be nosy
   But I went into a bank
   To get some bail for Arab
   And all the boys back in the tank
   They asked me for some collateral
   And I pulled down my pants
   They threw me in the alley
   When up comes this girl from France
   Who invited me to her house
   I went, but she had a friend
   Who knocked me out
   And robbed my boots
   And I was on the street again

6. Well, I rapped upon a house
   With the U.S. flag upon display
   I said, "Could you help me out
   I got some friends down the way"
   The man says, "Get out of here
   I'll tear you limb from limb"
   I said, "You know they refused Jesus, too"
   He said, "You're not Him
   Get out of here before I break your bones
   I ain't your pop"
   I decided to have him arrested
   And I went looking for a cop

7. I ran right outside
   And I hopped inside a cab
   I went out the other door
   This Englishman said, "Fab"
   As he saw me leap a hot dog stand
   And a chariot that stood
   Parked across from a building
   Advertising brotherhood
   I ran right through the front door
   Like a hobo sailor does
   But it was just a funeral parlor
   And the man asked me who I was

8. I repeated that my friends
   Were all in jail, with a sigh
   He gave me his card
   He said, "Call me if they die"
   I shook his hand and said goodbye
   Ran out to the street
   When a bowling ball came down the road
   And knocked me off my feet
   A pay phone was ringing
   It just about blew my mind
   When I picked it up and said hello
   This foot came through the line

9. Well, by this time I was fed up
   At tryin' to make a stab
   At bringin' back any help
   For my friends and Captain Arab
   I decided to flip a coin
   Like either heads or tails
   Would let me know if I should go
   Back to ship or back to jail
   So I hocked my sailor suit
   And I got a coin to flip
   It came up tails
   It rhymed with sails
   So I made it back to the ship

10. Well, I got back and took
    The parkin' ticket off the mast
    I was ripping it to shreds
    When this coastguard boat went past
    They asked me my name
    And I said, "Captain Kidd"
    They believed me but
    They wanted to know
    What exactly that I did
    I said for the Pope of Eruke
    I was employed
    They let me go right away
    They were very paranoid

11. Well, the last I heard of Arab
    He was stuck on a whale
    That was married to the deputy
    Sheriff of the jail
    But the funniest thing was
    When I was leavin' the bay
    I saw three ships a-sailin'
    They were all heading my way
    I asked the captain what his name was
    And how come he didn't drive a truck
    He said his name was Columbus
    I just said, "Good luck."

Ballad in Plain D

Words and Music by Bob Dylan

Additional lyrics

2. Through young summer's breeze, I stole her away
   From her mother and sister, though close did they stay.
   Each one of them suffering from the failures of their day,
   With strings of guilt they tried hard to guide us.

3. Of the two sisters, I loved the young.
   With sensitive instincts, she was the creative one.
   The constant scapegoat, she was easily undone
   By the jealousy of others around her.

4. For her parasite sister, I had no respect,
   Bound by her boredom, her pride to protect.
   Countless visions of the other she'd reflect
   As a crutch for her scenes and her society.

5. Myself, for what I did, I cannot be excused,
   The changes I was going through can't even be used,
   For the lies that I told her in hopes not to lose
   The could-be dream-lover of my lifetime.

6. With unknown consciousness, I possessed in my grip
   A magnificent mantelpiece, though its heart being chipped,
   Noticing not that I'd already slipped
   To a sin of love's false security.

7. From silhouetted anger to manufactured peace,
   Answers of emptiness, voice vacancies,
   Till the tombstones of damage read me no questions but, "Please,
   What's wrong and what's exactly the matter?"

8. And so it did happen like it could have been foreseen,
   The timeless explosion of fantasy's dream.
   At the peak of the night, the king and the queen
   Tumbled all down into pieces.

9. "The tragic figure!" her sister did shout,
   "Leave her alone, God damn you, get out!"
   And I in my armor, turning about
   And nailing her to the ruins of her pettiness.

10. Beneath a bare light bulb the plaster did pound
    Her sister and I in a screaming battleground.
    And she in between, the victim of sound,
    Soon shattered as a child 'neath her shadows.

11. All is gone, all is gone, admit it, take flight.
    I gagged twice, doubled, tears blinding my sight.
    My mind it was mangled, I ran into the night
    Leaving all of love's ashes behind me.

12. The wind knocks my window, the room it is wet.
    The words to say I'm sorry, I haven't found yet.
    I think of her often and hope whoever she's met
    Will be fully aware of how precious she is.

13. Ah, my friends from the prison, they ask unto me,
    "How good, how good does it feel to be free?"
    And I answer them most mysteriously,
    "Are birds free from the chains of the skyway?"

Ballad of a Thin Man

Words and Music by Bob Dylan

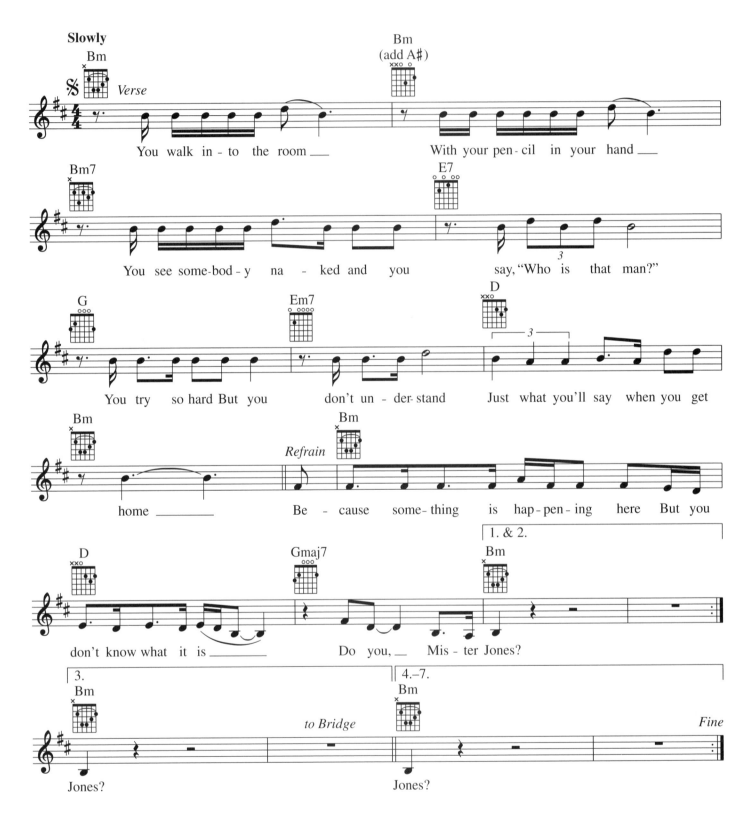

You have man - y con - tacts ___ A- mong the lum- ber- jacks To

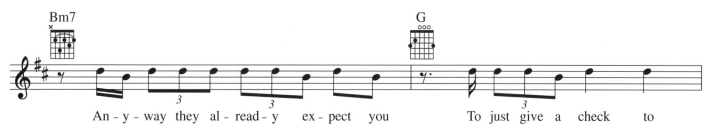

get you facts when some-one at-tacks your im-ag-i - na - tion But no-bod-y has an- y res-pect

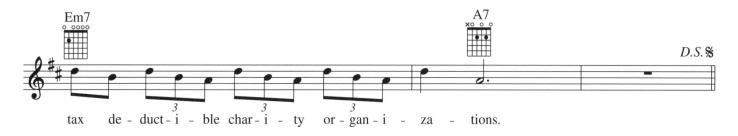

An - y - way they al - read - y ex - pect you To just give a check to

tax de - duct - i - ble char - i - ty or - gan - i - za - tions.

2. You raise up your head
   And you ask, "Is this where it is?"
   And somebody points to you and says,
   "It's his."
   And you say, "What's mine?"
   And somebody else says, "Where what is?"
   And you say, "Oh my God
   Am I here all alone?"

   Because something is happening here
   But you don't know what it is
   Do you, Mister Jones?

3. You hand in your ticket
   And you go watch the geek
   Who immediately walks up to you
   When he hears you speak.
   And says, "How does it feel
   To be such a freak?"
   And you say, "Impossible,"
   As he hands you a bone

   Because something is happening here
   But you don't know what it is
   Do you, Mister Jones?

   Bridge:
   You have many contacts
   Among the lumberjacks
   To get you facts
   When someone attacks your imagination
   But nobody has any respect
   Anyway they already expect you
   To just give a check
   To tax-deductible charity organizations

4. You've been with the professors
   And they've all liked your looks
   With great lawyers you have
   Discussed lepers and crooks
   You've been through all of
   F. Scott Fitzgerald's books
   You're very well read
   It's well known

   Because something is happening here
   But you don't know what it is
   Do you, Mister Jones?

5. Well, the sword swallower, he comes up to you
   And then he kneels
   He crosses himself
   And then he clicks his high heels
   And without further notice
   He asks you how it feels
   And he says, "Here is your throat back
   Thanks for the loan"

   Because something is happening here
   But you don't know what it is
   Do you, Mister Jones?

6. Now you see this one-eyed midget
   Shouting the word "NOW"
   And you say, "For what reason?"
   And he says, "How?"
   And you say, "What does this mean?"
   And he screams back, "You're a cow
   Give me some milk
   Or else go home"

   Because something is happening here
   But you don't know what it is
   Do you, Mister Jones?

7. Well, you walk into the room
   Like a camel and then you frown
   You put your eyes in your pocket
   And your nose on the ground
   There ought to be a law
   Against you comin' around
   You should be made
   To wear earphones

   Because something is happening here
   But you don't know what it is
   Do you, Mister Jones?

Bob Dylan's Blues

Words and Music by Bob Dylan

Bright

Well, the Lone Rang - er and Ton - to They are rid - in' down the line _

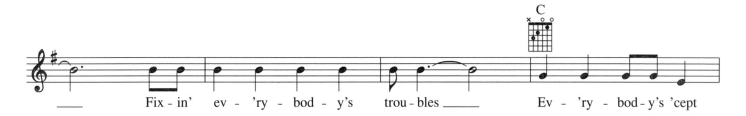

_____ Fix - in' ev - 'ry - bod - y's trou - bles _____ Ev - 'ry - bod - y's 'cept

repeat four times

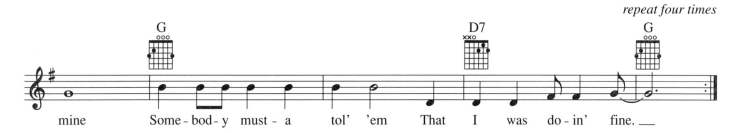

mine Some - bod - y must - a tol' 'em That I was do - in' fine. ___

Additional lyrics

2. Oh you five and ten cent women
   With nothin' in your heads
   I got a real gal I'm lovin'
   And Lord I'll love her till I'm dead
   Go away from my door and my window too
   Right now

3. Lord, I ain't goin' down to no race track
   See no sports car run
   I don't have no sports car
   And I don't even care to have one
   I can walk anytime around the block

4. Well, the wind keeps a-blowin' me
   Up and down the street
   With my hat in my hand
   And my boots on my feet
   Watch out so you don't step on me

5. Well, lookit here buddy
   You want to be like me
   Pull out your six-shooter
   And rob every bank you can see
   Tell the judge I said it was all right
   Yes!

The Ballad of Frankie Lee and Judas Priest

Words and Music by Bob Dylan

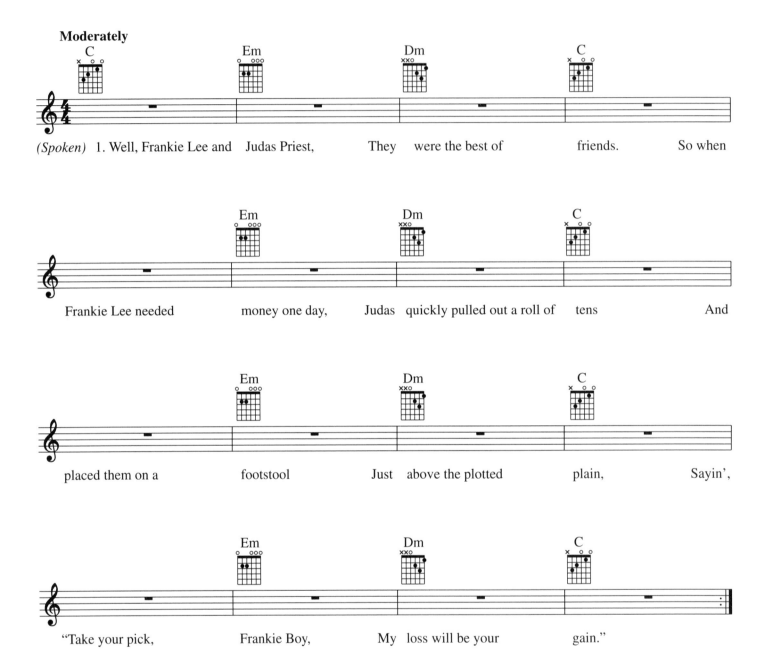

Moderately

(Spoken) 1. Well, Frankie Lee and Judas Priest, They were the best of friends. So when

Frankie Lee needed money one day, Judas quickly pulled out a roll of tens And

placed them on a footstool Just above the plotted plain, Sayin',

"Take your pick, Frankie Boy, My loss will be your gain."

Additional lyrics

2. Well, Frankie Lee, he sat right down
   And put his fingers to his chin,
   But with the cold eyes of Judas on him,
   His head began to spin.
   "Would ya please not stare at me like that," he said,
   "It's just my foolish pride,
   But sometimes a man must be alone
   And this is no place to hide."

3. Well, Judas, he just winked and said,
   "All right, I'll leave you here,
   But you'd better hurry up and choose
   Which of those bills you want,
   Before they all disappear."
   "I'm gonna start my pickin' right now,
   Just tell me where you'll be."

4. Judas pointed down the road
   And said, "Eternity!"
   "Eternity?" said Frankie Lee,
   With a voice as cold as ice.
   "That's right," said Judas Priest, "Eternity,
   Though you might call it 'Paradise.'"

5. "I don't call it anything,"
   Said Frankie Lee with a smile.
   "All right," said Judas Priest,
   "I'll see you after a while."

6. Well, Frankie Lee, he sat back down,
   Feelin' low and mean,
   When just then a passing stranger
   Burst upon the scene,
   Saying, "Are you Frankie Lee, the gambler,
   Whose father is deceased?
   Well, if you are,
   There's a fellow callin' you down the road
   And they say his name is Priest."

7. "Oh, yes, he is my friend,"
   Said Frankie Lee in fright,
   "I do recall him very well,
   In fact, he just left my sight."
   "Yes, that's the one," said the stranger,
   As quiet as a mouse,
   "Well, my message is, he's down the road,
   Stranded in a house."

8. Well, Frankie Lee, he panicked,
   He dropped ev'rything and ran
   Until he came up to the spot
   Where Judas Priest did stand.
   "What kind of house is this," he said,
   "Where I have come to roam?"
   "It's not a house," said Judas Priest,
   "It's not a house . . . it's a home."

9. Well, Frankie Lee, he trembled,
   He soon lost all control
   Over ev'rything which he had made
   While the mission bells did toll.
   He just stood there staring
   At that big house as bright as any sun,
   With four and twenty windows
   And a woman's face in ev'ry one.

10. Well, up the stairs ran Frankie Lee
    With a soulful, bounding leap,
    And, foaming at the mouth,
    He began to make his midnight creep.
    For sixteen nights and days he raved,
    But on the seventeenth he burst
    Into the arms of Judas Priest,
    Which is where he died of thirst.

11. No one tried to say a thing
    When they took him out in jest,
    Except, of course, the little neighbor boy
    Who carried him to rest.
    And he just walked along, alone,
    With his guilt so well concealed,
    And muttered underneath his breath,
    "Nothing is revealed."

12. Well, the moral of the story,
    The moral of this song,
    Is simply that one should never be
    Where one does not belong.
    So when you see your neighbor carryin' somethin',
    Help him with his load,
    And don't go mistaking Paradise
    For that home across the road.

Ballad of Hollis Brown

Words and Music by Bob Dylan

Additional lyrics

2. Your baby's eyes look crazy
   They're a-tuggin' at your sleeve
   Your baby's eyes look crazy
   They're a-tuggin' at your sleeve
   You walk the floor and wonder why
   With every breath you breathe

3. The rats have got your flour
   Bad blood it got your mare
   The rats have got your flour
   Bad blood it got your mare
   If there's anyone that knows
   Is there anyone that cares?

4. You prayed to the Lord above
   Oh please send you a friend
   You prayed to the Lord above
   Oh please send you a friend
   Your empty pockets tell yuh
   That you ain't a-got no friend

5. Your babies are crying louder
   It's pounding on your brain
   Your babies are crying louder now
   It's pounding on your brain
   Your wife's screams are stabbin' you
   Like the dirty drivin' rain

6. Your grass it is turning black
   There's no water in your well
   Your grass is turning black
   There's no water in your well
   You spent your last lone dollar
   On seven shotgun shells

7. Way out in the wilderness
   A cold coyote calls
   Way out in the wilderness
   A cold coyote calls
   Your eyes fix on the shotgun
   That's hangin' on the wall

8. Your brain is a-bleedin'
   And your legs can't seem to stand
   Your brain is a-bleedin'
   And your legs can't seem to stand
   Your eyes fix on the shotgun
   That you're holdin' in your hand

9. There's seven breezes a-blowin'
   All around the cabin door
   There's seven breezes a-blowin'
   All around the cabin door
   Seven shots ring out
   Like the ocean's pounding roar

10. There's seven people dead
    On a South Dakota farm
    There's seven people dead
    On a South Dakota farm
    Somewhere in the distance
    There's seven new people born

Billy

Words and Music by Bob Dylan

1. There's guns a - cross the riv - er aim - in' at ya ___

Law - man on your trail, ___ he'd like to catch ___ ya ___

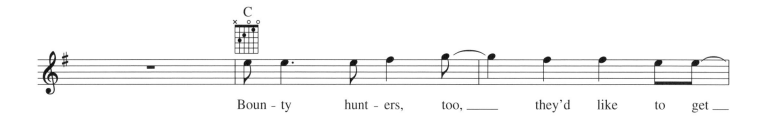

Boun - ty hunt - ers, too, ___ they'd like to get ___

___ ya ___ Bil - ly, they don't like ___

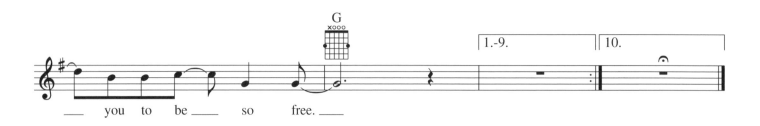

___ you to be ___ so free. ___

Additional lyrics

2. Campin' out all night on the berenda
   Dealin' cards 'til dawn in the hacienda
   Up to Boot Hill they'd like to send ya
   Billy, don't you turn your back on me.

3. Playin' around with some sweet señorita
   Into her dark hallway she will lead ya
   In some lonesome shadows she will greet ya
   Billy, you're so far away from home.

4. There's eyes behind the mirrors in empty places
   Bullet holes and scars between the spaces
   There's always one more notch and ten more paces
   Billy, and you're walkin' all alone.

5. They say that Pat Garrett's got your number
   So sleep with one eye open when you slumber
   Every little sound just might be thunder
   Thunder from the barrel of his gun.

6. Guitars will play your grand finale
   Down in some Tularosa alley,
   Maybe in the Rio Pecos valley
   Billy, you're so far away from home.

7. There's always some new stranger sneakin' glances
   Some trigger-happy fool willin' to take chances
   And some old whore from San Pedro to make advances
   Advances on your spirit and your soul.

8. The businessmen from Taos want you to go down
   They've hired Pat Garrett to force a showdown.
   Billy, don't it make ya feel so low-down
   To be shot down by the man who was your friend?

9. Hang on to your woman if you got one
   Remember in El Paso, once, you shot one.
   She may have been a whore, but she was a hot one
   Billy, you been runnin' for so long.

10. Guitars will play your grand finale
    Down in some Tularosa alley
    Maybe in the Rio Pecos valley
    Billy, you're so far away from home.

Black Crow Blues

Words and Music by Bob Dylan

Medium blues tempo

Additional lyrics

2. I was standin' at the side road
   Listenin' to the billboard knock.
   Standin' at the side road
   Listenin' to the billboard knock.
   Well, my wrist was empty
   But my nerves were kickin',
   Tickin' like a clock.

3. If I got anything you need, babe,
   Let me tell you in front.
   If I got anything you need, babe,
   Let me tell you in front.
   You can come to me sometime,
   Night time, day time,
   Any time you want.

4. Sometimes I'm thinkin' I'm
   Too high to fall.
   Sometimes I'm thinkin' I'm
   Too high to fall.
   Other times I'm thinkin' I'm
   So low I don't know
   If I can come up at all.

5. Black crows in the meadow
   Across a broad highway.
   Black crows in the meadow
   Across a broad highway.
   Though it's funny, honey,
   I just don't feel much like a
   Scarecrow today.

Black Diamond Bay

Words and Music by Bob Dylan and Jacques Levy

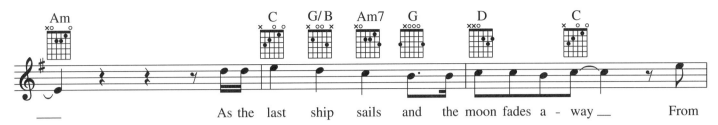

As the last ship sails and the moon fades a - way __ From

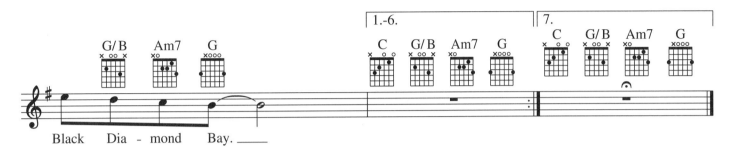

Black Dia - mond Bay. ____

Additional lyrics

2. As the mornin' light breaks open, the Greek comes down
And he asks for a rope and a pen that will write.
"Pardon, monsieur," the desk clerk says,
Carefully removes his fez,
"Am I hearin' you right?"
And as the yellow fog is liftin'
The Greek is quickly headin' for the second floor.
She passes him on the spiral staircase
Thinkin' he's the Soviet Ambassador,
She starts to speak, but he walks away
As the storm clouds rise and the palm branches sway
On Black Diamond Bay.

3. A soldier sits beneath the fan
Doin' business with a tiny man who sells him a ring.
Lightning strikes, the lights blow out.
The desk clerk wakes and begins to shout,
"Can you see anything?"
Then the Greek appears on the second floor
In his bare feet with a rope around his neck,
While a loser in the gambling room lights up a candle,
Says, "Open up another deck."
But the dealer says, "Attendez-vous, s'il vous plait,"
As the rain beats down and the cranes fly away
From Black Diamond Bay.

4. The desk clerk heard the woman laugh
As he looked around the aftermath and the soldier got tough.
He tried to grab the woman's hand,
Said, "Here's a ring, it cost a grand."
She said, "That ain't enough."
Then she ran upstairs to pack her bags
While a horse-drawn taxi waited at the curb.
She passed the door that the Greek had locked,
Where a handwritten sign read, "Do Not Disturb."
She knocked upon it anyway
As the sun went down and the music did play
On Black Diamond Bay.

5. "I've got to talk to someone quick!"
But the Greek said, "Go away," and he kicked the chair to the floor.
He hung there from the chandelier.
She cried, "Help, there's danger near
Please open up the door!"
Then the volcano erupted
And the lava flowed down from the mountain high above.
The soldier and the tiny man were crouched in the corner
Thinking of forbidden love.
But the desk clerk said, "It happens every day,"
As the stars fell down and the fields burned away
On Black Diamond Bay.

6. As the island slowly sank
The loser finally broke the bank in the gambling room.
The dealer said, "It's too late now.
You can take your money, but I don't know how
You'll spend it in the tomb."
The tiny man bit the soldier's ear
As the floor caved in and the boiler in the basement blew,
While she's out on the balcony, where a stranger tells her,
"My darling, je vous aime beaucoup."
She sheds a tear and then begins to pray
As the fire burns on and the smoke drifts away
From Black Diamond Bay.

7. I was sittin' home alone one night in L.A.,
Watchin' old Cronkite on the seven o'clock news.
It seems there was an earthquake that
Left nothin' but a Panama hat
And a pair of old Greek shoes.
Didn't seem like much was happenin',
So I turned it off and went to grab another beer.
Seems like every time you turn around
There's another hard-luck story that you're gonna hear
And there's really nothin' anyone can say
And I never did plan to go anyway
To Black Diamond Bay.

Blackjack Davey

Traditional, arranged by Bob Dylan

Moderately

guitar N.C.

Am

voice

1. Black Jack Da-vey come a - rid-in' on back, A-

Em

whis-tl-in' loud and mer-ry. _____ Made the woods a - round him ring, And he

G D   Am

charmed the heart of a la-dy, _____ Charmed the heart _ of a

la - dy. _____ 2. "How old are you, my pret-ty lit-tle miss, How

Em   Am

old are you, my hon-ey?" _____ She an-swered to him with a lov-in' smile, "I'll

G D   Am

be six-teen come Sun - day, _____ Be six-teen come Sun - day." _____

Additional lyrics

3. "Come and go with me, my pretty little miss,
   Come and go with me, my honey.
   Take you where the grass grows green,
   You never will want for money,
   You never will want for money.

4. "Pull off, pull off them high-heeled shoes
   All made of Spanish leather.
   Get behind me on my horse
   And we'll ride off together,
   We'll both go off together."

5. Well, she pulled off them high-heeled shoes
   Made of Spanish leather.
   Got behind him on his horse
   And they rode off together,
   They both rode off together.

6. At night the boss came home
   Inquiring about this lady.
   The servant spoke before she thought,
   "She's been with Black Jack Davey,
   Rode off with Black Jack Davey."

7. "Well, saddle for me my coal-black stud,
   He's speedier than the gray.
   I rode all day and I'll ride all night,
   And I'll overtake my lady,
   I'll bring back my lady."

8. Well, he rode all night 'til the broad daylight,
   'Til he came to a river ragin',
   And there he spied his darlin' bride
   In the arms of Black Jack Davey,
   Wrapped up with Black Jack Davey.

9. "Pull off, pull off them long blue gloves
   All made of the finest leather.
   Give to me your lily-white hand
   And we'll both go home together,
   We'll both go home together."

10. Well, she pulled off them long blue gloves
    All made of the finest leather,
    Gave to him her lily-white hand
    And said good-bye forever,
    Bid farewell forever.

11. "Would you forsake your house and home,
    Would you forsake your baby?
    Would you forsake your husband, too,
    To go with Black Jack Davey,
    Ride off with Black Jack Davey?"

12. "Well, I'll forsake my house and home,
    And I'll forsake my baby.
    I'll forsake my husband, too,
    For the love of Black Jack Davey,
    Love my Black Jack Davey."

13. "Last night I slept in a feather bed
    Between my husband and baby.
    Tonight I lay on the river banks
    In the arms of Black Jack Davey,
    Love my Black Jack Davey."

Blood in My Eyes

Traditional, arranged by Bob Dylan

Additional lyrics

2. I went back home, put on my tie,
   Gonna get that girl that money will buy.
   Hey, hey, babe, I got blood in my eyes for you,
   Hey, hey, babe, I got blood in my eyes for you.
   I got blood in my eyes for you, babe,
   I don't care what in the world you do.

3. She looked at me, begin to smile,
   Said, "Hey, hey, man, can't you wait a little while?"
   No, no, babe, I got blood in my eyes for you,
   No, no, babe, I got blood in my eyes for you.
   Got blood in my eyes for you, babe,
   I don't care what in the world you do.

Instrumental

4. No, no, ma'ma, I can't wait,
   You got my money, now you're trying to break this date.
   Hey, hey, babe, I got blood in my eyes for you,
   Hey, hey, babe, I got blood in my eyes for you.
   I got blood in my eyes for you, babe,
   I don't care what in the world you do.

5. I tell you something, tell you the facts,
   You don't want me, give my money back.
   Hey, hey, babe, I got blood in my eyes for you,
   Hey, hey, babe, I got blood in my eyes for you.
   I got blood in my eyes for you, babe,
   I don't care what in the world you do.

Instrumental

Blowin' in the Wind

Words and Music by Bob Dylan

1. How man – y roads must a man walk ____ down be –
2. How man – y times must a man look ____ up be –
3. How man – y years can a moun – tain ex – ist be –

fore ____ you call him a man? ____ Yes, 'n'
fore he can see the ____ sky? ____ Yes, 'n'
fore ____ it's washed to the sea? ____ Yes, 'n'

How man – y seas must a white dove ____ sail be –
How man – y ears must ____ one man ____ have be –
How man – y years can some peo – ple ex – ist be –

fore ____ she sleeps in the sand? ____ Yes, 'n'
fore he can hear peo – ple cry? ____ Yes, 'n'
fore they're al – lowed to be free? ____ Yes, 'n'

Bob Dylan's Dream

Words and Music by Bob Dylan

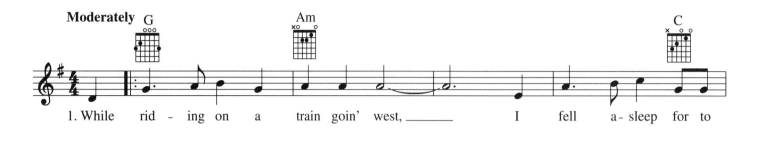

1. While rid - ing on a train goin' west, _____ I fell a- sleep for to

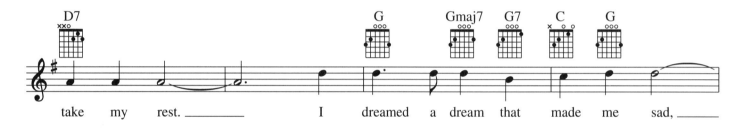

take my rest. _____ I dreamed a dream that made me sad, _____

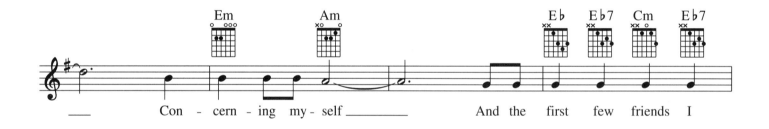

____ Con - cern - ing my- self _____ And the first few friends I

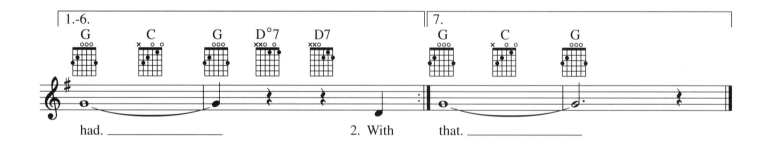

had. _____ 2. With that. _____

Additional lyrics

2. With half-damp eyes I stared to the room
   Where my friends and I spent many an afternoon,
   Where we together weathered many a storm,
   Laughin' and singin' till the early hours of the morn.

3. By the old wooden stove where our hats was hung,
   Our words were told, our songs were sung,
   Where we longed for nothin' and were quite satisfied
   Talkin' and a-jokin' about the world outside.

4. With haunted hearts through the heat and cold,
   We never thought we could ever get old.
   We thought we could sit forever in fun
   But our chances really was a million to one.

5. As easy it was to tell black from white,
   It was all that easy to tell wrong from right.
   And our choices were few and the thought never hit
   That the one road we traveled would ever shatter and split.

6. How many a year has passed and gone,
   And many a gamble has been lost and won,
   And many a road taken by many a friend,
   And each one I've never seen again.

7. I wish, I wish, I wish in vain,
   That we could sit simply in that room again,
   Ten thousand dollars at the drop of a hat,
   I'd give it all gladly if our lives could be like that.

Boots of Spanish Leather

Words and Music by Bob Dylan

Slowly
Refrain

1. Oh, I'm sail - in' a - way my ___ own true

love, I'm sail - in' a - way in the morn - ing. ___

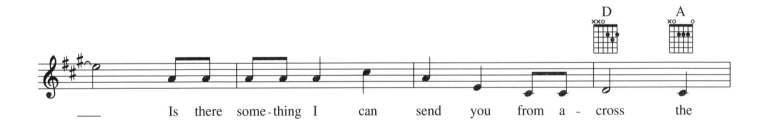

___ Is there some-thing I can send you from a - cross the

repeat eight times

sea, From the place that I'll be land - ing? ___

Additional lyrics

2. No, there's nothin' you can send me, my own true love,
There's nothin' I wish to be ownin'.
Just carry yourself back to me unspoiled,
From across that lonesome ocean.

3. Oh, but I just thought you might want something fine
Made of silver or of golden,
Either from the mountains of Madrid
Or from the coast of Barcelona.

4. Oh, but if I had the stars from the darkest night
And the diamonds from the deepest ocean,
I'd forsake them all for your sweet kiss,
For that's all I'm wishin' to be ownin'.

5. That I might be gone a long time
And it's only that I'm askin',
Is there something I can send you to remember me by,
To make your time more easy passin'.

6. Oh, how can, how can you ask me again,
It only brings me sorrow.
The same thing I want from you today,
I would want again tomorrow.

7. I got a letter on a lonesome day,
It was from her ship a-sailin',
Saying I don't know when I'll be comin' back again,
It depends on how I'm a-feelin'.

8. Well, if you, my love, must think that-a-way,
I'm sure your mind is roamin'.
I'm sure your heart is not with me,
But with the country to where you're goin'.

9. So take heed, take heed of the western wind,
Take heed of the stormy weather.
And yes, there's something you can send back to me,
Spanish boots of Spanish leather.

Brownsville Girl

Words and Music by Bob Dylan and Sam Shepard

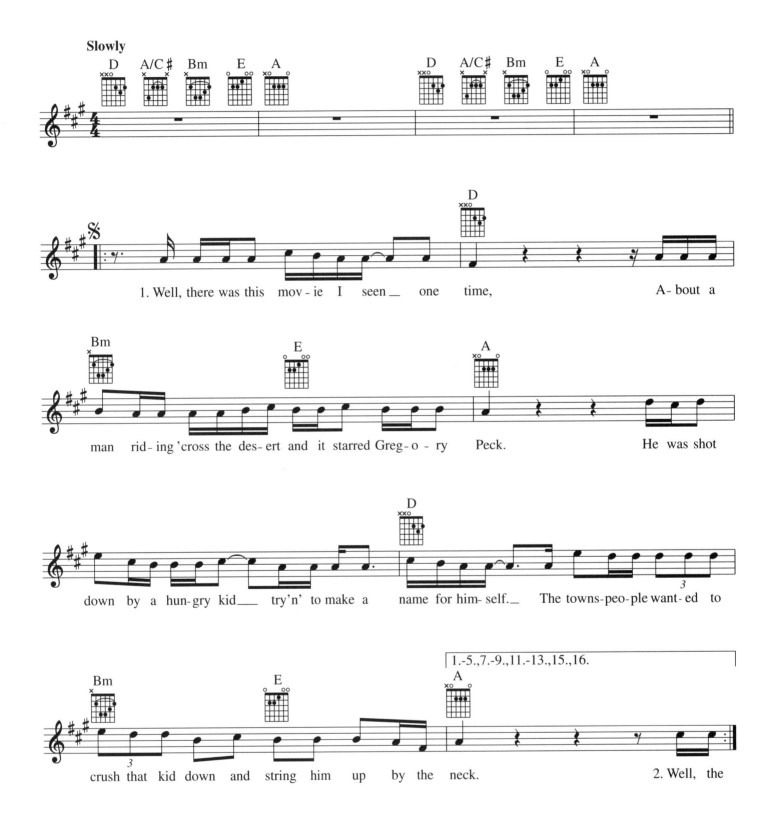

Slowly

1. Well, there was this mov-ie I seen __ one time, A- bout a man rid- ing 'cross the des- ert and it starred Greg-o - ry Peck. He was shot down by a hun-gry kid__ try'n' to make a name for him- self.__ The towns-peo-ple want-ed to crush that kid down and string him up by the neck. 2. Well, the

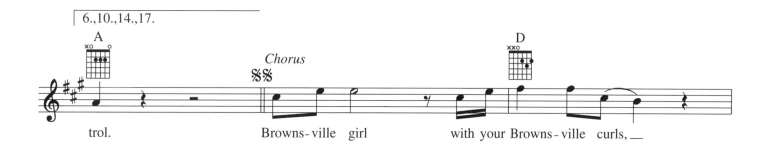

trol.   Browns-ville girl   with your Browns-ville curls, __

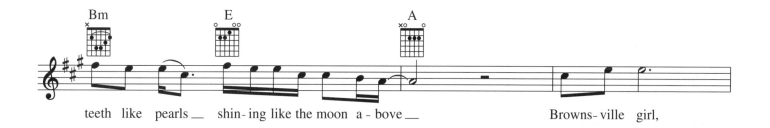

teeth like pearls __ shin-ing like the moon a-bove __   Browns-ville girl,

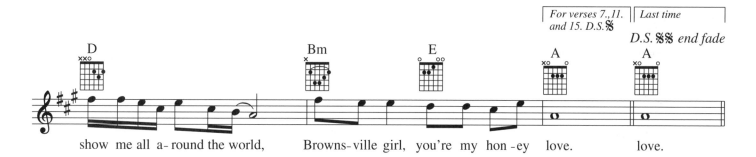

show me all a-round the world,   Browns-ville girl, you're my hon-ey love.   love.

Additional lyrics

2. Well, the marshal, now he beat that kid to a bloody pulp
   As the dying gunfighter lay in the sun and gasped for his last breath.
   Turn him loose, let him go, let him say he outdrew me fair and square,
   I want him to feel what it's like to every moment face his death.

3. Well, I keep seeing this stuff and it just comes a-rolling in
   And you know it blows right through me like a ball and chain.
   You know I can't believe we've lived so long and are still so far apart.
   The memory of you keeps callin' after me like a rollin' train.

4. I can still see the day that you came to me on the painted desert
   In your busted down Ford and your platform heels
   I could never figure out why you chose that particular place to meet
   Ah, but you were right. It was perfect as I got in behind the wheel.

5. Well, we drove that car all night into San Anton'
   And we slept near the Alamo, your skin was so tender and soft.
   Way down in Mexico you went out to find a doctor and you never came back.
   I would have gone on after you but I didn't feel like letting my head get blown off.

6. Well, we're drivin' this car and the sun is comin' up over the Rockies,
   Now I know she ain't you but she's here and she's got that dark rhythm in her soul.
   But I'm too over the edge and I ain't in the mood anymore to remember the times when I was your only man
   And she don't want to remind me. She knows this car would go out of control.

   Chorus

7. Well, we crossed the panhandle and then we headed towards Amarillo
    We pulled up where Henry Porter used to live. He owned a wreckin' lot outside of town about a mile.
    Ruby was in the backyard hanging clothes, she had her red hair tied back.
    She saw us come rolling up in a trail of dust.
    She said, "Henry ain't here but you can come on in, he'll be back in a little while."

8. Then she told us how times were tough and about how she was thinkin' of bummin' a ride back to where she started.
    But ya know, she changed the subject every time money came up.
    She said, "Welcome to the land of the living dead." You could tell she was so broken hearted.
    She said, "Even the swap meets around here are getting pretty corrupt."

9. "How far are y'all going?" Ruby asked us with a sigh.
    "We're going all the way 'til the wheels fall off and burn,
    'Til the sun peels the paint and the seat covers fade and the water moccasin dies."
    Ruby just smiled and said, "Ah, you know some babies never learn."

10. Something about that movie though, well I just can't get it out of my head
    But I can't remember why I was in it or what part I was supposed to play.
    All I remember about it was Gregory Peck and the way people moved
    And a lot of them seemed to be lookin' my way.

    Chorus

11. Well, they were looking for somebody with a pompadour.
    I was crossin' the street when shots rang out.
    I didn't know whether to duck or to run, so I ran.
    "We got him cornered in the churchyard," I heard somebody shout.

12. Well, you saw my picture in the Corpus Christi Tribune. Underneath it, it said, "A man with no alibi."
    You went out on a limb to testify for me, you said I was with you.
    Then when I saw you break down in front of the judge and cry real tears,
    It was the best acting I saw anybody do.

13. Now I've always been the kind of person that doesn't like to trespass but sometimes you just find yourself over the line.
    Oh if there's an original thought out there, I could use it right now.
    You know, I feel pretty good, but that ain't sayin' much. I could feel a whole lot better,
    If you were just here by my side to show me how.

14. Well, I'm standin' in line in the rain to see a movie starring Gregory Peck,
    Yeah, but you know it's not the one that I had in mind.
    He's got a new one out now, I don't even know what it's about
    But I'll see him in anything so I'll stand in line.

    Chorus

15. You know, it's funny how things never turn out the way you had 'em planned.
    The only thing we knew for sure about Henry Porter is that his name wasn't Henry Porter.
    And you know there was somethin' about you baby that I liked that was always too good for this world
    Just like you always said there was somethin' about me you liked that I left behind in the French Quarter.

16. Strange how people who suffer together have stronger connections than people who are most content.
    I don't have any regrets, they can talk about me plenty when I'm gone.
    You always said people don't do what they believe in, they just do what's most convenient, then they repent.
    And I always said, "Hang on to me, baby, and let's hope that the roof stays on."

17. There was a movie I seen one time, I think I sat through it twice.
    I don't remember who I was or where I was bound.
    All I remember about it was it starred Gregory Peck, he wore a gun and he was shot in the back.
    Seems like a long time ago, long before the stars were torn down.

    Chorus

Born in Time

Words and Music by Bob Dylan

Moderately

In the lone - ly night ___

In the blink - ing star - dust ___ of a pale blue light ___

You're com - in' thru to me in black and white_ When we were made_ of

dreams. You're blow - ing ___ down the shak - y street, ___

You're hear - ing my heart beat In ___ the rec - ord -

Broke Down Engine

Traditional, arranged by Bob Dylan

Moderate blues

1. Feel like a broke-down en - gine, ain't got no dri - vin' wheel,____

____ Feel like a broke-down en - gine, ain't got no dri - vin' wheel. __

____ You all been down and lone - some, you know just how a poor man feels. __

Additional lyrics

2. Been shooting craps and gambling, momma, and I done got broke,
   Been shooting craps and gambling, momma, and I done got broke.
   I done pawned my pistol, baby, my best clothes been sold.

   Lordy, Lord, Lordy, Lordy, Lord, Lordy, Lordy, Lordy,
   Lordy, Lord.

3. I went down in my praying ground, fell on my bended knees,
   I went down in my praying ground, fell on my bended knees.
   I ain't cryin' for no religion, Lord, give me back my good gal please.

4. If you give me back my baby, I won't worry you no more,
   Give me back my baby, I won't worry you no more.
   Don't have to put her in my house, Lordy, just lead her to my door.

   Lordy, Lord, Lordy, Lordy, Lord, Lordy, Lordy, Lordy,
   Lordy, Lord.

5. Can't you hear me, baby, rappin' on your door?
   Can't you hear me, baby, rappin' on your door?
   Now you hear me tappin', tappin' across your floor.

6. Feel like a broke-down engine, ain't got no drive at all,
   Feel like a broke-down engine, ain't got no drive at all.
   What make me love my woman, she can really do the Georgia Crawl.

7. Feel like a broke-down engine, ain't got no whistle or bell,
   Feel like a broke-down engine, ain't got no whistle or bell.
   If you're a real hot momma, come take away Daddy's weeping spell.

Buckets of Rain

Words and Music by Bob Dylan

Additional lyrics

2. I been meek
    And hard like an oak
    I seen pretty people disappear like smoke.
    Friends will arrive, friends will disappear,
    If you want me, honey baby,
    I'll be here.

3. Like your smile
    And your fingertips
    Like the way that you move your lips.
    I like the cool way you look at me,
    Everything about you is bringing me
    Misery.

4. Little red wagon
    Little red bike
    I ain't no monkey but I know what I like.
    I like the way you love me strong and slow,
    I'm takin' you with me, honey baby,
    When I go.

5. Life is sad
    Life is a bust
    All ya can do is do what you must.
    You do what you must do and ya do it well,
    I'll do it for you, honey baby,
    Can't you tell?

Can't Wait

Words and Music by Bob Dylan

Moderately slow, with a beat

I can't 1. wait, wait for you _ to change_ your

2.-5. *See additional lyrics*

mind _ It's late; I'm trying to walk the

line _ Well it's way past mid-night and there are

peo-ple all a-round_ Some on their way up,_ some on their way down_

The air burns _ and I'm trying _ to think _ straight _

And I _ don't know _ how much long-er I _ can wait_

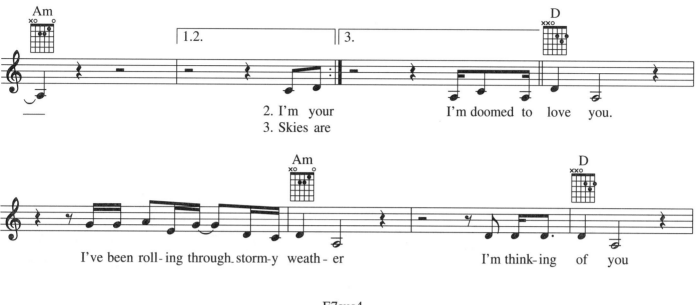

Am

| 1.2. | 3. | D

2. I'm your

3. Skies are

I'm doomed to love you.

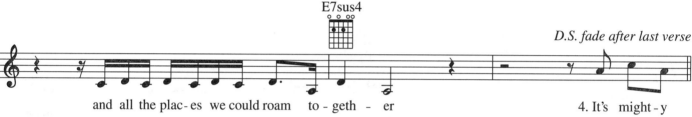

Am

I've been roll- ing through storm-y weath - er

D

I'm think- ing of you

E7sus4

D.S. fade after last verse

and all the plac- es we could roam to - geth - er

4. It's might- y

Additional lyrics

2. I'm your man; I'm trying to recover the sweet love that we knew
   You understand that my heart can't go on beating without you
   Well, your loveliness has wounded me, I'm reeling from the blow
   I wish I knew what it was keeps me loving you so
   I'm breathing hard, standing at the gate
   But I don't know how much longer I can wait

3. Skies are grey, I'm looking for anything that will bring a happy glow
   Night or day, it doesn't matter where I go anymore; I just go
   If I ever saw you coming I don't know what I would do
   I'd like to think I could control myself, but it isn't true
   That's how it is when things disintegrate
   And I don't know how much longer I can wait

   Bridge:
   I'm doomed to love you, I've been rolling through stormy weather
   I'm thinking of you and all the places we could roam together

4. It's mighty funny; the end of time has just begun
   Oh, honey, after all these years you're still the one
   While I'm strolling through the lonely graveyard of my mind
   I left my life with you somewhere back there along the line
   I thought somehow that I would be spared this fate
   But I don't know how much longer I can wait.

5. *Instrumental solo*

Canadee-i-o

Traditional, arranged by Bob Dylan

1. Well it's all of a fair ___ and ___ hand-some girl, ___ She's
all in her ten - der years. ___ She fell in love with a
sail - or boy, ___ It's true she loved him well. ___ For to
go off to sea with him Like she did not know how, ___
She longed to see that sea-port town _ Of Ca - na - dee-i - o. ___

Additional lyrics

2. So she bargained with the sailor boy,
   All for a piece of gold.
   Straightaway then he led her
   Down into the hold,
   Sayin', "I'll dress you up in sailor's clothes,
   Your jacket shall be blue.
   You'll see that seaport town
   Of Canadee-i-o."

3. Now, when the other sailors heard the news,
   Well, they fell into a rage,
   And with all the ship's company
   They were willing to engage,
   Saying, "We'll tie her hands and feet, my boys,
   Overboard we'll throw her.
   She'll never see that seaport town
   Called Canadee-i-o.

4. Now, when the captain he heard the news,
   Well, he too fell in a rage,
   And with the whole ship's company
   He was willing to engage,
   Sayin', "She'll stay in sailor's clothes,
   Her color shall be blue,
   She'll see that seaport town
   Called Canadee-i-o.

5. Now, when they come down to Canada,
   Scarcely 'bout half a year,
   She's married this bold captain
   Who called her his dear.
   She's dressed in silks and satins now,
   She cuts a gallant show,
   Finest of the ladies
   Down Canadee-i-o.

6. Come, all you fair and tender girls,
   Wheresoever you may be.
   I'd have you to follow your own true love
   Whene'er he goes to sea.
   For if the sailors prove false to you,
   Well, the captain, he might prove true.
   You'll see the honor I have gained
   By the wearing of the blue.

Cat's in the Well

Words and Music by Bob Dylan

Moderately bright

The cat's in the well, ___ the wolf is look-ing down. ___ The cat's in the well, ___ the wolf is look-ing down. ___ He got his big bush-y tail drag-ging all o-ver the ground. ___ The cat's in the well, ___ the gen-tle la-dy ___ is a-sleep. Cat's in the well, the gen-tle la-dy is a-sleep. She ain't hear-ing a thing, ___ the

si - lence is a - stick- in' her ____ deep. The

Bridge

cat's in the well and grief is show-ing its face ____ The world's

be - ing slaugh -tered __ and it's such a blood -y dis - grace._____

The cat's in the well, the horse is go-ing bump-e -ty bump. __

The cat's in the well, and the horse is go-ing bump-e -ty ____

bump. __ Back- al - ley Sal - ly is do -ing the A -

1.2.   3.

mer - i - can ____ jump. __ The

Additional lyrics

Bridge #2:
The cat's in the well, and pappa is reading the news.
His hair is falling out and all of his daughters need shoes.

The cat's in the well and the barn is full of bull
The cat's in the well and the barn is full of bull
The night is so long and the table is oh, so full

Bridge #3:
The cat's in the well and the servant is at the door.
The drinks are ready and the dogs are going to war.

The cat's in the well, the leaves are starting to fall
The cat's in the well, leaves are starting to fall
Goodnight, my love, may the Lord have mercy on us all.

Dead Man, Dead Man

Words and Music by Bob Dylan

Moderately

1. Ut - ter - ing i - dle words from a rep - ro - bate mind,

Cling - ing to strange prom - is - es, dy - ing on the vine,

Nev - er be - in' a - ble to sep - a - rate the good from the bad,

Ooh, I can't stand it, I can't stand it, It's mak - in' me feel so sad.

Chorus

Dead man, dead man,

When will you a - rise? Cob - webs in your mind,

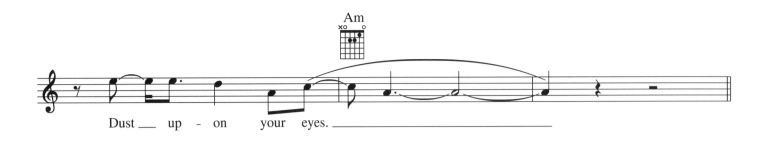

Dust __ up - on your eyes. _____

Verse

2. Sa - tan got you by the heel, there's a bird's nest in your hair. __

Do you have _ an - y faith at all? __ Do you have an - y love to share? __ The

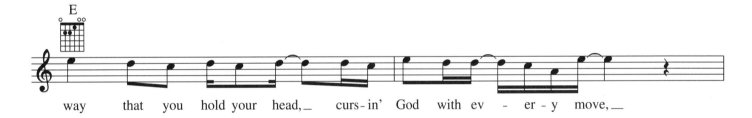

way that you hold your head, __ curs - in' God with ev - er - y move, __

Ooh, I can't stand it, I ___ can't stand it, What are you try'n' __ to prove? __

Chorus

Dead man, _____ dead __ man,

When will you a - rise? _____ Cob - webs in your mind, __

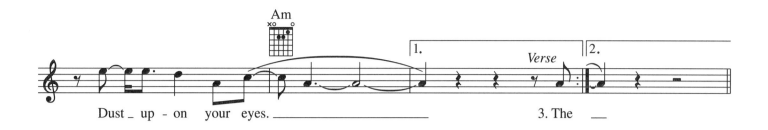

Dust — up - on your eyes. _____ 3. The _____

Ooh, I can't stand it, I ___ can't stand it. Ooh, I can't stand it, I ___ can't stand it.

Ooh, I can't stand it, I ___ can't stand it. Ooh, I can't stand it, I ___ can't stand it.

Additional lyrics

3. The glamour and the bright lights and the politics of sin,
   The ghetto that you build for me is the one you end up in,
   The race of the engine that overrules your heart,
   Ooh, I can't stand it, I can't stand it,
   Pretending that you're so smart.

   Chorus

4. What are you tryin' to overpower me with, the doctrine or the gun?
   My back is already to the wall, where can I run?
   The tuxedo that you're wearin', the flower in your lapel,
   Ooh, I can't stand it, I can't stand it,
   You wanna take me down to hell.

   Chorus

Catfish

Words and Music by Bob Dylan and Jacques Levy

Additional lyrics

2. Used to work on Mr. Finley's farm
   But the old man wouldn't pay
   So he packed his glove and took his arm
   An' one day he just ran away.

   Chorus

3. Come up where the Yankees are,
   Dress up in a pinstripe suit,
   Smoke a custom-made cigar,
   Wear an alligator boot.

   Chorus

4. Carolina born and bred,
   Love to hunt the little quail.
   Got a hundred-acre spread,
   Got some huntin' dogs for sale.

   Chorus

5. Reggie Jackson at the plate
   Seein' nothin' but the curve,
   Swing too early or too late
   Got to eat what Catfish serve.

   Chorus

6. Even Billy Martin grins
   When the Fish is in the game.
   Every season twenty wins
   Gonna make the Hall of Fame.

   Chorus

Changing of the Guards

Words and Music by Bob Dylan

Additional lyrics

3. The cold-blooded moon.
   The captain waits above the celebration
   Sending his thoughts to a beloved maid
   Whose ebony face is beyond communication.
   The captain is down but still believing that his love will be repaid.

4. They shaved her head.
   She was torn between Jupiter and Apollo.
   A messenger arrived with a black nightingale.
   I seen her on the stairs and I couldn't help but follow,
   Follow her down past the fountain where they lifted her veil.

5. I stumbled to my feet.
   I rode past destruction in the ditches
   With the stitches still mending 'neath a heart-shaped tattoo.
   Renegade priests and treacherous young witches
   Were handing out the flowers that I'd given to you.

6. The palace of mirrors
   Where dog soldiers are reflected,
   The endless road and the wailing of chimes,
   The empty rooms where her memory is protected,
   Where the angels' voices whisper to the souls of previous times.

7. She wakes him up
   Forty-eight hours later, the sun is breaking
   Near broken chains, mountain laurel and rolling rocks.
   She's begging to know what measures he now will be taking.
   He's pulling her down and she's clutching on to his long golden locks.

8. Gentlemen, he said,
   I don't need your organization, I've shined your shoes,
   I've moved your mountains and marked your cards
   But Eden is burning, either brace yourself for elimination
   Or else your hearts must have the courage for the changing of the guards.

9. Peace will come
   With tranquility and splendor on the wheels of fire
   But will bring us no reward when her false idols fall
   And cruel death surrenders with its pale ghost retreating
   Between the King and the Queen of Swords.

Delia

Traditional, arranged by Bob Dylan

Moderately

1. De - lia was a gam - bl - ing girl, gam - bled all a - round, __
De - lia was a gam - bl - ing girl, __ she laid her mon - ey
down. All the friends I ev - er had are gone. __

Additional lyrics

2. Delia's dear ol' mother took a trip out West.
   When she returned, little Delia gone to rest.
   All the friends I ever had are gone.

3. Delia's daddy weeped, Delia's momma moaned.
   Wouldn't have been so bad if the poor girl died at home.
   All the friends I ever had are gone.

4. Curtis' looking high, Curtis' looking low.
   He shot poor Delia down with a cruel forty-four.
   All the friends I ever had are gone.

5. High up on the housetops, high as I can see,
   Looking for them rounders, looking out for me.
   All the friends I ever had are gone.

6. Men in Atlanta, tryin' to pass for white,
   Delia's in the graveyard, boys, six feet out of sight.
   All the friends I ever had are gone.

7. Judge says to Curtis, "What's this noise about?"
   "All about them rounders, Judge, tryin' to cut me out."
   All the friends I ever had are gone.

8. Curtis said to the judge, "What might be my fine?"
   Judge says, "Poor boy, you got ninety-nine."
   All the friends I ever had are gone.

9. Curtis' in the jail house, drinking from an old tin cup.
   Delia's in the graveyard, she ain't gettin' up.
   All the friends I ever had are gone.

10. Delia, oh Delia, how can it be?
    You loved all them rounders, never did love me.
    All the friends I ever had are gone.

11. Delia, oh Delia, how could it be?
    You wanted all them rounders, never had time for me.
    All the friends I ever had are gone.

Chimes of Freedom

Words and Music by Bob Dylan

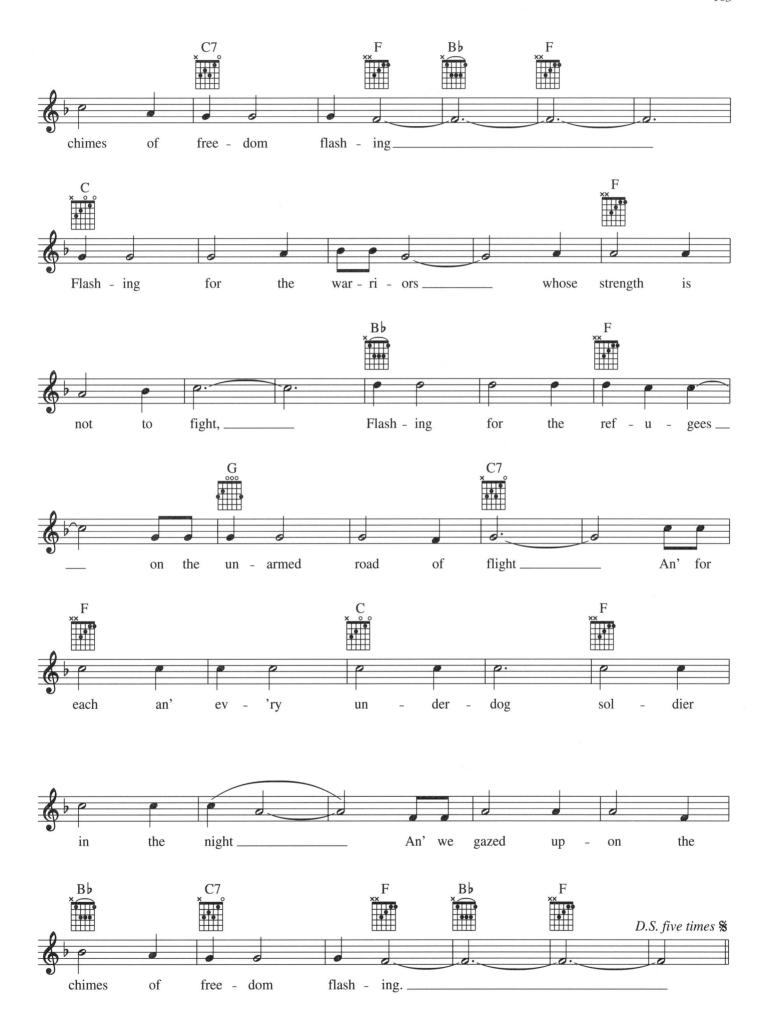

Additional lyrics

2. In the city's melted furnace, unexpectedly we watched
   With faces hidden while the walls were tightening
   As the echo of the wedding bells before the blowin' rain
   Dissolved into the bells of the lightning
   Tolling for the rebel, tolling for the rake
   Tolling for the luckless, the abandoned an' forsaked
   Tolling for the outcast, burnin' constantly at stake
   An' we gazed upon the chimes of freedom flashing.

3. Through the mad mystic hammering of the wild ripping hail
   The sky cracked its poems in naked wonder
   That the clinging of the church bells blew far into the breeze
   Leaving only bells of lightning and its thunder
   Striking for the gentle, striking for the kind
   Striking for the guardians and protectors of the mind
   An' the unpawned painter behind beyond his rightful time
   An' we gazed upon the chimes of freedom flashing.

4. Through the wild cathedral evening the rain unraveled tales
   For the disrobed faceless forms of no position
   Tolling for the tongues with no place to bring their thoughts
   All down in taken-for-granted situations
   Tolling for the deaf an' blind, tolling for the mute
   Tolling for the mistreated, mateless mother, the mistitled prostitute
   For the misdemeanor outlaw, chased an' cheated by pursuit
   An' we gazed upon the chimes of freedom flashing.

5. Even though a cloud's white curtain in a far-off corner flashed
   An' the hypnotic splattered mist was slowly lifting
   Electric light still struck like arrows, fired but for the ones
   Condemned to drift or else be kept from drifting
   Tolling for the searching ones, on their speechless, seeking trail
   For the lonesome-hearted lovers with too personal a tale
   An' for each unharmful, gentle soul misplaced inside a jail
   An' we gazed upon the chimes of freedom flashing.

6. Starry-eyed an' laughing as I recall when we were caught
   Trapped by no track of hours for they hanged suspended
   As we listened one last time an' we watched with one last look
   Spellbound an' swallowed 'til the tolling ended
   Tolling for the aching ones whose wounds cannot be nursed
   For the countless confused, accused, misused, strung-out ones an' worse
   An' for every hung-up person in the whole wide universe
   An' we gazed upon the chimes of freedom flashing.

Everything Is Broken

Words and Music by Bob Dylan

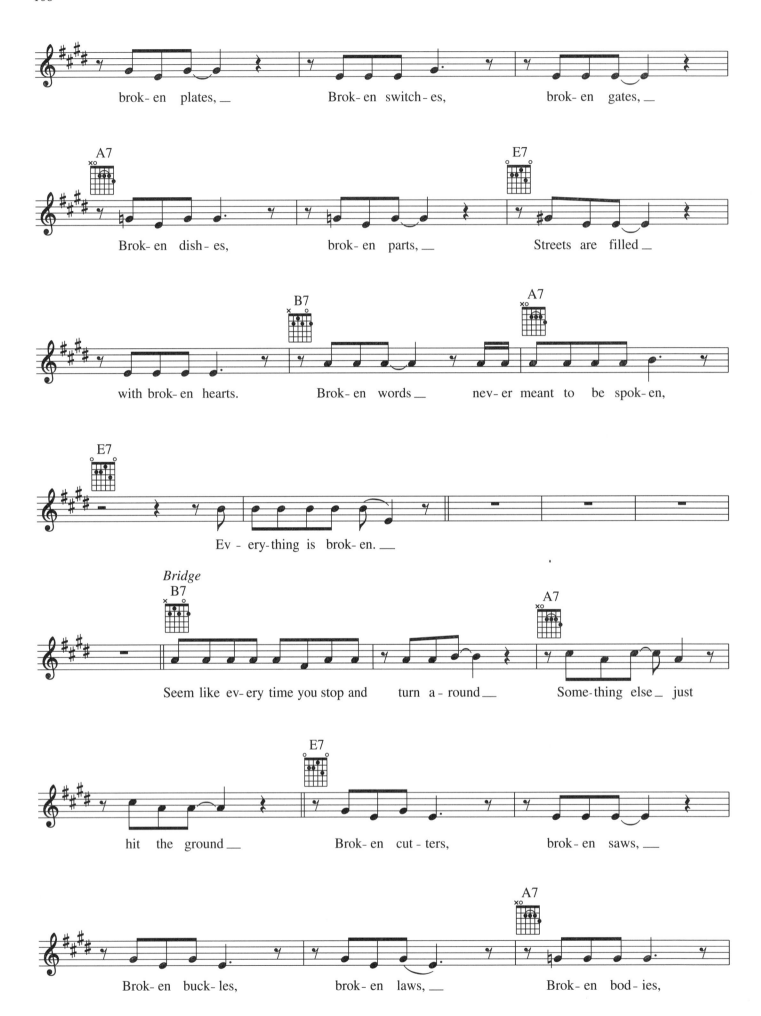

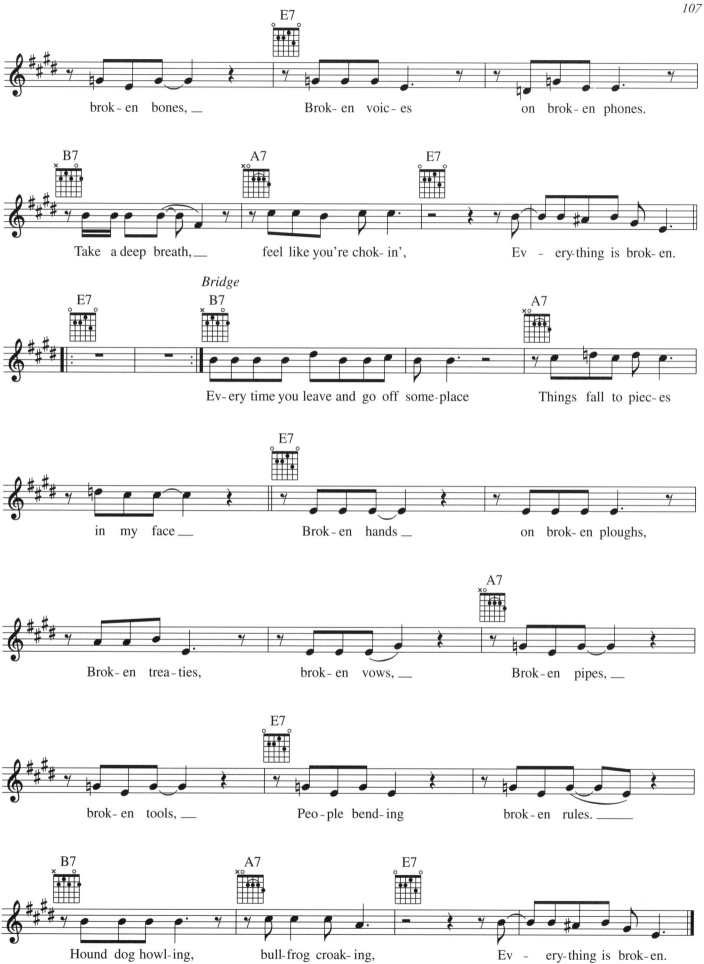

Clean-Cut Kid

Words and Music by Bob Dylan

No chord

Ev- ery-bo- dy wants to know why he could- n't ad- just __ Ad -

just to what, __ a dream that bust? __ He was a clean-cut kid __

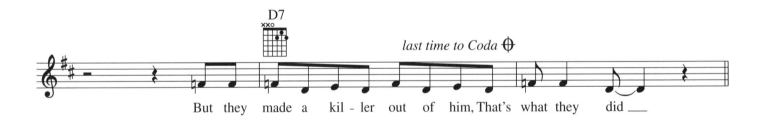

last time to Coda

But they made a kil- ler out of him, That's what they did __

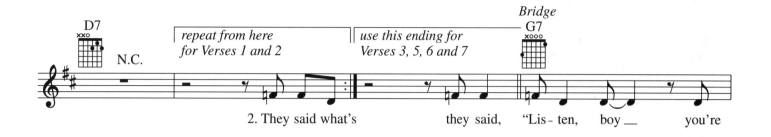

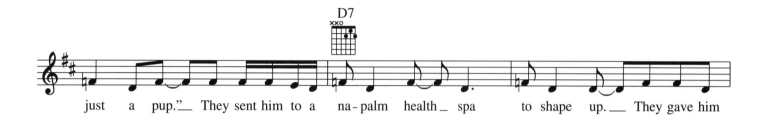

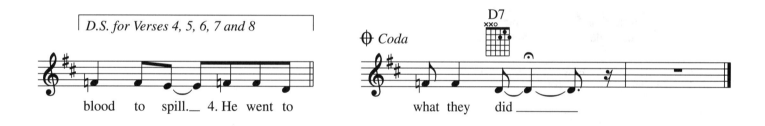

Additional lyrics

2. They said what's up is down, they said what isn't is
   They put ideas in his head he thought were his

   Chorus

3. He was on the baseball team, he was in the marching band
   When he was ten years old he had a watermelon stand

   Chorus

4. He went to church on Sunday, he was a Boy Scout
   For his friends he would turn his pockets inside out

   Chorus

   Bridge #1:
   They said, "Listen boy, you're just a pup"
   They sent him to a napalm health spa to shape up

   They gave him dope to smoke, drinks and pills,
   A jeep to drive, blood to spill

5. They said "Congratulations, you got what it takes"
   They sent him back into the rat race without any brakes

   Chorus

   Bridge #2:
   He bought the American dream but it put him in debt
   The only game he could play was Russian roulette

   He drank Coca-Cola, he was eating Wonder Bread,
   Ate Burger Kings, he was well fed

6. He went to Hollywood to see Peter O'Toole
   He stole a Rolls Royce and drove it in a swimming pool

   Chorus

   Bridge #3:
   He could've sold insurance, owned a restaurant or bar
   Could've been an accountant or a tennis star

   He was wearing boxing gloves, took a dive one day
   Off the Golden Gate Bridge into China Bay

7. His mama walks the floor, his daddy weeps and moans
   They gotta sleep together in a home they don't own

   Chorus

   Bridge #4:
   Well, everybody's asking why he couldn't adjust
   All he ever wanted was somebody to trust

   They took his head and turned it inside out
   He never did know what it was all about

8. He had a steady job, he joined the choir
   He never did plan to walk the high wire

   Chorus

Forever Young

Words and Music by Bob Dylan

May God bless and keep you al-ways,___ May your wish-es all come true,___ May you al-ways do for oth-ers and let oth-ers do _ for you. ___ May you build a lad-der to the stars_ And climb on ev-ery rung,___ May you stay_ for - ev - er young, ____ For - ev - er young, ____ for - ev - er young, ____

Clothes Line

Words and Music by Bob Dylan

Hang 'em on ___ the line. ___ It was Jan - u - ar - y the thir- ti - eth

And ev - 'ry- bod- y was___ feel- in' fine.

Additional lyrics

2. The next day everybody got up
   Seein' if the clothes were dry.
   The dogs were barking, a neighbor passed,
   Mama, of course, she said, "Hi!"
   "Have you heard the news?" he said, with a grin,
   "The Vice-President's gone mad!"
   "Where?" "Downtown." "When?" "Last night."
   "Hmm, say, that's too bad!"
   "Well, there's nothin' we can do about it," said the neighbor,
   "It's just somethin' we're gonna have to forget."
   "Yes, I guess so," said Ma,
   Then she asked me if the clothes was still wet.

3. I reached up, touched my shirt,
   And the neighbor said, "Are those clothes yours?"
   I said, "Some of 'em, not all of 'em."
   He said, "Ya always help out around here with the chores?"
   I said, "Sometime, not all the time."
   Then my neighbor, he blew his nose
   Just as Papa yelled outside,
   "Mama wants you t' come back in the house and bring them clothes."
   Well, I just do what I'm told,
   So, I did it, of course.
   I went back in the house and Mama met me
   And then I shut all the doors.

Cold Irons Bound

Words and Music by Bob Dylan

1. I'm beg - in - ning to hear voic - es and there's no one a - round

2.-6. See additional lyrics

Well, I'm all used up and the fields have turned brown

I went to church on Sun - day and she passed by

My love for her is tak - ing such a long time to die

Additional lyrics

2. The walls of pride are high and wide
   Can't see over to the other side
   It's such a sad thing to see beauty decay
   It's sadder still, to feel your heart torn away

   One look at you and I'm out of control
   Like the universe has swallowed me whole
   I'm twenty miles out of town in cold irons bound

3. There's too many people, too many to recall
   I thought some of 'm were friends of mine; I was wrong about 'm all
   Well, the road is rocky and the hillside's mud
   Up over my head nothing but clouds of blood

   I found my world, found my world in you
   But your love just hasn't proved true
   I'm twenty miles out of town in cold irons bound
   Twenty miles out of town in cold irons bound

4. *Instrumental solo*

5. Oh, the winds in Chicago have torn me to shreds
   Reality has always had too many heads
   Some things last longer than you think they will
   There are some kind of things you can never kill

   It's you and you only, I'm been thinking about
   But you can't see in and it's hard lookin' out
   I'm twenty miles out of town in cold irons bound

6. Well the fat's in the fire and the water's in the tank
   The whiskey's in the jar and the money's in the bank
   I tried to love and protect you because I cared
   I'm gonna remember forever the joy that we shared

   Looking at you and I'm on my bended knee
   You have no idea what you do to me
   I'm twenty miles out of town in cold irons bound
   Twenty miles out of town in cold irons bound

Girl of the North Country

Words and Music by Bob Dylan

Moderato, gently

1. Well, if you're trav - 'lin' in the north coun - try fair,

Where the winds hit heav - y on the bor - der - line, _____ Re -

mem - ber me to one who lives there,

She once was _____ a true love of mine.

Additional lyrics

2. Well, if you go when the snowflakes storm,
   When the rivers freeze and summer ends,
   Please see if she's wearing a coat so warm,
   To keep her from the howlin' winds.

3. Please see for me if her hair hangs long,
   If it rolls and flows all down her breast.
   Please see for me if her hair hangs long,
   That's the way I remember her best.

4. I'm a-wonderin' if she remembers me at all.
   Many times I've often prayed
   In the darkness of my night,
   In the brightness of my day.

5. So if you're travelin' in the north country fair,
   Where the winds hit heavy on the borderline,
   Remember me to one who lives there.
   She once was a true love of mine.

Corrina, Corrina

Traditional, arranged by Bob Dylan

Additional lyrics

2. I got a bird that whistles,
   I got a bird that sings.
   I got a bird that whistles,
   I got a bird that sings.
   But I ain' a-got Corrina,
   Life don't mean a thing.

   Corrina, Corrina,
   Gal, you're on my mind.
   Corrina, Corrina,
   Gal, you're on my mind.
   I'm a-thinkin' 'bout you, baby,
   I just can't keep from crying.

Country Pie
Words and Music by Bob Dylan

Covenant Woman

Words and Music by Bob Dylan

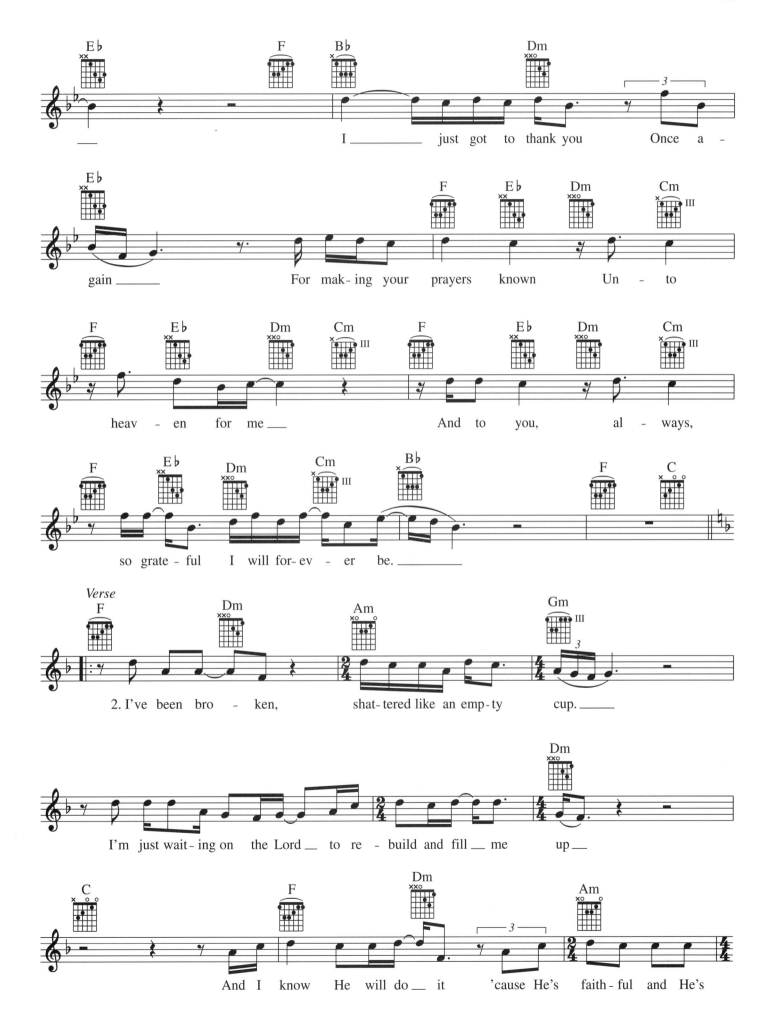

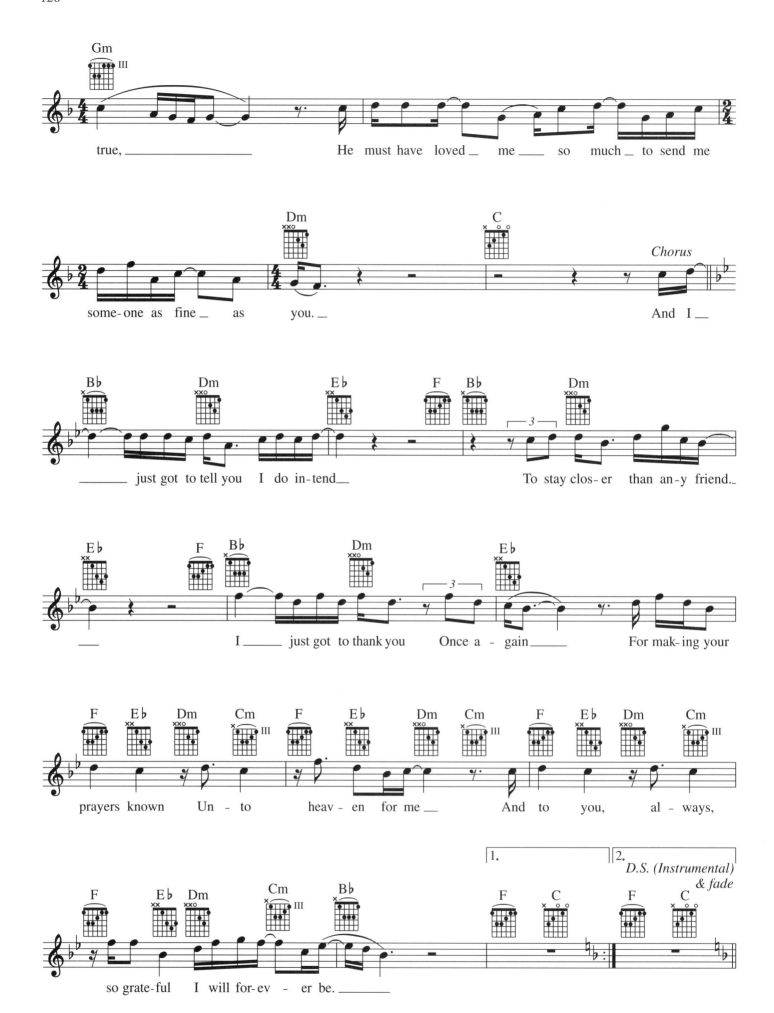

Additional lyrics

2. Covenant woman, intimate little girl
Who knows those most secret things of me that are hidden from the world.
You know we are strangers in a land we're passing through.
I'll always be right by your side, I've got a covenant too.

And I just got to tell you
I do intend
To stay closer than any friend.
I just got to thank you
Once again
For making your prayers known
Unto heaven for me
And to you, always, so grateful
I will forever be.

Dark Eyes

Words and Music by Bob Dylan

Additional lyrics

2. A cock is crowing far away and another soldier's deep in prayer,
   Some mother's child has gone astray, she can't find him anywhere.
   But I can hear another drum beating for the dead that rise,
   Whom nature's beast fears as they come and all I see are dark eyes.

3. They tell me to be discreet for all intended purposes,
   They tell me revenge is sweet and from where they stand, I'm sure it is.
   But I feel nothing for their game where beauty goes unrecognized,
   All I feel is heat and flame and all I see are dark eyes.

4. Oh, the French girl, she's in paradise and a drunken man is at the wheel,
   Hunger pays a heavy price to the falling gods of speed and steel.
   Oh, time is short and the days are sweet and passion rules the arrow
   that flies,
   A million faces at my feet but all I see are dark eyes.

Day of the Locusts

Words and Music by Bob Dylan

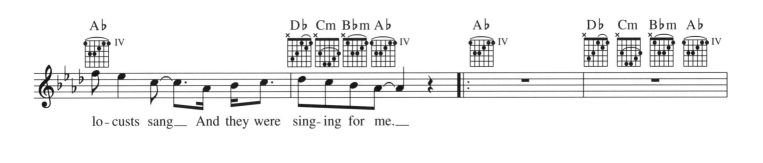

lo-custs sang__ And they were sing-ing for me.__

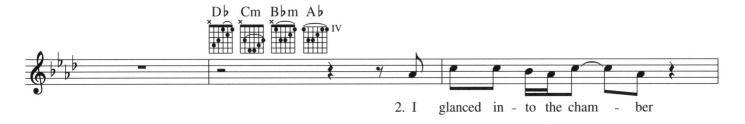

2. I glanced in - to the cham - ber

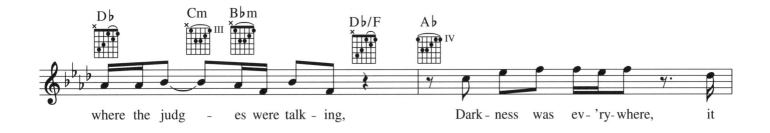

where the judg - es were talk - ing, Dark - ness was ev-'ry-where, it

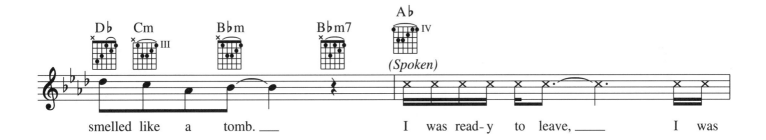

smelled like a tomb. __ I was read-y to leave, ____ I was

al - read-y walk - in', ____ But the next time I looked there was

light in the room.__ And the lo-custs sang, yeah, it give me a chill, Oh,__ the

lo - custs sang ___ such a sweet mel- o - dy. ____ Oh, the lo - custs sang ___ their

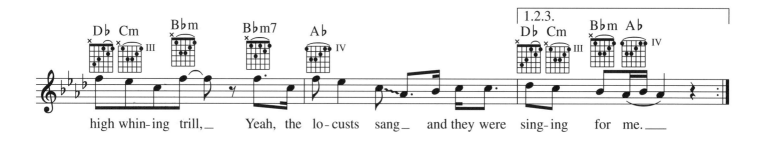

high whin-ing trill, ___ Yeah, the lo - custs sang ___ and they were sing-ing for me. ___

4. Final Ending

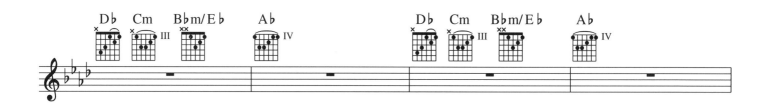

sing - ing for me ___ well, sing - ing for me. ___

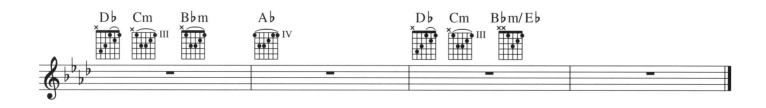

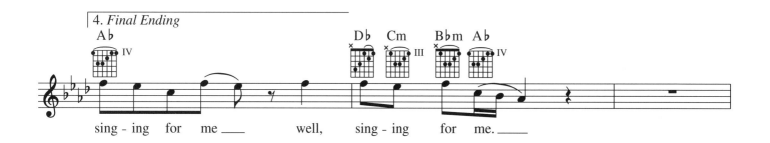

Additional lyrics

3. Outside of the gates the trucks were unloadin',
   The weather was hot, a-nearly 90 degrees.
   The man standin' next to me, his head was exploding,
   Well, I was prayin' the pieces wouldn't fall on me.
   Yeah, the locusts sang off in the distance,
   Yeah, the locusts sang such a sweet melody.
   Oh, the locusts sang off in the distance,
   And the locusts sang and they were singing for me.

4. I put down my robe, picked up my diploma,
   Took hold of my sweetheart and away we did drive,
   Straight for the hills, the black hills of Dakota,
   Sure was glad to get out of there alive.
   And the locusts sang, well, it give me a chill,
   Yeah, the locusts sang such a sweet melody.
   And the locusts sang with a high whinin' trill,
   Yeah, the locusts sang and they was singing for me,
   Singing for me, well, singing for me.

Dear Landlord

Words and Music by Bob Dylan

Additional lyrics

2. Dear landlord,
   Please heed these words that I speak.
   I know you've suffered much,
   But in this you are not so unique.
   All of us, at times, we might work too hard
   To have it too fast and too much,
   And anyone can fill his life up
   With things he can see but he just cannot touch.

3. Dear landlord,
   Please don't dismiss my case.
   I'm not about to argue,
   I'm not about to move to no other place.
   Now, each of us has his own special gift
   And you know this was meant to be true,
   And if you don't underestimate me,
   I won't underestimate you.

Death Is Not the End

Words and Music by Bob Dylan

Moderately slow

When you're

sad and when you're lone - ly and you have - n't got a ___ friend Just re -
See additional lyrics

mem - ber that death is not the end ___ And

all that you've held sa - cred, falls down and does not mend Just re -

Additional lyrics

2. When you're standing at the crossroads that you cannot comprehend
   Just remember that death is not the end
   And all your dreams have vanished and you don't know what's up the bend
   Just remember that death is not the end
   Not the end, not the end
   Just remember that death is not the end

3. When the storm clouds gather 'round you, and heavy rains descend
   Just remember that death is not the end
   And there's no one there to comfort you, with a helpin' hand to lend
   Just remember that death is not the end
   Not the end, not the end
   Just remember that death is not the end

   Oh, the tree of life is growing
   Where the spirit never dies
   And the bright light of salvation shines
   In dark and empty skies

4. When the cities are on fire with the burning flesh of men
   Just remember that death is not the end
   And you search in vain to find just one law abiding citizen
   Just remember that death is not the end
   Not the end, not the end
   Just remember that death is not the end

Hazel

Words and Music by Bob Dylan

Moderately, with a two feel

Ha - zel, dirt - y - blonde hair

I would-n't be a - shamed to be seen with you an-y-where.

You got some-thing I want _____ plen-ty of _____

Ooh, _____ a lit-tle touch of your love. ___

Ha - zel, star-dust in your eye

You're go - in' some-where_ and so____ am I.

Now — don't ——— make me — play this wait - ing game. —

You've — got some-thing I want — plen - ty of ———

Ooh, —————— a lit - tle touch of your love. ——

The Death of Emmett Till

Words and Music by Bob Dylan

Additional lyrics

2. Some men they dragged him to a barn and there they beat him up.
   They said they had a reason, but I can't remember what.
   They tortured him and did some evil things too evil to repeat.
   There were screaming sounds inside the barn, there was laughing sounds out on the street.

3. Then they rolled his body down a gulf amidst a bloody red rain
   And they threw him in the waters wide to cease his screaming pain.
   The reason that they killed him there, and I'm sure it ain't no lie,
   Was just for the fun of killin' him and to watch him slowly die.

4. And then to stop the United States of yelling for a trial,
   Two brothers they confessed that they had killed poor Emmett Till.
   But on the jury there were men who helped the brothers commit this awful crime,
   And so this trial was a mockery, but nobody seemed to mind.

5. I saw the morning papers but I could not bear to see
   The smiling brothers walkin' down the courthouse stairs.
   For the jury found them innocent and the brothers they went free,
   While Emmett's body floats the foam of a Jim Crow southern sea.

6. If you can't speak out against this kind of thing, a crime that's so unjust,
   Your eyes are filled with dead men's dirt, your mind is filled with dust.
   Your arms and legs they must be in shackles and chains, and your blood it must refuse to flow,
   For you let this human race fall down so God-awful low!

7. This song is just a reminder to remind your fellow man
   That this kind of thing still lives today in that ghost-robed Ku Klux Klan.
   But if all of us folks that thinks alike, if we gave all we could give,
   We could make this great land of ours a greater place to live.

Desolation Row
Words and Music by Bob Dylan

2. Cinderella, she seems so easy,
   "It takes one to know one," she smiles,
   And puts her hands in her back pockets
   Bette Davis style
   And in comes Romeo, he's moaning,
   "You Belong to Me I Believe"
   And someone says," You're in the wrong place, my friend
   You better leave."
   And the only sound that's left
   After the ambulances go
   Is Cinderella sweeping up
   On Desolation Row

3. Now the moon is almost hidden
   The stars are beginning to hide
   The fortunetelling lady
   Has even taken all her things inside
   All except for Cain and Abel
   And the hunchback of Notre Dame
   Everybody is making love
   Or else expecting rain
   And the Good Samaritan, he's dressing
   He's getting ready for the show
   He's going to the carnival tonight
   On Desolation Row

4. Now Ophelia, she's 'neath the window
   For her I feel so afraid
   On her twenty-second birthday
   She already is an old maid
   To her, death is quite romantic
   She wears an iron vest
   Her profession's her religion
   Her sin is her lifelessness
   And though her eyes are fixed upon
   Noah's great rainbow
   She spends her time peeking
   Into Desolation Row

5. Einstein, disguised as Robin Hood
   With his memories in a trunk
   Passed this way an hour ago
   With his friend, a jealous monk
   He looked so immaculately frightful
   As he bummed a cigarette
   Then he went off sniffing drainpipes
   And reciting the alphabet
   Now you would not think to look at him
   But he was famous long ago
   For playing the electric violin
   On Desolation Row

6. Dr. Filth, he keeps his world
   Inside of a leather cup
   But all his sexless patients
   They're trying to blow it up
   Now his nurse, some local loser
   She's in charge of the cyanide hole
   And she also keeps the cards that read
   "Have Mercy on His Soul."
   They all play on penny whistles
   You can hear them blow
   If you lean your head out far enough
   From Desolation Row

7. Across the street they've nailed the curtains
   They're getting ready for the feast
   The Phantom of the Opera
   A perfect image of a priest
   They're spoonfeeding Casanova
   To get him to feel more assured
   Then they'll kill him with self-confidence
   After poisoning him with words
   And the Phantom's shouting to skinny girls
   "Get Outa Here If You Don't Know
   Casanova is just being punished for going
   To Desolation Row"

8. Now at midnight all the agents
   And the superhuman crew
   Come out and round up everyone
   That knows more than they do
   Then they bring them to the factory
   Where the heart-attack machine
   Is strapped across their shoulders
   And then the kerosene
   Is brought down from the castles
   By insurance men who go
   Check to see that nobody is escaping
   To Desolation Row

9. Praise be to Nero's Neptune
   The Titanic sails at dawn
   And everybody's shouting
   "Which Side Are You On?"
   And Ezra Pound and T. S. Eliot
   Fighting in the captain's tower
   While calypso singers laugh at them
   And fishermen hold flowers
   Between the windows of the sea
   Where lovely mermaids flow
   And nobody has to think too much
   About Desolation Row

10. Yes, I received your letter yesterday
    (About the time the door knob broke)
    When you asked how I was doing
    Was that some kind of joke?
    All these people that you mention
    Yes, I know them, they're quite lame
    I had to rearrange their faces
    And give them all another name
    Right now I can't read too good
    Don't send me no more letters no
    Not unless you mail them
    From Desolation Row

Diamond Joe

Traditional, arranged by Bob Dylan

Moderately

1. Now there's a man you'll hear a-bout ____ Most

an-y-where ____ you go, ____ And his hold-ings are in

Tex - as, ____ And his name is Dia - mond Joe. ____

____ 2. He car - ries all his mon - ey ____ In a

dia - mond stud - ded jar, ____ And he nev - er took much

trou - ble ____ With the pro - cess of the law. ____

Additional lyrics

3. I hired out to Diamond Joe, boys,
   Did offer him my hand,
   He gave a string of horses
   So old they could not stand.

4. And I nearly starved to death, boys,
   He did mistreat me so,
   And I never saved a dollar
   In the pay of Diamond Joe.

5. Now his bread it was corn dodger
   And his meat you couldn't chaw,
   Nearly drove me crazy
   With the waggin' of his jaw.

6. And the tellin' of his story,
   Mean to let you know
   That there never was a rounder
   That could lie like Diamond Joe.

Instrumental

7. Now, I tried three times to quit him,
   But he did argue so
   I'm still punchin' cattle
   In the pay of Diamond Joe.

8. And when I'm called up yonder
   And it's my time to go,
   Give my blankets to my buddies
   Give the fleas to Diamond Joe.

Dignity

Words and Music by Bob Dylan

Moderate shuffle beat

1. Fat man look-in' in a ___ blade of steel ___ Thin man look-in' at his last meal

Hol-low man look-in' in a cot-ton-field ___ For dig-ni-ty ___

Wise man look-in' in a blade of grass

Young man look-in' in the shad-ows that pass ___

Poor man look-in' through paint-ed glass For dig-ni-ty

2.-4. *See additional lyrics*

Additional lyrics

2. Blind man breakin' out of a trance
   Puts both his hands in the pockets of chance
   Hopin' to find one circumstance
   Of dignity

   I went to the wedding of Mary-lou
   She said "I don't want nobody see me talkin' to you"
   Said she could get killed if she told me what she knew
   About dignity

   I went down where the vultures feed
   I would've got deeper, but there wasn't any need
   Heard the tongues of angels and the tongues of men
   Wasn't any difference to me

   Chilly wind sharp as a razor blade
   House on fire, debts unpaid
   Gonna stand at the window, gonna ask the maid
   Have you seen dignity?

3. Drinkin' man listens to the voice he hears
   In a crowded room full of covered up mirrors
   Lookin' into the lost forgotten years
   For dignity

   Met Prince Phillip at the home of the blues
   Said he'd give me information if his name wasn't used
   He wanted money up front, said he was abused
   By dignity

Footprints runnin' cross the sliver sand
Steps goin' down into tattoo land
I met the sons of darkness and the sons of light
In the bordertowns of despair

Got no place to fade, got no coat
I'm on the rollin' river in a jerkin' boat
Tryin' to read a note somebody wrote
About dignity

4. Sick man lookin' for the doctor's cure
   Lookin' at his hands for the lines that were
   And into every masterpiece of literature
   For dignity

   Englishman stranded in the blackheart wind
   Combin' his hair back, his future looks thin
   Bites the bullet and he looks within
   For dignity

   Someone showed me a picture and I just laughed
   Dignity never been photographed
   I went into the red, went into the black
   Into the valley of dry bone dreams

   So many roads, so much at stake
   So many dead ends, I'm at the edge of the lake
   Sometimes I wonder what it's gonna take
   To find dignity

Heart of Mine

Words and Music by Bob Dylan

Moderately, with an easy beat

Heart of mine be still, ___

You can play with fire ___ but you'll get the bill. ___

Don't let her know ___ Don't let her know that you

love her. Don't be a fool, don't be blind Heart of mine.

Heart of mine go back home,

You got no rea-son to wan-der, no rea-son to roam.

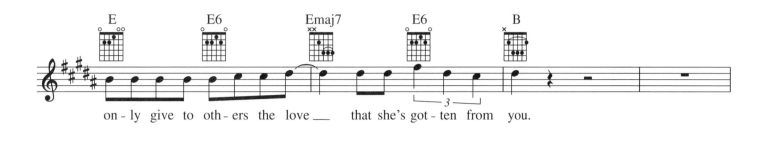

on - ly give to oth - ers the love ___ that she's got - ten from you.

Don't let her know___ don't let her know where you're go - ing. Don't_

___ un - tie the ties that bind _____ Heart of mine.

Heart of mine so ma - li - cious and so full of guile,_

Give you an inch and you'll take a mile. __

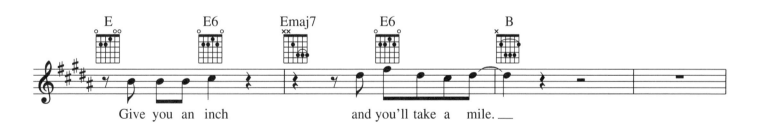

Don't let your - self fall ___ Don't let your - self stum - ble. If you can't_

D.S. (Instrumental) & fade

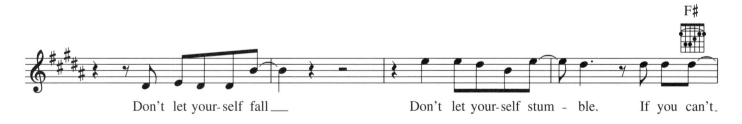

___ do the time,_ don't do the crime Heart of mine.

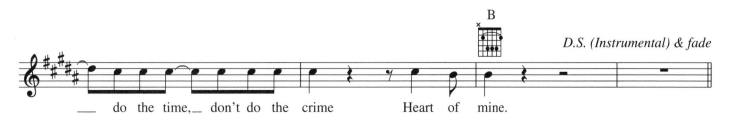

Dirge

Words and Music by Bob Dylan

Additional lyrics

2. I hate that foolish game we played and the need that was expressed
   And the mercy that you showed to me, who ever would have guessed?
   I went out on Lower Broadway and I felt that place within,
   That hollow place where martyrs weep and angels play with sin.

3. Heard your songs of freedom and man forever stripped,
   Acting out his folly while his back is being whipped.
   Like a slave in orbit, he's beaten 'til he's tame,
   All for a moment's glory and it's a dirty, rotten shame.

4. There are those who worship loneliness, I'm not one of them,
   In this age of fiberglass I'm searching for a gem.
   The crystal ball up on the wall hasn't shown me nothing yet,
   I've paid the price of solitude, but at last I'm out of debt.

5. Can't recall a useful thing you ever did for me
   'Cept pat me on the back one time when I was on my knees.
   We stared into each other's eyes 'til one of us would break,
   No use to apologize, what diff'rence would it make?

6. So sing your praise of progress and of the Doom Machine,
   The naked truth is still taboo whenever it can be seen.
   Lady Luck, who shines on me, will tell you where I'm at,
   I hate myself for lovin' you, but I should get over that.

Dirt Road Blues

Words and Music by Bob Dylan

Pac - ing 'round the room __ hop - ing may - be she'd come

back   Well, I __ been pray - ing for __ sal - va - tion __

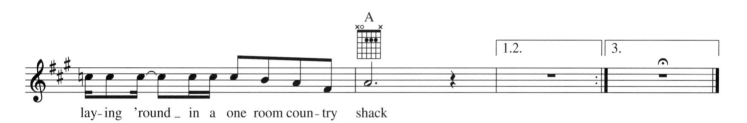

lay - ing 'round _ in a one room coun - try   shack

Additional lyrics

3. Gon' walk down that dirt road until my eyes begin to bleed
   Gon' walk down that dirt road until my eyes begin to bleed
   'Til there's nothing left to see, 'til the chains have been shattered and I've been freed,

4. I been lookin' at my shadow, I been watching the colors up above
   Lookin' at my shadow watching the colors up above
   Rolling through the rain and hail, looking for the sunny side of love

5. *Instrumental*

6. Gon' walk on down that dirt road 'til I'm right beside the sun
   Gon' walk on down until I'm right beside the sun
   I'm gonna have to put up a barrier to keep myself away from everyone.

Disease of Conceit

Words and Music by Bob Dylan

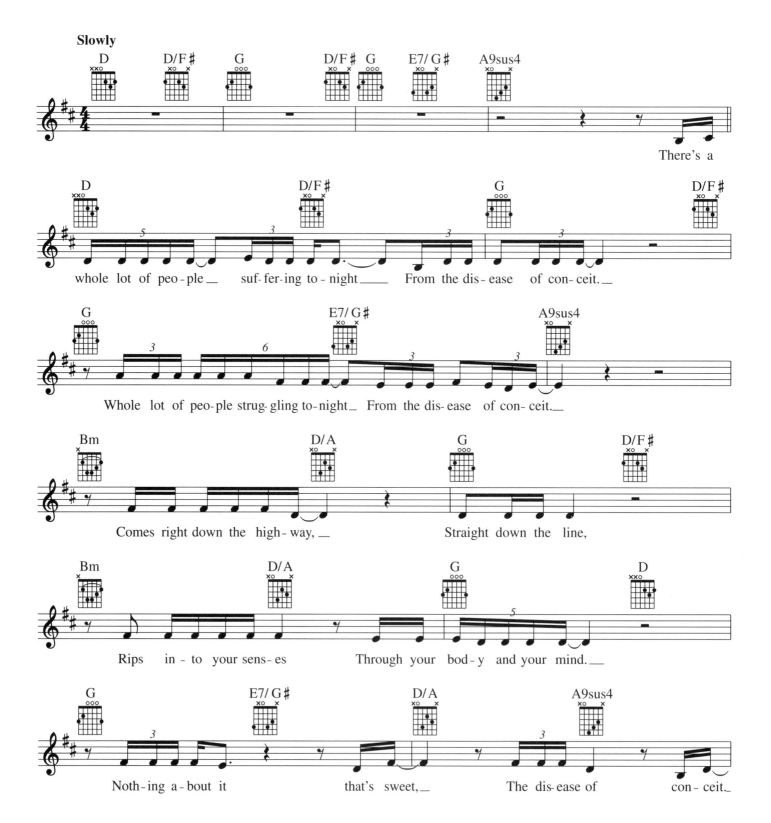

Do Right to Me Baby

Words and Music by Bob Dylan

Moderately

Verse

1. Don't wan - na judge no - bod - y, don't wan - na be judged,

Don't wan - na touch no - bod - y, don't wan - na be touched.

Don't wan - na hurt no - bod - y, don't wan - na be hurt,

Don't wan - na treat no - bod - y like they was _____ dirt.

Chorus

But if you

do right to me, ba - by, I'll do right to you, too. ___ Ya got to

do un - to oth - ers like you'd have ___ them, like you'd have___

___ them, do un - to you. ___

1.-4. **5.** *repeat & fade*

Verse

2. Don't wan - na

Additional lyrics

2. Don't wanna shoot nobody, don't wanna be shot,
   Don't wanna buy nobody, don't wanna be bought.
   Don't wanna bury nobody, don't wanna be buried,
   Don't wanna marry nobody if they're already married.

Chorus

3. Don't wanna burn nobody, don't wanna be burned,
   Don't wanna learn from nobody what I gotta unlearn.
   Don't wanna cheat nobody, don't wanna be cheated,
   Don't wanna defeat nobody if they already been defeated.

Chorus

4. Don't wanna wink at nobody, don't wanna be winked at,
   Don't wanna be used by nobody for a doormat.
   Don't wanna confuse nobody, don't wanna be confused,
   Don't wanna amuse nobody, don't wanna be amused.

Chorus

5. Don't wanna betray nobody, don't wanna be betrayed,
   Don't wanna play with nobody, don't wanna be waylaid.
   Don't wanna miss nobody, don't wanna be missed,
   Don't put my faith in nobody, not even a scientist.

Chorus

Don't Fall Apart on Me Tonight

Words and Music by Bob Dylan

Do you re-mem-ber___ St. James Street Where you blew Jack-ie P.'s mind? You were so

fine, Clark Ga- ble would have fell at your feet And laid his life on the

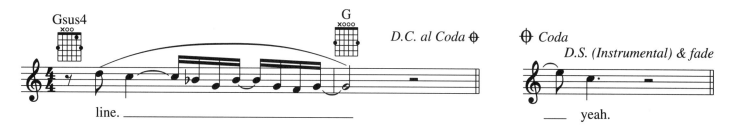

line. ___

D.C. al Coda ⊕   ⊕ _Coda_

D.S. (Instrumental) & fade

___ yeah.

Additional lyrics

2. Come over here from over there, girl,
   Sit down here. You can have my chair.
   I can't see us goin' anywhere, girl.
   The only place open is a thousand miles away and I can't take you there.
   I wish I'd have been a doctor,
   Maybe I'd have saved some life that had been lost,
   Maybe I'd have done some good in the world
   'Stead of burning every bridge I crossed.

   Don't fall apart on me tonight,
   I just don't think that I could handle it.
   Don't fall apart on me tonight,
   Yesterday's just a memory,
   Tomorrow is never what it's supposed to be
   And I need you, oh, yeah.

3. I ain't too good at conversation, girl,
   So you might not know exactly how I feel,
   But if I could, I'd bring you to the mountaintop, girl,
   And build you a house made out of stainless steel.
   But it's like I'm stuck inside a painting
   That's hanging in the Louvre,
   My throat start to tickle and my nose itches
   But I know that I can't move.

   Don't fall apart on me tonight,
   I just don't think that I could handle it.
   Don't fall apart on me tonight,
   Yesterday's gone but the past lives on,
   Tomorrow's just one step beyond
   And I need you, oh, yeah.

Bridge:
Who are these people who are walking towards you?
Do you know them or will there be a fight?
With their humorless smiles so easy to see through,
Can they tell you what's wrong from what's right?

Do you remember St. James Street
Where you blew Jackie P.'s mind?
You were so fine, Clark Gable would have fell at your feet
And laid his life on the line.

4. Let's try to get beneath the surface waste, girl,
    No more booby traps and bombs,
    No more decadence and charm,
    No more affection that's misplaced, girl,
    No more mudcake creatures lying in your arms.
    What about that millionaire with the drumsticks in his pants?
    He looked so baffled and so bewildered
    When he played and we didn't dance.

    Don't fall apart on me tonight,
    I just don't think that I could handle it.
    Don't fall apart on me tonight,
    Yesterday's just a memory,
    Tomorrow is never what it's supposed to be
    And I need you, yeah.

Don't Think Twice, It's All Right

Words and Music by Bob Dylan

Don't Ya Tell Henry

Words and Music by Bob Dylan

Moderate rock

1. I went down to the riv - er on a Sat - ur - day morn, __ A -
2.-4. *See additional lyrics*

look - in' a - round __ just to see who's born. __ I found a lit - tle chick - en

down on his knees, __ I went up and yelled __ to him,

"Please, please, please!" He said, "Don't __ ya tell Hen - ry, Don't

__ ya tell Hen - ry, Don't __ ya tell Hen - ry,

No chord

Ap - ple's got __ your fly." __

Additional lyrics

2. I went down to the corner at a-half past ten,
   I's lookin' around, I wouldn't say when.
   I looked down low, I looked above,
   And who did I see but the one I love.
   She said, "Don't ya tell Henry,
   Don't ya tell Henry,
   Don't ya tell Henry,
   Apple's got your fly."

3. Now, I went down to the beanery at half past twelve,
   A-lookin' around just to see myself.
   I spotted a horse and a donkey, too,
   I looked for a cow and I saw me a few.
   They said, "Don't ya tell Henry,
   Don't ya tell Henry,
   Don't ya tell Henry,
   Apple's got your fly."

4. Now, I went down to the pumphouse the other night,
   A-lookin' around, it was outa sight.
   I looked high and low for that big ol' tree,
   I did go upstairs but I didn't see nobody but me.
   I said, "Don't ya tell Henry,
   Don't ya tell Henry,
   Don't ya tell Henry,
   Apple's got your fly."

Down Along the Cove

Words and Music by Bob Dylan

Down a - long the cove, I spied my
Down a - long the cove, I spied my
Down a - long the cove, We walked to -

true love com - in' my way. ___
lit - tle bun - dle of joy.
geth - er hand in hand.

Down a - long the cove, I spied my true
Down a - long the cove, I spied my lit-
Down a - long the cove, We walked to - geth-

___ love com - in' my way. _____
tle bun - dle of joy. _____
er hand in hand. _____

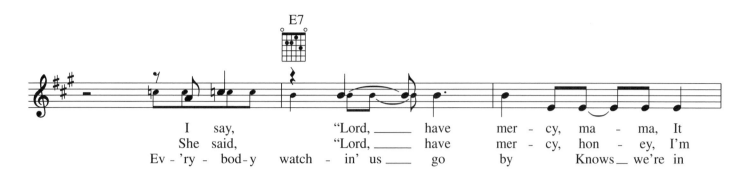

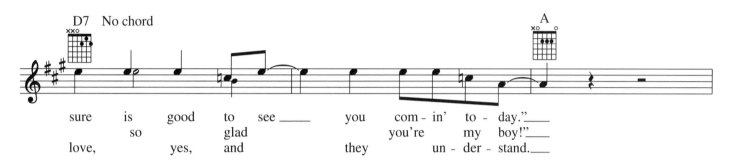

I   say,   "Lord, _____ have   mer - cy, ma - ma, It
She   said,   "Lord, _____ have   mer - cy, hon - ey, I'm
Ev - 'ry - bod - y watch - in' us ____ go   by   Knows __ we're in

sure   is   good   to   see ____   you   com - in' to - day." ____
        so   glad   you're   my   boy!" ____
love,   yes,   and   they   un - der - stand. ___

Down in the Flood

Words and Music by Bob Dylan

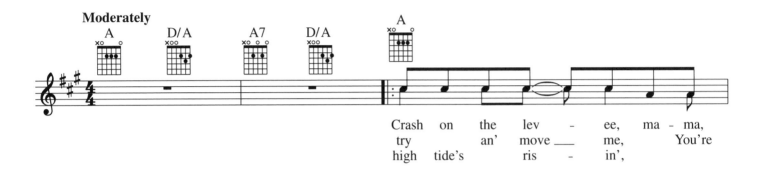

Crash on the lev - ee, ma - ma,
try an' move ___ me, You're
high tide's ris - in',

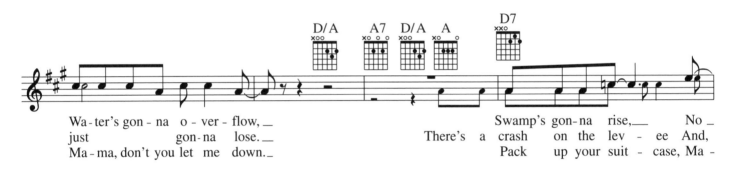

Wa - ter's gon - na o - ver - flow, ___
just gon - na lose. ___
Ma - ma, don't you let me down. ___

Swamp's gon - na rise, ___ No
There's a crash on the lev - ee And,
Pack up your suit - case, Ma -

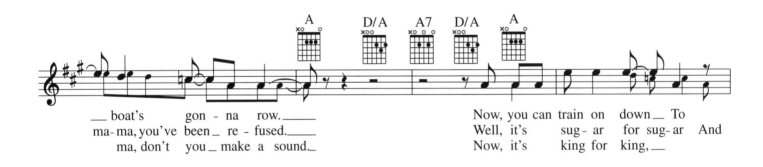

___ boat's gon - na row. ___
ma - ma, you've been ___ re - fused. ___
ma, don't you ___ make a sound. ___

Now, you can train on down ___ To
Well, it's sug - ar for sug - ar And
Now, it's king for king, ___

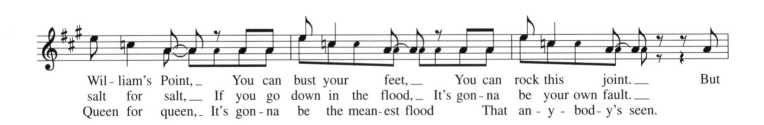

Wil - liam's Point, ___ You can bust your feet, ___ You can rock this joint. ___ But
salt for salt, ___ If you go down in the flood, ___ It's gon - na be your own fault. ___
Queen for queen, ___ It's gon - na be the mean - est flood That an - y - bod - y's seen.

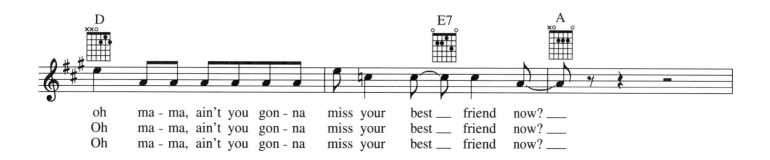

oh   ma - ma, ain't you gon - na   miss your   best __ friend   now? __
Oh   ma - ma, ain't you gon - na   miss your   best __ friend   now? __
Oh   ma - ma, ain't you gon - na   miss your   best __ friend   now? __

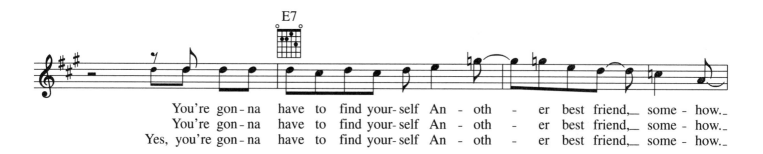

You're gon - na   have to find your- self An - oth - er best friend,__ some - how.__
You're gon - na   have to find your- self An - oth - er best friend,__ some - how.__
Yes, you're gon - na have to find your- self An - oth - er best friend,__ some - how.__

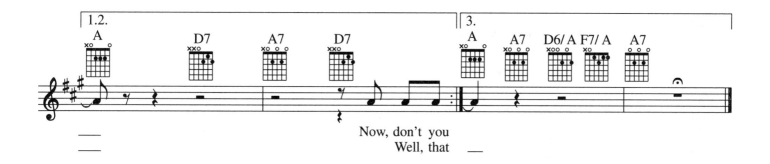

 __
 __   Now, don't you
               Well, that __

Down the Highway

Words and Music by Bob Dylan

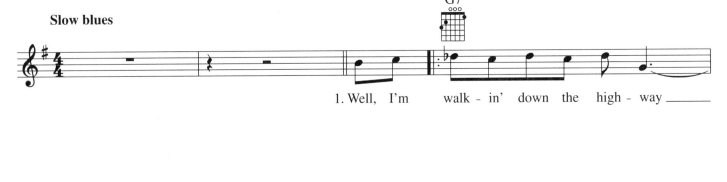

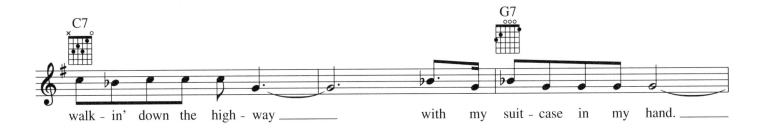

Additional lyrics

2. Well, your streets are gettin' empty,
   Lord, your highway's gettin' filled.
   And your streets are gettin' empty
   And your highway's gettin' filled.
   Well, the way I love that woman,
   I swear it's bound to get me killed.

3. Well, I been gamblin' so long,
   Lord, I ain't got much more to lose.
   Yes, I been gamblin' so long,
   Lord, I ain't got much more to lose.
   Right now I'm havin' trouble,
   Please don't take away my highway shoes.

4. Well, I'm bound to get lucky, baby,
   Or I'm bound to die tryin'.
   Yes, I'm a-bound to get lucky, baby,
   Lord, Lord I'm a-bound to die tryin'.
   Well, meet me in the middle of the ocean
   And we'll leave this ol' highway behind.

5. Well, the ocean took my baby,
   My baby stole my heart from me.
   Yes, the ocean took my baby,
   My baby took my heart from me.
   She packed it all up in a suitcase,
   Lord, she took it away to Italy, Italy.

6. So, I'm a-walkin' down your highway
   Just as far as my poor eyes can see.
   Yes, I'm a-walkin' down your highway
   Just as far as my eyes can see.
   From the Golden Gate Bridge
   All the way to the Statue of Liberty.

Drifter's Escape

Words and Music by Bob Dylan

Moderately

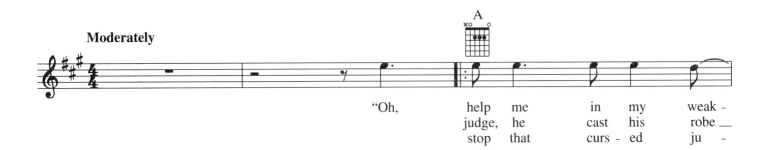

"Oh,   help   me   in   my   weak-
judge,   he   cast   his   robe
stop   that   curs-ed   ju-

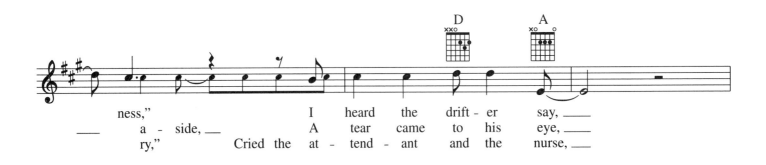

ness,"   I   heard   the   drift-er   say,
a-side,   A   tear   came   to   his   eye,
ry,"   Cried   the   at-tend-ant   and   the   nurse,

As   they   car-ried   him   from   the   court-room,   And   were   tak-
"You   fail   to   un-der-stand,"   he   said,   "Why   must
"The   trial   was   bad   e-nough,   But   this

ing   him   a-way.   "My   trip
you   e-ven   try?"   Out-
is   ten   times   worse."   Just   then

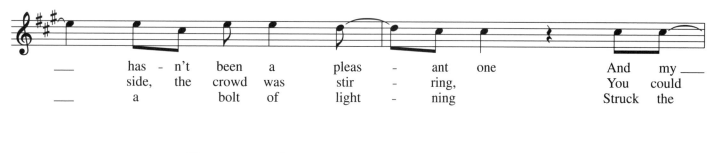

has - n't been a pleas - ant one And my ___
side, the crowd was stir - ring, You could
a bolt of light - ning Struck the

___ time it is - n't long, ___ And I ___
hear it from the door. ___ In - side, __
court - house out of shape, ___ And while ev -

___ still do not know___ What it was ___ that I've done wrong."
___ the judge was step - ping down, While the ju - ry cried for more. __
'ry - bod - y knelt to pray The drift - er did es - cape. __

|1.2.| |3.|

Well, the
"Oh,

Driftin' Too Far from Shore

Words and Music by Bob Dylan

Moderately, with a beat

1. I did-n't know that you'd be leav-in' Or who you thought you were talk-in'

to. I fig-ure may-be we're e - ven Or

may-be I'm one up on you. ___ I send you all my mon-

ey Just like I did be-fore. ___ I tried to reach you

hon - ey, But you're drift - in' too far from shore. ___

Drift-in' too far from shore ___ Drift-in' too far from shore ___

Drift - in' too far from shore ____

Drift - in' too far from shore ____

Coda

Drift - in' too far from shore ____

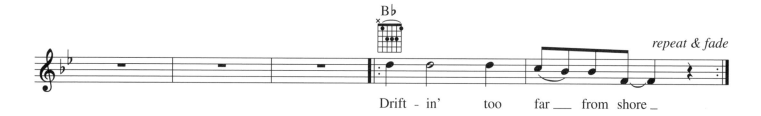

repeat & fade

Drift - in' too far ___ from shore _

Additional lyrics

2. I ain't gonna get lost in this current,
   I don't like playing cat and mouse.
   No gentleman likes making love to a servant.
   Especially when he's in his father's house.

   I never could guess your weight, baby,
   Never needed to call you my whore.
   I always thought you were straight, baby,
   But you're driftin' too far from shore.

   Driftin' too far from shore
   Driftin' too far from shore
   Driftin' too far from shore
   Driftin' too far from shore

3. Well these times and these tunnels are haunted,
   The bottom of the barrel is too.
   I waited years sometimes for what I wanted.
   Everybody can't be as lucky as you.

   Never no more do I wonder,
   Why you don't never play with me any more.
   At any moment you could go under,
   'Cause you're driftin' too far from shore.

   Driftin' too far from shore
   Driftin' too far from shore
   Driftin' too far from shore
   Driftin' too far from shore

4. You and me we had completeness,
   I give you all of what I could provide
   We weren't on the wrong side, sweetness,
   We were the wrong side.

   I've already ripped out the phones honey.
   You can't walk the streets in a war.
   I can finish this alone honey,
   You're driftin' too far from shore.

Emotionally Yours

Words and Music by Bob Dylan

Moderately slow

Come ba - by, find _ me,
Come ba - by, rock _ me,

come ba-by, re-mind _ me _
come ba - by, lock _ me _

of _ where I once be - gun. _
in - to the shad-ows of your heart.

Come ba - by, show _ me,
Come ba - by, teach _ me,

show me you know _ me,
come ba - by, reach _ me,

tell me you're the one. _
let the mu - sic start. _

I could be learn - ing,
I could be dream-ing

you could be yearn-ing
but I keep be - liev-ing

to see be-hind closed
you're the one I'm liv - in'

doors.
for.

But I will al - ways be e - mo - tion - al - ly yours.
And I will al - ways be e -

Eternal Circle

Words and Music by Bob Dylan

Additional lyrics

2. Through a bullet of light
   Her face was reflectin'
   The fast fading words
   That rolled from my tongue
   With a long-distance look
   Her eyes was on fire
   But the song it was long
   And there was more to be sung.

3. My eyes danced a circle
   Across her clear outline
   With her head tilted sideways
   She called me again
   As the tune drifted out
   She breathed hard through the echo
   But the song it was long
   And it was far to the end.

4. I glanced at my guitar
   And played it pretendin'
   That of all the eyes out there
   I could see none
   As her thoughts pounded hard
   Like the pierce of an arrow
   But the song it was long
   And it had to get done.

5. As the tune finally folded
   I laid down the guitar
   Then looked for the girl
   Who'd stayed for so long
   But her shadow was missin'
   For all of my searchin'
   So I picked up my guitar
   And began the next song.

Every Grain of Sand

Words and Music by Bob Dylan

Moderately slow, in 2

1. In the

time of my con - fes - sion, in the hour of my deep - est need __
flow - ers of in - dul - gence and the weeds of yes - ter - year, __

__ When the pool of tears be - neath my feet flood ev - ery new - born __
__ Like crim - 'nals they have choked the breath of con - science and good __

seed There's a dy - in' voice with - in me reach - ing out some -
cheer. The __ sun - beat down up - on the steps of time to light my

where, Toil - ing in the dan - ger and in the mor - als __ of __ de -
way To ease the pain of i - dle - ness and the mem - o - ry __ of __ de -

188

Highlands

Words and Music by Bob Dylan

Additional lyrics

2. Windows were shakin' all night in my dreams
   Everything was exactly the way that it seems
   Woke up this morning and I looked at the same old page
   Same ol' rat race
   Life in the same ol' cage.

3. I don't want nothing from anyone, ain't that much to take
   Wouldn't know the difference between a real blonde and a fake
   Feel like a prisoner in a world of mystery
   I wish someone would come
   And push back the clock for me

4. Well my heart's in the Highlands wherever I roam
   That's where I'll be when I get called home
   The wind, it whispers to the buckeyed trees in rhyme
   Well my heart's in the Highland,
   I can only get there one step at a time.

5. I'm listening to Neil Young, I gotta turn up the sound
   Someone's always yelling turn it down
   Feel like I'm drifting
   Drifting from scene to scene
   I'm wondering what in the devil could it all possibly mean?

6. Insanity is smashing up against my soul
   You can say I was on anything but a roll
   If I had a conscience, well I just might blow my top
   What would I do with it anyway
   Maybe take it to the pawn shop

7. My heart's in the Highlands at the break of dawn
   By the beautiful lake of the Black Swan
   Big white clouds, like chariots that swing down low
   Well my heart's in the Highlands
   Only place left to go

8. I'm in Boston town, in some restaurant
   I got no idea what I want
   Well, maybe I do but I'm just really not sure
   Waitress comes over
   Nobody in the place but me and her

9. It must be a holiday, there's nobody around
   She studies me closely as I sit down
   She got a pretty face and long white shiny legs
   She says, "What'll it be?"
   I say, "I don't know, you got any soft boiled eggs?"

10. She looks at me, says, "I'd bring you some
    But we're out of 'm, you picked the wrong time to come"
    Then she says, "I know you're an artist, draw a picture of me!"
    I say, "I would if I could, but,
    I don't do sketches from memory."

11. "Well," she says, "I'm right here in front of you, or haven't you looked?"
    I say, "All right, I know, but I don't have my drawing book!"
    She gives me a napkin, she says, "You can do it on that"
    I say, "Yes I could but,
    I don't know where my pencil is at!"

12. She pulls one out from behind her ear
    She says, "All right now, go ahead, draw me, I'm standing right here."
    I make a few lines, and I show it for her to see
    Well she takes a napkin and throws it back
    And says, "That don't look a thing like me!"

13. I said, "Oh, kind miss, it most certainly does"
    She says, "You must be jokin'." I say, "I wish I was!"
    Then she says, "You don't read women authors, do you?"
    Least that's what I think I hear her say,
    "Well," I say, "how would you know and what would it matter anyway?"

14. "Well," she says, "you just don't seem like you do!"
    I said, "You're way wrong."
    She says, "Which ones have you read then?" I say, "I read Erica Jong!"
    She goes away for a minute and I slide up out of my chair
    I step outside back to the busy street, but nobody's going anywhere

15. Well my heart's in the Highlands, with the horses and hounds
    Way up in the border country, far from the towns
    With the twang of the arrow and a snap of the bow
    My heart's in the Highlands
    Can't see any other way to go

16. Every day is the same thing out the door
    Feel further away then ever before
    Some things in life, it gets too late to learn
    Well, I'm lost somewhere
    I must have made a few bad turns

17. I see people in the park forgetting their troubles and woes
    They're drinking and dancing, wearing bright colored clothes
    All the young men with their young women looking so good
    Well, I'd trade places with any of them
    In a minute, if I could

18. I'm crossing the street to get away from a mangy dog
    Talking to myself in a monologue
    I think what I need might be a full length leather coat
    Somebody just asked me
    If I registered to vote

19. The sun is beginning to shine on me
    But it's not like the sun that used to be
    The party's over, and there's less and less to say
    I got new eyes
    Everything looks far away

20. Well, my heart's in the Highlands at the break of day
    Over the hills and far away
    There's a way to get there, and I'll figure it out somehow
    But I'm already there in my mind
    And that's good enough for now

Farewell

Words and Music by Bob Dylan

Additional lyrics

2. Oh the weather is against me and the wind blows hard
   And the rain she's a-turnin' into hail.
   I still might strike it lucky on a highway goin' west,
   Though I'm travelin' on a path beaten trail.

   Refrain

3. I will write you a letter from time to time,
   As I'm ramblin' you can travel with me too.
   With my head, my heart and my hands, my love,
   I will send what I learn back home to you.

   Refrain

4. I will tell you of the laughter and of troubles,
   Be them somebody else's or my own.
   With my hands in my pockets and my coat collar high,
   I will travel unnoticed and unknown.

   Refrain

5. I've heard tell of a town where I might as well be bound,
   It's down around the old Mexican plains.
   They say that the people are all friendly there
   And all they ask of you is your name.

   Refrain

Farewell Angelina

Words and Music by Bob Dylan

Moderato

1. Fare - well An - ge - li - na the bells of the crown _____ are be - ing stol - en by ban - dits I must fol - low the sound _____ The tri - an - gle ting - les and the trum-pets play slow _____ Fare - well An - ge - li - na the sky is on fire _____ and I must go. _____ 2. There's no need for an - ger there's no need for blame _____ There's noth - ing to prove _ ev - 'ry -

things's still the same _____ Just a ta - ble stand-ing emp - ty by the

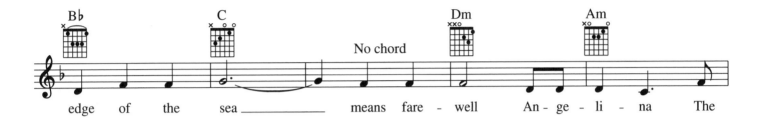

edge of the sea _____ means fare - well An - ge - li - na The

For Verses 2 & 4

sky _____ is trem - bling and I must leave. _____

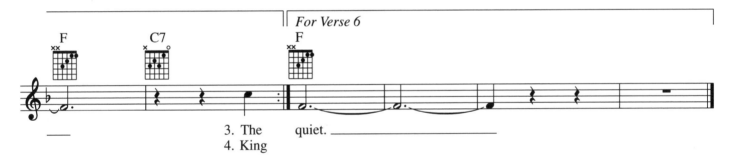

For Verse 6

_____ 3. The quiet. _____
4. King

Additional lyrics

3. The jacks and queens
   Have forsaked the courtyard
   Fifty-two gypsies
   Now file past the guards
   In the space where the deuce
   And the ace once ran wild
   Farewell Angelina
   The sky is folding
   I'll see you in a while.

4. See the cross-eyed pirates sitting
   Perched in the sun
   Shooting tin cans
   With a sawed-off shotgun
   And the neighbors they clap
   And they cheer with each blast
   Farewell Angelina
   The sky's changing color
   And I must leave fast.

5. King Kong, little elves
   On the rooftoops they dance
   Valentino-type tangos
   While the make-up man's hands
   Shut the eyes of the dead
   Not to embarrass anyone
   Farewell Angelina
   The sky is embarrassed
   And I must be gone.

6. The machine guns are roaring
   The puppets heave rocks
   The fiends nail time bombs
   To the hands of the clocks
   Call me any name you like
   I will never deny it
   Farewell Angelina
   The sky is erupting
   I must go where it's quiet.

Father of Night

Words and Music by Bob Dylan

Moderately fast

Fa - ther of night, Fa - ther of day, Fa - ther, who tak - eth the
Fa - ther of day, Fa - ther of night, Fa - ther of black, __
Fa - ther of grain, Fa - ther of wheat, Fa - ther of cold __ and

dark - ness a - way, Fa - ther, who teach - eth the bird to fly, __
Fa - ther of white, Fa - ther, who build the moun - tain so high, __ Who
Fa - ther of heat, Fa - ther of air and Fa - ther of trees, __ Who

to Coda

Build - er of rain - bows __ up in the sky, Fa - ther of lone - li - ness __
shap - eth the cloud __ up in the sky, Fa - ther of time, __

__ and pain, Fa - ther of love and Fa - ther of rain.
Fa - ther of dreams, __ Fa - ther, who turn - eth the

1.

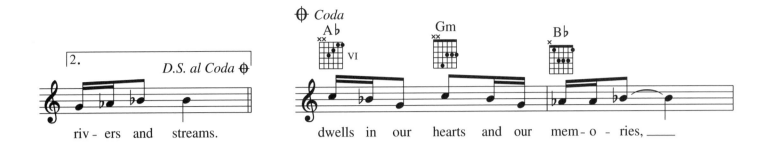

riv - ers and streams.

dwells in our hearts and our mem - o - ries, _____

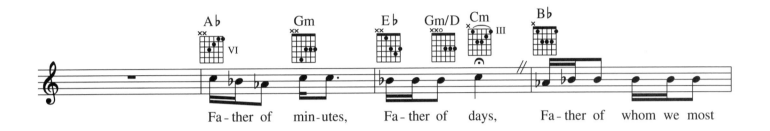

Fa - ther of min - utes, Fa - ther of days, Fa - ther of whom we most

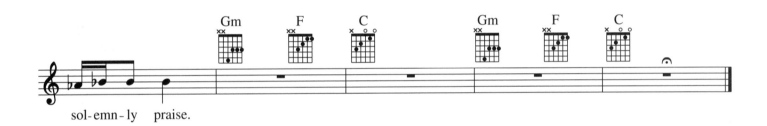

sol - emn - ly praise.

Foot of Pride

Words and Music by Bob Dylan

Moderate beat, quasi recitative

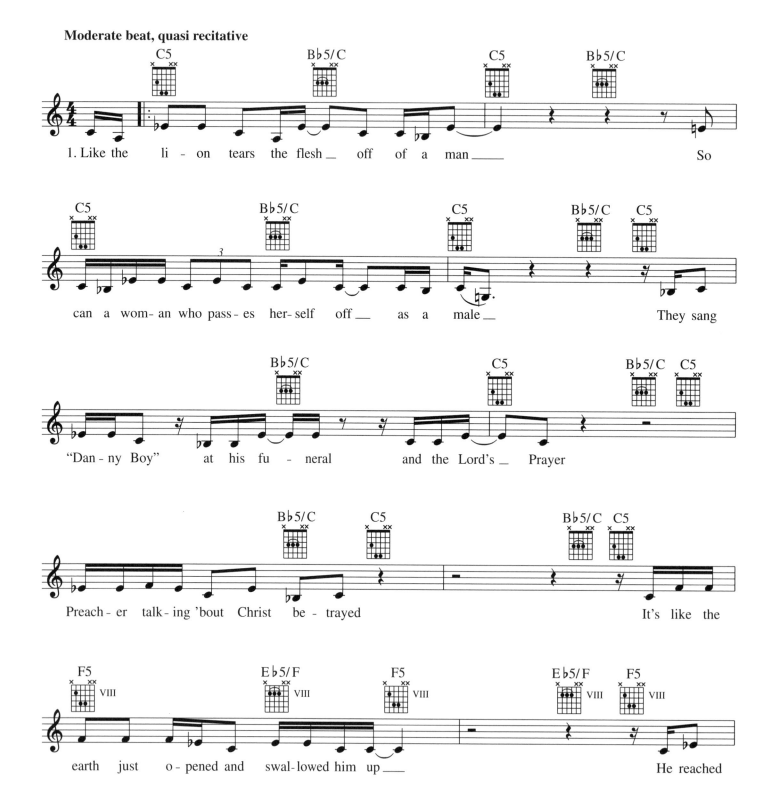

1. Like the li - on tears the flesh __ off of a man __ So
can a wom- an who pass- es her- self off __ as a male __ They sang
"Dan - ny Boy" at his fu - neral and the Lord's __ Prayer
Preach- er talk- ing 'bout Christ be - trayed It's like the
earth just o - pened and swal- lowed him up __ He reached

Additional lyrics

2. Hear ya got a brother named James, don't forget faces or names
   Sunken cheeks and his blood is mixed
   He looked straight into the sun and said revenge is mine
   But he drinks, and drinks can be fixed
   Sing me one more song, about ya love me to the moon and the stranger
   And your fall by the sword love affair with Erroll Flynn
   In these times of compassion when conformity's in fashion
   Say one more stupid thing to me before the final nail is driven in

   Chorus

3. There's a retired businessman named Red, cast down from heaven and he's out of his head
   He feeds off of everyone that he can touch
   He said he only deals in cash or sells tickets to a plane crash
   He's not somebody that you play around with much
   Miss Delilah is his, a Philistine is what she is
   She'll do wondrous works with your fate
   Feed you coconut bread, spice buns in your bed
   If you don't mind sleepin' with your head face down in a grave

   Chorus

4. Well, they'll choose a man for you to meet tonight
   You'll play the fool and learn how to walk through doors
   How to enter into the gates of paradise
   No, how to carry a burden too heavy to be yours
   Yeah, from the stage they'll be tryin' to get water outta rocks
   A whore will pass the hat, collect a hundred grand and say thanks
   They like to take all this money from sin, build big universities to study in
   Sing "Amazing Grace" all the way to the Swiss banks

   Chorus

5. They got some beautiful people out there, man
   They can be a terror to your mind and show you how to hold your tongue
   They got mystery written all over their forehead
   They kill babies in the crib and say only the good die young
   They don't believe in mercy
   Judgment on them is something that you'll never see
   They can exalt you up or bring you down main route
   Turn you into anything that they want you to be

   Chorus

6. Yes, I guess I loved him too
   I can still see him in my mind climbin' that hill
   Did he make it to the top, well he probably did and dropped
   Struck down by the strength of the will
   Ain't nothin' left here partner, just the dust of a plague that has left this whole town afraid
   From now on, this'll be where you're from
   Let the dead bury the dead. Your time will come
   Let hot iron blow as he raised the shade

   Chorus

Honey, Just Allow Me One More Chance

Words and Music by H. Thomas and Bob Dylan

Frankie & Albert

Traditional, arranged by Bob Dylan

1. Fran-kie was a good girl, Ev-'ry-bod-y knows. Paid one hun-dred dol-lars For Al-bert's new suit of clothes. He was her man _____ but he done her wrong. 2. Al-bert said, _ "I'm leav-ing you, _ Won't be gone for long. Don't wait up for me, A-wor-ry 'bout me when I'm gone." _ He was her man ____ but he done her wrong.

Additional lyrics

3. Frankie went down to the corner saloon,
   Get a bucket of beer.
   Said to the bartender,
   "Has my lovin' man been here?"
   He was her man but he done her wrong.

   Instrumental

4. "Well, I ain't gonna tell you no stories,
   I ain't gonna tell you no lies.
   I saw Albert an hour ago
   With a gal named Alice Bly."
   He was her man but he done her wrong.

5. Frankie went down to 12th Street,
   Lookin' up through the window high.
   She saw her Albert there,
   Lovin' up Alice Bly.
   He was her man but he done her wrong.

   Instrumental

6. Frankie pulled out a pistol,
   Pulled out a forty-four.
   Gun went off a-rootie-toot-toot
   And Albert fell on the floor.
   He was her man but he done her wrong.

7. Frankie got down upon her knees,
   Took Albert into her lap.
   Started to hug and kiss him,
   But there was no bringin' him back.
   He was her man but he done her wrong.

   Instrumental

8. "Gimme a thousand policemen,
   Throw me into a cell.
   I shot my Albert dead,
   And now I'm goin' to hell.
   He was my man but he done me wrong."

9. Judge said to the jury,
   "Plain as a thing can be,
   A woman shot her lover down,
   Murder in the second degree."
   He was her man but he done her wrong.

   Instrumental

10. Frankie went to the scaffold,
    Calm as a girl could be,
    Turned her eyes up towards the heavens,
    Said, "Nearer, my God, to Thee."
    He was her man but he done her wrong.

Froggie Went a Courtin'

Traditional, arranged by Bob Dylan

Additional lyrics

3. Said, "Miss Mouse, are you within?" Uh-huh,
   Said he, "Miss Mouse, are you within?" Uh-huh.
   Said, "Miss Mouse, are you within?"
   "Yes, kind sir, I sit and spin," Uh-huh.

4. He took Miss Mousey on his knee, Uh-huh,
   Took Miss Mousey on his knee, Uh-huh.
   Took Miss Mousey on his knee,
   Said, "Miss Mousey, will you marry me?" Uh-huh.

5. "Without my uncle Rat's consent, Uh-huh,
   "Without my uncle Rat's consent, Uh-huh.
   "Without my uncle Rat's consent,
   I wouldn't marry the president," Uh-huh.

6. Uncle Rat laughed and he shook his fat sides, Uh-huh,
   Uncle Rat laughed and he shook his fat sides, Uh-huh.
   Uncle Rat laughed and he shook his fat sides,
   To think his niece would be a bride, Uh-huh.

7. Uncle Rat went runnin' downtown, Uh-huh,
   Uncle Rat went runnin' downtown, Uh-huh.
   Uncle Rat went runnin' downtown
   To buy his niece a wedding gown, Uh-huh.

8. Where shall the wedding supper be? Uh-huh,
   Where shall the wedding supper be? Uh-huh.
   Where shall the wedding supper be?
   Way down yonder in a hollow tree, Uh-huh.

9. What should the wedding supper be? Uh-huh,
   What should the wedding supper be? Uh-huh.
   What should the wedding supper be?
   Fried mosquito in a black-eye pea, Uh-huh.

10. Well, first to come in was a flyin' moth, Uh-huh,
    First to come in was a flyin' moth, Uh-huh.
    First to come in was a flyin' moth,
    She laid out the table cloth, Uh-huh.

11. Next to come in was a juney bug, Uh-huh,
    Next to come in was a juney bug, Uh-huh.
    Next to come in was a juney bug,
    She brought the water jug, Uh-huh.

12. Next to come in was a bumbley bee, Uh-huh,
    Next to come in was a bumbley bee, Uh-huh.
    Next to come in was a bumbley bee,
    Sat mosquito on his knee, Uh-huh.

13. Next to come in was a broken black flea, Uh-huh,
    Next to come in was a broken black flea, Uh-huh.
    Next to come in was a broken black flea,
    Danced a jig with the bumbley bee, Uh-huh.

14. Next to come in was Mrs. Cow, Uh-huh,
    Next to come in was Mrs. Cow, Uh-huh.
    Next to come in was Mrs. Cow,
    She tried to dance but she didn't know how, Uh-huh.

15. Next to come in was a little black tick, Uh-huh,
    Next to come in was a little black tick, Uh-huh.
    Next to come in was a little black tick,
    She ate so much she made us sick, Uh-huh.

16. Next to come in was a big black snake, Uh-huh,
    Next to come in was a big black snake, Uh-huh.
    Next to come in was a big black snake,
    Ate up all of the wedding cake, Uh-huh.

17. Next to come was the old gray cat, Uh-huh,
    Next to come was the old gray cat, Uh-huh.
    Next to come was the old gray cat,
    Swallowed the mouse and ate up the rat, Uh-huh.

18. Mr. Frog went a-hoppin' up over the brook, Uh-huh,
    Mr. Frog went a-hoppin' up over the brook, Uh-huh.
    Mr. Frog went a-hoppin' up over the brook,
    A lily-white duck come and swallowed him up, Uh-huh.

19. A little piece of cornbread layin' on a shelf, Uh-huh,
    A little piece of cornbread layin' on a shelf, Uh-huh.
    A little piece of cornbread layin' on a shelf,
    If you want anymore, you can sing it yourself, Uh-huh.

Instrumental

From a Buick 6

Words and Music by Bob Dylan

Moderato

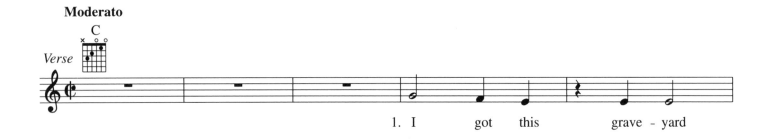

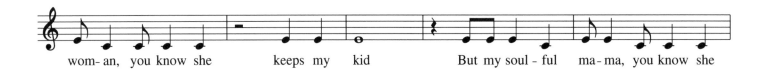

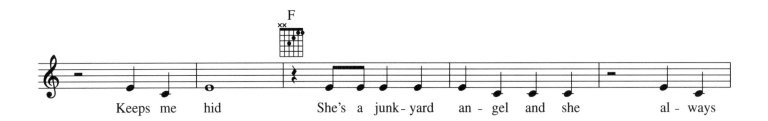

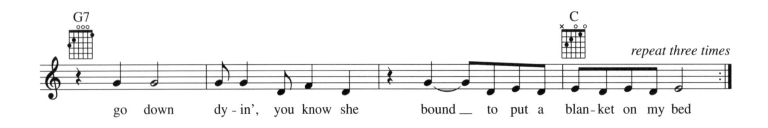

Additional lyrics

2. Well, when the pipeline gets broken and I'm lost on the river bridge
   I'm cracked up on the highway and on the water's edge
   She comes down the thruway ready to sew me up with thread
   Well, if I go down dyin', you know she bound to put a blanket on my bed.

3. Well, she don't make me nervous, she don't talk too much
   She walks like Bo Diddley and she don't need no crutch
   She keeps this four-ten all loaded with lead
   Well, if I go down dyin', you know she bound to put a blanket on my bed.

4. Well, you know I need a steam shovel mama to keep away the dead
   I need a dump truck mama to unload my head
   She brings me everything and more, and just like I said
   Well, if I go down dyin', you know she bound to put a blanket on my bed.

Gates of Eden

Words and Music by Bob Dylan

Additional lyrics

2. The lamppost stands with folded arms
   Its iron claws attached
   To curbs 'neath holes where babies wail
   Though it shadows metal badge
   All and all can only fall
   With a crashing but meaningless blow
   No sound ever comes from the Gates of Eden

3. The savage soldier sticks his head in sand
   And then complains
   Unto the shoeless hunter who's gone deaf
   But still remains
   Upon the beach where hound dogs bay
   At ships with tattooed sails
   Heading for the Gates of Eden

4. With a time-rusted compass blade
   Aladdin and his lamp
   Sits with Utopian hermit monks
   Side saddle on the Golden Calf
   And on their promises of paradise
   You will not hear a laugh
   All except inside the Gates of Eden

5. Relationships of ownership
   They whisper in the wings
   To those condemned to act accordingly
   And wait for succeeding kings
   And I try to harmonize with songs
   The lonesome sparrow sings
   There are no kings inside the Gates of Eden

6. The motorcycle black madonna
   Two-wheeled gypsy queen
   And her silver-studded phantom cause
   The gray flannel dwarf to scream
   As he weeps to wicked birds of prey
   Who pick up on his bread crumb sins
   And there are no sins inside the Gates of Eden

7. The kingdoms of Experience
   In the precious wind they rot
   While paupers change possessions
   Each one wishing for what the other has got
   And the princess and the prince
   Discuss what's real and what is not
   It doesn't matter inside the Gates of Eden

8. The foreign sun, it squints upon
   A bed that is never mine
   As friends and other strangers
   From their fates try to resign
   Leaving men wholly, totally free
   To do anything they wish to do but die
   And there are no trials inside the Gates of Eden

9. At dawn my lover comes to me
   And tells me of her dreams
   With no attempts to shovel the glimpse
   Into the ditch of what each one means
   At times I think there are no words
   But these to tell what's true
   And there are no truths outside the Gates of Eden

George Jackson

Words and Music by Bob Dylan

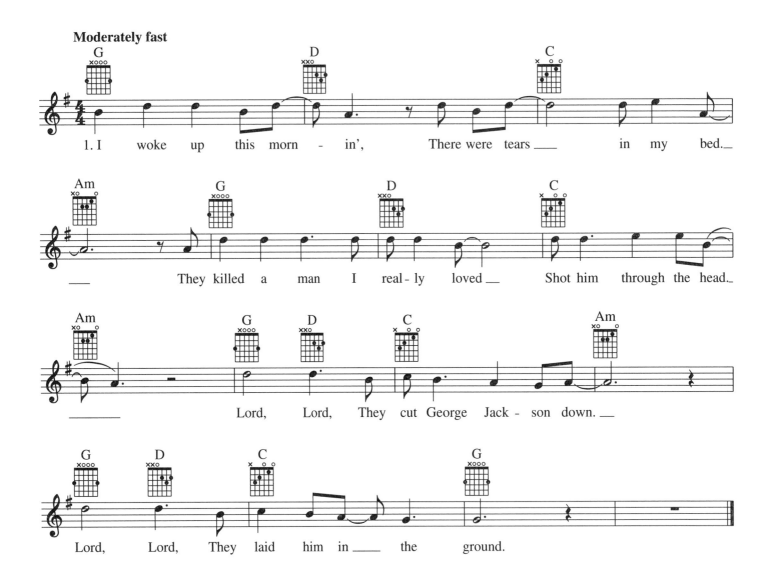

Moderately fast

1. I woke up this morn - in', There were tears ___ in my bed. ___

They killed a man I real - ly loved ___ Shot him through the head. ___

Lord, Lord, They cut George Jack - son down. ___

Lord, Lord, They laid him in ___ the ground.

Additional lyrics

2. Sent him off to prison
   For a seventy-dollar robbery.
   Closed the door behind him
   And they threw away the key.
   Lord, Lord, They cut George Jackson down.
   Lord, Lord,
   They laid him in the ground.

3. He wouldn't take shit from no one
   He wouldn't bow down or kneel.
   Authorities, they hated him
   Because he was just too real.
   Lord, Lord,
   They cut George Jackson down.
   Lord, Lord,
   They laid him in the ground.

4. Prison guards, they cursed him
   As they watched him from above
   But they were frightened of his power
   They were scared of his love.
   Lord, Lord,
   So they cut George Jackson down.
   Lord, Lord,
   They laid him in the ground.

5. Sometimes I think this whole world
   Is one big prison yard.
   Some of us are prisoners
   The rest of us are guards.
   Lord, Lord,
   They cut George Jackson down.
   Lord, Lord,
   They laid him in the ground.

Get Your Rocks Off!

Words and Music by Bob Dylan

Additional lyrics

2. Well, you know, there late one night up on Blueberry Hill,
   One man turned to the other man and said, with a blood-curdlin' chill, he said:
   "Get your rocks off! (Get 'em off!)
   Get your rocks off! (Get 'em off!)
   Get your rocks off! (Get 'em off!)
   Get your rocks off-a me! (Get 'em off!)"

3. Well, you know, we was layin' down around Mink Muscle Creek,
   One man said to the other man, he began to speak, he said:
   "Get your rocks off! (Get 'em off!)
   Get your rocks off! (Get 'em off!)
   Get your rocks off! (Get 'em off!)
   Get your rocks off-a me! (Get 'em off!)"

4. Well, you know, we was cruisin' down the highway in a Greyhound bus.
   All kinds-a children in the side road, they was hollerin' at us, sayin':
   "Get your rocks off! (Get 'em off!)
   Get your rocks off! (Get 'em off!)
   Get your rocks off! (Get 'em off!)
   Get your rocks off-a me!"

God Knows

Words and Music by Bob Dylan

Additional lyrics

Bridge #2:
God knows it's terrifying,
God sees it all unfold,
There's a million reasons for you to be crying
You been so bold and so cold.

God knows that when you see it,
God knows you've got to weep,
God knows the secrets of your heart,
He'll tell them to you when you're asleep.

God knows there's a river,
God knows how to make it flow,
God knows you ain't gonna be taking
Nothing with you when you go.

God knows there's a purpose,
God knows there's a chance,
God knows you can rise above the darkest hour
Of any circumstance.

God knows there's a heaven,
God knows it's out of sight,
God knows we can get all the way from here to there
Even if we've got to walk a million miles by candlelight.

I Threw It All Away

Words and Music by Bob Dylan

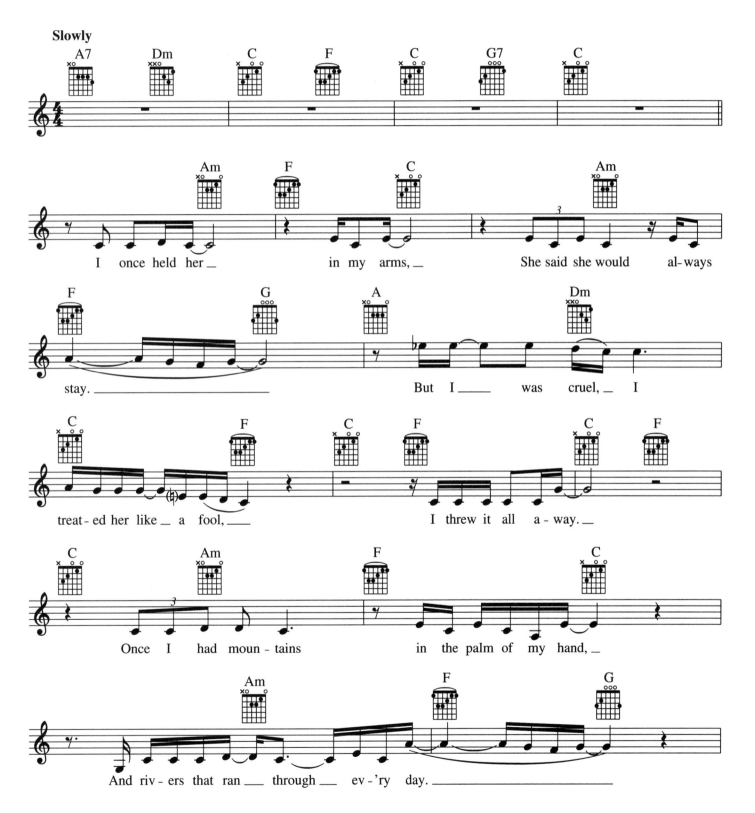

Slowly

I once held her __ in my arms, __ She said she would al-ways stay. _____ But I ___ was cruel, __ I treat-ed her like __ a fool, ___ I threw it all a-way. __ Once I had moun-tains in the palm of my hand, __ And riv-ers that ran __ through __ ev-'ry day. _____

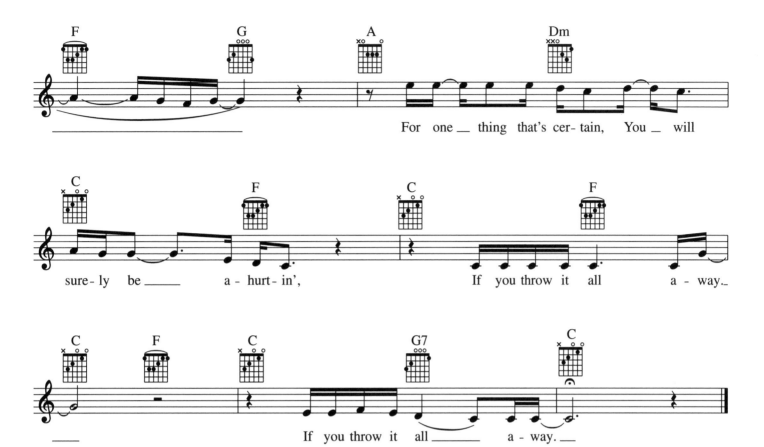

For one __ thing that's cer-tain, You __ will

sure-ly be _____ a-hurt-in', If you throw it all a-way. __

____ If you throw it all _____ a-way. __

Goin' to Acapulco

Words and Music by Bob Dylan

Slowly, with a beat

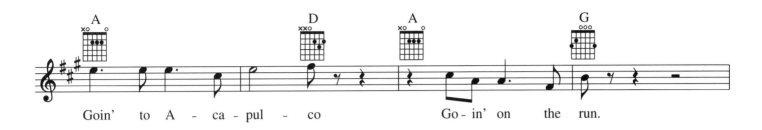

Goin' to A - ca - pul - co   Go - in' on   the   run.

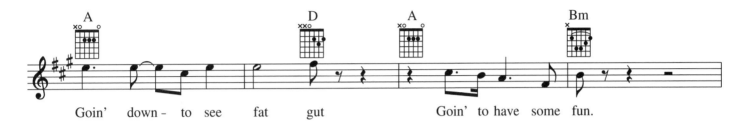

Goin' down - to see fat gut   Goin' to have some fun.

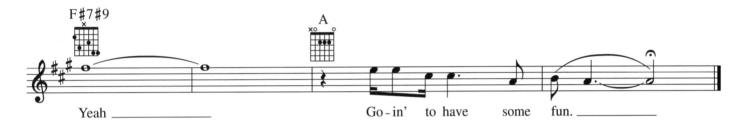

Yeah _____   Go - in' to have   some fun. _____

Additional lyrics

2. Now, whenever I get up
   And I ain't got what I see
   I just make it down to Rose Marie's
   'Bout a quarter after three.

   There are worse ways of getting there
   And I ain't complainin' none.
   If the clouds don't drop and the train don't stop
   I'm bound to meet the sun.

   Goin'to Acapulco
   Goin'on the run.
   Goin'down to see some girl
   Goin'to have some fun.
   Yeah
   Goin'to have some fun.

3. Now, if someone offers me a joke
   I just say no thanks.
   I try to tell it like it is
   And keep away from pranks.

   Well, sometime you know when the well breaks down
   I just go pump on it some.
   Rose Marie, she likes to go to big places
   And just set there waitin' for me to come.

   Goin'to Acapulco
   Goin'on the run.
   Goin'down to see some girl
   Goin'to have some fun.
   Yeah
   Goin'to have some fun.

Going, Going, Gone

Words and Music by Bob Dylan

Slowly

I've just reached_ a place ___ Where the wil-low don't bend.

There's not much more to be said It's ___ the top of the end. I'm ___

go - ing, ___ I'm go - ing, _ I'm gone. _

I'm clos - in' the book _ On the pag - es and the text

And I don't real - ly care What ___ hap - pens next. ___ I'm just

go - ing, I'm go - ing, ___ I'm gone. _

Golden Loom

Words and Music by Bob Dylan

Additional lyrics

2. First we wash our feet near the immortal shrine
   And then our shadows meet and then we drink the wine.
   I see the hungry clouds up above your face
   And then the tears roll down, what a bitter taste.
   And then you drift away on a summer's day where the wildflowers bloom
   With your golden loom.

3. I walk across the bridge in the dismal light
   Where all the cars are stripped between the gates of night.
   I see the trembling lion with the lotus flower tail
   And then I kiss your lips as I lift your veil.
   But you're gone and then all I seem to recall is the smell of perfume
   And your golden loom.

Gonna Change My Way of Thinking

Words and Music by Bob Dylan

Moderately slow rock beat

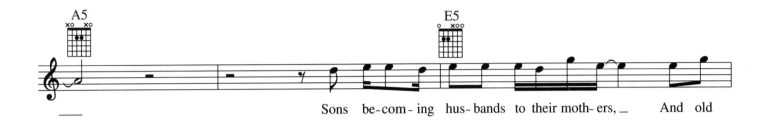

Sons be-com-ing hus-bands to their moth-ers, __ And old

men turn-ing __ young daugh-ters in-to whores. ___

Additional lyrics

3. Stripes on your shoulders,
   Stripes on your back and on your hands.
   Stripes on your shoulders,
   Stripes on your back and on your hands.
   Swords piercing your side,
   Blood and water flowing through the land.

4. Well don't know which one is worse,
   Doing your own thing or just being cool.
   Well don't know which one is worse,
   Doing your own thing or just being cool.
   You remember only about the brass ring,
   You forget all about the golden rule.

5. You can mislead a man,
   You can take ahold of his heart with your eyes.
   You can mislead a man,
   You can take ahold of his heart with your eyes.
   But there's only one authority,
   And that's the authority on high.

6. I got a God-fearing woman,
   One I can easily afford.
   I got a God-fearing woman,
   One I can easily afford.
   She can do the Georgia crawl,
   She can walk in the spirit of the Lord.

7. Jesus said, "Be ready,
   For you know not the hour in which I come."
   Jesus said, "Be ready,
   For you know not the hour in which I come."
   He said, "He who is not for Me is against Me,"
   Just so you know where He's coming from.

8. There's a kingdom called Heaven,
   A place where there is no pain of birth.
   There's a kingdom called Heaven,
   A place where there is no pain of birth.
   Well the Lord created it, mister,
   About the same time He made the earth.

Got My Mind Made Up

Words and Music by Bob Dylan and Tom Petty

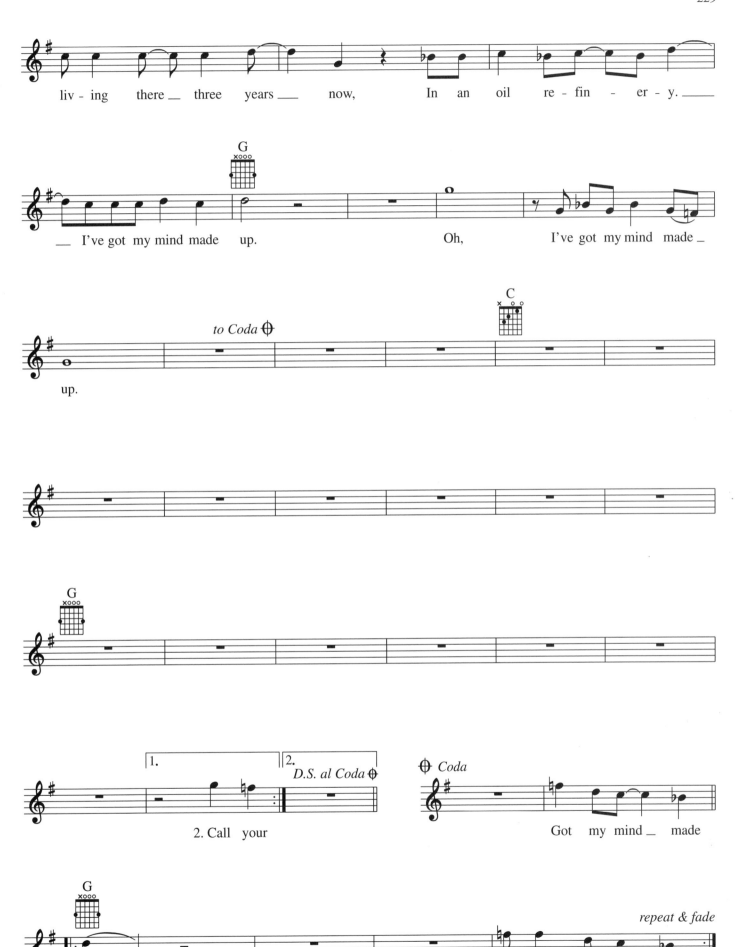

liv - ing there __ three years __ now, In an oil re - fin - er - y. ____

G

__ I've got my mind made up. Oh, I've got my mind made _

to Coda ⊕

C

up.

G

1.

2. *D.S. al Coda* ⊕

⊕ *Coda*

2. Call your

Got my mind __ made

G

repeat & fade

up ____

I've got my mind made

Additional lyrics

2. Call your Ma in Tallahassee
   Tell her her baby's on the line.
   Tell her not to worry
   Everything is gonna be fine.

   Well, I gave you all my money
   All my connections, too.
   There ain't nothin' in this world, girl
   You can say I didn't give to you.
   I've got my mind made up.
   I've got my mind made up.

3. You will be alright, girl,
   Someone's watchin' over you.
   He won't do nothin' to you
   Baby that I wouldn't do.

   Well, if you don't want to see me,
   Look the other way.
   You don't have to feed me,
   I ain't your dog that's gone astray.
   I got my mind made up
   I got my mind made up
   I got my mind made up
   I got my mind made up
   I got my mind made up

If Not for You

Words and Music by Bob Dylan

Gotta Serve Somebody

Words and Music by Bob Dylan

____ some-bod- y.　　　　Well, it　may　be　the　dev - il　or ____ it __

____ may　be　the　Lord　But you're gon- na have to serve some-bod- y.　　　2. You

|1.-6.|　|7.|

Additional lyrics

2. You might be a rock 'n' roll addict prancing on the stage,
   You might have drugs at your command, women in a cage,
   You may be a business man or some high degree thief,
   They may call you Doctor or they may call you Chief

   But you're gonna have to serve somebody, yes indeed
   You're gonna have to serve somebody,
   Well, it may be the devil or it may be the Lord
   But you're gonna have to serve somebody.

3. You may be a state trooper, you might be a young Turk,
   You may be the head of some big TV network,
   You may be rich or poor, you may be blind or lame,
   You may be living in another country under another name

   But you're gonna have to serve somebody, yes indeed
   You're gonna have to serve somebody,
   Well, it may be the devil or it may be the Lord
   But you're gonna have to serve somebody.

4. You may be a construction worker working on a home,
   You may be living in a mansion or you might live in a dome,
   You might own guns and you might even own tanks,
   You might be somebody's landlord, you might even own
   banks

   But you're gonna have to serve somebody, yes indeed
   You're gonna have to serve somebody,
   Well, it may be the devil or it may be the Lord
   But you're gonna have to serve somebody.

5. You may be a preacher with your spiritual pride,
   You may be a city councilman taking bribes on the side,
   You may be workin' in a barbershop, you may know how to
   cut hair,
   You may be somebody's mistress, may be somebody's heir

   But you're gonna have to serve somebody, yes indeed
   You're gonna have to serve somebody,
   Well, it may be the devil or it may be the Lord
   But you're gonna have to serve somebody.

6. Might like to wear cotton, might like to wear silk,
   Might like to drink whiskey, might like to drink milk,
   You might like to eat caviar, you might like to eat bread,
   You may be sleeping on the floor, sleeping in a king-sized bed

   But you're gonna have to serve somebody, yes indeed
   You're gonna have to serve somebody,
   Well, it may be the devil or it may be the Lord
   But you're gonna have to serve somebody.

7. You may call me Terry, you may call me Timmy,
   You may call me Bobby, you may call me Zimmy,
   You may call me R.J., you may call me Ray,
   You may call me anything but no matter what you say

   You're gonna have to serve somebody, yes indeed
   You're gonna have to serve somebody.
   Well, it may be the devil or it may be the Lord
   But you're gonna have to serve somebody.

The Groom's Still Waiting at the Altar

Words and Music by Bob Dylan

Moderately slow funky blues

1. Prayed in the ghet-to with my face in the ce-ment, Heard the last moan of a box-er, seen the mas-sa-cre of the in-no-cent, Felt a-round for the light switch, be-came naus-e-at-ed. She was walk-ing down the hall-way while the walls de-te-ri-o-rat-ed. East of the Jor-dan, hard as the Rock of Gib-ral-tar, I see the

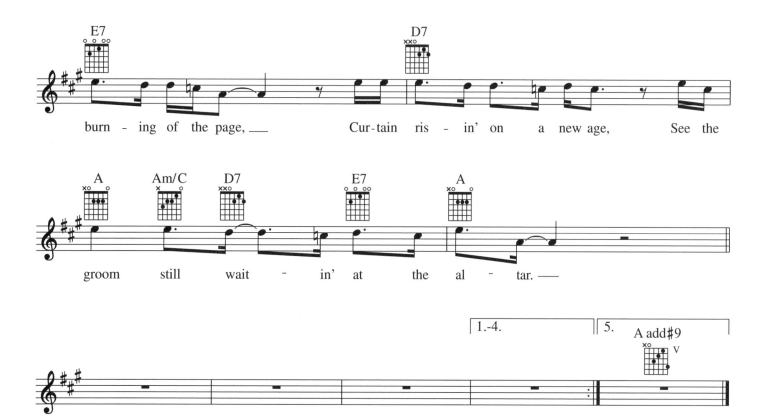

burn - ing of the page, ___ Cur-tain ris - in' on a new age, See the

groom still wait - in' at the al - tar. __

1.-4.   5. A add♯9

Additional lyrics

2. Try to be pure at heart, they arrest you for robbery,
   Mistake your shyness for aloofness, your shyness for snobbery,
   Got the message this morning, the one that was sent to me
   About the madness of becomin' what one was never meant to be.

   West of the Jordan, east of the Rock of Gibraltar,
   I see the burning of the stage,
   Curtain risin' on a new age,
   See the groom still waitin' at the altar.

3. Don't know what I can say about Claudette that wouldn't come back to haunt me,
   Finally had to give her up 'bout the time she began to want me.
   But I know God has mercy on them who are slandered and humiliated.
   I'd a-done anything for that woman if she didn't make me feel so obligated.

   West of the Jordan, west of the Rock of Gibraltar,
   I see the burning of the cage,
   Curtain risin' on a new stage,
   See the groom still waitin' at the altar.

4. Put your hand on my head, baby, do I have a temperature?
   I see people who are supposed to know better standin' around like furniture.
   There's a wall between you and what you want and you got to leap it,
   Tonight you got the power to take it, tomorrow you won't have the power to keep it.

   West of the Jordan, east of the Rock of Gibraltar,
   I see the burning of the stage,
   Curtain risin' on a new age,
   See the groom still waitin' at the altar.

5. Cities on fire, phones out of order,
   They're killing nuns and soldiers, there's fighting on the border.
   What can I say about Claudette?
   Ain't seen her since January,
   She could be respectably married or running a whorehouse in Buenos Aires.

   West of the Jordan, west of the Rock of Gibraltar,
   I see the burning of the stage,
   Curtain risin' on a new age,
   See the groom still waitin' at the altar.

In Search of Little Sadie

Words and Music by Bob Dylan

Freely

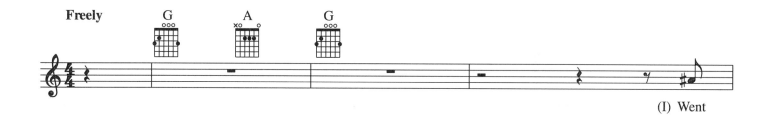

(I) Went

out last night just to take a lit-tle round, I met my Lit-tle Sa-die and I brought her down.___ I

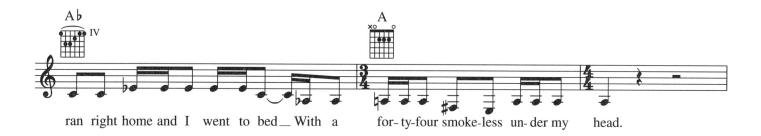

ran right home and I went to bed___ With a for-ty-four smoke-less un-der my head.

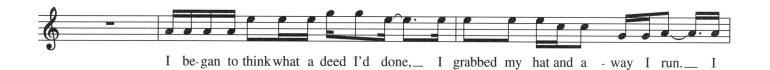

I be-gan to think what a deed I'd done,___ I grabbed my hat and a-way I run.___ I

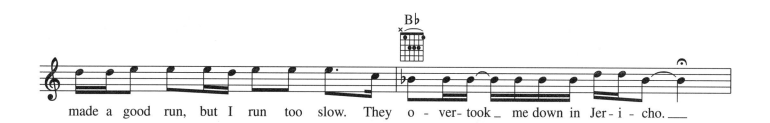

made a good run, but I run too slow. They o-ver-took___ me down in Jer-i-cho.___

Guess I'm Doin' Fine

Words and Music by Bob Dylan

Well, I ain't got _____ my child - hood Or friends I

once __ did know, _____ No, I ain't got _____ my child -

hood Or friends I once __ did know. _____ But

I still _____ got my voice left, I can take it an - y -

where __ I go. _____ Hey, hey, _____ so I

guess I'm _____ (spoken) do - in' fine.

Additional lyrics

2. And I've never had much money
   But I'm still around somehow.
   No, I've never had much money
   But I'm still around somehow.
   Many times I've bended
   But I ain't never yet bowed.
   Hey, hey, so I guess I'm doin' fine.

3. Trouble, oh trouble,
   I've trouble on my mind
   Trouble, oh trouble,
   Trouble on my mind.
   But the trouble in the world, Lord,
   Is much more bigger than mine.
   Hey, hey, so I guess I'm doin' fine.

4. And I never had no armies
   To jump at my command.
   No, I ain't got no armies
   To jump at my command.
   But I don't need no armies,
   I got me one good friend.
   Hey, hey, so I guess I'm doin' fine.

5. I been kicked and whipped and trampled on,
   I been shot at just like you.
   I been kicked and whipped and trampled on,
   I been shot at just like you.
   But as long as the world keeps a-turnin',
   I just keep a-turnin' too.
   Hey, hey, so I guess I'm doin' fine.

6. Well, my road might be rocky,
   The stones might cut my face.
   My road it might be rocky,
   The stones might cut my face.
   But as some folks ain't got no road at all,
   They gotta stand in the same old place.
   Hey, hey, so I guess I'm doin' fine.

Gypsy Lou

Words and Music by Bob Dylan

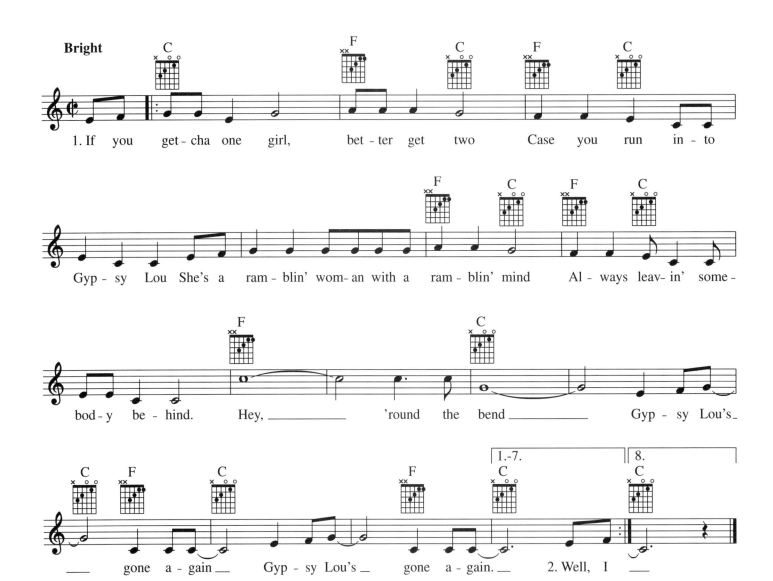

Bright

1. If you get-cha one girl, bet-ter get two Case you run in-to

Gyp - sy Lou She's a ram - blin' wom-an with a ram - blin' mind Al - ways leav - in' some-

bod - y be - hind. Hey, _____ 'round the bend _____ Gyp - sy Lou's_

___ gone a - gain __ Gyp - sy Lou's _ gone a - gain. __ 2. Well, I __

1.-7.   **8.**

Additional lyrics

2. Well, I seen the whole country through
   Just to find Gypsy Lou
   Seen it up, seen it down
   Followin' Gypsy Lou around.
   Hey, 'round the bend
   Gypsy Lou's gone again
   Gypsy Lou's gone again.

3. Well, I gotta stop and take some rest
   My poor feet are second best
   My poor feet are wearin' thin
   Gypsy Lou's gone again.
   Hey, gone again
   Gypsy Lou's 'round the bend
   Gypsy Lou's 'round the bend.

4. Well, seen her up in old Cheyenne
   Turned my head and away she ran
   From Denver Town to Wichita
   Last I heard she's in Arkansas.
   Hey, 'round the bend
   Gypsy Lou's gone again
   Gypsy Lou's gone again.

5. Well, I tell you what if you want to do
   Tell you what, you'll wear out your shoes
   If you want to wear out your shoes
   Try and follow Gypsy Lou.
   Hey, gone again
   Gypsy Lou's 'round the bend
   Gypsy Lou's 'round the bend.

6. Well, Gypsy Lou, I been told
   Livin' down on Gallus Road
   Gallus Road, Arlington
   Moved away to Washington.
   Hey, 'round the bend
   Gypsy Lou's gone again
   Gypsy Lou's gone again.

7. Well, I went down to Washington
   Then she went to Oregon
   I skipped the ground and hopped a train
   She's back in Gallus Road again.
   Hey, I can't win
   Gypsy Lou's gone again
   Gypsy Lou's gone again.

8. Well, the last I heard of Gypsy Lou
   She's in a Memphis calaboose
   She left one too many a boy behind
   He committed suicide.
   Hey, you can't win
   Gypsy Lou's gone again
   Gypsy Lou's gone again.

Had a Dream About You, Baby

Words and Music by Bob Dylan

Additional lyrics

4. You kiss me, baby, in the coffee shop
   You make me nervous, you gotta stop

   Chorus

5. You got a rag wrapped around your head
   Wearing a long dress fire engine red

   Chorus

Handy Dandy

Words and Music by Bob Dylan

Additional lyrics

Bridge #2:
He's got that clear crystal fountain
He's got that soft silky skin
He's got that fortress on the mountain
With no doors, no windows, no thieves can break in

Handy Dandy, sitting with a girl named Nancy in a garden feelin' kind of lazy
He says, "Ya want a gun? I'll give you one." She says, "Boy, you talking crazy."
Handy Dandy, just like sugar and candy
Handy Dandy, pour him another brandy

Handy Dandy, he got a basket of flowers and a bag full or sorrow
He finishes his drink, he gets up from the table he says, "Okay, boys, I'll see you tomorrow."
Handy Dandy, Handy Dandy, just like sugar and candy
Handy Dandy, just like sugar and candy

A Hard Rain's A-Gonna Fall

Words and Music by Bob Dylan

Moderato

Oh, where have you been, my blue-eyed son? Oh,

where have you been, my dar-ling young one? 1. I've

stum- bled on the side of __ twelve mis- ty moun-tains,
walked and I've crawled on __ six crook- ed high-ways,
stepped in the mid- dle of __ sev- en sad for- ests,
been out in front of a doz- en dead o- ceans, 2. I've / 3. I've / 4. I've

5. I've been ten thou-sand miles in the mouth of a grave-yard, And it's a hard,

and it's a hard, it's a hard, and it's a hard, and it's a

hard rain's _____ a gon-na fall. _____

Additional lyrics

2. Oh, what did you see, my blue-eyed son?
   Oh, what did you see, my darling young one?

   I saw a newborn baby with wild wolves all around it,
   I saw a highway of diamonds with nobody on it,
   I saw a black branch with blood that kept drippin',
   I saw a room full of men with their hammers a-bleedin',
   I saw a white ladder all covered with water,
   I saw ten thousand talkers whose tongues were all broken,

   I saw guns and sharp swords in the hands of young children,
   And it's a hard, and it's a hard, it's a hard, it's a hard,
   And it's a hard rain's a-gonna fall.

3. And what did you hear, my blue-eyed son?
   And what did you hear, my darling young one?

   I heard the sound of a thunder, it roared out a warnin',
   Heard the roar of a wave that could drown the whole world,
   Heard one hundred drummers whose hands were a-blazin',
   Heard ten thousand whisperin' and nobody listenin',
   Heard one person starve, I heard many people laughin',
   Heard the song of a poet who died in the gutter,
   Heard the sound of a clown who cried in the alley,
   And it's a hard, and it's a hard, it's a hard, it's a hard,
   And it's a hard rain's a-gonna fall.

4. Oh, who did you meet, my blue-eyed son?
   Who did you meet, my darling young one?

   I met a young child beside a dead pony,
   I met a white man who walked a black dog,
   I met a young woman whose body was burning,
   I met a young girl, she gave me a rainbow,
   I met one man who was wounded in love,
   I met another man who was wounded with hatred,
   And it's a hard, it's a hard, it's a hard, it's a hard,
   It's a hard rain's a-gonna fall.

5. Oh, what'll you do now, my blue-eyed son?
   Oh, what'll you do now, my darling young one?

   I'm a-goin' back out 'fore the rain starts a-fallin',
   I'll walk to the depths of the deepest black forest,
   Where the people are many and their hands are all empty,
   Where the pellets of poison are flooding their waters,
   Where the home in the valley meets the damp dirty prison,
   Where the executioner's face is always well hidden,
   Where hunger is ugly, where souls are forgotten,
   Where black is the color, where none is the number,
   And I'll tell it and think it and speak it and breathe it,
   And reflect it from the mountain so all souls can see it,
   Then I'll stand on the ocean until I start sinkin',
   But I'll know my song well before I start singin',
   And it's a hard, it's a hard, it's a hard, it's a hard,
   It's a hard rain's a-gonna fall.

Hard Times

Traditional, arranged by Bob Dylan

Additional lyrics

2. While we seek mirth and beauty and music light and gay,
   There are frail forms fainting at the door.
   Though their voices are silent, their pleading looks will say,
   Oh, hard times, come again no more.
   'Tis the song, the sigh of the weary.
   Hard times, hard times, come again no more.
   Many days you have lingered all around my cabin door.
   Oh, hard times, come again no more.

3. There's a pale drooping maiden who toils her life away
   With a worn heart, whose better days are o'er.
   Though her voice it would be merry, 'tis sighing all the day,
   Oh, hard times, come again no more.
   'Tis the song, the sigh of the weary.
   Hard times, hard times, come again no more.
   Many days you have lingered all around my cabin door.
   Oh, hard times, come again no more.

   'Tis the song, the sigh of the weary.
   Hard times, hard times, come again no more.
   Many days you have lingered all around my cabin door.
   Oh, hard times, come again no more.

Hero Blues

Words and Music by Bob Dylan

Highway 61 Revisited

Words and Music by Bob Dylan

Bright (in 4)

1. Oh God said to A - bra-ham, "Kill me a son," Abe says, "Man you must be put - tin' me on"__ God say, "No." Abe say, "What?" God say, "You can do what you want Abe, but the next time you see me com - in' you bet-ter run" Well Abe says, "Where do you want this kill - in' done?" God says, "Out on High - way Six - ty - one."

repeat four times

Additional lyrics

2. Well Georgia Sam he had a bloody nose
   Welfare Department they wouldn't give him no clothes
   He asked poor Howard where can I go
   Howard said there's only one place I know
   Sam said tell me quick man I got to run
   Ol' Howard just pointed with his gun
   And said that way down on Highway 61.

3. Well Mack the Finger said to Louie the King
   I got forty red white and blue shoe strings
   And a thousand telephones that don't ring
   Do you know where I can get rid of these things
   And Louie the King said let me think for a minute son
   And he said yes I think it can be easily done
   Just take everything down to Highway 61.

4. Now the fifth daughter on the twelfth night
   Told the first father that things weren't right
   My complexion she said is much too white
   He said come here and step into the light he says hmm you're right
   Let me tell the second mother this has been done
   But the second mother was with the seventh son
   And they were both out on Highway 61.

5. Now the rovin' gambler he was very bored
   He was tryin' to create a next world war
   He found a promoter who nearly fell off the floor
   He said I never engaged in this kind of thing before
   But yes I think it can be very easily done
   We'll just put some bleachers out in the sun
   And have it on Highway 61.

Hurricane

Words and Music by Bob Dylan and Jacques Levy

Moderately

1. Pis - tol shots ring out in the bar - room night __ En - ter Pat - ty Val - en-tine from the

up - per hall. __ She sees the bar-tend - er in a pool of blood, __

Cries out, "My God, they killed __ them all!" ____ Here comes the sto - ry of the

Hur - ri - cane, __ The man the au-thor-i - ties came __ to blame __

For some-thin' that he nev - er done. Put in a pris - on cell, but

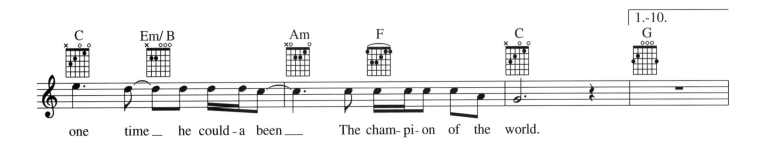

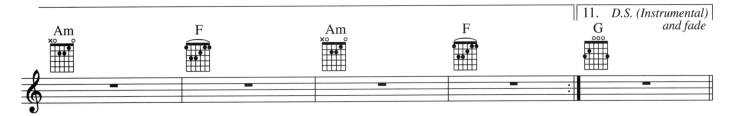

one   time ___ he could-a been ___   The cham- pi- on   of   the   world.

Additional lyrics

2. Three bodies lyin' there does Patty see
   And another man named Bello, movin' around mysteriously.
   "I didn't do it," he says, and he throws up his hands
   "I was only robbin' the register, I hope you understand.
   I saw them leavin'," he says, and he stops
   "One of us had better call up the cops."
   And so Patty calls the cops
   And they arrive on the scene with their red lights flashin'
   In the hot New Jersey night.

3. Meanwhile, far away in another part of town
   Rubin Carter and a couple of friends are drivin' around.
   Number one contender for the middleweight crown
   Had no idea what kinda shit was about to go down
   When a cop pulled him over to the side of the road
   Just like the time before and the time before that.
   In Paterson that's just the way things go.
   If you're black you might as well not show up on the street
   'Less you wanna draw the heat.

4. Alfred Bello had a partner and he had a rap for the cops.
   Him and Arthur Dexter Bradley were just out prowlin' around
   He said, "I saw two men runnin' out, they looked like middleweights
   They jumped into a white car with out-of-state plates."
   And Miss Patty Valentine just nodded her head.
   Cop said, "Wait a minute, boys, this one's not dead"
   So they took him to the infirmary
   And though this man could hardly see
   They told him that he could identify the guilty men.

5. Four in the mornin' and they haul Rubin in,
   Take him to the hospital and they bring him upstairs.
   The wounded man looks up through his one dyin' eye
   Says, "Wha'd you bring him in here for? He ain't the guy!"
   Yes, here's the story of the Hurricane,
   The man the authorities came to blame
   For somethin' that he never done.
   Put in a prison cell, but one time he could-a been
   The champion of the world.

6. Four months later, the ghettos are in flame,
   Rubin's in South America, fightin' for his name
   While Arthur Dexter Bradley's still in the robbery game
   And the cops are puttin' the screws to him, lookin' for somebody to blame.
   "Remember that murder that happened in a bar?"
   "Remember you said you saw the getaway car?"
   "You think you'd like to play ball with the law?"
   "Think it might-a been that fighter that you saw runnin' that night?"
   "Don't forget that you are white."

7. Arthur Dexter Bradley said, "I'm really not sure."
   Cops said, "A poor boy like you could use a break
   We got you for the motel job and we're talkin' to your friend Bello
   Now you don't wanta have to go back to jail, be a nice fellow.
   You'll be doin' society a favor.
   That sonofabitch is brave and gettin' braver.
   We want to put his ass in stir
   We want to pin this triple murder on him
   He ain't no Gentleman Jim."

8. Rubin could take a man out with just one punch
   But he never did like to talk about it all that much.
   "It's my work," he'd say, "and I do it for pay.
   And when it's over I'd just as soon go on my way
   Up to some paradise
   Where the trout streams flow and the air is nice
   And ride a horse along a trail."
   But then they took him to the jailhouse
   Where they try to turn a man into a mouse.

9. All of Rubin's cards were marked in advance
   The trial was a pig-circus, he never had a chance.
   The judge made Rubin's witnesses drunkards from the slums
   To the white folks who watched he was a revolutionary bum
   And to the black folks he was just a crazy nigger.
   No one doubted that he pulled the trigger
   And though they could not produce the gun,
   The D.A. said he was the one who did the deed
   And the all-white jury agreed.

10. Rubin Carter was falsely tried.
    The crime was murder "one," guess who testified?
    Bello and Bradley and they both baldly lied
    And the newspapers, they all went along for the ride.
    How can the life of such a man
    Be in the palm of some fool's hand?
    To see him obviously framed
    Couldn't help but make me feel ashamed to live in a land
    Where justice is a game.

11. Now all the criminals in their coats and their ties
    Are free to drink martinis and watch the sun rise
    While Rubin sits like Buddha in a ten-foot cell
    An innocent man in a living hell.
    That's the story of the Hurricane,
    But it won't be over till they clear his name
    And give him back the time he's done.
    Put in a prison cell, but one time he could-a been
    The champion of the world.

It Takes a Lot to Laugh, It Takes a Train to Cry

Words and Music by Bob Dylan

Medium slow blues tempo

1. Well, I ride on the mail train, babe, Can't buy a thrill.

Well, I've been up all night, Lean-in' on the win-dow sill.

Well if I die on top of the hill And

if I don't make it You know my ba-by will.

repeat two times

Additional lyrics

2. Don't the moon look good, mama,
   Shinin' through the trees?
   Don't the brakeman look good, mama,
   Flagging down the "Double E"?
   Don't the sun look good
   Goin' down over the sea?
   Don't my gal look fine
   When she's comin' after me?

3. Now the wintertime is coming,
   The windows are filled with frost.
   I went to tell everybody,
   But I could not get across.
   Well, I wanna be your lover, baby,
   I don't wanna be your boss.
   Don't say I never warned you
   When your train gets lost.

I Am a Lonesome Hobo

Words and Music by Bob Dylan

Additional lyrics

2. Well, once I was rather prosperous,
   There was nothing I did lack.
   I had fourteen-karat gold in my mouth
   And silk upon my back.
   But I did not trust my brother,
   I carried him to blame,
   Which led me to my fatal doom,
   To wander off in shame.

3. Kind ladies and kind gentlemen,
   Soon I will be gone,
   But let me just warn you all,
   Before I do pass on;
   Stay free from petty jealousies,
   Live by no man's code,
   And hold your judgment for yourself
   Lest you wind up on this road.

I and I

Words and Music by Bob Dylan

Additional lyrics

2. Think I'll go out and go for a walk,
   Not much happenin' here, nothin' ever does.
   Besides, if she wakes up now, she'll just want me to talk
   I got nothin' to say, 'specially about whatever was.

   Chorus

3. Took an untrodden path once, where the swift don't win the race,
   It goes to the worthy, who can divide the word of truth.
   Took a stranger to teach me, to look into justice's beautiful face
   And to see an eye for an eye and a tooth for a tooth.

   Chorus

4. Outside of two men on a train platform there's nobody in sight,
   They're waiting for spring to come, smoking down the track.
   The world could come to an end tonight, but that's all right.
   She should still be there sleepin' when I get back.

   Chorus

5. Noontime, and I'm still pushin' myself along the road, the darkest part,
   Into the narrow lanes, I can't stumble or stay put.
   Someone else is speakin' with my mouth, but I'm listening only to my heart.
   I've made shoes for everyone, even you, while I still go barefoot.

   Chorus

I Believe in You

Words and Music by Bob Dylan

Moderately slow

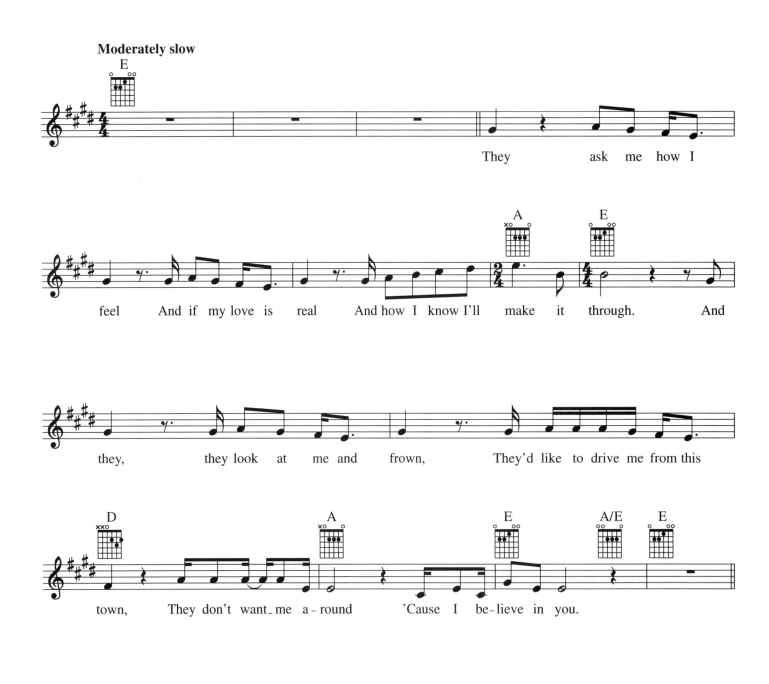

They ask me how I feel And if my love is real And how I know I'll make it through. And they, they look at me and frown, They'd like to drive me from this town, They don't want me a-round 'Cause I be-lieve in you. They show me to the door, They say don't come back no

269

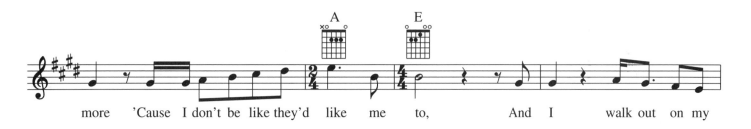

more 'Cause I don't be like they'd like me to, And I walk out on my

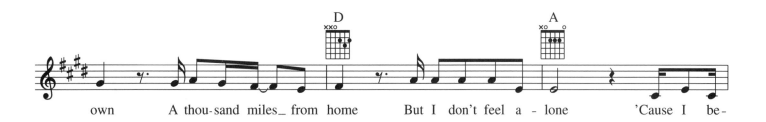

own A thou-sand miles_ from home But I don't feel a - lone 'Cause I be-

lieve in you. I be - lieve in you e - ven through the tears_ and the

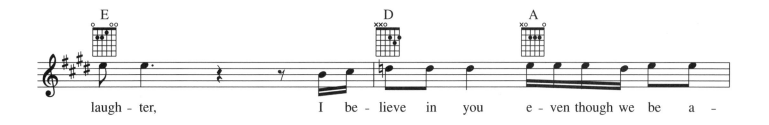

laugh - ter, I be - lieve in you e - ven though we be a -

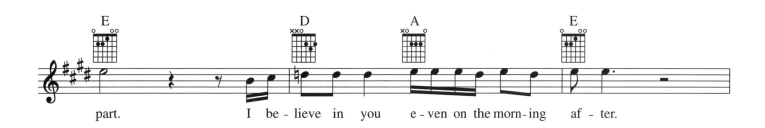

part. I be - lieve in you e - ven on the morn - ing af - ter.

Oh, when the dawn is near-ing Oh, when the night is dis-ap-pear-ing

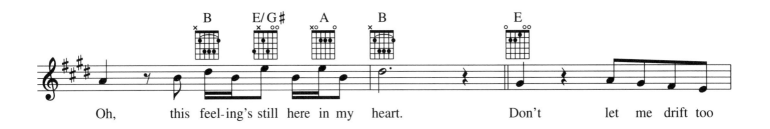

Oh, this feel-ing's still here in my heart. Don't let me drift too

far, Keep me where you are Where I will al-ways be re - newed. And

that which you've giv-en me __ to - day Is worth more than I could

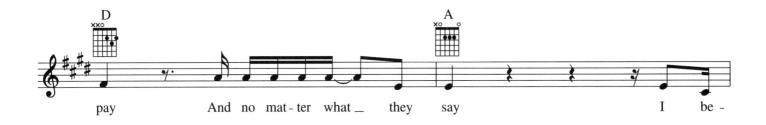

pay And no mat-ter what __ they say I be -

lieve in you. I be - lieve in you when win-ter turn __ to

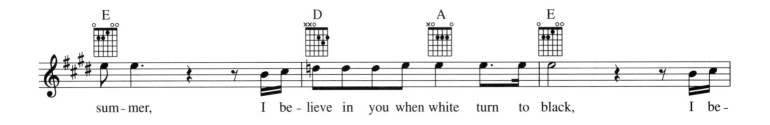

sum - mer, I be - lieve in you when white turn to black, I be -

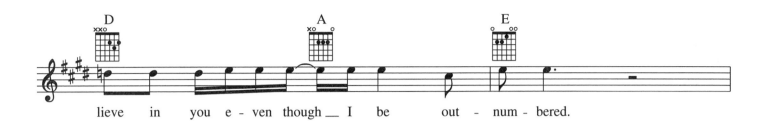

lieve in you e - ven though __ I be out - num - bered.

Oh, though the earth may shake me Oh, though my friends for - sake me

Oh, e - ven that could- n't make me go back. Don't let me change my

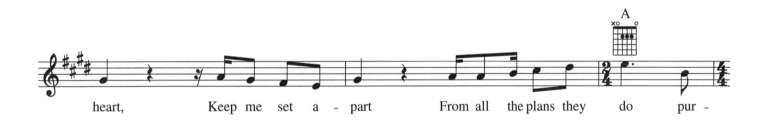

heart, Keep me set a - part From all the plans they do pur -

sue. And I, I don't mind the pain Don't mind the driv- ing

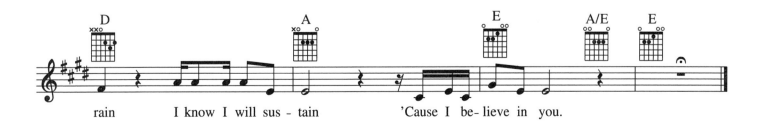

rain I know I will sus - tain 'Cause I be- lieve in you.

I Don't Believe You
(She Acts Like We Never Have Met)
Words and Music by Bob Dylan

Additional lyrics

2. It's all new t' me,
   Like some mystery,
   It could even be like a myth.
   Yet it's hard t' think on,
   That she's the same one
   That last night I was with.
   From darkness, dreams're deserted,
   Am I still dreamin' yet?
   I wish she'd unlock
   Her voice once an' talk,
   'Stead of acting like we never have met.

3. If she ain't feelin' well,
   Then why don't she tell
   'Stead of turnin' her back t' my face?
   Without any doubt,
   She seems too far out
   For me t' return t' her chase.
   Though the night ran swirling an' whirling,
   I remember her whispering yet.
   But evidently she don't
   An' evidently she won't,
   She just acts like we never have met.

4. If I didn't have t' guess,
   I'd gladly confess
   T' anything I might've tried.
   If I was with 'er too long
   Or have done something wrong,
   I wish she'd tell me what it is, I'll run an' hide.
   Though her skirt it swayed as a guitar played,
   Her mouth was watery and wet.
   But now something has changed
   For she ain't the same,
   She just acts like we never have met.

5. I'm leavin' today,
   I'll be on my way
   Of this I can't say very much.
   But if you want me to,
   I can be just like you
   An' pretend that we never have touched.
   An' if anybody asks me, "Is it easy to forget?"
   I'll say, "It's easily done,
   You just pick anyone,
   An' pretend that you never have met!"

I Dreamed I Saw St. Augustine

Words and Music by Bob Dylan

Additional lyrics

2. "Arise, arise," he cried so loud,
   In a voice without restraint,
   "Come out, ye gifted kings and queens
   And hear my sad complaint.
   No martyr is among ye now
   Whom you can call your own,
   So go on your way accordingly
   But know you're not alone."

3. I dreamed I saw St. Augustine,
   Alive with fiery breath,
   And I dreamed I was amongst the ones
   That put him out to death.
   Oh, I awoke in anger,
   So alone and terrified,
   I put my fingers against the glass
   And bowed my head and cried.

I Pity the Poor Immigrant

Words and Music by Bob Dylan

ev - 'ry _____ breath, Who

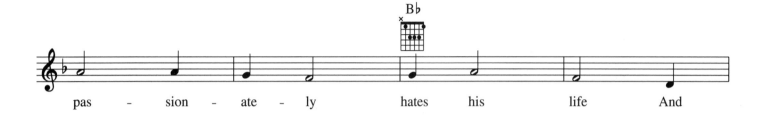

pas - sion - ate - ly hates his life And

like - wise, fears _____ his _____ death. _____

Additional lyrics

2. I pity the poor immigrant
   Whose strength is spent in vain,
   Whose heaven is like Ironsides,
   Whose tears are like rain,
   Who eats but is not satisfied,
   Who hears but does not see,
   Who falls in love with wealth itself
   And turns his back on me.

3. I pity the poor immigrant
   Who tramples through the mud,
   Who fills his mouth with laughing
   And who builds his town with blood,
   Whose visions in the final end
   Must shatter like the glass.
   I pity the poor immigrant
   When his gladness comes to pass.

I Shall Be Free

Words and Music by Bob Dylan

Moderate country boogie

1. Well, I took me a wom-an late last night, __ I's three-fourths drunk, she looked up-tight. __ She took off her wheel, took off her bell, Took off her wig, said, "How do I smell?" I hot-footed it... bare na-ked... out the win-dow!

1.-10. 2. Well,

11.

Additional lyrics

2. Well, sometimes I might get drunk,
   Walk like a duck and stomp like a skunk.
   Don't hurt me none, don't hurt my pride
   'Cause I got my little lady right by my side.
   (Right there
   Proud as can be)

3. I's out there paintin' on the old woodshed
   When a can a black paint it fell on my head.
   I went down to scrub and rub
   But I had to sit in back of the tub.
   (Cost a quarter
   And I had to get out quick . . .
   Someone wanted to come in and take a sauna)

4. Well, my telephone rang it would not stop,
   It's President Kennedy callin' me up.
   He said, "My friend, Bob, what do we need to make the country grow?"
   I said, "My friend, John, Brigitte Bardot,
   Anita Ekberg, Sophia Loren."
   (Put 'em all in the same room with Ernest Borgnine!)

5. Well, I got a woman sleeps on a cot,
   She yells and hollers and squeals a lot.
   Licks my face and tickles my ear,
   Bends me over and buys me beer.
   (She's a honeymooner
   A June crooner
   A spoon feeder
   And a natural leader)

6. Oh, there ain't no use in me workin' so heavy,
   I got a woman who works on the levee.
   Pumping that water up to her neck,
   Every week she sends me a monthly check.
   (She's a humdinger
   Folk singer
   Dead ringer
   For a thing-a-muh jigger)

7. Late one day in the middle of the week,
   Eyes were closed I was half asleep.
   I chased me a woman up the hill,
   Right in the middle of an air raid drill.
   It was Little Bo Peep!
   (I jumped a fallout shelter
   I jumped a bean stalk
   I jumped a ferris wheel)

8. Now, the man on the stand he wants my vote,
   He's a-runnin' for office on the ballot note.
   He's out there preachin' in front of the steeple,
   Tellin' me he loves all kinds-a people.
   (He's eatin' bagels
   He's eatin' pizza
   He's eatin' chitlins
   He's eatin' bullshit!)

9. Oh, set me down on a television floor,
   I'll flip the channel to number four.
   Out of the shower comes a grown-up man
   With a bottle of hair oil in his hand.
   (It's that greasy kid stuff.
   What I want to know, Mr. Football Man, is
   What do you do about Willy Mays and Yul Brynner,
   Charles de Gaulle
   And Robert Louis Stevenson?)

10. Well, the funniest woman I ever seen
    Was the great-granddaughter of Mr. Clean.
    She takes about fifteen baths a day,
    Wants me to grow a cigar on my face.
    (She's a little bit heavy!)

11. Well, ask me why I'm drunk alla time,
    It levels my head and eases my mind.
    I just walk along and stroll and sing,
    I see better days and I do better things.
    (I catch dinosaurs
    I make love to Elizabeth Taylor . . .
    Catch hell from Richard Burton!)

I Shall Be Released

Words and Music by Bob Dylan

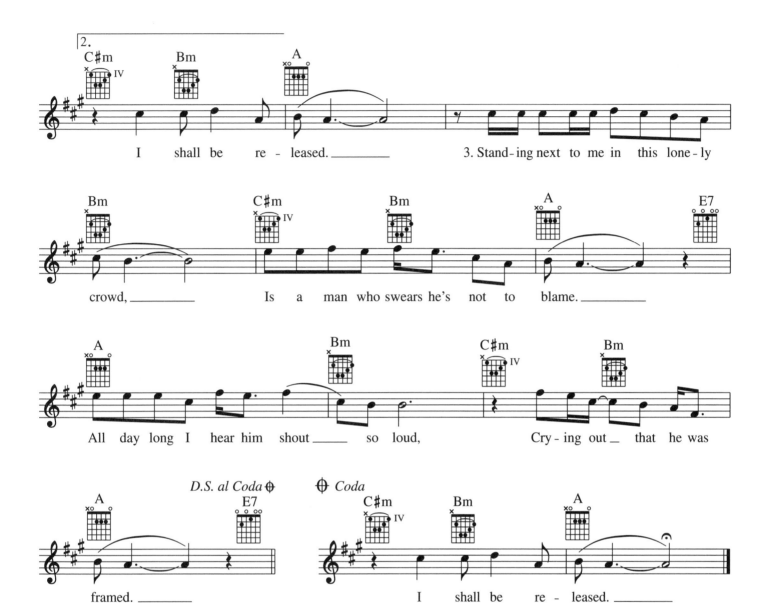

I shall be re - leased. _____ 3. Stand-ing next to me in this lone-ly

crowd, _____ Is a man who swears he's not to blame. _____

All day long I hear him shout _____ so loud, Cry - ing out _ that he was

D.S. al Coda ⊕   ⊕ *Coda*

framed. _____   I shall be re - leased. _____

I Wanna Be Your Lover

Words and Music by Bob Dylan

I wan-na be your lov - er, baby, ___ I wan - na be ___ your

man. I wan-na be your lov - er, ba - by, I don't wan - na be

hers, I wan - na be yours. _____

Additional lyrics

2. Well, the undertaker in his midnight suit
   Says to the masked man, "Ain't you cute!"
   Well, the mask man he gets up on the shelf
   And he says, "You ain't so bad yourself."

   Chorus

3. Well, jumpin' Judy can't go no higher.
   She had bullets in her eyes, and they fire.
   Rasputin he's so dignified,
   He touched the back of her head an' he died.

   Chorus

4. Well, Phaedra with her looking glass,
   Stretchin' out upon the grass.
   She gets all messed up and she faints
   That's 'cause she's so obvious and you ain't.

   Chorus

I Want You

Words and Music by Bob Dylan

Moderately bright (quasi in 2)

Verse

1. The

guilt - y un - der - tak - er sighs, __ The lone - some or - gan
drunk - en pol - i - ti - cian leaps __ Up - on the street __ where

grind - er cries, __ The sil - ver sax - o - phones __ say I __ should
moth - ers weep __ And the sav - iors who are fast __ a - sleep, __ They

re - fuse you. _____ The cracked bells and
wait for you. _____ And I wait for them to

washed - out horns_ Blow in - to my face with scorn, __ But it's
in - ter - rupt_ Me drink - in' from my bro - ken cup __ And

3. Well, I return to the Queen of Spades
   And talk with my chambermaid.
   She knows that I'm not afraid
   To look at her.
   She is good to me
   And there's nothing she doesn't see.
   She knows where I'd like to be
   But it doesn't matter.
   I want you, I want you,
   I want you so bad,
   Honey, I want you.

4. Now your dancing child with his Chinese suit,
   He spoke to me, I took his flute.
   No, I wasn't very cute to him,
   Was I?
   But I did it, though, because he lied
   Because he took you for a ride
   And because time was on his side
   And because I . . .
   I want you, I want you,
   I want you so bad,
   Honey, I want you.

John Wesley Harding

Words and Music by Bob Dylan

I'd Hate to Be You On That Dreadful Day

Words and Music by Bob Dylan

Moderate boogie-rock

1. Well, your clock is gon - na stop at Saint Pe - ter's gate. __ Ya gon - na
4. have to walk __ na - ked, Can't ride in no car. __ You're gon - na

ask him what time it is, He's gon - na say, "It's too late!" __ Hey, hey! I'd
let ev - 'ry - bod - y see _____ just what you __ are. __

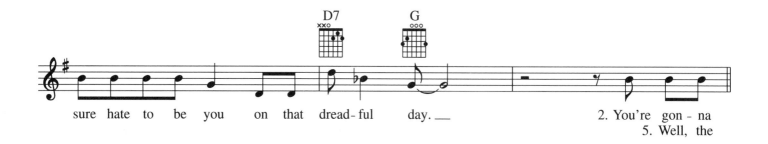

sure hate to be you on that dread - ful day. __ 2. You're gon - na
5. Well, the

start to sweat __ and you ain't gon - na stop. __ You're gon - na have a night - mare and
good wine's a - flow - in' for five cents a quart. __ You're gon - na look in your mon - ey - bags and

I'd Have You Any Time

Words and Music by Bob Dylan and George Harrison

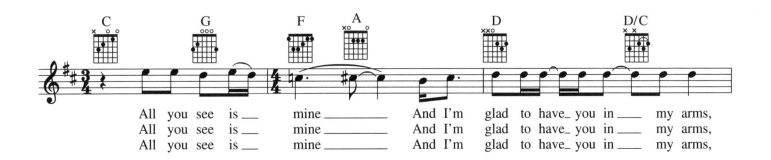

All you see is __ mine _____ And I'm glad to have__ you in __ my arms,
All you see is __ mine _____ And I'm glad to have__ you in __ my arms,
All you see is __ mine _____ And I'm glad to have__ you in __ my arms,

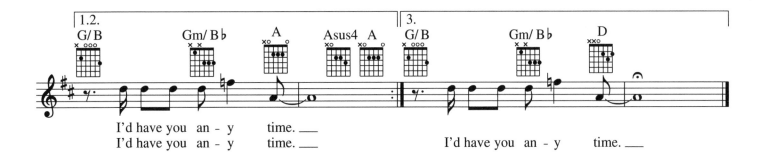

I'd have you an - y time. __
I'd have you an - y time. __

I'd have you an - y time. __

I'll Be Your Baby Tonight

Words and Music by Bob Dylan

Moderately

Close your eyes, _____ close the door, _____
(Shut the) light, _____ shut the shade, _____

You don't have to wor-ry _____ an-y - more. ___
You don't have _____ to be a - fraid. ___

I'll _____ be your _____ ba - by to -

night. _____ Shut the

Well, that mock - ing - bird's gon - na sail __ a - way, _____

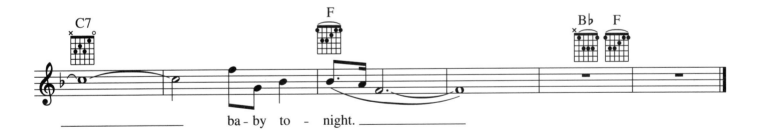

I'll Keep It with Mine

Words and Music by Bob Dylan

Slow, but not draggy

1. You will search, babe, __ At an - y __ cost. But how

long, babe, __ Can you search for what's not lost? Ev - 'ry - bod - y

will help you, Some peo-ple are __ ver - y __ kind. __

Chorus

But if I __ can save you an - y time, __

Come __ on, give it to me, I'll __ keep it with __ mine. __

1.-2. | 3.

2. I can't
3. The

Additional lyrics

2. I can't help it
   If you might think I'm odd,
   If I say I'm not loving you for what you are
   But for what you're not.
   Everybody will help you
   Discover what you set out to find.
   But if I can save you any time,
   Come on, give it to me,
   I'll keep it with mine.

3. The train leaves
   At half past ten,
   But it'll be back tomorrow,
   Same time again.
   The conductor he's weary,
   He's still stuck on the line.
   But if I can save you any time,
   Come on, give it to me,
   I'll keep it with mine.

I'll Remember You

Words and Music by Bob Dylan

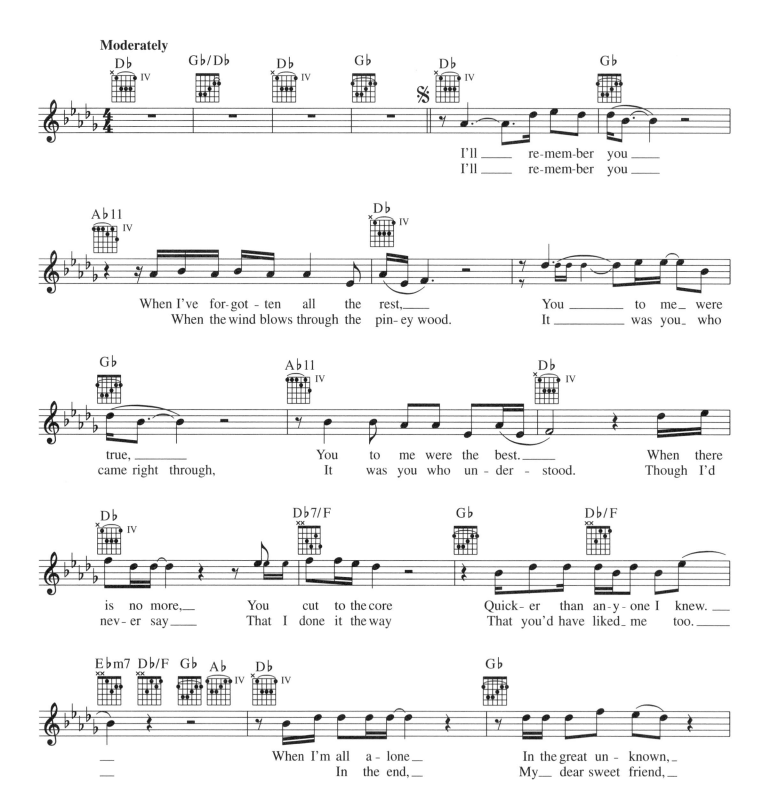

Idiot Wind

Words and Music by Bob Dylan

Additional lyrics

2. I ran into the fortune-teller, who said beware of lightning that might strike
I haven't known peace and quiet for so long I can't remember what it's like.
There's a lone soldier on the cross, smoke pourin' out of a boxcar door,
You didn't know it, you didn't think it could be done, in the final end he won the wars
After losin' every battle.

I woke up on the roadside, daydreamin' 'bout the way things sometimes are
Visions of your chestnut mare shoot through my head and are makin' me see stars.
You hurt the ones that I love best and cover up the truth with lies.
One day you'll be in the ditch, flies buzzin' around your eyes,
Blood on your saddle.

Idiot wind, blowing through the flowers on your tomb,
Blowing through the curtains in your room.
Idiot wind, blowing every time you move your teeth,
You're an idiot, babe.
It's a wonder that you still know how to breathe.

3. It was gravity which pulled us down and destiny which broke us apart
You tamed the lion in my cage but it just wasn't enough to change my heart.
Now everything's a little upside down, as a matter of fact the wheels have stopped,
What's good is bad, what's bad is good, you'll find out when you reach the top
You're on the bottom.

I noticed at the ceremony, your corrupt ways had finally made you blind.
I can't remember your face anymore, your mouth has changed, your eyes don't look into mine.
The priest wore black on the seventh day and sat stone-faced while the building burned.
I waited for you on the running boards, near the cypress trees, while the springtime turned
Slowly into autumn.

Idiot wind, blowing like a circle around my skull,
From the Grand Coulee Dam to the Capitol.
Idiot wind, blowing every time you move your teeth,
You're an idiot, babe.
It's a wonder that you still know how to breathe.

4. I can't feel you anymore, I can't even touch the books you've read
Every time I crawl past your door, I been wishin' I was somebody else instead.
Down the highway, down the tracks, down the road to ecstasy,
I followed you beneath the stars, hounded by your memory
And all your ragin' glory.

I been double-crossed now for the very last time and now I'm finally free,
I kissed goodbye the howling beast on the borderline which separated you from me.
You'll never know the hurt I suffered nor the pain I rise above,
And I'll never know the same about you, your holiness or your kind of love,
And it makes me feel so sorry.

Idiot wind, blowing through the buttons of our coats,
Blowing through the letters that we wrote.
Idiot wind, blowing through the dust upon our shelves,
We're idiots, babe.
It's a wonder we can even feed ourselves.

Knockin' on Heaven's Door

Words and Music by Bob Dylan

If Dogs Run Free

Words and Music by Bob Dylan

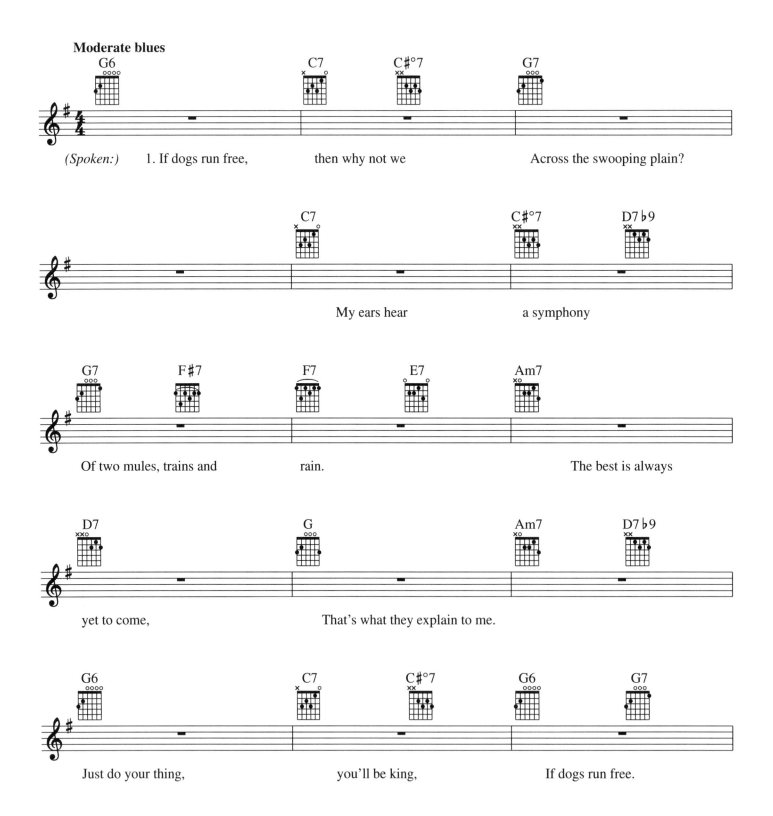

Moderate blues

(Spoken:)   1. If dogs run free,   then why not we   Across the swooping plain?

My ears hear   a symphony

Of two mules, trains and   rain.   The best is always

yet to come,   That's what they explain to me.

Just do your thing,   you'll be king,   If dogs run free.

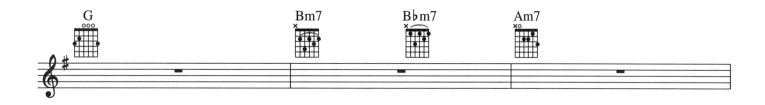

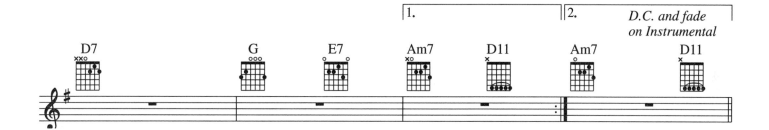

Additional lyrics

2. If dogs run free, why not me
   Across the swamp of time?
   My mind weaves a symphony
   And tapestry of rhyme.
   Oh, winds which rush my tale to thee
   So it may flow and be,
   To each his own, it's all unknown,
   If dogs run free.

3. If dogs run free, then what must be,
   Must be, and that is all.
   True love can make a blade of grass
   Stand up straight and tall.
   In harmony with the cosmic sea,
   True love needs no company,
   It can cure the soul, it can make it whole,
   If dogs run free.

If You See Her, Say Hello

Words and Music by Bob Dylan

Moderately slow

1. If you see ___ her, say ___ hel - lo, she

might be in ___ Tan - gier ___ She left here _ last ear - ly spring, _ is

liv - in' there, _ I hear _____ Say for me _ that I'm_

___ al - right_ though things get kind of slow_ She might think_ that I've for-got-

ten her, don't tell her it is - n't so. ___

Additional lyrics

2. We had a falling-out, like lovers often will
   And to think of how she left that night, it still brings me a chill
   And though our separation, it pierced me to the heart
   She still lives inside of me, we've never been apart.

3. If you get close to her, kiss her once for me
   I always have respected her for busting out and gettin' free
   Oh, whatever makes her happy, I won't stand in the way
   Though the bitter taste still lingers on from the night I tried to make her stay.

4. I see a lot of people as I make the rounds
   And I hear her name here and there as I go from town to town
   And I've never gotten used to it, I've just learned to turn it off
   Either I'm too sensitive or else I'm gettin' soft.

5. Sundown, yellow moon, I replay the past
   I know every scene by heart, they all went by so fast
   If she's passin' back this way, I'm not that hard to find
   Tell her she can look me up if she's got the time.

In the Garden

Words and Music by Bob Dylan

Moderately slow, with a gospel beat

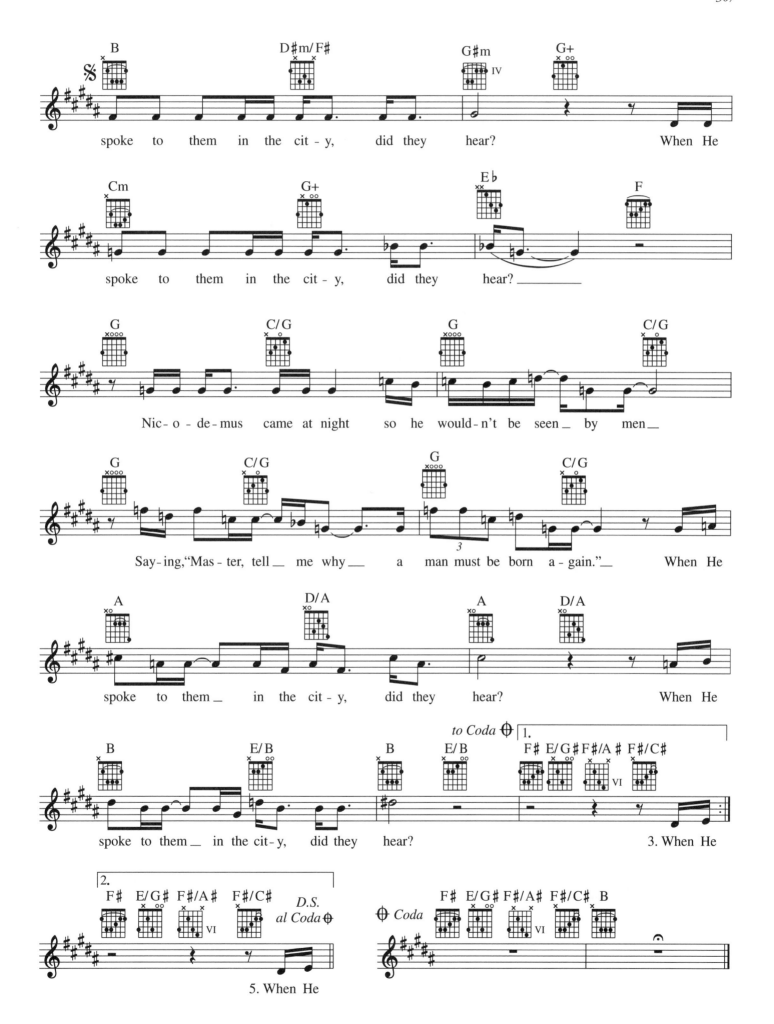

3. When He healed the blind and crippled, did they see?
   When He healed the blind and crippled, did they see?
   When He said, "Pick up your bed and walk, why must you criticize?
   Same thing My Father do, I can do likewise."
   When He healed the blind and crippled, did they see?
   When He healed the blind and crippled, did they see?

4. Did they speak out against Him, did they dare?
   Did they speak out against Him, did they dare?
   The multitude wanted to make Him king, put a crown upon His head
   Why did He slip away to a quiet place instead?
   Did they speak out against Him, did they dare?
   Did they speak out against Him, did they dare?

5. When He rose from the dead, did they believe?
   When He rose from the dead, did they believe?
   He said, "All power is given to Me in heaven and on earth."
   Did they know right then and there what that power was worth?
   When He rose from the dead, did they believe?
   When He rose from the dead, did they believe?

Lay, Lady, Lay
Words and Music by Bob Dylan

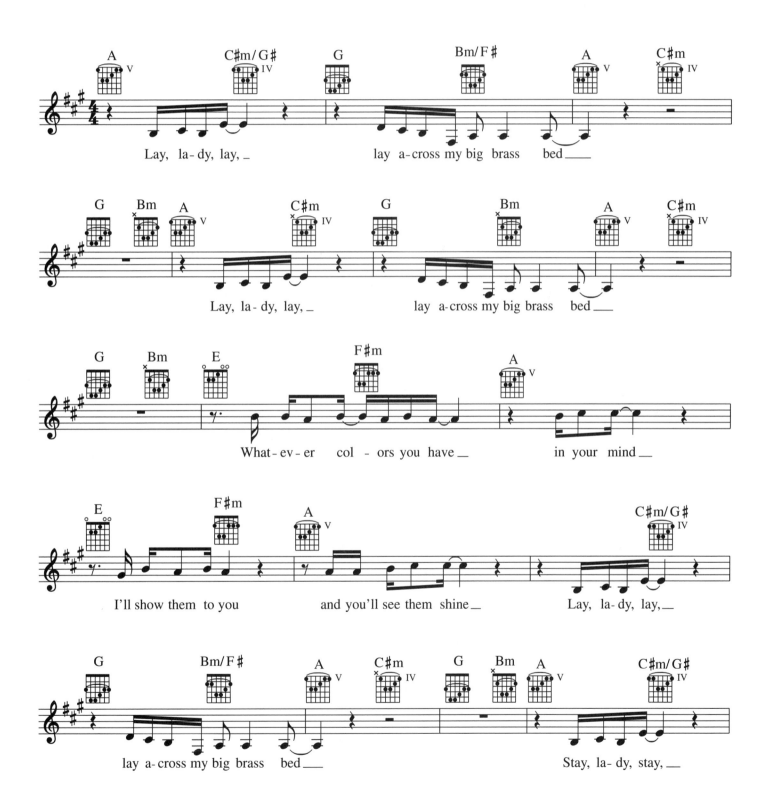

In the Summertime

Words and Music by Bob Dylan

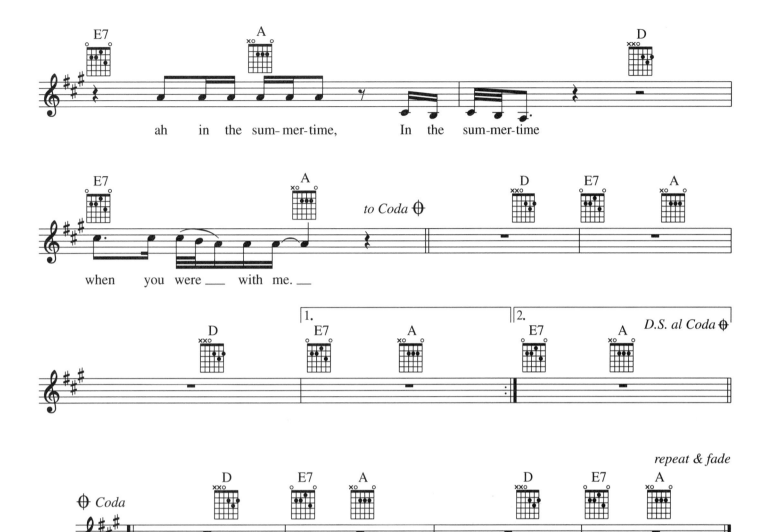

ah in the sum-mer-time, In the sum-mer-time

to Coda ⊕

when you were ___ with me. ___

1.

2.

D.S. al Coda ⊕

repeat & fade

⊕ *Coda*

Additional lyrics

2. I got the heart and you got the blood,
   We cut through iron and we cut through mud.
   Then came the warnin' that was before the flood
   That set everybody free.
   Fools they made a mock of sin,
   Our loyalty they tried to win
   But you were closer to me than my next of kin
   When they didn't want to know or see.

   Chorus

3. Strangers, they meddled in our affairs,
   Poverty and shame was theirs.
   But all that sufferin' was not to be compared
   With the glory that is to be.
   And I'm still carrying the gift you gave,
   It's a part of me now, it's been cherished and saved,
   It'll be with me unto the grave
   And then unto eternity.

   Chorus

Is Your Love in Vain?

Words and Music by Bob Dylan

Isis

Words and Music by Bob Dylan and Jacques Levy

Additional lyrics

2. I came to a high place of darkness and light.
   The dividing line ran through the center of town.
   I hitched up my pony to a post on the right,
   Went in to a laundry to wash my clothes down.

3. A man in the corner approached me for a match.
   I knew right away he was not ordinary.
   He said, "Are you lookin' for somethin' easy to catch?"
   I said, "I got no money." He said, "That ain't necessary."

4. We set out that night for the cold in the North.
   I gave him my blanket, he gave me his word.
   I said, "Where are we goin'?" He said we'd be back by the fourth.
   I said, "That's the best news that I've ever heard."

5. I was thinkin' about turquoise, I was thinkin' about gold,
   I was thinkin' about diamonds and the world's biggest necklace.
   As we rode through the canyons, through the devilish cold,
   I was thinkin' about Isis, how she thought I was so reckless.

6. How she told me that one day we would meet up again,
   And things would be different the next time we wed,
   If I only could hang on and just be her friend.
   I still can't remember all the best things she said.

7. We came to the pyramids all embedded in ice.
   He said, "There's a body I'm tryin' to find.
   If I carry it out it'll bring a good price."
   'Twas then that I knew what he had on his mind.

8. The wind it was howlin' and the snow was outrageous.
   We chopped through the night and we chopped through the dawn.
   When he died I was hopin' that it wasn't contagious,
   But I made up my mind that I had to go on.

9. I broke into the tomb, but the casket was empty.
   There was no jewels, no nothin', I felt I'd been had.
   When I saw that my partner was just bein' friendly,
   When I took up his offer I must-a been mad.

10. I picked up his body and I dragged him inside,
    Threw him down in the hole and I put back the cover.
    I said a quick prayer and I felt satisfied.
    Then I rode back to find Isis just to tell her I love her.

11. She was there in the meadow where the creek used to rise.
    Blinded by sleep and in need of a bed,
    I came in from the East with the sun in my eyes.
    I cursed her one time then I rode on ahead.

12. She said, "Where ya been?" I said, "No place special."
    She said, "You look different." I said, "Well, not quite."
    She said, "You been gone." I said, "That's only natural."
    She said, "You gonna stay?" I said, "Yeah, I jes might."

13. Isis, oh, Isis, you mystical child.
    What drives me to you is what drives me insane.
    I still can remember the way that you smiled
    On the fifth day of May in the drizzlin' rain.

It Ain't Me, Babe

Words and Music by Bob Dylan

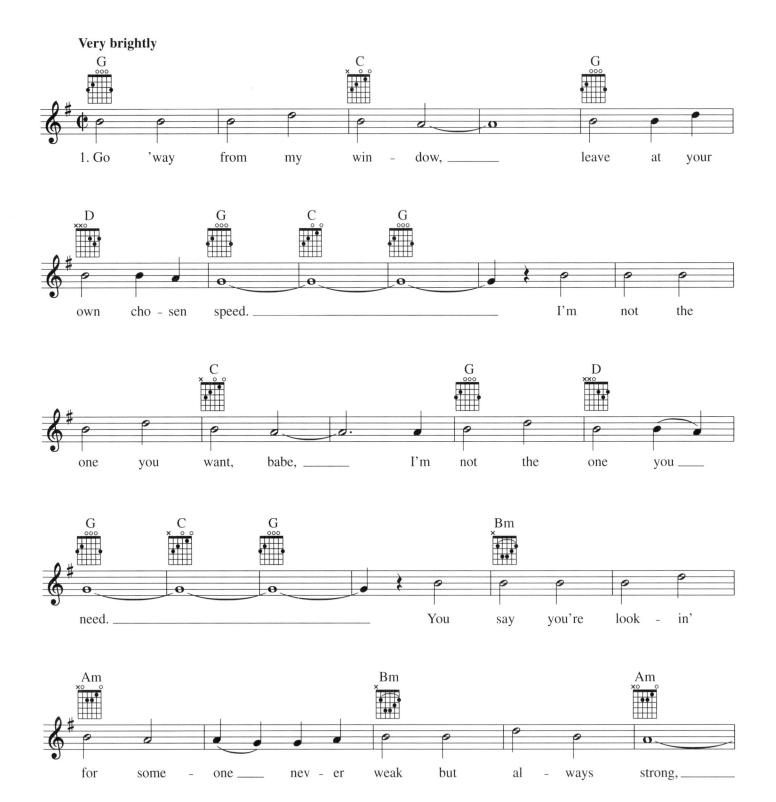

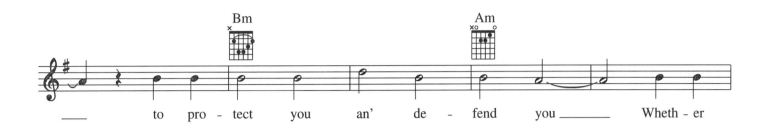

to pro - tect you an' de - fend you _____ Wheth - er

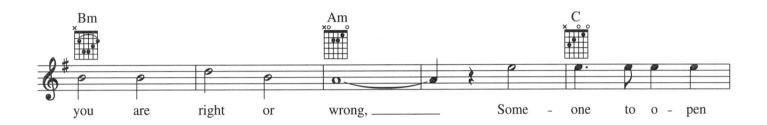

you are right or wrong, _____ Some - one to o - pen

each and ev - 'ry door, _____ *Chorus* But it ain't me, babe, _____

No, no, no, _____ it ain't me, babe, _____ It ain't me you're

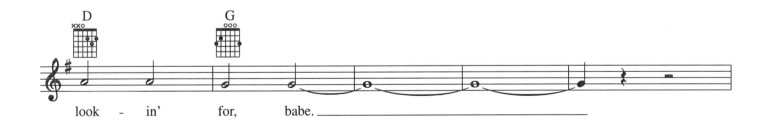

look - in' for, babe. _____

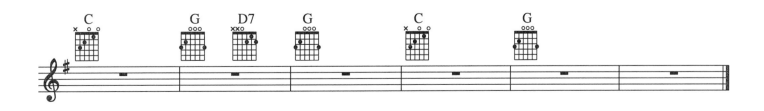

Additional lyrics

2. Go lightly from the ledge, babe,
   Go lightly on the ground.
   I'm not the one you want, babe,
   I will only let you down.
   You say you're lookin' for someone
   Who will promise never to part,
   Someone to close his eyes for you,
   Someone to close his heart,
   Someone who will die for you an' more,
   But it ain't me, babe,
   No, no, no, it ain't me, babe,
   It ain't me you're lookin' for, babe.

3. Go melt back into the night, babe,
   Everything inside is made of stone.
   There's nothing in here moving
   An' anyway I'm not alone.
   You say you're looking for someone
   Who'll pick you up each time you fall,
   To gather flowers constantly
   An' to come each time you call,
   A lover for your life an' nothing more,
   But it ain't me, babe,
   No, no, no, it ain't me, babe,
   It ain't me you're lookin' for, babe.

Lily, Rosemary and the Jack of Hearts

Words and Music by Bob Dylan

Additional lyrics

2. He moved across the mirrored room, "Set it up for everyone," he said,
   Then everyone commenced to do what they were doin' before he turned their heads.
   Then he walked up to a stranger and he asked him with a grin,
   "Could you kindly tell me, friend, what time the show begins?"
   Then he moved into the corner, face down like the Jack of Hearts.

3. Backstage the girls were playin' five-card stud by the stairs,
   Lily had two queens, she was hopin' for a third to match her pair.
   Outside the streets were fillin' up, the window was open wide,
   A gentle breeze was blowin', you could feel it from inside.
   Lily called another bet and drew up the Jack of Hearts.

4. Big Jim was no one's fool, he owned the town's only diamond mine,
   He made his usual entrance lookin' so dandy and so fine.
   With his bodyguards and silver cane and every hair in place,
   He took whatever he wanted to and he laid it all to waste.
   But his bodyguards and silver cane were no match for the Jack of Hearts.

5. Rosemary combed her hair and took a carriage into town,
   She slipped in through the side door lookin' like a queen without a crown.
   She fluttered her false eyelashes and whispered in his ear,
   "Sorry, darlin', that I'm late," but he didn't seem to hear.
   He was starin' into space over at the Jack of Hearts.

6. "I know I've seen that face before," Big Jim was thinkin' to himself,
   "Maybe down in Mexico or a picture up on somebody's shelf."
   But then the crowd began to stamp their feet and the house lights did dim
   And in the darkness of the room there was only Jim and him,
   Starin' at the butterfly who just drew the Jack of Hearts.

7. Lily was a princess, she was fair-skinned and precious as a child,
   She did whatever she had to do, she had that certain flash every time she smiled.
   She'd come away from a broken home, had lots of strange affairs
   With men in every walk of life which took her everywhere.
   But she'd never met anyone quite like the Jack of Hearts.

8. The hangin' judge came in unnoticed and was being wined and dined,
   The drillin' in the wall kept up but no one seemed to pay it any mind.
   It was known all around that Lily had Jim's ring
   And nothing would ever come between Lily and the king.
   No, nothin' ever would except maybe the Jack of Hearts.

9. Rosemary started drinkin' hard and seein' her reflection in the knife,
   She was tired of the attention, tired of playin' the role of Big Jim's wife.
   She had done a lot of bad things, even once tried suicide,
   Was lookin' to do just one good deed before she died.
   She was gazin' to the future, riding on the Jack of Hearts.

10. Lily washed her face, took her dress off and buried it away.
    "Has your luck run out?" she laughed at him, "Well, I guess you must have known it would someday.
    Be careful not to touch the wall, there's a brand-new coat of paint,
    I'm glad to see you're still alive, you're lookin' like a saint."
    Down the hallway footsteps were comin' for the Jack of Hearts.

11. The backstage manager was pacing all around by his chair.
    "There's something funny going on," he said, "I can just feel it in the air."
    He went to get the hangin' judge, but the hangin' judge was drunk,
    As the leading actor hurried by in the costume of a monk.
    There was no actor anywhere better than the Jack of Hearts.

12. Lily's arms were locked around the man that she dearly loved to touch,
    She forgot all about the man she couldn't stand who hounded her so much.
    "I've missed you so," she said to him, and he felt she was sincere,
    But just beyond the door he felt jealousy and fear.
    Just another night in the life of the Jack of Hearts.

13. No one knew the circumstance but they say that it happened pretty quick,
    The door to the dressing room burst open and a cold revolver clicked.
    And Big Jim was standin' there, ya couldn't say surprised,
    Rosemary right beside him, steady in her eyes.
    She was with Big Jim but she was leanin' to the Jack of Hearts.

14. Two doors down the boys finally made it through the wall
    And cleaned out the bank safe, it's said that they got off with quite a haul.
    In the darkness by the riverbed they waited on the ground
    For one more member who had business back in town.
    But they couldn't go no further without the Jack of Hearts.

15. The next day was hangin' day, the sky was overcast and black,
    Big Jim lay covered up, killed by a penknife in the back.
    And Rosemary on the gallows, she didn't even blink,
    The hangin' judge was sober, he hadn't had a drink.
    The only person on the scene missin' was the Jack of Hearts.

16. The cabaret was empty now, a sign said, "Closed for repair,"
    Lily had already taken all of the dye out of her hair.
    She was thinkin' 'bout her father, who she very rarely saw,
    Thinkin' 'bout Rosemary and thinkin' about the law.
    But, most of all she was thinkin' 'bout the Jack of Hearts.

It's All Over Now, Baby Blue

Words and Music by Bob Dylan

Additional lyrics

2. The highway is for gamblers, better use your sense.
   Take what you have gathered from coincidence.
   The empty-handed painter from your streets
   Is drawing crazy patterns on your sheets.
   This sky, too, is folding under you
   And it's all over now, Baby Blue.

3. All your seasick sailors, they are rowing home.
   All your reindeer armies, are all going home.
   The lover who just walked out your door
   Has taken all his blankets from the floor.
   The carpet, too, is moving under you
   And it's all over now, Baby Blue.

4. Leave your stepping stones behind, something calls for you.
   Forget the dead you've left, they will not follow you.
   The vagabond who's rapping at your door
   Is standing in the clothes that you once wore.
   Strike another match, go start anew
   And it's all over now, Baby Blue.

It's Alright, Ma
(I'm Only Bleeding)
Words and Music by Bob Dylan

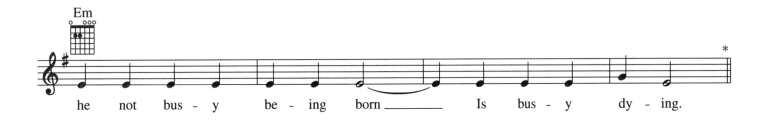

he not bus - y be - ing born _____ Is bus - y dy - ing.

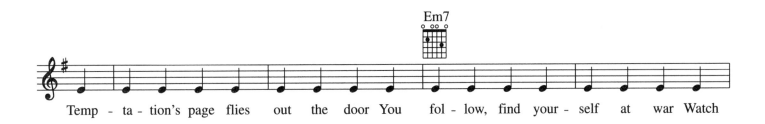

Temp - ta - tion's page flies out the door You fol - low, find your - self at war Watch

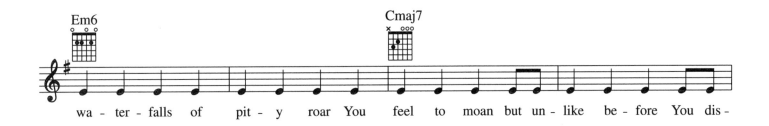

wa - ter - falls of pit - y roar You feel to moan but un - like be - fore You dis -

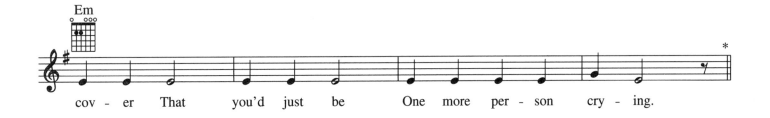

cov - er That you'd just be One more per - son cry - ing.

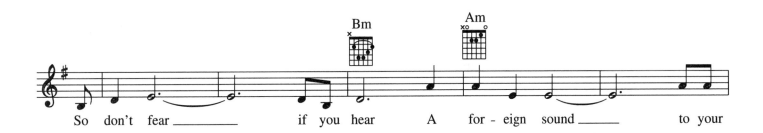

So don't fear _____ if you hear A for - eign sound _____ to your

repeat four times

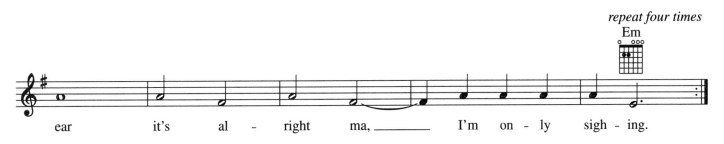

ear it's al - right ma, _____ I'm on - ly sigh - ing.

* The asterisks denote ad lib guitar breaks which occur at these points in the Dylan recording.

Additional lyrics

2. As some warn victory, some downfall
   Private reasons great or small
   Can be seen in the eyes of those that call
   To make all that should be killed to crawl
   While others say don't hate nothing at all
   Except hatred.

   Disillusioned words like bullets bark
   As human gods aim for their mark
   Made everything from toy guns that spark
   To flesh-colored Christs that glow in the dark
   It's easy to see without looking too far
   That not much is really sacred.

   While preachers preach of evil fates
   Teachers teach that knowledge waits
   Can lead to hundred-dollar plates
   Goodness hides behind its gates
   But even the president of the United States
   Sometimes must have to stand naked.

   An' though the rules of the road have been lodged
   It's only people's games that you got to dodge
   And it's alright, Ma, I can make it.

3. Advertising signs that con you
   Into thinking you're the one
   That can do what's never been done
   That can win what's never been won
   Meantime life outside goes on
   All around you.

   You lose yourself, you reappear
   You suddenly find you got nothing to fear
   Alone you stand with nobody near
   When a trembling distant voice, unclear
   Startles your sleeping ears to hear
   That somebody thinks they really found you.

   A question in your nerves is lit
   Yet you know there is no answer fit to satisfy
   Insure you not to quit
   To keep it in your mind and not forget
   That it is not he or she or them or it
   That you belong to.

   Although the masters make the rules
   For the wise men and the fools
   I got nothing, Ma, to live up to.

4. For them that must obey authority
   That they do not respect in any degree
   Who despise their jobs, their destinies
   Speak jealously of them that are free
   Cultivate their flowers to be
   Nothing more than something they invest in.

   While some on principles baptized
   To strict party platform ties
   Social clubs in drag disguise
   Outsiders they can freely criticize
   Tell nothing except who to idolize
   And then say God bless him.

   While one who sings with his tongue on fire
   Gargles in the rat race choir
   Bent out of shape from society's pliers
   Cares not to come up any higher
   But rather get you down in the hole
   That he's in.

   But I mean no harm nor put fault
   On anyone that lives in a vault
   But it's alright, Ma, if I can't please him.

5. Old lady judges watch people in pairs
   Limited in sex, they dare
   To push fake morals, insult and stare
   While money doesn't talk, it swears
   Obscenity, who really cares
   Propaganda, all is phony.

   While them that defend what they cannot see
   With a killer's pride, security
   It blows the minds most bitterly
   For them that think death's honesty
   Won't fall upon them naturally
   Life sometimes must get lonely.

   My eyes collide head-on with stuffed graveyards
   False gods, I scuff
   At pettiness which plays so rough
   Walk upside-down inside handcuffs
   Kick my legs to crash it off
   Say okay, I have had enough what else can you show me?

   And if my thought-dreams could be seen
   They'd probably put my head in a guillotine
   But it's alright, Ma, it's life, and life only.

Lone Pilgrim

Words and Music by B.F. White and Adgar M. Pace

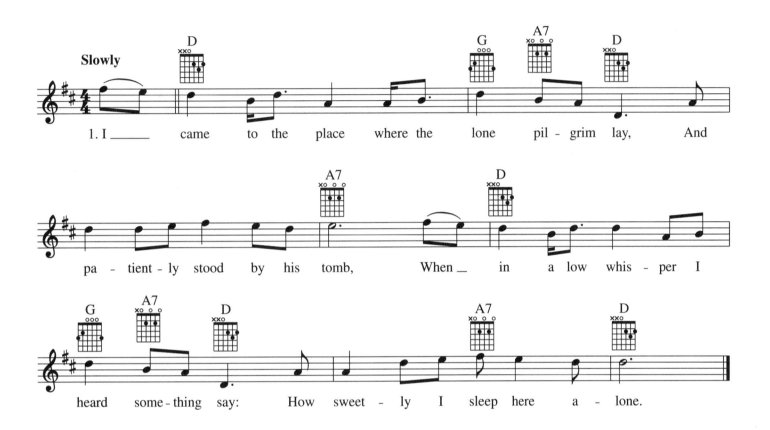

1. I _____ came to the place where the lone pil - grim lay, And

pa - tient - ly stood by his tomb, When __ in a low whis - per I

heard some - thing say: How sweet - ly I sleep here a - lone.

Additional lyrics

2. The tempest may howl and the loud thunder roar
   And gathering storms may arise,
   But calm is my feeling, at rest is my soul,
   The tears are all wiped from my eyes.

3. The call of my master compelled me from home,
   No kindred or relative nigh.
   I met the contagion and sank to the tomb,
   My soul flew to mansions on high.

4. Go tell my companion and children most dear
   To weep not for me now I'm gone.
   The same hand that led me through seas most severe
   Has kindly assisted me home.

Publisher and performance rights society unknown.

Jack-A-Roe

Traditional, arranged by Bob Dylan

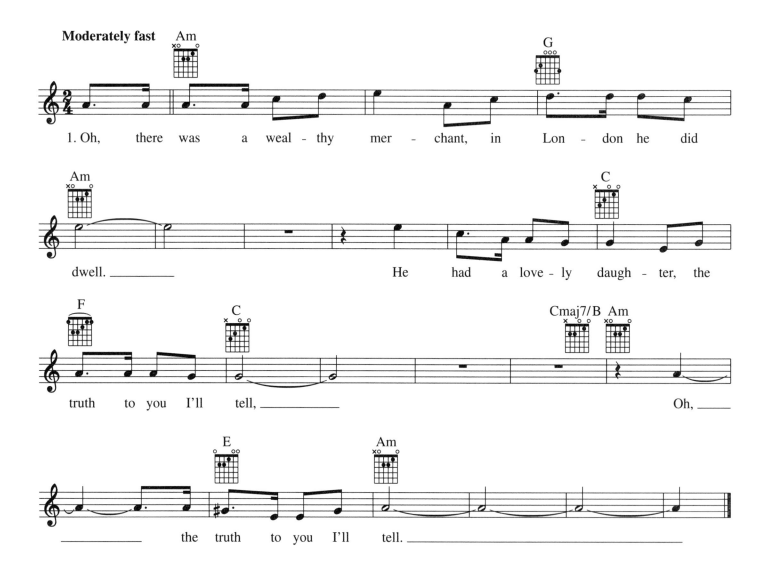

Moderately fast

1. Oh, there was a weal-thy mer-chant, in Lon-don he did dwell. _____ He had a love-ly daugh-ter, the truth to you I'll tell, _____ Oh, _____ _____ the truth to you I'll tell. _____

Additional lyrics

2. She had sweethearts a-plenty and men of high degree.
   There was none but Jackie Frazier, her true love e'er to be,
   Oh, her true love e'er to be.

3. "Oh daughter, oh daughter, your body I will confine.
   If none but Jack the sailor would ever suit your mind,
   Oh, would ever suit your mind."

4. "This body you may imprison, my heart you can't confine.
   There's none but Jack the sailor would have this heart of mine,
   Oh, would have this heart of mine.

5. Now Jackie's gone sailing with trouble on his mind.
   To leave his native country and his darling girl behind,
   Oh, his darling girl behind.

6. She went into the tailor shop and dressed in men's array,
   Then she went into the vessel to convey herself away,
   Oh, convey herself away.

7. "Before you step onboard, sir, your name I'd like to know."
   She smiled all in her countenance, said, "They call me Jack-A-Roe,
   Oh, they call me Jack-A-Roe."

8. "Your waist is light and slender, your fingers neat and small,
   Your cheeks too red and rosy for to face the cannonball,
   Oh, to face the cannonball."

9. "I know my waist is slender and my fingers they are small,
   But they would not make me tremble for to see ten thousand fall,
   Oh, to see ten thousand fall."

10. The war soon being over, they hunted all around.
    Among the dead and dying her darling love she found,
    Oh, her darling love she found.

11. She picked him up all in her arms and carried him to town,
    And sent for her physician to quickly heal his wounds,
    Oh, to quickly heal his wounds.

12. This couple, they got married, so well they did agree,
    This couple they got married, so why not you and me,
    Oh, so why not you and me.

Jim Jones

Traditional, arranged by Bob Dylan

1. Come and lis-ten for __ a mo-ment, lads, __ And hear me tell __ my tale. __

__ How a-cross the sea __ from Eng-land __ I

was con-demned to sail. Now the ju-ry found __ me

guil-ty, __ Then says the judge, __ says he, ___ "Oh, for

life, Jim Jones, I'm send-ing you __ A-cross the storm-y

sea. _____ But take a tip __ be -

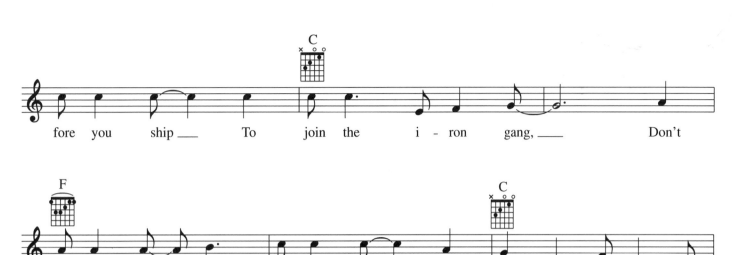

fore you ship ___ To join the i - ron gang, ___ Don't

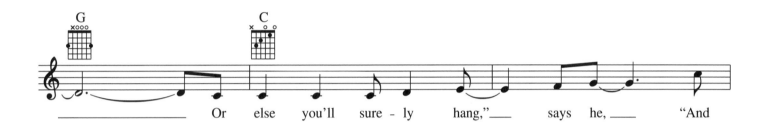

get too gay ___ in Bot'- ny Bay, ___ Or else you'll sure - ly hang, ___

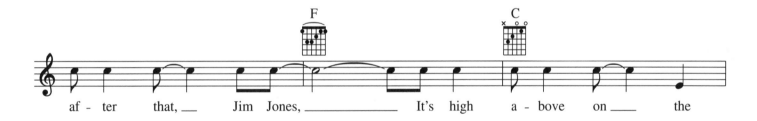

___ Or else you'll sure - ly hang," ___ says he, ___ "And

af - ter that, ___ Jim Jones, _____ It's high a - bove on ___ the

gal - lows tree ___ The ___ crows will pick your bones." _____

Additional lyrics

2. And our ship was high upon the sea
   When pirates came along,
   But the soldiers on our convict ship
   Were full five hundred strong,
   For they opened fire and somehow drove
   That pirate ship away,
   But I'd rather have joined that pirate ship
   Than gone to Botany Bay.
   With the storms ragin' round us,
   And the winds a-blowin' gale,
   I'd rather have drowned in misery
   Than gone to New South Wales.
   There's no time for mischief there, they say,
   Remember that, says they,
   Or they'll flog the poaching out of you,
   Down in Botany Bay.

3. Now it's day and night and the irons clang,
   And like poor galley slaves
   We toil and toil, and when we die
   Must fill dishonored graves.
   And it's by and by I'll slip my chains,
   Well, into the bush I'll go,
   And I'll join the bravest rankers there,
   Jack Donohue and co.
   And some dark night, when everything
   Is silent in the town,
   I'll shoot those tyrants one and all,
   I'll gun the floggers down.
   Oh, I'll give the land a little shock,
   Remember what I say,
   And they'll yet regret they've sent Jim Jones
   In chains to Botany Bay.

Love Henry

Traditional, arranged by Bob Dylan

Capo on sixth fret

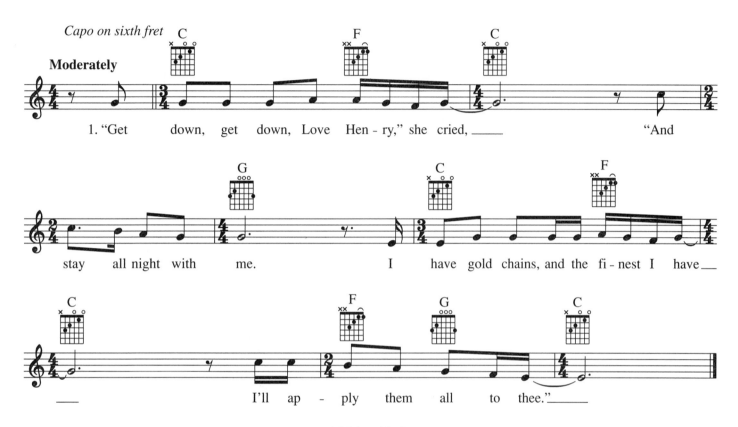

Moderately

1. "Get down, get down, Love Hen - ry," she cried, _____ "And

stay all night with me. I have gold chains, and the fi - nest I have_____

_____ I'll ap - ply them all to thee."_____

Additional lyrics

2. "I can't get down and I shan't get down,
   Or stay all night with thee.
   Some pretty little girl in Cornersville
   I love far better than thee."

3. He layed his head on a pillow of down.
   Kisses she gave him three.
   With a penny knife that she held in her hand
   She murdered mortal he.

Instrumental

4. "Get well, get well, Love Henry," she cried,
   "Get well, get well," said she.
   "Oh don't you see my own heart's blood
   Come flowin' down so free?"

5. She took him by his long yellow hair,
   And also by his feet.
   She plunged him into well water, where
   It runs both cold and deep.

6. "Lie there, lie there, Love Henry," she cried,
   "Til the flesh rots off your bones.
   Some pretty little girl in Cornersville
   Will mourn for your return."

Instrumental

7. "Hush up, hush up, my parrot," she cried,
   "Don't tell no news on me;
   Or these costly beads around my neck,
   I'll apply them all to thee."

8. "Fly down, fly down, pretty parrot," she cried,
   "And light on my right knee.
   The doors to your cage shall be decked with gold
   And hung on a willow tree."

9. "I won't fly down, I can't fly down
   And light on your right knee.
   A girl who would murder her own true love
   Would kill a little bird like me."

Joey

Words and Music by Bob Dylan and Jacques Levy

1. Born in Red Hook, Brook-lyn, in the year __ of __ who knows when

O- pened up his eyes to the tune of an ac-cor-di-on _____

Al-ways on the out - side of what-ev-er side there was When they

asked him why _ it had to be that way, _ "Well," he an-swered, "Just be-cause." _

Lar - ry was the old - est, Jo - ey was next _ to last. ___

Additional lyrics

2. There was talk they killed their rivals, but the truth was far from that
   No one ever knew for sure where they were really at.
   When they tried to strangle Larry, Joey almost hit the roof.
   He went out that night to seek revenge, thinkin' he was bulletproof.

   The war broke out at the break of dawn, it emptied out the streets
   Joey and his brothers suffered terrible defeats
   Till they ventured out behind the lines and took five prisoners.
   They stashed them away in a basement, called them amateurs.

   The hostages were tremblin' when they heard a man exclaim,
   "Let's blow this place to kingdom come, let Con Edison take the blame."
   But Joey stepped up, he raised his hand, said, "We're not those kind of men.
   It's peace and quiet that we need to go back to work again."

   Chorus

3. The police department hounded him, they called him Mr. Smith
   They got him on conspiracy, they were never sure who with.
   "What time is it?" said the judge to Joey when they met
   "Five to ten," said Joey. The judge says, "That's exactly what you get."

   He did ten years in Attica, reading Nietzsche and Wilhelm Reich
   They threw him in the hole one time for tryin' to stop a strike.
   His closest friends were black men 'cause they seemed to understand
   What it's like to be in society with a shackle on your hand.

   When they let him out in '71 he'd lost a little weight
   But he dressed like Jimmy Cagney and I swear he did look great.
   He tried to find the way back into the life he left behind
   To the boss he said, "I have returned and now I want what's mine."

   Chorus

4. It was true that in his later years he would not carry a gun
   "I'm around too many children," he'd say, "they should never know of one."
   Yet he walked right into the clubhouse of his lifelong deadly foe,
   Emptied out the register, said, "Tell 'em it was Crazy Joe."

   One day they blew him down in a clam bar in New York
   He could see it comin' through the door as he lifted up his fork.
   He pushed the table over to protect his family
   Then he staggered out into the streets of Little Italy.

   Chorus

5. Sister Jacqueline and Carmela and mother Mary all did weep.
   I heard his best friend Frankie say, "He ain't dead, he's just asleep."
   Then I saw the old man's limousine head back towards the grave
   I guess he had to say one last goodbye to the son that he could not save.

   The sun turned cold over President Street and the town of Brooklyn mourned
   They said a mass in the old church near the house where he was born.
   And someday if God's in heaven overlookin' His preserve
   I know the men that shot him down will get what they deserve.

   Chorus

Man in the Long Black Coat

Words and Music by Bob Dylan

Moderately bright, in 6

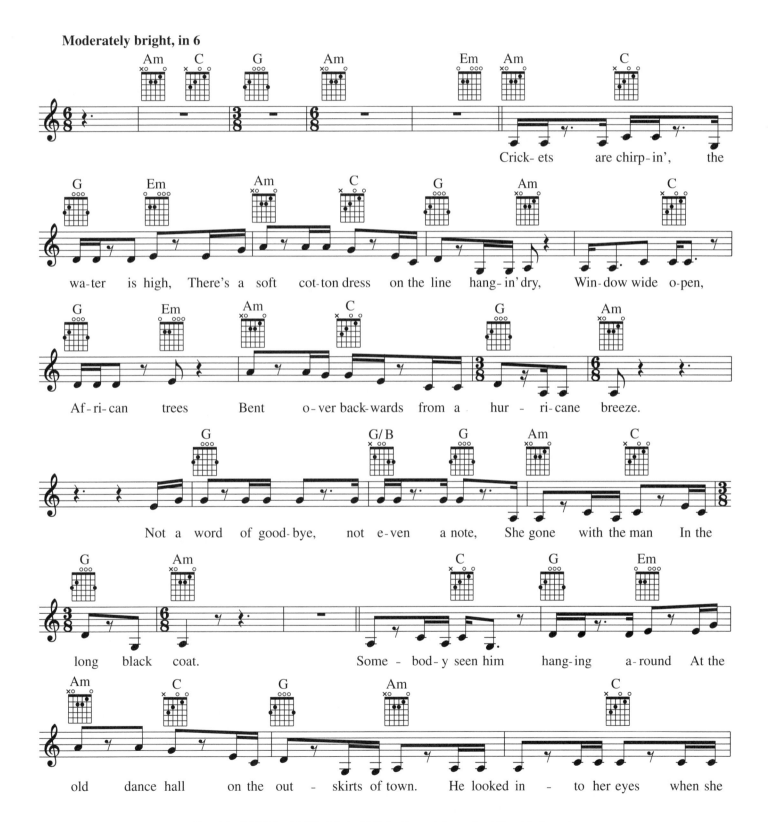

Crick- ets are chirp- in', the wa- ter is high, There's a soft cot-ton dress on the line hang- in' dry, Win- dow wide o-pen, Af- ri- can trees Bent o- ver back-wards from a hur – ri- cane breeze. Not a word of good- bye, not e-ven a note, She gone with the man In the long black coat. Some - bod- y seen him hang-ing a- round At the old dance hall on the out - skirts of town. He looked in - to her eyes when she

John Brown

Words and Music by Bob Dylan

Moderate rock

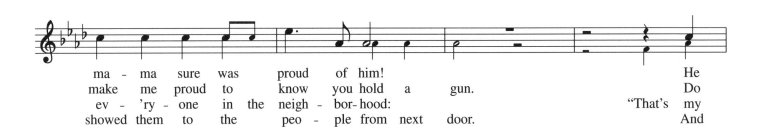

1. John Brown went off to war to fight on a for-eign shore. His
2. son, you look so fine, I'm glad you're a son of mine, you
3. that old train pulled out, John's _ ma be-gan to shout, tell-in'
4. let-ter once in a while and her face broke in-to a smile as she

ma-ma sure was proud of him! He
make me proud to know you hold a gun. Do
ev-'ry-one in the neigh-bor-hood: "That's my
showed them to the peo-ple from next door. And

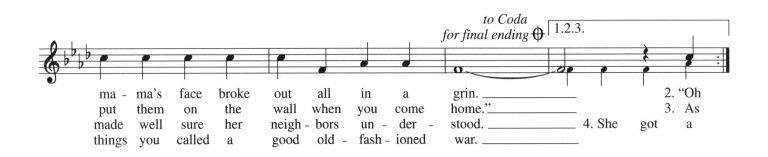

stood straight and tall in his un-i-form and all. His
what the cap-tain says, lots of med-als you will get, and we'll
son that's a-bout to go, he's a sol-dier now, you know." She
she bragged a-bout her son with his un-i-form and gun, and these

to Coda for final ending

1.2.3.

ma-ma's face broke out all in a grin. _____ 2. "Oh
put them on the wall when you come home." _____ 3. As
made well sure her neigh-bors un-der-stood. _____ 4. She got a
things you called a good old-fash-ioned war. _____

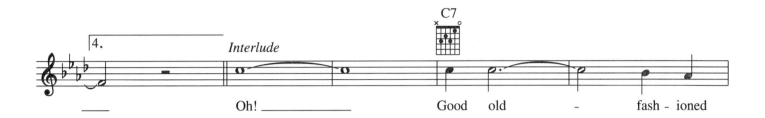

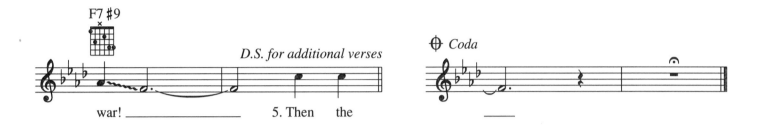

Additional lyrics

5. Then the letters ceased to come, for a long time they did not come.
   They ceased to come for about ten months or more.
   Then a letter finally came saying, "Go down and meet the train.
   Your son's a-coming home from the war."

6. She smiled and went right down, she looked everywhere around
   But she could not see her soldier son in sight.
   But as all the people passed, she saw her son at last,
   When she did she could hardly believe her eyes.

7. Oh his face was all shot up and his hand was all blown off
   And he wore a metal brace around his waist.
   He whispered kind of slow, in a voice she did not know,
   While she couldn't even recognize his face!

   Oh! Lord! Not even recognize his face.

8. "Oh tell me, my darling son, pray tell me what they done.
   How is it you come to be this way?"
   He tried his best to talk but his mouth could hardly move
   And the mother had to turn her face away.

9. "Don't you remember, Ma, when I went off to war
   You thought it was the best thing I could do?
   I was on the battleground, you were home . . . acting proud.
   You wasn't there standing in my shoes."

10. "Oh, and I thought when I was there, God, what am I doing here?
    I'm a-tryin' to kill somebody or die tryin'.
    But the thing that scared me most was when my enemy came close
    And I saw that his face looked just like mine."

    Oh! Lord! Just like mine!

11. "And I couldn't help but think, through the thunder rolling and stink,
    That I was just a puppet in a play.
    And through the roar and smoke, this string is finally broke,
    And a cannon ball blew my eyes away."

12. As he turned away to walk, his Ma was still in shock
    At seein' the metal brace that helped him stand.
    But as he turned to go, he called his mother close
    And he dropped his medals down into her hand.

Jokerman

Words and Music by Bob Dylan

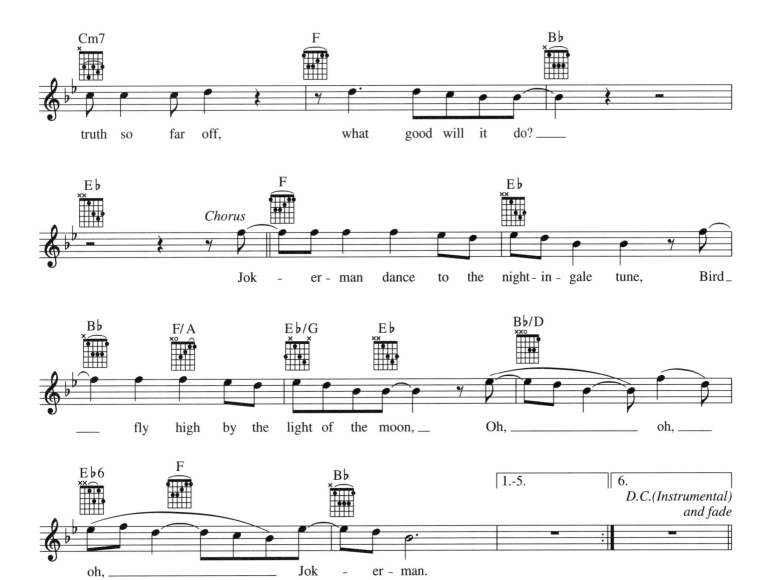

truth so far off, what good will it do? ____

Chorus

Jok - er - man dance to the night - in - gale tune, Bird ___

____ fly high by the light of the moon, __ Oh, _____ oh, ____

oh, _____ Jok - er - man.

1.-5.

6.
D.C.(Instrumental)
and fade

Additional lyrics

2. So swiftly the sun sets in the sky,
   You rise up and say goodbye to no one.
   Fools rush in where angels fear to tread,
   Both of their futures, so full of dread, you don't show one.
   Shedding off one more layer of skin,
   Keeping one step ahead of the persecutor within.

   Chorus

3. You're a man of the mountains, you can walk on the clouds,
   Manipulator of crowds, you're a dream twister.
   You're going to Sodom and Gomorrah
   But what do you care? Ain't nobody there would want to marry your sister.
   Friend to the martyr, a friend to the woman of shame,
   You look into the fiery furnace, see the rich man without any name.

   Chorus

4. Well, the Book of Leviticus and Deuteronomy,
   The law of the jungle and the sea are your only teachers.
   In the smoke of the twilight on a milk-white steed,
   Michelangelo indeed could've carved out your features.
   Resting in the fields, far from the turbulent space,
   Half asleep near the stars with a small dog licking your face.

   Chorus

5. Well, the rifleman's stalking the sick and the lame,
   Preacherman seeks the same, who'll get there first is uncertain.
   Nightsticks and water cannons, tear gas, padlocks,
   Molotov cocktails and rocks behind every curtain,
   False-hearted judges dying in the webs that they spin,
   Only a matter of time 'til night comes steppin' in.

   Chorus

6. It's a shadowy world, skies are slippery gray,
   A woman just gave birth to a prince today and dressed him in scarlet.
   He'll put the priest in his pocket, put the blade to the heat,
   Take the motherless children off the street
   And place them at the feet of a harlot.
   Oh, Jokerman, you know what he wants,
   Oh, Jokerman, you don't show any response.

   Chorus

Mixed Up Confusion

Words and Music by Bob Dylan

Additional lyrics

2. Well, my hat's in my hand
   Babe, I'm walkin' down the line

3. An' I'm lookin' for a woman
   Whose head's mixed up like mine

4. Well, my head's full of questions
   My temp'rature's risin' fast

5. Well, I'm lookin' for some answers
   But I don't know who to ask

6. But I'm walkin' and wonderin'
   And my poor feet don't ever stop

7. Seein' my reflection
   I'm hung over, hung down, hung up!

Just Like a Woman

Words and Music by Bob Dylan

Just Like Tom Thumb's Blues

Words and Music by Bob Dylan

Moderato (in 4)

1. When you're lost in the rain ___ in Juar - ez _____ And it's East - er time

too _____ And your grav - i - ty fails ___ And neg - a -

tiv - i - ty don't ___ pull you through_____ Don't put on an - y airs When you're

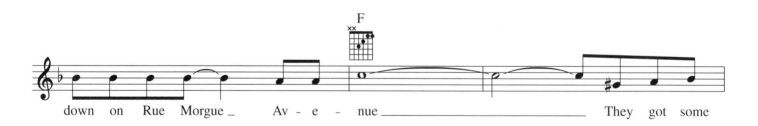

down on Rue Morgue ___ Av - e - nue _____ They got some

repeat five times

hun - gry wom - en there And they real - ly make a mess out - ta you _____

Additional lyrics

2. Now if you see Saint Annie
   Please tell her thanks a lot
   I cannot move
   My fingers are all in a knot
   I don't have the strength
   To get up and take another shot
   And my best friend, my doctor
   Won't even say what it is I've got

3. Sweet Melinda
   The peasants call her the goddess of gloom
   She speaks good English
   And she invites you up into her room
   And you're so kind
   And careful not to go to her too soon
   And she takes your voice
   And leaves you howling at the moon

4. Up on Housing Project Hill
   It's either fortune or fame
   You must pick up one or the other
   Though neither of them are to be what they claim
   If you're lookin' to get silly
   You better go back to from where you came
   Because the cops don't need you
   And man they expect the same

5. Now all the authorities
   They just stand around and boast
   How they blackmailed the sergeant-at-arms
   Into leaving his post
   And picking up Angel who
   Just arrived here from the coast
   Who looked so fine at first
   But left looking just like a ghost

6. I started out on burgundy
   But soon hit the harder stuff
   Everybody said they'd stand behind me
   When the game got rough
   But the joke was on me
   There was nobody even there to call my bluff
   I'm going back to New York City
   I do believe I've had enough

Lay Down Your Weary Tune

Words and Music by Bob Dylan

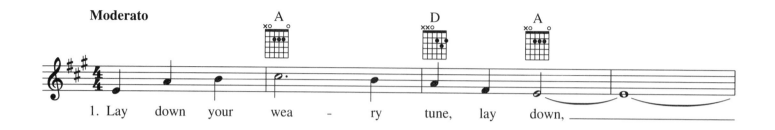

1. Lay down your wea - ry tune, lay down, _____

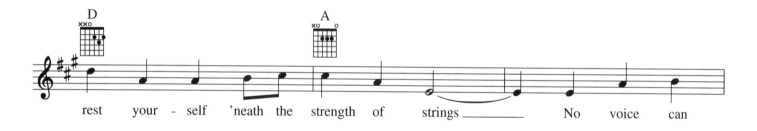

_____ Lay down the song you strum, _____ And

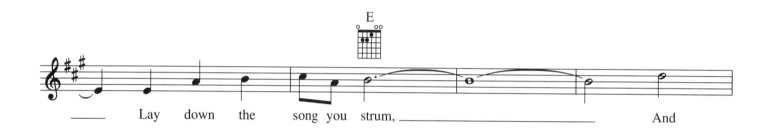

rest your - self 'neath the strength of strings _____ No voice can

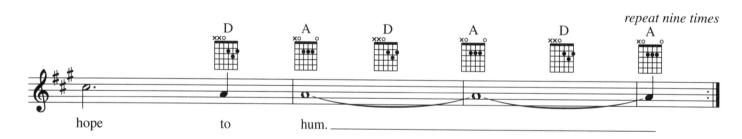

hope to hum. _____

Additional lyrics

2. Struck by the sounds before the sun,
   I knew the night had gone.
   The morning breeze like a bugle blew
   Against the drums of dawn.

3. Lay down your weary tune, lay down,
   Lay down the song you strum,
   And rest yourself 'neath the strength of strings
   No voice can hope to hum.

4. The ocean wild like an organ played,
   The seaweed's wove its strands.
   The crashin' waves like cymbals clashed
   Against the rocks and sands.

5. Lay down your weary tune, lay down,
   Lay down the song you strum,
   And rest yourself 'neath the strength of strings
   No voice can hope to hum.

6. I stood unwound beneath the skies
   And clouds unbound by laws.
   The cryin' rain like a trumpet sang
   And asked for no applause.

7. Lay down your weary tune, lay down,
   Lay down the song you strum,
   And rest yourself 'neath the strength of strings
   No voice can hope to hum.

8. The last of leaves fell from the trees
   And clung to a new love's breast.
   The branches bare like a banjo played
   To the winds that listened best.

9. I gazed down in the river's mirror
   And watched its winding strum.
   The water smooth ran like a hymn
   And like a harp did hum.

10. Lay down your weary tune, lay down,
    Lay down the song you strum,
    And rest yourself 'neath the strength of strings
    No voice can hope to hum.

Lenny Bruce

Words and Music by Bob Dylan

Moderately slow, with expression

1. Len - ny Bruce is dead but his ghost lives on and on

Nev - er did get an - y Gold - en Globe a - ward, nev - er made it to Syn - a - non.

He was an out - law, that's for sure,

More of an out - law than you ___ ev - er

were. Len - ny Bruce is gone but his

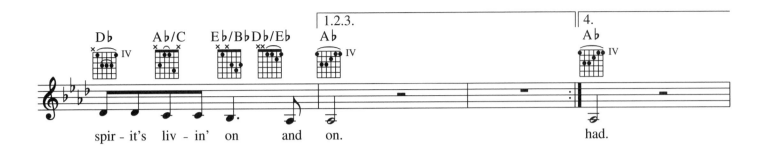

spir - it's liv - in' on   and   on.   had.

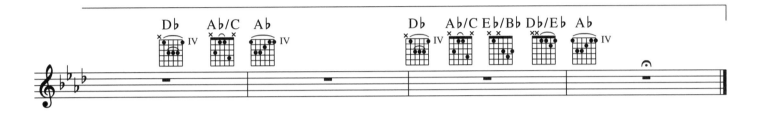

Additional lyrics

2. Maybe he had some problems, maybe some things that he couldn't work out
   But he sure was funny and he sure told the truth and he knew what he was talkin' about.
   Never robbed any churches nor cut off any babies' heads,
   He just took the folks in high places and he shined a light in their beds.
   He's on some other shore, he didn't wanna live anymore.

3. Lenny Bruce is dead but he didn't commit any crime
   He just had the insight to rip off the lid before its time.
   I rode with him in a taxi once, only for a mile and a half,
   Seemed like it took a couple of months.
   Lenny Bruce moved on and like the ones that killed him, gone.

4. They said that he was sick 'cause he didn't play by the rules
   He just showed the wise men of his day to be nothing more than fools.
   They stamped him and they labeled him like they do with pants and shirts,
   He fought a war on a battlefield where every victory hurts.
   Lenny Bruce was bad, he was the brother that you never had.

Leopard-Skin Pill-Box Hat

Words and Music by Bob Dylan

Additional lyrics

2. Well, you look so pretty in it
   Honey, can I jump on it sometime?
   Yes, I just wanna see
   If it's really that expensive kind
   You know it balances on your head
   Just like a mattress balances
   On a bottle of wine
   Your brand new leopard-skin pill-box hat

3. Well, if you wanna see the sun rise
   Honey, I know where
   We'll go out and see it sometime
   We'll both just sit there and stare
   Me with my belt
   Wrapped around my head
   And you just sittin' there
   In your brand new leopard-skin pill-box hat

4. Well, I asked the doctor if I could see you
   It's bad for your health, he said
   Yes, I disobeyed his orders
   I came to see you
   But I found him there instead
   You know, I don't mind him cheatin' on me
   But I sure wish he'd take that off his head
   Your brand new leopard-skin pill-box hat

5. Well, I see you got a new boyfriend
   You know, I never seen him before
   Well, I saw him
   Makin' love to you
   You forgot to close the garage door
   You might think he loves you for your money
   But I know what he really loves you for
   It's your brand new leopard-skin pill-box hat

Let Me Die in My Footsteps

Words and Music by Bob Dylan

Additional lyrics

3. I don't know if I'm smart but I think I can see
   When someone is pullin' the wool over me
   And if this war comes and death's all around
   Let me die on this land 'fore I die underground.
   Let me die in my footsteps
   Before I go down under the ground.

4. There's always been people that have to cause fear
   They've been talking of the war now for many long years
   I have read all their statements and I've not said a word
   But now Lawd God, let my poor voice be heard.
   Let me die in my footsteps
   Before I go down under the ground.

5. If I had rubies and riches and crowns
   I'd buy the whole world and change things around
   I'd throw all the guns and the tanks in the sea
   For they are mistakes of a past history.
   Let me die in my footsteps
   Before I go down under the ground.

6. Let me drink from the waters where the mountain streams flood
   Let me smell of wildflowers flow free through my blood
   Let me sleep in your meadows with the green grassy leaves
   Let me walk down the highway with my brother in peace.
   Let me die in my footsteps
   Before I go down under the ground.

7. Go out in your country where the land meets the sun
   See the craters and the canyons where the waterfalls run
   Nevada, New Mexico, Arizona, Idaho
   Let every state in this union seep in your souls.
   And you'll die in your footsteps
   Before you go down under the ground.

License to Kill

Words and Music by Bob Dylan

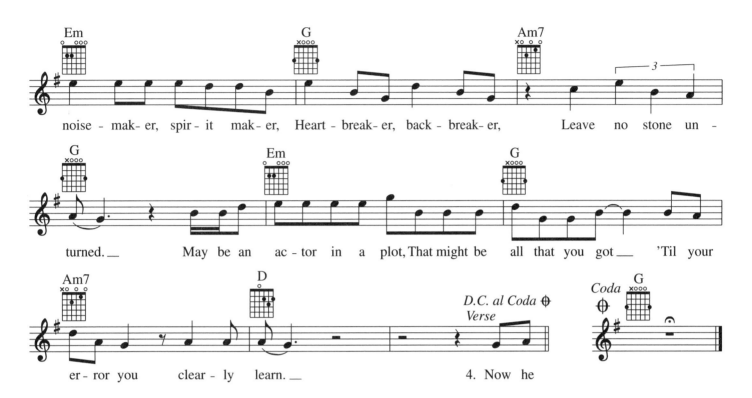

noise - mak- er, spir- it mak- er, Heart - break- er, back - break- er, Leave no stone un - turned. __ May be an ac - tor in a plot, That might be all that you got __ 'Til your er - ror you clear - ly learn. __ 4. Now he

Additional lyrics

2. Now, they take him and they teach him and they groom him for life
   And they set him on a path where he's bound to get ill,
   Then they bury him with stars,
   Sell his body like they do used cars.

   Chorus:
   Now, there's a woman on my block,
   She just sit there facin' the hill.
   She say who gonna take away his license to kill?

3. Now, he's hell-bent for destruction, he's afraid and confused,
   And his brain has been mismanaged with great skill.
   All he believes are his eyes
   And his eyes, they just tell him lies.

   Chorus:
   But there's a woman on my block,
   Sitting there in a cold chill.
   She say who gonna take away his license to kill?

   Bridge:
   Ya may be a noisemaker, spirit maker,
   Heartbreaker, backbreaker,
   Leave no stone unturned.
   May be an actor in a plot,
   That might be all that you got
   'Til your error you clearly learn.

4. Now he worships at an altar of a stagnant pool
   And when he sees his reflection, he's fulfilled.
   Oh, man is opposed to fair play,
   He wants it all and he wants it his way.

   Chorus:
   Now, there's a woman on my block,
   She just sit there as the night grows still.
   She say who gonna take away his license to kill?

Like a Rolling Stone

Words and Music by Bob Dylan

Additional lyrics

2. You've gone to the finest school all right, Miss Lonely
   But you know you only used to get juiced in it
   And nobody has ever taught you how to live on the street
   And now you find out you're gonna have to get used to it
   You said you'd never compromise
   With the mystery tramp, but now you realize
   He's not selling any alibis
   As you stare into the vacuum of his eyes
   And ask him do you want to make a deal?

Refrain

3. You never turned around to see the frowns on the jugglers and the clowns
   When they all come down and did tricks for you
   You never understood that it ain't no good
   You shouldn't let other people get your kicks for you
   You used to ride on the chrome horse with your diplomat
   Who carried on his shoulder a Siamese cat
   Ain't it hard when you discover that
   He really wasn't where it's at
   After he took from you everything he could steal.

Refrain

4. Princess on the steeple and all the pretty people
   They're drinkin', thinkin' that they got it made
   Exchanging all kinds of precious gifts and things
   But you'd better lift your diamond ring, you'd better pawn it babe
   You used to be so amused
   At Napoleon in rags and the language that he used
   Go to him now, he calls you, you can't refuse
   When you got nothing, you got nothing to lose
   You're invisible now, you got no secrets to conceal.

Refrain

One More Weekend

Words and Music by Bob Dylan

Moderately slow blues

Slip-pin' and _ slid - in' like a wea-sel on the run,
Come on down to my ship, hon-ey, _ ride _ on _ deck,

I'm look-in' good to see you, yeah, and we can have _ some fun. _
We'll fly o - ver the o - cean _ just like you sus-pect. _

One more week-end, one more week-end _ with you. _
One more week-end, one more week-end _ with you. _

One _ more _ week-end, one more week-end _ 'll do. _

We'll fly the night a - way _

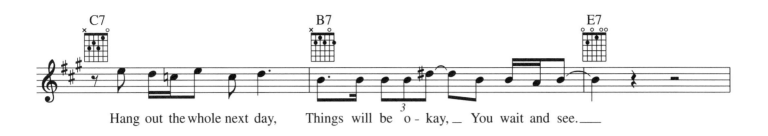

Hang out the whole next day, Things will be o-kay, __ You wait and see. __

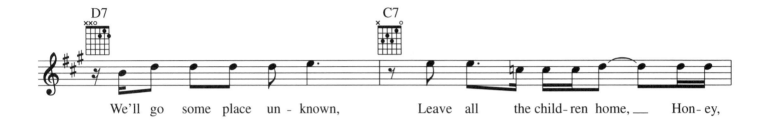

We'll go some place un-known, Leave all the child-ren home, __ Hon-ey,

Why not go a-lone __ Just you and me. __ Com-in' and go-in' __

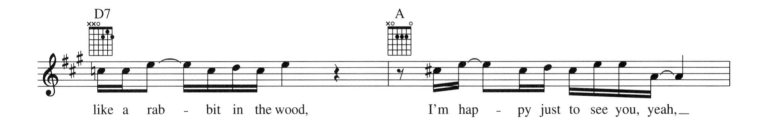

like a rab - bit in the wood, I'm hap - py just to see you, yeah, __

look-in' so good. __ One more week-end, one __ more week-end __ with you, __

__ One more week-end, one more week-end __ 'll do

Little Maggie

Traditional, arranged by Bob Dylan

Moderately

1. Oh, where is lit – tle Mag – gie? __ O – ver yon – der she stands.

Ri – fle on her shoul- der, __ Six – shoot- er in her hand. __

2. How can I ev – er stand it, __ Just to see them two blue eyes,

Shin – in' like some dia – monds, _ Like some dia – monds in the sky.

Additional lyrics

3. Rather be in some lonely hollow
   Where the sun don't ever shine,
   Than to see you be another man's darling,
   And to know that you'll never be mine.

4. Well, it's march me away to the station
   With my suitcase in my hand.
   Yes, march me away to the station,
   I'm off to some far-distant land.

5. Sometimes I have a nickel,
   And sometimes I have a dime.
   Sometimes I have ten dollars,
   Just to pay for little Maggie's wine.

6. Pretty flowers are made for blooming,
   Pretty stars are made to shine.
   Pretty girls are made for boy's love.
   Little Maggie was made for mine.

7. Well, yonder stands little Maggie
   With a dram glass in her hand.
   She's a-drinkin' down her troubles
   Over courtin' some other man.

Little Sadie

Words and Music by Bob Dylan

Moderately

(I) went out last night just to take a lit-tle round, I

met my Lit-tle Sa-die and I brought her down. I run right home and I went to bed With a

last time to Final ending

for-ty-four smoke-less un-der my head.

Final ending

I went

Additional lyrics

2. I began to think what a deed I'd done,
   I grabbed my hat and away I run.
   I made a good run, but I run too slow.
   They overtook me down in Jericho.

3. Standing on a corner ringin' my bell,
   Up stepped the sheriff from Thomasville.
   He said, "Young man, is you name Brown?
   Remember the night you blowed Little Sadie down?"

4. "Oh, yes sir, my name is Lee,
   I murdered little Sadie in the first degree.
   First degree and second degree,
   If you've got any papers will you serve them to me?"

5. Well, they took me downtown and they dressed me in black,
   They put me on a train and they sent me back.
   I had no one for to go my bail,
   They crammed me back into the county jail.

6. The judge and the jury, they took their stand.
   The judge had the papers in his right hand.
   Forty-one days, forty-one nights,
   Forty-one years to wear the ball and the stripes.

Living the Blues

Words and Music by Bob Dylan

But I can't de - ny ____ this feel -ing that I ____

car - ry for you deep down in - side. _____ If you

see me this way, __ You'd come back and you'd stay, __ Oh, how __ could you re -

fuse. I've been liv - ing the blues _____ ev - 'ry night with-out you. __

I've been liv - ing the

blues _____ ev - 'ry night with-out you, _____ I've been liv - ing the blues_

ev - 'ry night with-out you. _____

Lo and Behold!

Words and Music by Bob Dylan

Moderately

(Spoken:) 1. I pulled out for San Anton', I never felt so good.

My woman said she'd meet me there And of course, I knew she

would. The coachman, he hit me for my hook And he asked me my

name. I give it to him right away, Then I hung my head in shame.

(Sung:) Lo and be - hold! Lo and be - hold! Look - in' for __ my

lo and be - hold, Get me out - a here, my dear man! __

Additional lyrics

2. I come into Pittsburgh
   At six-thirty flat.
   I found myself a vacant seat
   An' I put down my hat.
   "What's the matter, Molly, dear,
   What's the matter with your mound?"
   "What's it to ya, Moby Dick?
   This is chicken town!"
   Lo and behold! Lo and behold!
   Lookin' for my lo and behold,
   Get me outa here, my dear man!

3. I bought my girl
   A herd of moose,
   One she could call her own.
   Well, she came out the very next day
   To see where they had flown.
   I'm goin' down to Tennessee,
   Get me a truck 'r somethin'.
   Gonna save my money and rip it up!
   Lo and behold! Lo and behold!
   Lookin' for my lo and behold,
   Get me outa here, my dear man!

4. Now, I come in on a ferris wheel
   An' boys, I sure was slick.
   I come in like a ton of bricks,
   Laid a few tricks on 'em.
   Goin' back to Pittsburgh,
   Count up to thirty,
   Round that horn and ride that herd,
   Gonna thread up!
   Lo and behold! Lo and behold!
   Lookin' for my lo and behold,
   Get me outa here, my dear man!

The Lonesome Death of Hattie Carroll

Words and Music by Bob Dylan

But you who phil - o - so - phize dis - grace and crit - i - cize all fears, _____ Take the rag a - way from your face. Now ain't the time for your tears. _____

Additional lyrics

2. William Zanzinger, who at twenty-four years
   Owns a tobacco farm of six hundred acres
   With rich wealthy parents who provide and protect him
   And high office relations in the politics of Maryland,
   Reacted to his deed with a shrug of his shoulders
   And swear words and sneering, and his tongue it was snarling,
   In a matter of minutes on bail was out walking.

   Chorus

3. Hattie Carroll was a maid of the kitchen.
   She was fifty-one years old and gave birth to ten children
   Who carried the dishes and took out the garbage
   And never sat once at the head of the table
   And didn't even talk to the people at the table
   Who just cleaned up all the food from the table
   And emptied the ashtrays on a whole other level,
   Got killed by a blow, lay slain by a cane
   That sailed through the air and came down through the room,
   Doomed and determined to destroy all the gentle.
   And she never done nothing to William Zanzinger.

   Chorus

4. In the courtroom of honor, the judge pounded his gavel
   To show that all's equal and that the courts are on the level
   And that the strings in the books ain't pulled and persuaded
   And that even the nobles get properly handled
   Once that the cops have chased after and caught 'em
   And that the ladder of law has no top and no bottom,
   Stared at the person who killed for no reason
   Who just happened to be feelin' that way without warnin'.
   And he spoke through his cloak, most deep and distinguished,
   And handed out strongly, for penalty and repentance,
   William Zanzinger with a six-month sentence.

   Chorus:
   Oh, but you who philosophize disgrace and criticize all fears,
   Bury the rag deep in your face
   For now's the time for your tears.

Señor
(Tales of Yankee Power)
Words and Music by Bob Dylan

Moderately slow

Se - ñor,　　　se - ñor,　　　do you
ñor,　　　se - ñor,　　　do you

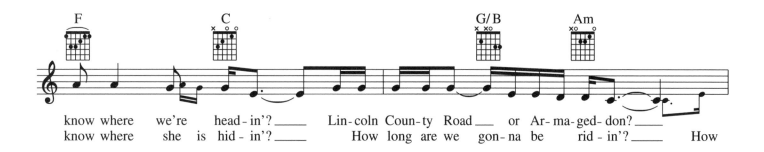

know where　we're　head - in'? _____ Lin-coln Coun-ty Road ___ or Ar-ma-ged-don? _____
know where　she is　hid - in'? _____ How long are we gon-na be rid - in'? ___ How

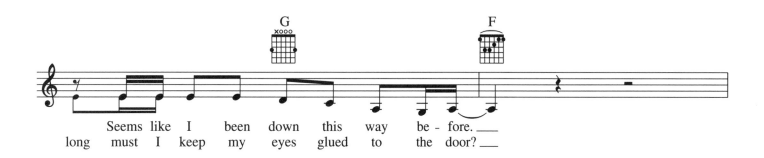

Seems like I　been down this way be - fore. ___
long must I keep my eyes glued to the door? ___

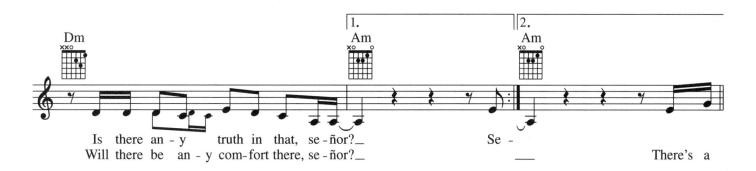

Is there an - y　truth in that, se -ñor?_　　Se -
Will there be an - y com-fort there, se - ñor?_　　　　　There's a

Can't stand the sus - pense an - y - more.
I just got - ta pick my - self up off the floor. Can you

1.
tell me who to con - tact here, se - ñor?

2.
Well, the I'm read - y when you_ are, se -

ñor. Se - ñor, se - ñor, let's

dis - con - nect __ these ca - bles, O - ver - turn __ these ta - bles.

This place don't make sense to me __ no more. Can you

D.S. (Instrumental) & fade

tell me what we're wait - ing for, se - ñor? __

Long Ago, Far Away

Words and Music by Bob Dylan

Moderate hard rock

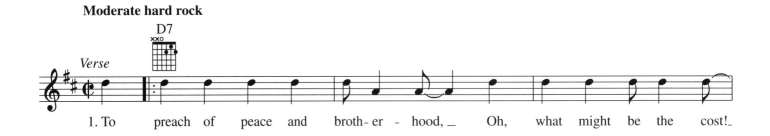

1. To preach of peace and broth-er-hood, _ Oh, what might be the cost! _

_ A man he did it long a - go _ And they

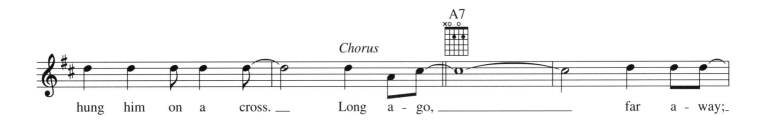

hung him on a cross. _ Long a - go, _____ far a - way; _

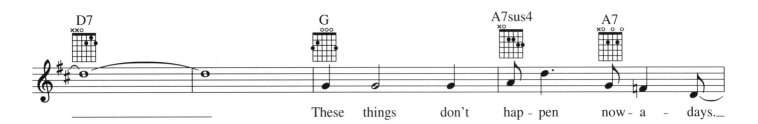

_____ These things don't hap - pen now - a - days. _

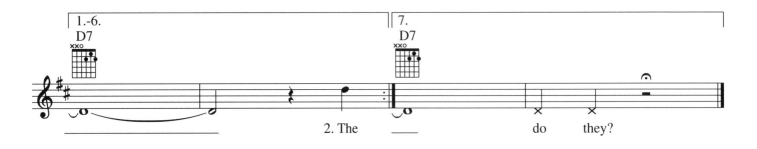

2. The ___ do they?

Additional lyrics

2. The chains of slaves
   They dragged the ground
   With heads and hearts hung low.
   But it was during Lincoln's time
   And it was long ago.
   Long ago, far away;
   Things like that don't happen
   No more, nowadays.

3. The war guns they went off wild,
   The whole world bled its blood.
   Men's bodies floated on the edge
   Of oceans made of mud.
   Long ago, far away;
   Those kind of things don't happen
   No more, nowadays.

4. One man had much money,
   One man had not enough to eat,
   One man lived just like a king,
   The other man begged on the street.
   Long ago, far away;
   These things don't happen
   No more, nowadays.

5. One man died of a knife so sharp,
   One man died from the bullet of a gun,
   One man died of a broken heart
   To see the lynchin' of his son.
   Long ago, far away;
   Things like that don't happen
   No more, nowadays.

6. Gladiators killed themselves,
   It was during the Roman times.
   People cheered with bloodshot grins
   As eye and minds went blind.
   Long ago, far away;
   Things like that don't happen
   No more, nowadays.

7. And to talk of peace and brotherhood,
   Oh, what might be the cost!
   A man he did it long ago
   And they hung him on a cross.
   Long ago, far away;
   Things like that don't happen
   No more, nowadays, do they?

Long Time Gone

Words and Music by Bob Dylan

Moderate rock

1. My par - ents raised me ten - der - ly, I was their on - ly son. ____

____ My mind got mixed with ramb - lin' When I was all so

young, ____ And I left my home the first time When

I was twelve and one. ____ I'm a

long time a - com - in', Maw, An' I'll be a long time

1.-7. || 8.

gone. ____ 2. On the gone. ____

Additional lyrics

2. On the western side of Texas,
   On the Texas plains,
   I tried to find a job o'work
   But they said I's young of age.
   My eyes they burned when I heard,
   "Go home where you belong!"
   I'm a long time a-comin',
   An' I'll be a long time gone.

3. I remember when I's ramblin'
   Around with the carnival trains,
   Different towns, different people,
   Somehow they're all the same.
   I remember children's faces best,
   I remember travelin' on.
   I'm a long time a-comin',
   I'll be a long time gone.

4. I once loved a fair young maid
   An' I ain't too big to tell,
   If she broke my heart a single time,
   She broke it ten or twelve.
   I walked and talked all by myself,
   I did not tell no one.
   I'm a long time a-comin', babe,
   An' I'll be a long time gone.

5. Many times by the highwayside,
   I tried to flag a ride.
   With bloodshot eyes and gritting teeth,
   I'd watch the cars roll by.
   The empty air hung in my head
   I's thinkin' all day long.
   I'm a long time a-comin',
   An' I'll be a long time gone.

6. You might see me on your crossroads
   When I'm a-passin' through.
   Remember me how you wished to
   As I'm a-driftin' from your view.
   I ain't got the time to think about it,
   I got too much to get done.
   Well, I'm a long time comin'
   An' I'll be a long time gone.

7. If I can't help somebody
   With a word or song,
   If I can't show somebody
   They are travelin' wrong.
   But I know I ain't no prophet
   An' I ain't no prophet's son.
   I'm just a long time a-comin'
   An' I'll be a long time gone.

8. So you can have your beauty,
   It's skin deep and it only lies.
   And you can have your youth,
   It'll rot before your eyes.
   Just give to me my gravestone
   With it clearly carved upon:
   "I's a long time a-comin',
   An' I'll be a long time gone."

Long-Distance Operator

Words and Music by Bob Dylan

Slow rock blues

1. Long - dis-tance op - er - a - tor, __ Place this call, it's not for

fun.

Long - dis-tance op - er - a - tor, __

Please, place this call, ___ you know it's not for fun. __

I got-ta

get a mes-sage __ to my ba - by,

You know, ___ she's not just

an - y - one.

|1.-3.| |4.|

2. There are
3. If a
4. Ev - 'ry

Additional lyrics

2. There are thousands in the phone booth,
   Thousands at the gate.
   There are thousands in the phone booth,
   Thousands at the gate.
   Ev'rybody wants to make a long-distance call
   But you know they're just gonna have to wait.

3. If a call comes from Louisiana,
   Please, let it ride.
   If a call comes from Louisiana,
   Please, let it ride.
   This phone booth's on fire,
   It's getting hot inside.

4. Ev'rybody wants to be my friend,
   But nobody wants to get higher.
   Ev'rybody wants to be my friend,
   But nobody wants to get higher.
   Long-distance operator,
   I believe I'm stranglin' on this telephone wire.

Love Minus Zero/No Limit

Words and Music by Bob Dylan

Additional lyrics

2. In the dime stores and bus stations,
   People talk of situations,
   Read books, repeat quotations,
   Draw conclusions on the wall.
   Some speak of the future,
   My love she speaks softly,
   She knows there's no success like failure
   And that failure's no success at all.

3. The cloak and dagger dangles,
   Madams light the candles.
   In ceremonies of the horsemen,
   Even the pawn must hold a grudge.
   Statues made of match sticks,
   Crumble into one another,
   My love winks, she does not bother,
   She knows too much to argue or to judge.

4. The bridge at midnight trembles,
   The country doctor rambles,
   Bankers' nieces seek perfection,
   Expecting all the gifts that wise men bring.
   The wind howls like a hammer,
   The night blows cold and rainy,
   My love she's like some raven
   At my window with a broken wing.

Love Sick

Words and Music by Bob Dylan

Additional lyrics

3. I see, I see lovers in the meadow
   I see, I see silhouettes in the window
   I watch them 'til they're gone and they leave me hanging on
   To a shadow

   I'm sick of love; I hear the clock tick
   This kind of love; I'm love sick

4. *Instrumental*

5. Sometimes the silence can be like the thunder
   Sometimes I wanna take to the road and plunder
   Could you ever be true?
   I think of you
   And I wonder

   I'm sick of love; I wish I'd never met you
   I'm sick of love; I'm trying to forget you

   Just don't know what to do
   I'd give anything to
   Be with you

Seven Days

Words and Music by Bob Dylan

Moderately (in 2)

Sev - en days, _____ sev - en more days she'll be com - in', I'll be wait - ing ___ at the sta - tion for her to ar - rive ___ Sev - en more days, all I got - ta do is sur - vive. ___ She been gone ___ ev - er since I been a child ___ Ev - er

394

Maggie's Farm

Words and Music by Bob Dylan

Medium bright

1. I ain't gon - na work on Mag - gie's farm no more. ____

No, I ain't gon - na work on Mag - gie's farm no more. ____

Well, I wake in the morn - ing, Fold my hands and pray for

rain. I got a head full of i - de - as ____ That are driv - in' me in -

sane. __ It's a shame the way she makes me scrub the floor. ____ I

repeat four times

ain't gon - na work on Mag - gie's farm no more. ____

Additional lyrics

2. I ain't gonna work for Maggie's brother no more.
No, I ain't gonna work for Maggie's brother no more.
Well, he hands you a nickel,
He hands you a dime,
He asks you with a grin
If you're havin' a good time,
Then he fines you every time you slam the door.
I ain't gonna work for Maggie's brother no more.

3. I ain't gonna work for Maggie's pa no more.
No, I ain't gonna work for Maggie's pa no more.
Well, he puts his cigar
Out in your face just for kicks.
His bedroom window
It is made out of bricks.
The National Guard stands around his door.
Ah, I ain't gonna work for Maggie's pa no more.

4. I ain't gonna work for Maggie's ma no more.
No, I ain't gonna work for Maggie's ma no more.
Well, she talks to all the servants
About man and God and law.
Everybody says
She's the brains behind pa.
She's sixty-eight, but she says she's twenty-four.
I ain't gonna work for Maggie's ma no more.

5. I ain't gonna work on Maggie's farm no more.
No, I ain't gonna work on Maggie's farm no more.
Well, I try my best
To be just like I am,
But everybody wants you
To be just like them.
They sing while you slave and I just get bored.
I ain't gonna work on Maggie's farm no more.

Make You Feel My Love

Words and Music by Bob Dylan

Moderately slow

When the rain __ is blow-ing in your face

And the whole_ world is on your case I could of - fer you a

warm em - brace To make __ you feel my love ____

1. When the eve-ning sha-dows and the stars ap - pear
2. *Instrumental solo*

And there is no one there to dry __ your tears __ I could hold you for a

mil - lion years To make you feel my love ____

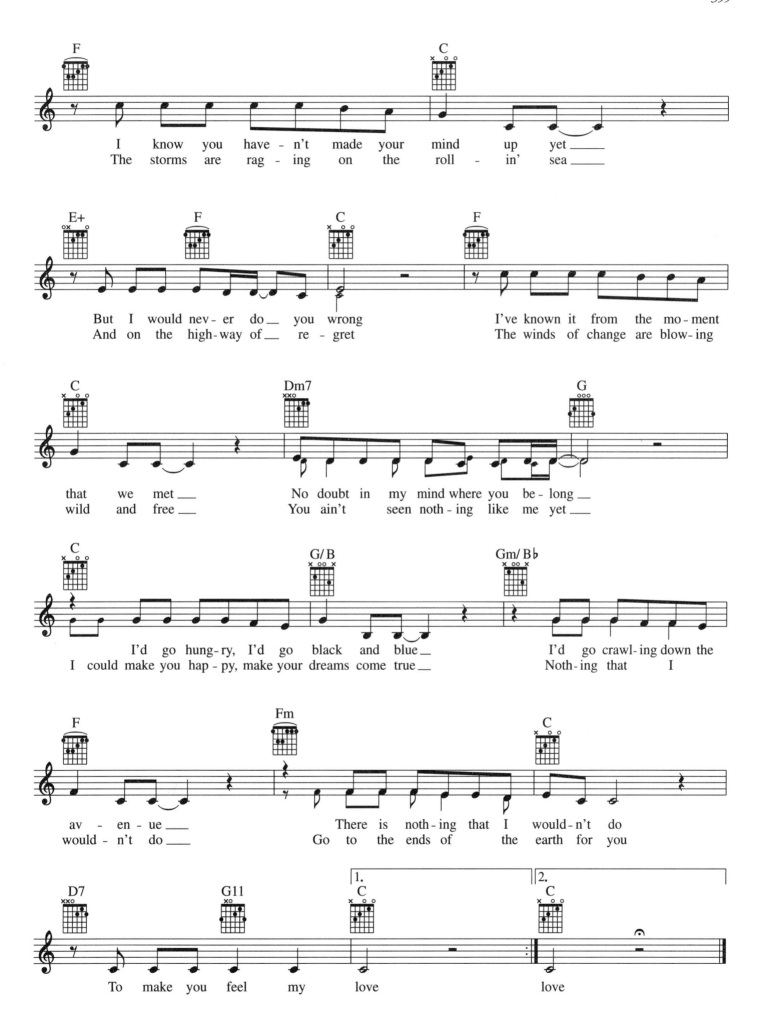

Mama, You Been on My Mind

Words and Music by Bob Dylan

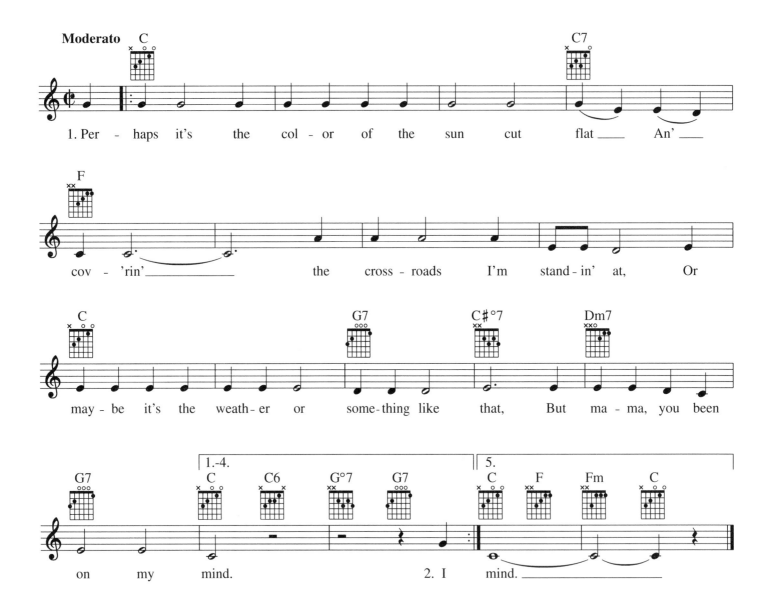

Additional lyrics

2. I don't mean trouble, please don't put me down or get upset,
   I am not pleadin' or sayin', "I can't forget."
   I do not walk the floor bowed down an' bent, but yet,
   Mama, you been on my mind.

3. Even though my mind is hazy an' my thoughts they might be narrow,
   Where you been don't bother me nor bring me down in sorrow.
   It don't even matter to me where you're wakin' up tomorrow,
   But mama, you're just on my mind.

4. I am not askin' you to say words like "yes" or "no,"
   Please understand me, I got no place for you t' go.
   I'm just breathin' to myself, pretendin' not that I don't know,
   Mama, you been on my mind.

5. When you wake up in the mornin', baby, look inside your mirror.
   You know I won't be next to you, you know I won't be near.
   I'd just be curious to know if you can see yourself as clear
   As someone who has had you on his mind.

Man Gave Names to All the Animals

Words and Music by Bob Dylan

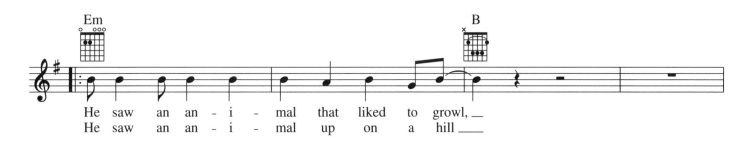

He saw an an - i - mal that liked to growl, __
He saw an an - i - mal up - on a hill ___

Big fur - ry paws and he liked to howl, __
Chew - ing up so much grass un - til she was filled. __

Great big fur - ry back __ and fur - ry hair. _____
He saw milk com - in' out ___ but he did - n't know how. _____

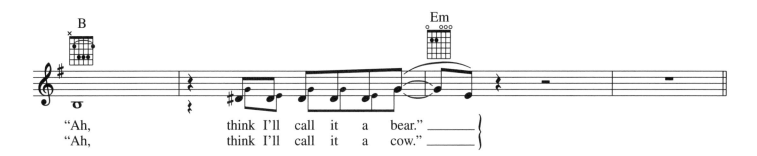

"Ah, think I'll call it a bear." _____ }
"Ah, think I'll call it a cow." _____ }

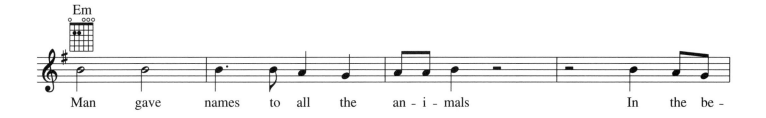

Man gave names to all the an - i - mals In the be -

gin - ning, in the be - gin - ning. Man gave

The Man in Me

Words and Music by Bob Dylan

Moderately slow, with a beat

The man in me will do __ near - ly an - y task, __ And
as for com - pen - sa - tion, there's _ lit - tle he __ would ask. __ Take a
wom - an like you __ To get through __ to the man in me. __
Storm clouds are rag - ing all a - round my door, __ I think to my - self I might not
take it an - y - more. __ Take a wom-an like your kind __ To

Man of Peace

Words and Music by Bob Dylan

Additional lyrics

2. He got a sweet gift of gab, he got a harmonious tongue,
    He knows every song of love that ever has been sung.
    Good intentions can be evil,
    Both hands can be full of grease.
    You know that sometimes Satan comes as a man of peace.

3. Well, first he's in the background, then he's in the front,
    Both eyes are looking like they're on a rabbit hunt.
    Nobody can see through him,
    No, not even the Chief of Police.
    You know that sometimes Satan comes as a man of peace.

4. Well, he catch you when you're hoping for a glimpse of the sun,
    Catch you when your troubles feel like they weigh a ton.
    He could be standing next to you,
    The person that you'd notice least.
    I hear that sometimes Satan comes as a man of peace.

5. Well, he can be fascinating, he can be dull,
    He can ride down Niagara Falls in the barrels of your skull.
    I can smell something cooking,
    I can tell there's going to be a feast.
    You know that sometimes Satan comes as a man of peace.

6. He's a great humanitarian, he's a great philanthropist,
    He knows just where to touch you, honey, and how you like to be kissed.
    He'll put both his arms around you,
    You can feel the tender touch of the beast.
    You know that sometimes Satan comes as a man of peace.

7. Well, the howling wolf will howl tonight, the king snake will crawl,
    Trees that've stood for a thousand years suddenly will fall.
    Wanna get married? Do it now,
    Tomorrow all activity will cease.
    You know that sometimes Satan comes as a man of peace.

8. Somewhere Mama's weeping for her blue-eyed boy,
    She's holding them little white shoes and that little broken toy
    And he's following a star,
    The same one them three men followed from the East.
    I hear that sometimes Satan comes as a man of peace.

Masters of War

Words and Music by Bob Dylan

Additional lyrics

2. You that never done nothin'
   But build to destroy
   You play with my world
   Like it's your little toy
   You put a gun in my hand
   And you hide from my eyes
   And you turn and run farther
   When the fast bullets fly

3. Like Judas of old
   You lie and deceive
   A world war can be won
   You want me to believe
   But I see through your eyes
   And I see through your brain
   Like I see through the water
   That runs down my drain

4. You fasten the triggers
   For the others to fire
   Then you set back and watch
   When the death count gets higher
   You hide in your mansion
   As young people's blood
   Flows out of their bodies
   And is buried in the mud

5. You've thrown the worst fear
   That can ever be hurled
   Fear to bring children
   Into the world
   For threatening my baby
   Unborn and unnamed
   You ain't worth the blood
   That runs in your veins

6. How much do I know
   To talk out of turn
   You might say that I'm young
   You might say I'm unlearned
   But there's one thing I know
   Though I'm younger than you
   Even Jesus would never
   Forgive what you do

7. Let me ask you one question
   Is your money that good
   Will it buy you forgiveness
   Do you think that it could
   I think you will find
   When your death takes its toll
   All the money you made
   Will never buy back your soul

8. And I hope that you die
   And your death'll come soon
   I will follow your casket
   In the pale afternoon
   And I'll watch while you're lowered
   Down to your deathbed
   And I'll stand o'er your grave
   'Til I'm sure that you're dead

Maybe Someday

Words and Music by Bob Dylan

Moderately

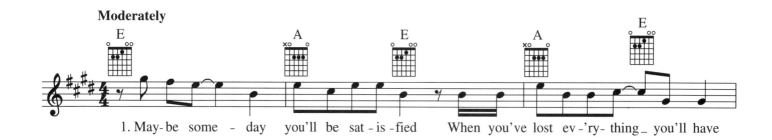

1. May-be some - day you'll be sat - is - fied When you've lost ev -'ry- thing _ you'll have

noth - ing left to hide. When you're through run-ning o - ver things like you're walk- ing 'cross the tracks,

May- be you'll beg me (like a dog) to take you back. _ May-be some-day you'll find out ev-ery-

bod- y's some - bod- y's fool, May - be then you'll real - ize _ what it would have

tak- en to keep me cool. May- be some - day when you're by your-self a - lone You'll

know the love_ that I had for you _ was nev - er my own. _ had for you. _

repeat & fade

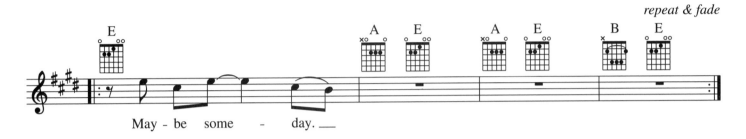

May - be some - day. ___

Additional lyrics

2. Maybe someday you'll have nowhere to turn,
You'll look back and wonder 'bout the bridges you have burned.
You'll look back sometime when the lights grow dim
And you'll see you look much better with me than you do with him.
Through hostile cities and unfriendly towns,
Thirty pieces of silver, no money down.
Maybe someday, you will understand
That something for nothing is everybody's plan.

3. Maybe someday you'll remember what you felt
When there was blood on the moon in the cotton belt.
When both of us, baby, were going though some sort of a test
Neither one of us could do what we do best.
I should have known better, baby, I should have called your bluff.
I guess I was too off the handle, not sentimental enough.
Maybe someday, you'll believe me when I say
That I wanted you, baby, in every kind of way.

4. Maybe someday you'll hear a voice from on high
Sayin' "For whose sake did you live, for whose sake did you die?"
Forgive me, baby, for what I didn't do
For not breakin' down no bedroom door to get at you.
Always was a sucker for the right cross.
Never wanted to go home 'til the last cent was lost.
Maybe someday you will look back and see
That I made it so easy for you to follow me.

5. Maybe someday there'll be nothing to tell.
I'm just as happy as you, baby, I just can't say it so well.
Never slumbered or slept or waited for lightning to strike.
There's no excuse for you to say that we don't think alike.
You said you were goin' to Frisco, stay a couple of months.
I always liked San Francisco, I was there for a party once.
Maybe someday you'll see that it's true
There was no greater love than what I had for you.

Meet Me in the Morning

Words and Music by Bob Dylan

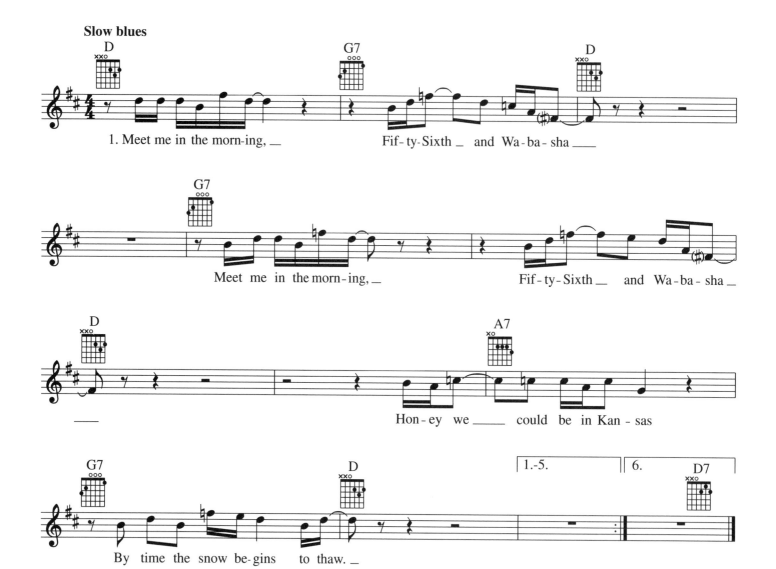

1. Meet me in the morn-ing, __ Fif-ty-Sixth __ and Wa-ba-sha ___

Meet me in the morn-ing, __ Fif-ty-Sixth __ and Wa-ba-sha __

___ Hon-ey we ___ could be in Kan-sas

By time the snow be-gins to thaw. __

Additional lyrics

2. They say the darkest hour is right before the dawn
   They say the darkest hour is right before the dawn
   But you wouldn't know it by me
   Every day's been darkness since you been gone.

3. Little rooster crowin', there must be something on his mind
   Little rooster crowin', there must be something on his mind
   Well, I feel just like that rooster
   Honey, ya treat me so unkind.

4. The birds are flyin' low babe, honey I feel so exposed
   Well, the birds are flyin' low babe, honey I feel so exposed
   Well now, I ain't got any matches
   And the station doors are closed.

5. Well, I struggled through barbed wire, felt the hail fall from above
   Well, I struggled through barbed wire, felt the hail fall from above
   Well, you know I even outran the hound dogs
   Honey, you know I've earned your love.

6. Look at the sun sinkin' like a ship
   Look at the sun sinkin' like a ship
   Ain't that just like my heart, babe
   When you kissed my lips?

Million Dollar Bash

Words and Music by Bob Dylan

1. Well, that big dumb blonde With her wheel in the gorge __ And

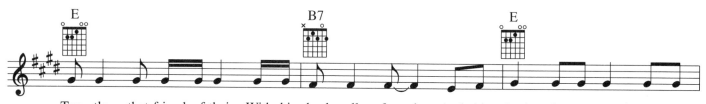

Tur - tle, that friend of theirs With his checks all forged_ And his cheeks in a chunk With his

cheese in the cash They're all gon - na be there At that mil - lion dol - lar bash.

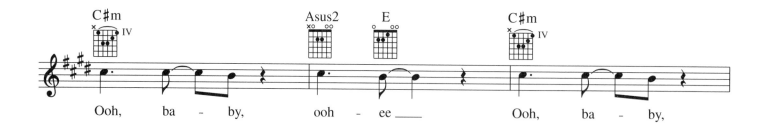

Ooh, ba - by, ooh - ee ___ Ooh, ba - by,

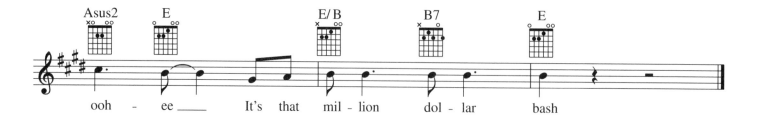

ooh - ee ___ It's that mil - lion dol - lar bash

Additional lyrics

2. Ev'rybody from right now
   To over there and back
   The louder they come
   The harder they crack
   Come now, sweet cream
   Don't forget to flash
   We're all gonna meet
   At that million dollar bash
   Ooh, baby, ooh-ee
   Ooh, baby, ooh-ee
   It's that million dollar bash

3. Well, I took my counselor
   Out to the barn
   Silly Nelly was there
   She told him a yarn
   Then along came Jones
   Emptied the trash
   Ev'rybody went down
   To that million dollar bash
   Ooh, baby, ooh-ee
   Ooh, baby, ooh-ee
   It's that million dollar bash

4. Well, I'm hittin' it too hard
   My stones won't take
   I get up in the mornin'
   But it's too early to wake
   First it's hello, goodbye
   Then push and then crash
   But we're all gonna make it
   At that million dollar bash
   Ooh, baby, ooh-ee
   Ooh, baby, ooh-ee
   It's that million dollar bash

5. Well, I looked at my watch
   I looked at my wrist
   Punched myself in the face
   With my fist
   I took my potatoes
   Down to be mashed
   Then I made it over
   To that million dollar bash
   Ooh, baby, ooh-ee
   Ooh, baby, ooh-ee
   It's that million dollar bash.

Million Miles

Words and Music by Bob Dylan

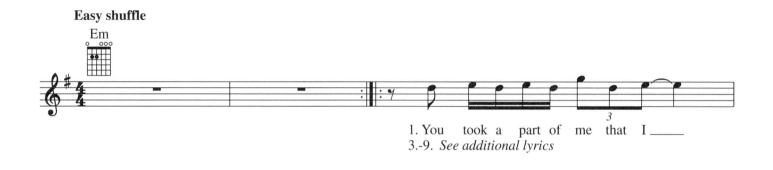

1. You took a part of me that I _____
3.-9. *See additional lyrics*

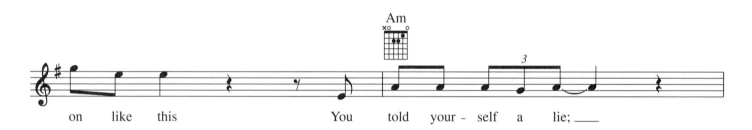

real - ly miss _____ I keep ask - ing my - self how long it can go

on like this You told your - self a lie; _____

that's all right ma - ma, I told my - self one too _____

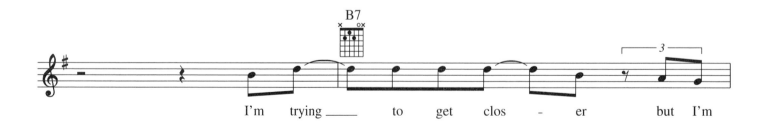

I'm trying _____ to get clos - er but I'm

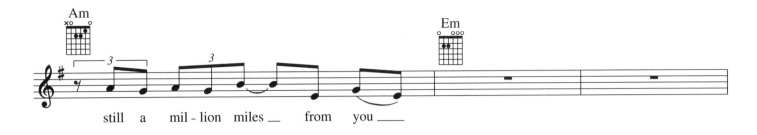

still a mil - lion miles ___ from you ___

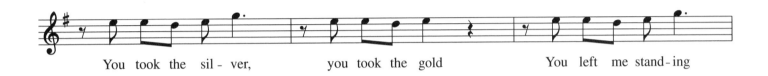

You took the sil - ver, you took the gold You left me stand-ing

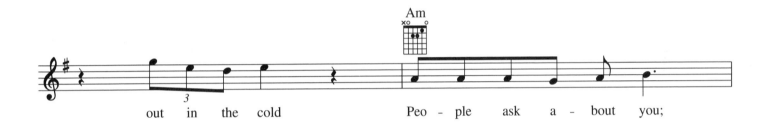

out in the cold Peo - ple ask a - bout you;

I did-n't tell them ev - ery - thing ___ I knew ___

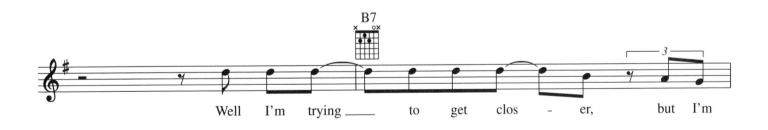

Well I'm trying _____ to get clos - er, but I'm

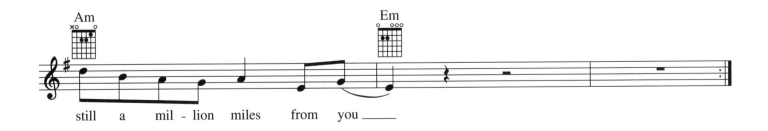

still a mil - lion miles from you _____

Additional lyrics

3. I'm drifting in and out of dreamless sleep
   Throwing all my memories in a ditch so deep
   Did so many things I never did intend to do
   Well I'm trying to get closer, but I'm still a million miles from you

4. I need your love so bad, turn your lamp down low
   I need every bit of it for the places that I go
   Sometimes I wonder just what it's all coming to
   Well I'm tryin' to get closer, but I'm still a million miles from you

5. Well I don't dare close my eyes and I don't dare wink
   Maybe in the next life I'll be able to hear myself think
   Feel like talking to somebody but I just don't know who
   Well, I'm tryin' to get closer but I'm still a million miles from you

6. The last thing you said before you hit the street
   "Gonna find me a janitor to sweep me off my feet"
   I said, "That's all right mama.... you..... you do what you gotta do"
   Well, I'm tryin' to get closer; I'm still a million miles from you

7. Rock me, pretty baby, rock me 'til everything gets real
   Rock me for a little while, rock me 'til there's nothing left to feel
   And I'll rock you too
   I'm tryin' to get closer but I'm still a million miles from you

8. Well, there's voices in the night trying to be heard
   I'm sitting here listening to every mind polluting word
   I know plenty of people who would put me up for a day or two
   Yes, I'm tryin' to get closer but I'm still a million miles from you

9. *Instrumental*

Shelter from the Storm

Words and Music by Bob Dylan

Moderately, in 2

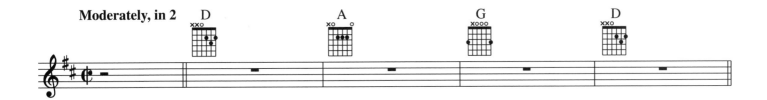

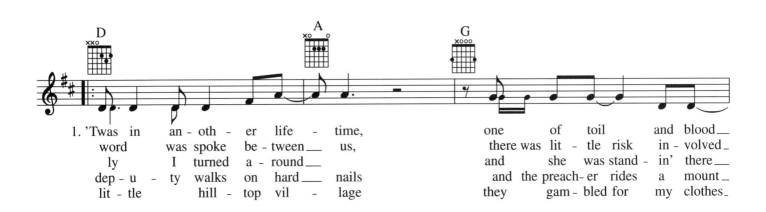

1. 'Twas in an - oth - er life - time,   one of toil and blood___
word was spoke be - tween___ us,   there was lit - tle risk in - volved___
ly I turned a - round___   and she was stand - in' there___
dep - u - ty walks on hard___ nails   and the preach - er rides a mount___
lit - tle hill - top vil - lage   they gam - bled for my clothes___

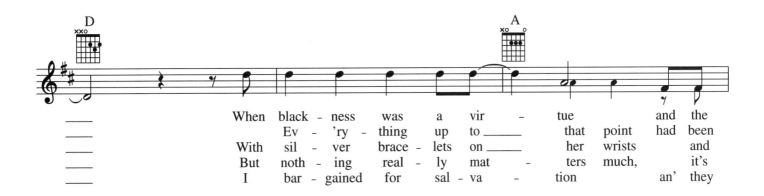

___ When black - ness was a vir - tue and the
___ Ev - 'ry - thing up to___ that point had been
___ With sil - ver brace - lets on___ her wrists and
___ But noth - ing real - ly mat - ters much, it's
___ I bar - gained for sal - va - tion an' they

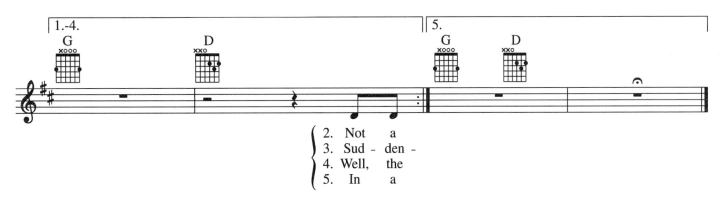

Minstrel Boy

Words and Music by Bob Dylan

Moderately slow

Who's gon - na throw that min - strel boy a coin? Who's gon - na

let it roll? ___ Who's gon-na throw that min - strel boy a coin? Who's gon - na

last time to Final ending

let it down eas - y to save his soul? ___ Oh,
Well, he

Luck - y's been driv - in' a long, long time
deep in num - ber and long heavy in toil,

And now he's stuck on top ___ of the hill. ___
Might - y Mock - ing-bird, he still has such a heavy load.

With twelve for - ward gears, It's been a long hard climb, and with
Be - neath his bound 'ries, What more than I can tell, with

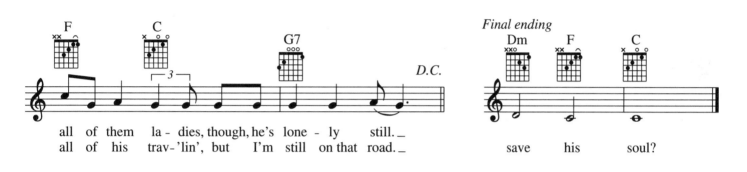

all of them la - dies, though, he's lone - ly still. _
all of his trav-'lin', but I'm still on that road. _

Final ending

save his soul?

D.C.

Money Blues

Words and Music by Bob Dylan and Jacques Levy

Moderate blues

Additional lyrics

2. Went out last night
   Bought two eggs and a slice of ham,
   Went out last night
   Bought two eggs and a slice of ham.
   Bill came to three dollars and ten cents
   And I didn't even get no jam.

3. Man came around
   Askin' for the rent,
   Man came around
   Askin' for the rent.
   Well, I looked into the drawer
   But the money's all been spent.

4. Well, well
   Ain't got no bank account,
   Well, well
   Ain't got no bank account.
   Went down to start one
   But I didn't have the right amount.

5. Everything's inflated
   Like a tire on a car,
   Everything's inflated
   Like a tire on a car.
   Well, the man came and took my Chevy back
   I'm glad I hid my old guitar.

6. Come to me, mama
   Ease my money crisis now,
   Come to me, mama
   Ease my money crisis now.
   I need something to support me
   And only you know how.

Most Likely You Go Your Way and I'll Go Mine

Words and Music by Bob Dylan

Moderately, with a beat

Most of the Time

Words and Music by Bob Dylan

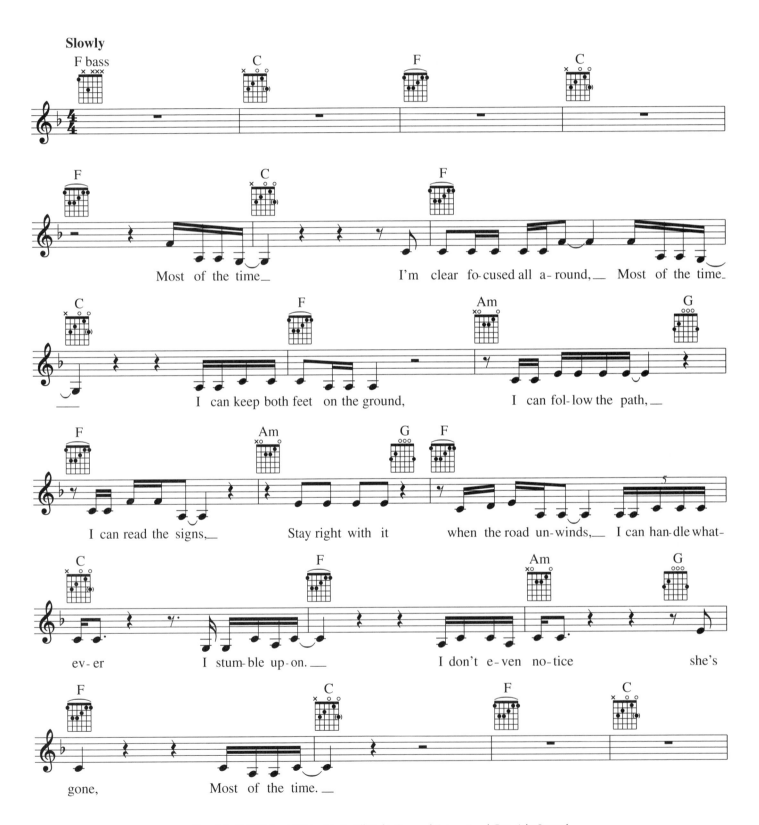

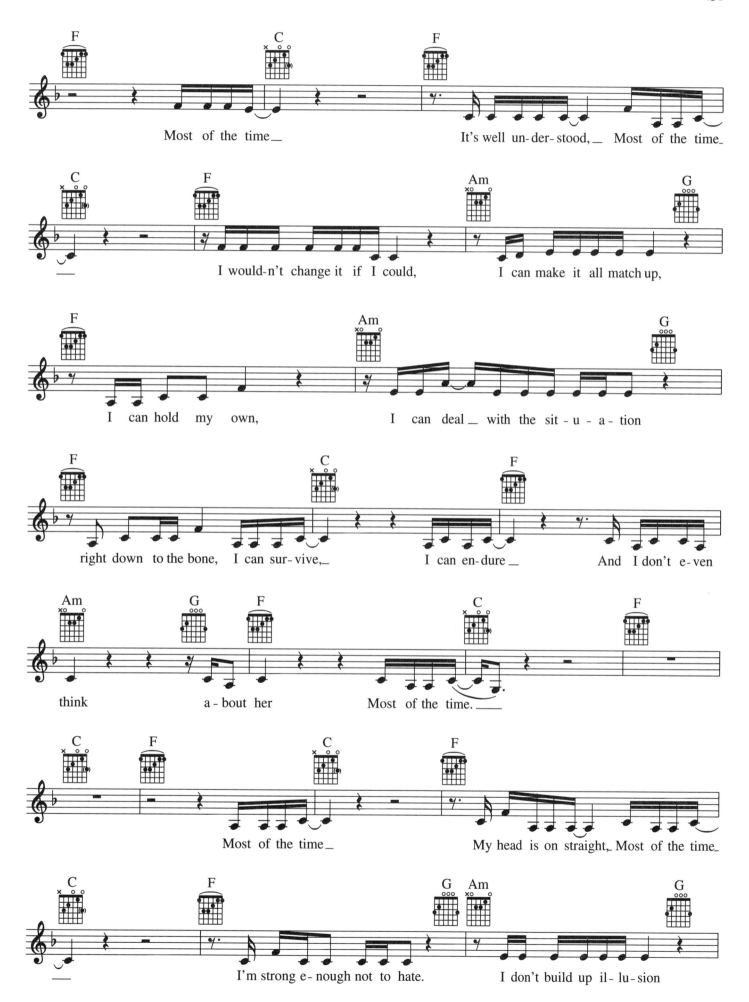

Motorpsycho Nightmare

Words and Music by Bob Dylan

Additional lyrics

2. I fell down
   To my bended knees,
   Saying, "I dig farmers,
   Don't shoot me, please!"
   He cocked his rifle
   And began to shout,
   "You're that travelin' salesman
   That I have heard about."
   I said, "No! No! No!
   I'm a doctor and it's true,
   I'm a clean-cut kid
   And I been to college, too."

3. Then in comes his daughter
   Whose name was Rita.
   She looked like she stepped out of
   La Dolce Vita.
   I immediately tried to cool it
   With her dad,
   And told him what a
   Nice, pretty farm he had.
   He said, "What do doctors
   Know about farms, pray tell?"
   I said, "I was born
   At the bottom of a wishing well."

4. Well, by the dirt 'neath my nails
   I guess he knew I wouldn't lie.
   "I guess you're tired,"
   He said, kinda sly.
   I said, "Yes, ten thousand miles
   Today I drove."
   He said, "I got a bed for you
   Underneath the stove.
   Just one condition
   And you go to sleep right now,
   That you don't touch my daughter
   And in the morning, milk the cow."

5. I was sleepin' like a rat
   When I heard something jerkin'.
   There stood Rita
   Lookin' just like Tony Perkins.
   She said, "Would you like to take a shower?
   I'll show you up to the door."
   I said, "Oh, no! no!
   I've been through this before."
   I knew I had to split
   But I didn't know how,
   When she said,
   "Would you like to take that shower, now?"

6. Well, I couldn't leave
   Unless the old man chased me out,
   'Cause I'd already promised
   That I'd milk his cows.
   I had to say something
   To strike him very weird,
   So I yelled out,
   "I like Fidel Castro and his beard."
   Rita looked offended
   But she got out of the way,
   As he came charging down the stairs
   Sayin', "What's that I heard you say?"

7. I said, "I like Fidel Castro,
   I think you heard me right,"
   And ducked as he swung
   At me with all his might.
   Rita mumbled something
   'Bout her mother on the hill,
   As his fist hit the icebox,
   He said he's going to kill me
   If I don't get out the door
   In two seconds flat,
   "You unpatriotic,
   Rotten doctor Commie rat."

8. Well, he threw a Reader's Digest
   At my head and I did run,
   I did a somersault
   As I seen him get his gun
   And crashed through the window
   At a hundred miles an hour,
   And landed fully blast
   In his garden flowers.
   Rita said, "Come back!"
   As he started to load
   The sun was comin' up
   And I was runnin' down the road.

9. Well, I don't figure I'll be back
   There for a spell,
   Even though Rita moved away
   And got a job in a motel.
   He still waits for me,
   Constant, on the sly.
   He wants to turn me in
   To the F.B.I.
   Me, I romp and stomp,
   Thankful as I romp,
   Without freedom of speech,
   I might be in the swamp.

Mozambique

Words and Music by Bob Dylan and Jacques Levy

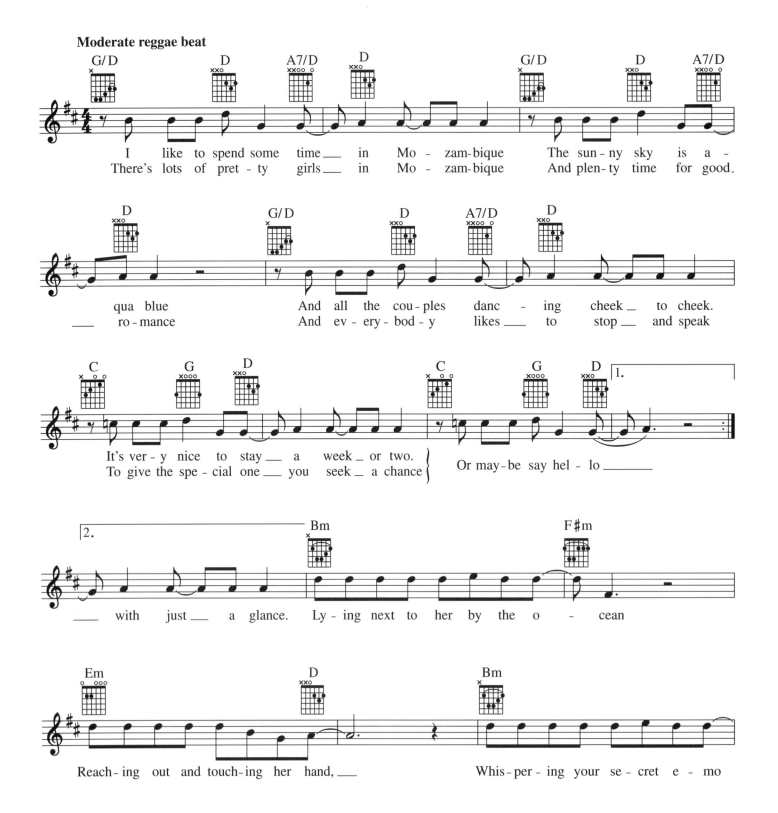

Mr. Tambourine Man

Words and Music by Bob Dylan

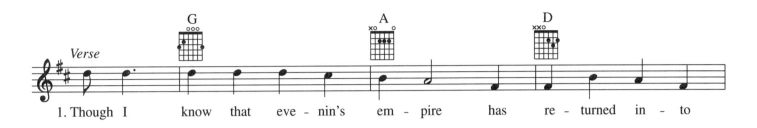

Verse

1. Though I know that eve‑nin's em‑pire has re‑turned in‑to

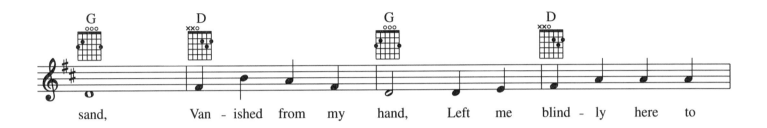

sand, Van‑ished from my hand, Left me blind‑ly here to

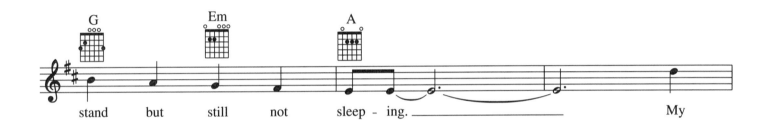

stand but still not sleep‑ing. _____ My

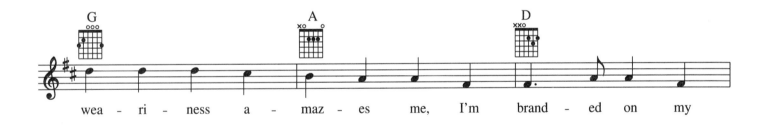

wea‑ri‑ness a‑maz‑es me, I'm brand‑ed on my

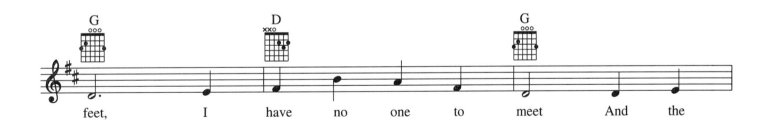

feet, I have no one to meet And the

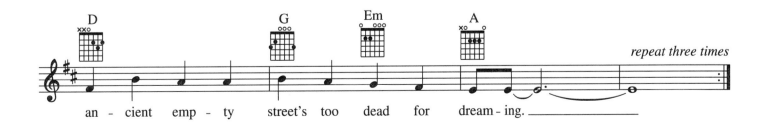

repeat three times

an‑cient emp‑ty street's too dead for dream‑ing. _____

Additional lyrics

2. Take me on a trip upon your magic swirlin' ship,
   My senses have been stripped, my hands can't feel to grip,
   My toes too numb to step, wait only for my boot heels
   To be wanderin'.
   I'm ready to go anywhere, I'm ready for to fade
   Into my own parade, cast your dancing spell my way,
   I promise to go under it.

   Refrain

3. Though you might hear laughin', spinnin', swingin' madly across the sun,
   It's not aimed at anyone, it's just escapin' on the run
   And but for the sky there are no fences facin'.
   And if you hear vague traces of skippin' reels of rhyme
   To your tambourine in time, it's just a ragged clown behind,
   I wouldn't pay it any mind, it's just a shadow you're
   Seein' that he's chasing.

   Refrain

4. Then take me disappearin' through the smoke rings of my mind,
   Down the foggy ruins of time, far past the frozen leaves,
   The haunted, frightened trees, out to the windy beach,
   Far from the twisted reach of crazy sorrow.
   Yes, to dance beneath the diamond sky with one hand waving free,
   Silhouetted by the sea, circled by the circus sands,
   With all memory and fate driven deep beneath the waves,
   Let me forget about today until tomorrow.

   Refrain

Shooting Star

Words and Music by Bob Dylan

Seen a shoot-ing star to-night And I thought of you.__ You were try-ing to break in-to an-oth-er world A world I nev-er knew.__ I al-ways kind of won-dered if you ev-er made it through.__ Seen a shoot-ing star to-night And I thought of you.__ Seen a shoot-ing star to-night

And I thought of me.___ If I was still the same If I ev-er be-came___ what you

want-ed me to be ___ Did I miss the mark or o-ver-step the line

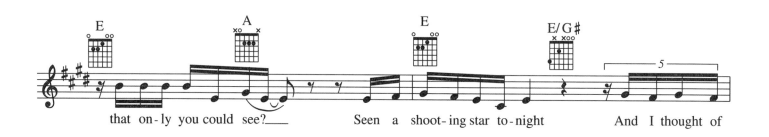

that on-ly you could see?___ Seen a shoot-ing star to-night And I thought of

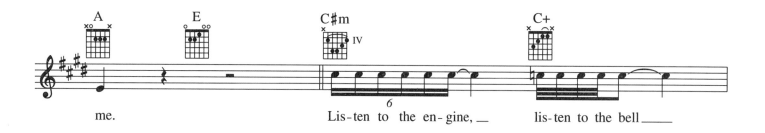

me. Lis-ten to the en-gine, ___ lis-ten to the bell ___

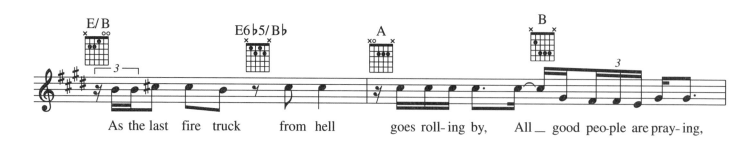

As the last fire truck from hell goes roll-ing by, All ___ good peo-ple are pray-ing,

It's the last temp-ta-tion ___ the last ac-count The last

My Back Pages

Words and Music by Bob Dylan

1. Crim - son flames tied through my ears Rol - lin'
2.-6. *See additional lyrics*

high and might - y traps Pounced with

fire on flam - ing roads Us - ing i - deas as my

maps "We'll meet on edg - es, soon," said

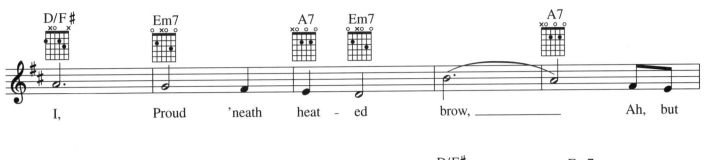

I, Proud 'neath heat - ed brow, _____ Ah, but

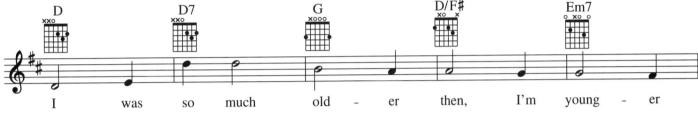

I was so much old - er then, I'm young - er

than that now. _____

Additional lyrics

2. Half-wracked prejudice leaped forth
"Rip down all hate," I screamed
Lies that life is black and white
Spoke from my skull. I dreamed
Romantic facts of musketeers
Foundationed deep, somehow.
Ah, but I was so much older then,
I'm younger than that now.

3. Girls' faces formed the forward path
From phony jealousy
To memorizing politics
Of ancient history
Flung down by corpse evangelists
Unthought of, though, somehow.
Ah, but I was so much older then,
I'm younger than that now.

4. A self-ordained professor's tongue
Too serious to fool
Spouted out that liberty
Is just equality in school
"Equality," I spoke the word
As if a wedding vow.
Ah, but I was so much older then,
I'm younger than that now.

5. In a soldier's stance, I aimed my hand
At the mongrel dogs who teach
Fearing not that I'd become my enemy
In the instant that I preach
My pathway led by confusion boats
Mutiny from stern to bow.
Ah, but I was so much older then,
I'm younger than that now.

6. Yes, my guard stood hard when abstract threats
Too noble to neglect
Deceived me into thinking
I had something to protect
Good and bad, I define these terms
Quite clear, no doubt, somehow.
Ah, but I was so much older then,
I'm younger than that now.

Neighborhood Bully

Words and Music by Bob Dylan

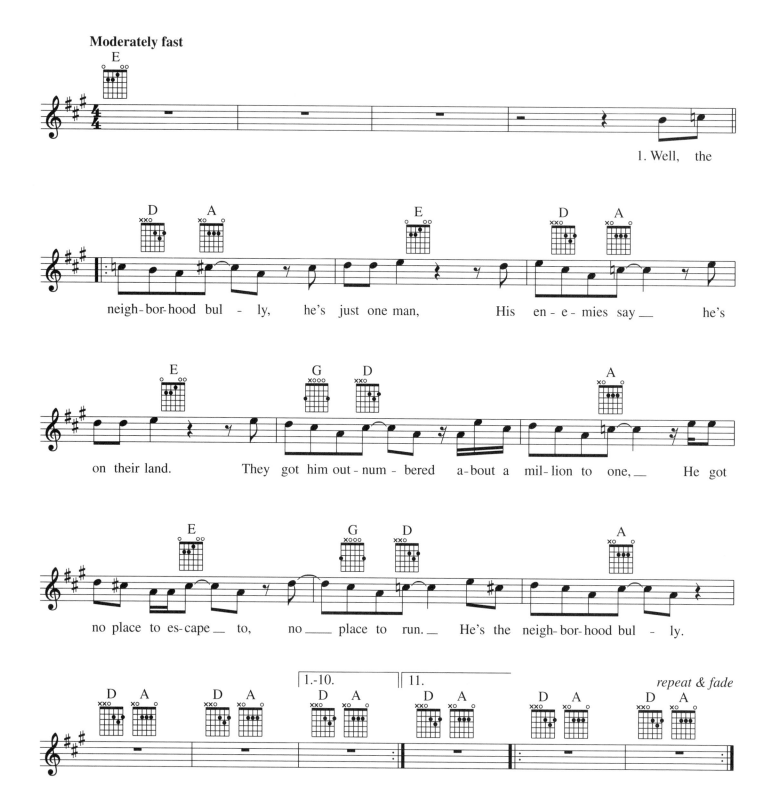

Additional lyrics

2. The neighborhood bully just lives to survive,
   He's criticized and condemned for being alive.
   He's not supposed to fight back, he's supposed to have thick skin,
   He's supposed to lay down and die when his door is kicked in.
   He's the neighborhood bully.

3. The neighborhood bully been driven out of every land,
   He's wandered the earth an exiled man.
   Seen his family scattered, his people hounded and torn,
   He's always on trial for just being born.
   He's the neighborhood bully.

4. Well, he knocked out a lynch mob, he was criticized,
   Old women condemned him, said he should apologize.
   Then he destroyed a bomb factory, nobody was glad.
   The bombs were meant for him.
   He was supposed to feel bad.
   He's the neighborhood bully.

5. Well, the chances are against it and the odds are slim
   That he'll live by the rules that the world makes for him,
   'Cause there's a noose at his neck and a gun at his back
   And a license to kill him is given out to every maniac.
   He's the neighborhood bully.

6. He got no allies to really speak of.
   What he gets he must pay for, he don't get it out of love.
   He buys obsolete weapons and he won't be denied
   But no one sends flesh and blood to fight by his side.
   He's the neighborhood bully.

7. Well, he's surrounded by pacifists who all want peace,
   They pray for it nightly that the bloodshed must cease.
   Now, they wouldn't hurt a fly.
   To hurt one they would weep.
   They lay and they wait for this bully to fall asleep.
   He's the neighborhood bully.

8. Every empire that's enslaved him is gone,
   Egypt and Rome, even the great Babylon.
   He's made a garden of paradise in the desert sand,
   In bed with nobody, under no one's command.
   He's the neighborhood bully.

9. Now his holiest books have been trampled upon,
   No contract he signed was worth what it was written on.
   He took the crumbs of the world and he turned it into wealth,
   Took sickness and disease and he turned it into health.
   He's the neighborhood bully.

10. What's anybody indebted to him for?
    Nothin', they say.
    He just likes to cause war.
    Pride and prejudice and superstition indeed,
    They wait for this bully like a dog waits to feed.
    He's the neighborhood bully.

11. What has he done to wear so many scars?
    Does he change the course of rivers?
    Does he pollute the moon and stars?
    Neighborhood bully, standing on the hill,
    Running out the clock, time standing still,
    Neighborhood bully.

Never Gonna Be the Same Again

Words and Music by Bob Dylan

Moderately slow

Now you're here be-side __ me, ba - by,
Sor - ry if I hurt you, ba - by,

You're a liv-ing dream.
Sor - ry if I did.
And ev - ery time you get this close __ It
Sor - ry if I touched the place __ Where

makes me want to scream.
your se - crets are hid.
You touched me and you knew That I _____ was
But you meant more than ev - ery-thing, __ And

warm for you __ and then,
I could not pre - tend,
I ain't nev-er gon-na be the same a - gain. __

I ain't nev-er gon-na be the same a - gain. __

Never Say Goodbye

Words and Music by Bob Dylan

New Morning

Words and Music by Bob Dylan

This must be the day that all of my __ dreams come true __

So hap - py just to be a - live _____ Un - der - neath __ the sky __ of blue
So hap - py just to be a - live _____ Un - der - neath __ the sky __ of blue

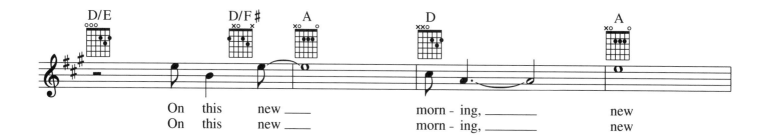

On this new ____ morn - ing, _____ new
On this new ____ morn - ing, _____ new

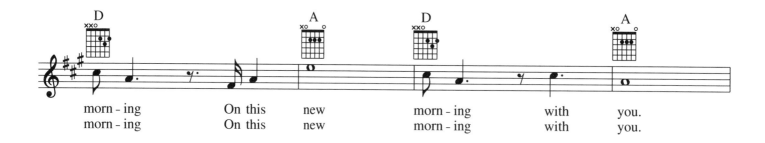

morn - ing On this new morn - ing with you.
morn - ing On this new morn - ing with you.

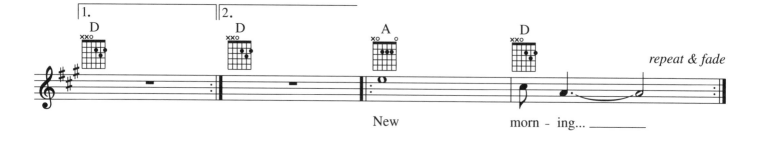

repeat & fade

New morn - ing... _____

Sign on the Window

Words and Music by Bob Dylan

Sign on the win - dow says __ "Lone - ly,"

Sign on the door said "No Com - pa - ny __ Al- lowed," _____

Sign on the street says "Y' Don't Own _____ Me,"

Sign on the porch says "Three's A Crowd," __ Sign on the porch says

"Three's A __ Crowd." __

Her and her boy-friend went to Cal-i-for - ia, Her and her boy-friend

New Pony

Words and Music by Bob Dylan

Slowly, with a beat

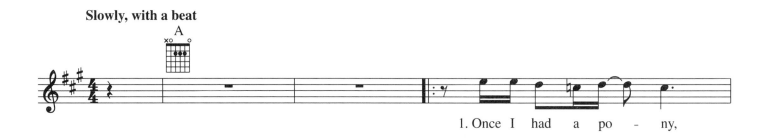

1. Once I had a po - ny,

her name _ was Lu - ci - fer _ I had a po - ny,

her name _ was Lu - ci - fer _ She broke her leg _

_ and she need - ed shoot - ing _ I swear it hurt me more than it could ev - er have hurt - ed

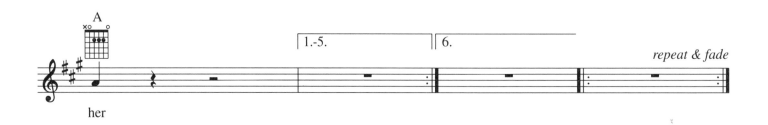

repeat & fade

1.-5.   6.

her

Additional lyrics

2. Sometimes I wonder what's going on in the mind of Miss X
   Sometimes I wonder what's going on in the mind of Miss X
   You know she got such a sweet disposition
   I never know what the poor girl's gonna do to me next

3. I got a new pony, she knows how to fox-trot, lope and pace
   Well, I got a new pony, she knows how to fox-trot, lope and pace
   She got great big hind legs
   And long black shaggy hair above her face

4. Well now, it was early in the mornin', I seen your shadow in the door
   It was early in the mornin', I seen your shadow in the door
   Now, I don't have to ask nobody
   I know what you come here for

5. They say you're usin' voodoo, your feet walk by themselves
   They say you're usin' voodoo, I seen your feet walk by themselves
   Oh, baby, that god you been prayin' to
   Is gonna give ya back what you're wishin' on someone else

6. Come over here pony, I, I wanna climb up one time on you
   Come over here pony, I, I wanna climb up one time on you
   Well, you're so bad and nasty
   But I love you, yes I do

No Time to Think

Words and Music by Bob Dylan

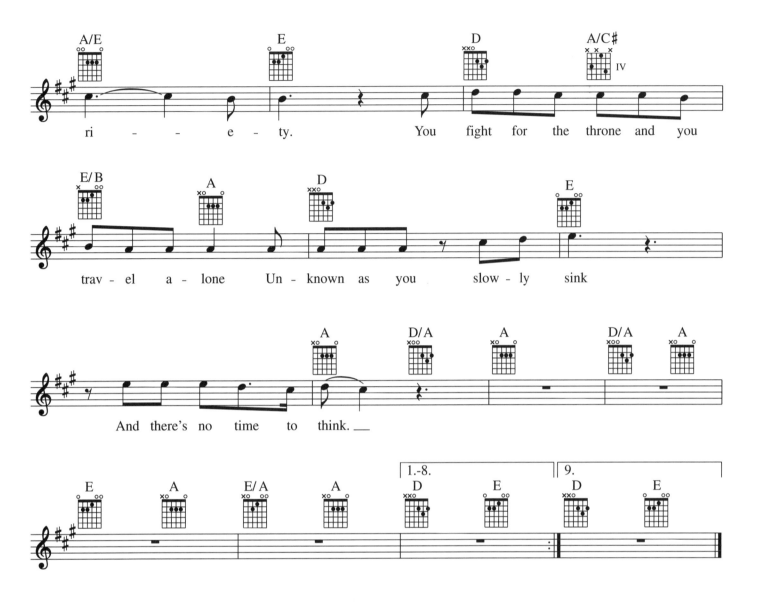

Additional lyrics

2. In the Federal City you been blown and shown pity,
   In secret, for pieces of change.
   The empress attracts you but oppression distracts you
   And it makes you feel violent and strange.

   Memory, ecstasy, tyranny, hypocrisy
   Betrayed by a kiss on a cool night of bliss
   In the valley of the missing link
   And you have no time to think.

3. Judges will haunt you, the country priestess will want you
   Her worst is better than best.
   I've seen all these decoys through a set of deep turquoise eyes
   And I feel so depressed.

   China doll, alcohol, duality, mortality.
   Mercury rules you and destiny fools you
   Like the plague, with a dangerous wink
   And there's no time to think.

4. Your conscience betrayed you when some tyrant waylaid you
   Where the lion lies down with the lamb.
   I'd have paid off the traitor and killed him much later
   But that's just the way that I am.

   Paradise, sacrifice, mortality, reality.
   But the magician is quicker and his game
   Is much thicker than blood and blacker than ink
   And there's no time to think.

5. Anger and jealousy's all that he sells us,
   He's content when you're under his thumb.
   Madmen oppose him, but your kindness throws him
   To survive it you play deaf and dumb.

   Equality, liberty, humility, simplicity.
   You glance through the mirror and there's eyes staring clear
   At the back of your head as you drink
   And there's no time to think.

6. Warlords of sorrow and queens of tomorrow
   Will offer their heads for a prayer.
   You can't find no salvation, you have no expectations
   Anytime, anyplace, anywhere.

   Mercury, gravity, nobility, humility.
   You know you can't keep her and the water gets deeper
   That is leading you onto the brink
   But there's no time to think.

7. You've murdered your vanity, buried your sanity
   For pleasure you must now resist.
   Lovers obey you but they cannot sway you
   They're not even sure you exist.

   Socialism, hypnotism, patriotism, materialism.
   Fools making laws for the breaking of jaws
   And the sound of the keys as they clink
   But there's no time to think.

8. The bridge that you travel on goes to the Babylon girl
   With the rose in her hair.
   Starlight in the East and you're finally released
   You're stranded but with nothing to share.

   Loyalty, unity, epitome, rigidity.
   You turn around for one real last glimpse of Camille
   'Neath the moon shinin' bloody and pink
   And there's no time to think.

9. Bullets can harm you and death can disarm you
   But no, you will not be deceived.
   Stripped of all virtue as you crawl through the dirt,
   You can give but you cannot receive.

   No time to choose when the truth must die,
   No time to lose or say goodbye,
   No time to prepare for the victim that's there,
   No time to suffer or blink
   And no time to think.

Silvio

Words and Music by Bob Dylan and Robert Hunter

to Coda ⊕

Sil - vi - o   I   got - ta go _____   Find   out   some-thing on - ly

dead men   know ___

Hon - est as   the next jade   rol - ling that stone   When I   come (a)-knock- in' don't
give what I got un - til   I   got no more   I   take what I get un - til

throw me no bone _____   I'm an old boll wee - vil look- ing   for a   home ___
I ev - en the ___ score   You know I   love you and   fur - ther - more ___

If   you don't like it   you can   leave me a - lone ___   I can snap my   fin - gers and re -
When it's time   to   go you got   an o - pen door ___   I can tell you fan - cy, I can

quire the rain ___ From a   clear blue   sky and turn it   off   a - gain ___   I can
tell   you plain ___ You give some-thing up for ev - ry - thing you gain ___

stroke your   bo - dy and re - lieve your   pain ___   And   charm the ___ whis - tle off an
Since ev - ery plea-sure's got an   edge of   pain ___   Pay   for your tick - et and

Nobody 'Cept You

Words and Music by Bob Dylan

There's noth - ing ____ 'round here I be- lieve ____ in _____ 'Cept
Noth - ing 'round here I care to try ____ for _____ 'Cept

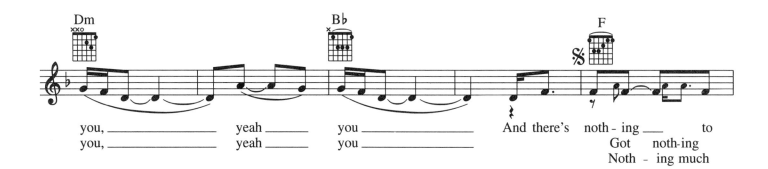

you, _____ yeah _____ you _____ And there's noth - ing ____ to
you, _____ yeah _____ you _____ Got noth-ing
Noth - ing much

me that's sa - cred _____ 'Cept you, _____ yeah
left to live or die for _____ 'Cept you, _____ yeah
mat-ters or seems to please me _____ 'Cept you, _____ yeah

you _____ You're the one that reach - es me __ You're the
you _____ There's a hymn I used to hear In the
you _____ Noth - ing hyp - no - tiz - es me __ Or

one that I ad – mire ___ Ev – 'ry time ___ we meet ___ to – geth- er My
church- es all the time ___ Make me feel ___ so good ___ in – side So
holds me in a spell ___ Ev – 'ry- thing ___ runs by ___ me Just like

soul feels like it's on fire ___ Noth-ing mat – ters to me And there's
peace - ful, so sub – lime ___ And there's noth-ing to re – mind me of that
wa – ter from a well ___ Ev – 'ry – bod- y wants my at – ten – tion Ev –'ry- bod-y's

to Coda ⊕

noth-ing I de – sire _____ 'Cept you, _____ yeah _____
Old fa – mil – iar chime _____ 'Cept you, _____ uh – huh
got some - thing to sell _____ 'Cept you, _____ yeah _____

1.   2.

you _____

you _____   Used to play in the cem- e – ter – y

Dance and sing and run when I was a child _____ Nev - er seemed strange _____

___ But now I just ___ pass mourn- ful- ly ___ by _____ That place ___ where the

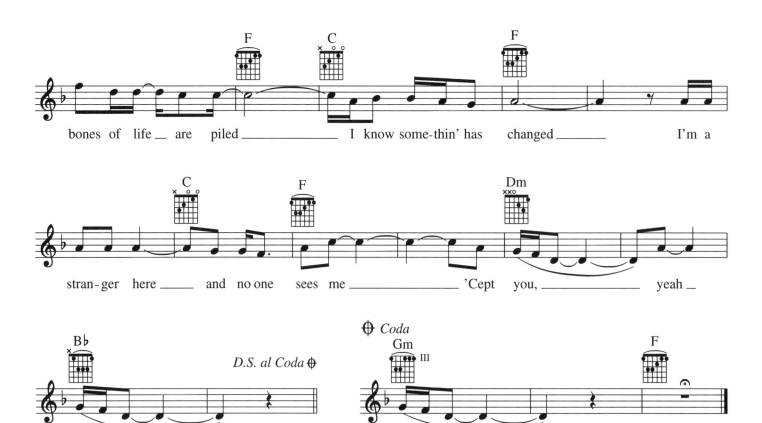

bones of life __ are piled _____ I know some-thin' has changed _____ I'm a

stran-ger here _____ and no one sees me _____ 'Cept you, _____ yeah __

D.S. al Coda ⊕

you _____

⊕ *Coda*

you _____

Time Passes Slowly

Words and Music by Bob Dylan

to go an - y - where. ____

Time pass - es slow - ly up here in the day -

light, We stare straight a - head and try so hard ____ to stay ____

____ right, Like the red rose of sum - mer that blooms in the

day, Time pass - es slow - ly and fades a - way. ____

North Country Blues

Words and Music by Bob Dylan

Medium tempo

1. Come gath - er 'round friends, And I'll tell you a tale,

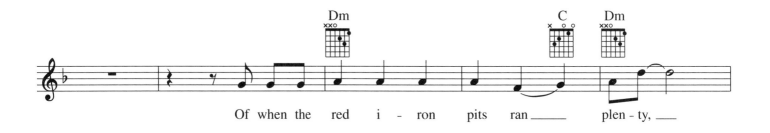

Of when the red i - ron pits ran ____ plen - ty, ____

But the card - board filled win - dows And

old men on the bench - es Tell you now that the

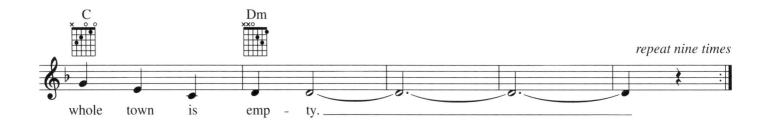

repeat nine times

whole town is emp - ty. ____

Additional lyrics

2. In the north end of town,
   My own children are grown
   But I was raised on the other.
   In the wee hours of youth,
   My mother took sick
   And I was brought up by my brother.

3. The iron ore poured
   As the years passed the door,
   The drag lines an' the shovels they was a-humming.
   'Til one day my brother
   Failed to come home
   The same as my father before him.

4. Well a long winter's wait,
   From the window I watched.
   My friends they couldn't have been kinder.
   And my schooling was cut
   As I quit in the spring
   To marry John Thomas, a miner.

5. Oh the years passed again
   And the givin' was good,
   With the lunch bucket filled every season.
   What with three babies born,
   The work was cut down
   To a half a day's shift with no reason.

6. Then the shaft was soon shut
   And more work was cut,
   And the fire in the air, it felt frozen.
   'Til a man come to speak
   And he said in one week
   That number eleven was closin'.

7. They complained in the East,
   They are paying too high.
   They say that your ore ain't worth digging.
   That it's much cheaper down
   In the South American towns
   Where the miners work almost for nothing.

8. So the mining gates locked
   And the red iron rotted
   And the room smelled heavy from drinking.
   Where the sad, silent song
   Made the hour twice as long
   As I waited for the sun to go sinking.

9. I lived by the window
   As he talked to himself,
   This silence of tongues it was building.
   Then one morning's wake,
   The bed it was bare,
   And I's left alone with three children.

10. The summer is gone,
    The ground's turning cold,
    The stores one by one they're a-foldin'.
    My children will go
    As soon as they grow.
    Well, there ain't nothing here now to hold them.

Not Dark Yet

Words and Music by Bob Dylan

Moderately slow, with a beat

1. Shad-ows are fall-ing
2.-5. *See additional lyrics*

and I've been here all day

It's too hot to sleep __

time is run-ning a-way __

Feel like my soul has __ turned __

__ in-to steel __

I've still got the scars __ that the

sun did-n't heal __

There's not e-ven room e-nough

to be __ an-y-where

It's not dark yet, __

1.2.3.4.

but it's __ get-ting there

5.

but it's __ get-ting there

Additional lyrics

2. Well my sense of humanity has gone down the drain
    Behind every beautiful thing there's been some kind of pain
    She wrote me a letter and she wrote it so kind
    She put down in writing what was in her mind
    I just don't see why I should even care
    It's not dark yet, but it's getting there

3. Well, I've been to London and I've been to gay Paree
    I've followed the river and I got to the sea
    I've been down on the bottom of a world full of lies
    I ain't looking for nothing in anyone's eyes
    Sometimes my burden seems more than I can bear
    It's not dark yet, but it's getting there

4. *Instrumental*

5. I was born here and I'll die here against my will
    I know it looks like I'm moving, but I'm standing still
    Every nerve in my body is so vacant and numb
    I can't even remember what it was I came here to get away from
    Don't even hear a murmur of a prayer
    It's not dark yet, but it's getting there.

Nothing Was Delivered

Words and Music by Bob Dylan

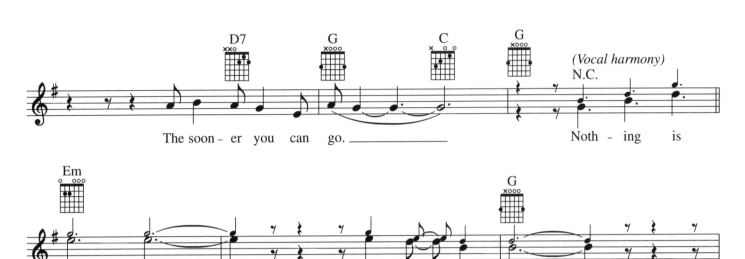

The soon - er you can go. _____ Noth - ing is

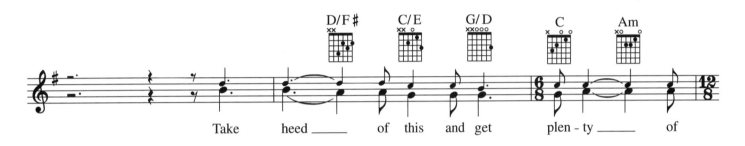

bet - ter, _____ noth - ing __ is best, _____

Take heed _____ of this and get plen - ty _____ of

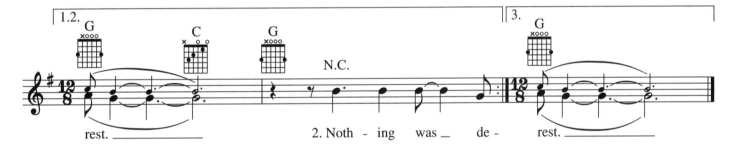

rest. _____ 2. Noth - ing was _ de - rest. _____

Additional lyrics

2. Nothing was delivered
   But I can't say I sympathize
   With what your fate is going to be,
   Yes, for telling all those lies.
   Now you must provide some answers
   For what you sell has not been received,
   And the sooner you come up with them,
   The sooner you can leave.

   Nothing is better, nothing is best,
   Take heed of this and get plenty rest.

3. (Now you know)
   Nothing was delivered
   And it's up to you to say
   Just what you had in mind
   When you made ev'rybody pay.
   No, nothing was delivered,
   Yes, 'n' someone must explain
   That as long as it takes to do this
   Then that's how long that you'll remain.

   Nothing is better, nothing is best,
   Take heed of this and get plenty rest.

Obviously Five Believers

Words and Music by Bob Dylan

Additional lyrics

3. I got my black dog barkin'
   Black dog barkin'
   Yes it is now
   Yes it is now
   Outside my yard
   Yes, I could tell you what he means
   If I just didn't have to try so hard

4. Your mama's workin'
   Your mama's moanin'
   She's cryin' you know
   She's tryin' you know
   You better go now
   Well, I'd tell you what she wants
   But I just don't know how

5. Fifteen jugglers
   Fifteen jugglers
   Five believers
   Five believers
   All dressed like men
   Tell yo' mama not to worry because
   They're just my friends

6. Early in the mornin'
   Early in the mornin'
   I'm callin' you to
   I'm callin' you to
   Please come home
   Yes, I could make it without you
   If I just did not feel so all alone

Odds and Ends

Words and Music by Bob Dylan

Moderately slow rock blues

I

plan it all __ and I take my place _ You break your prom - ise all
take your file __ and you bend my head __ I nev-er can re - mem -ber an - y-

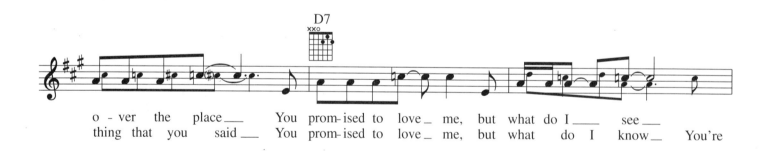

o - ver the place ___ You prom-ised to love _ me, but what do I ___ see ___
thing that you said ___ You prom-ised to love _ me, but what do I know __ You're

Just you com-in' _____ and spill-in' juice o - ver me
al - ways spill-in' juice on me like you got some place to go

Oh, Sister

Words and Music by Bob Dylan and Jacques Levy

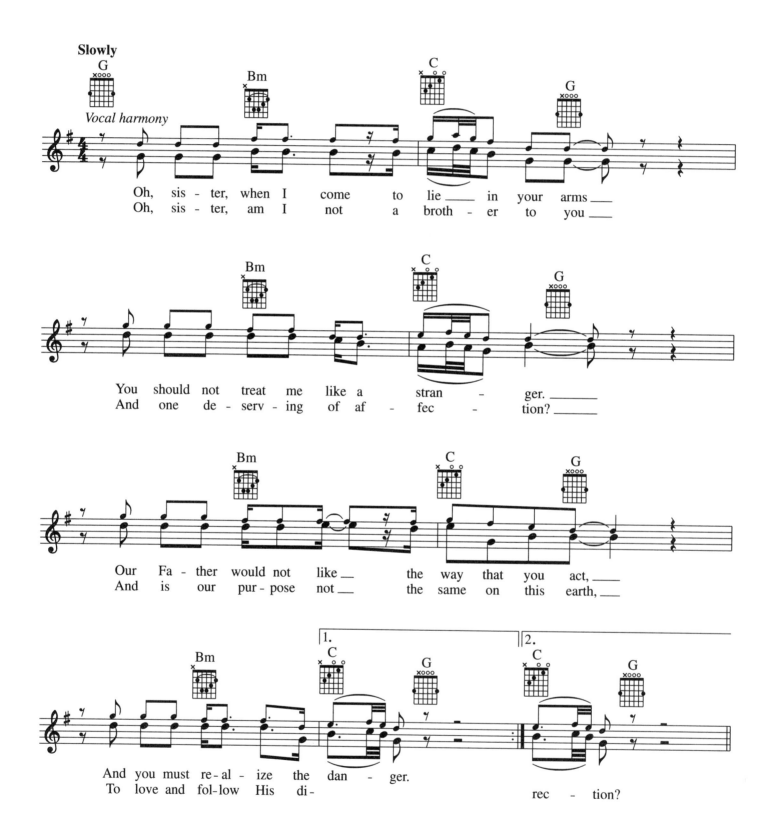

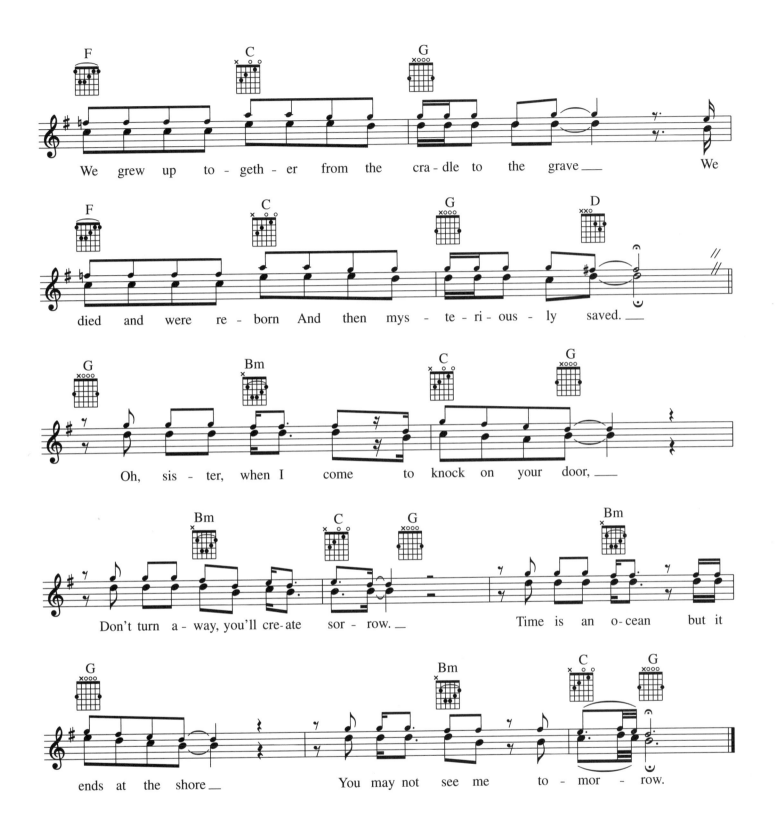

On a Night Like This

Words and Music by Bob Dylan

Moderately bright, with a beat

On a night like this ____
So glad you came a - round, _
So glad you've come to stay ____
I can't get an - y sleep, _

Hold on to me so tight
Hold on to me, pret - ty miss
The air is so cold out - side

And heat up some
Say you'll nev - er go a -
And the

cof - fee grounds. ____
way to stray. ____
snow's so deep. ____

We got much to talk a - bout _
Run your fin - gers down my spine _
Build a fire, throw on logs _

And
Bring
And

much to rem - i - nisce, ____
me a touch of bliss ____
lis - ten to it hiss ____

It sure is right ____
It sure feels right ____
And let it burn, ____ burn, burn, burn

On a night ____ like this. ____
On a night ____ like this. ____
On a night ____ like this. ____

1. 2.

N.C.

On a night like this _
On a night like this _

On the Road Again

Words and Music by Bob Dylan

Additional lyrics

2. Well, I go to pet your monkey
   I get a face full of claws
   I ask who's in the fireplace
   And you tell me Santa Claus
   The milkman comes in
   He's wearing a derby hat
   Then you ask why I don't live here
   Honey, how come you have to ask me that?

3. Well, I asked for something to eat
   I'm hungry as a hog
   So I get brown rice, seaweed
   And a dirty hot dog
   I've got a hole
   Where my stomach disappeared
   Then you ask why I don't live here
   Honey, I gotta think you're really weird.

4. Your grandpa's cane
   It turns into a sword
   Your grandma prays to pictures
   That are pasted on a board
   Everything inside my pockets
   Your uncle steals
   Then you ask why I don't live here
   Honey, I can't believe that you're for real.

5. Well, there's fist fights in the kitchen
   They're enough to make me cry
   The mailman comes in
   Even he's gotta take a side
   Even the butler
   He's got something to prove
   Then you ask why I don't live here
   Honey, how come you don't move?

One More Cup of Coffee
(Valley Below)
Words and Music by Bob Dylan

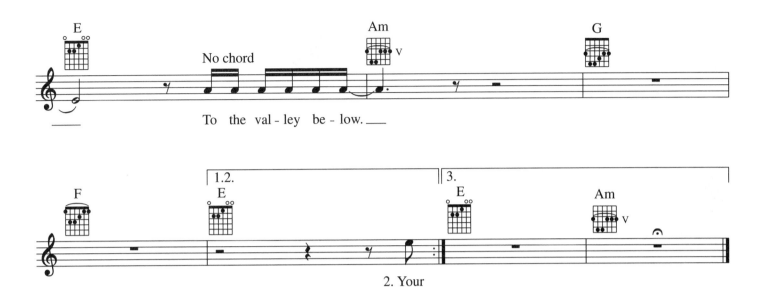

To the val - ley be - low. ___

1.2.

3.

2. Your

3. Your

Additional lyrics

2. Your daddy he's an outlaw
   And a wanderer by trade
   He'll teach you how to pick and choose
   And how to throw the blade.
   He oversees his kingdom
   So no stranger does intrude
   His voice it trembles as he calls out
   For another plate of food.

Chorus

3. Your sister sees the future
   Like your mama and yourself.
   You've never learned to read or write
   There's no books upon your shelf.
   And your pleasure knows no limits
   Your voice is like a meadowlark
   But your heart is like an ocean
   Mysterious and dark.

Chorus

One More Night
Words and Music by Bob Dylan

One of Us Must Know
(Sooner or Later)
Words and Music by Bob Dylan

did - n't mean ___ to treat you so bad ___
could-n't see ___ what you could show me ___ Your
could-n't see ___ when it start-ed snow in' ___ Your

You should-n't take_ it so per - son - al ___ I did - n't mean ___
scarf had kept_ your mouth well hid ___ I could-n't see ___
voice was all ___ that I heard ___ I could-n't see ___

to make you so sad ___ You just hap - pened to be
how you could know me ___ But you said you knew_ me and I be -
where we were go - in' ___ But you said you knew an' I

there, that's all ___ When I saw you say "good - bye" _
lieved you did ___ When you whis-pered
took your word ___ And then you told me lat - er,

One Too Many Mornings

Words and Music by Bob Dylan

1. Down the street the dogs are bark - in' And the day is a - get - tin'

dark. _____ As the night comes in a - fall - in', The dogs - 'll lose their

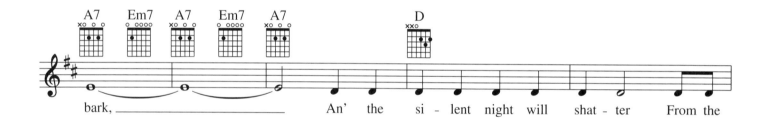

bark, _____ An' the si - lent night will shat - ter From the

sounds in - side my mind, _____ For I'm one too man - y

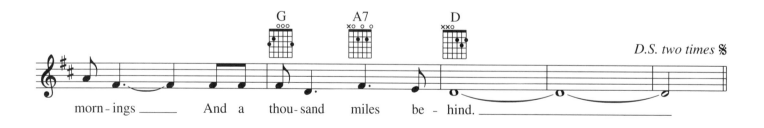

D.S. two times

morn - ings _____ And a thou - sand miles be - hind. _____

Additional lyrics

2. From the crossroads of my doorstep,
   My eyes they start to fade,
   As I turn my head back to the room
   Where my love and I have laid.
   An' I gaze back to the street,
   The sidewalk and the sign,
   And I'm one too many mornings
   An' a thousand miles behind.

3. It's a restless hungry feeling
   That don't mean no one no good,
   When ev'rything I'm a-sayin'
   You can say it just as good.
   You're right from your side,
   I'm right from mine.
   We're both just too many mornings
   An' a thousand miles behind.

Only a Hobo

Words and Music by Bob Dylan

Moderate country waltz

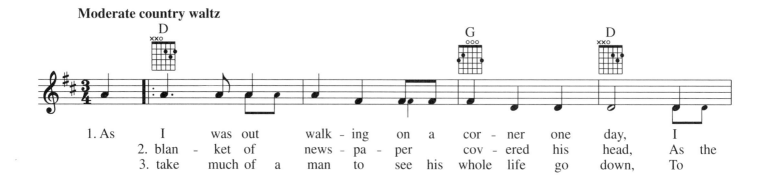

1. As I was out walk - ing on a cor - ner one day, I
2. blan - ket of news - pa - per cov - ered his head, As the
3. take much of a man to see his whole life go down, To

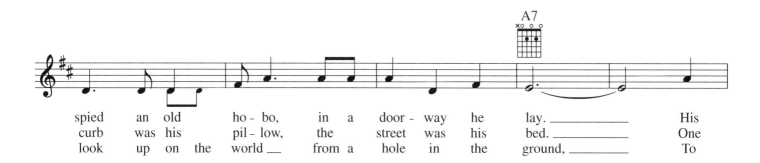

spied an old ho - bo, in a door - way he lay. _____ His
curb was his pil - low, the street was his bed. _____ One
look up on the world _ from a hole in the ground, _____ To

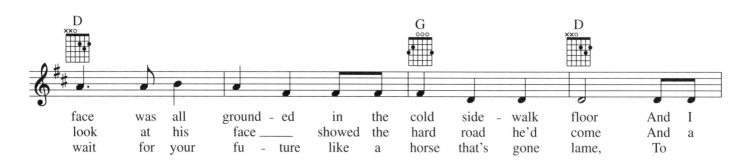

face was all ground - ed in the cold side - walk floor, And I
look at his face _____ showed the hard road he'd come And a
wait for your fu - ture like a horse that's gone lame, To

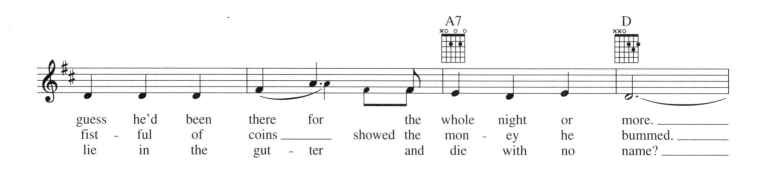

guess he'd been there for the whole night or more. _____
fist - ful of coins _____ showed the mon - ey he bummed. _____
lie in the gut - ter and die with no name? _____

On - ly a ho - bo, but one more is gone Leav - in' no - bod - y to sing his sad song _____ Leav - in' no - bod - y to car - ry him home

On - ly a ho - bo, but one more is gone. _____

2. A
3. Does it gone. _____

Only a Pawn in Their Game

Words and Music by Bob Dylan

* *Repeat as often as necessary to accommodate additional lyrics.*

Additional lyrics

2. A South politician preaches to the poor white man,
   "You got more than the blacks, don't complain.
   You're better than them, you been born with white skin," they explain.
   And the Negro's name
   Is used it is plain
   For the politician's gain
   As he rises to fame
   And the poor white remains
   On the caboose of the train
   But it ain't him to blame
   He's only a pawn in their game.

3. The deputy sheriffs, the soldiers, the governors get paid,
   And the marshals and cops get the same,
   But the poor white man's used in the hands of them all like a tool.
   He's taught in his school
   From the start by the rule
   That the laws are with him
   To protect his white skin
   To keep up his hate
   So he never thinks straight
   'Bout the shape that he's in
   But it ain't him to blame
   He's only a pawn in their game.

4. From the poverty shacks, he looks from the cracks to the tracks,
   And the hoof beats pound in his brain.
   And he's taught how to walk in a pack
   Shoot in the back
   With his fist in a clinch
   To hang and to lynch
   To hide 'neath the hood
   To kill with no pain
   Like a dog on a chain
   He ain't got no name
   But it ain't him to blame
   He's only a pawn in their game.

5. Today, Medgar Evers was buried from the bullet he caught.
   They lowered him down as a king.
   But when the shadowy sun sets on the one
   That fired the gun
   He'll see by his grave
   On the stone that remains
   Carved next to his name
   His epitaph plain:
   Only a pawn in their game.

Open the Door, Homer

Words and Music by Bob Dylan

door, Ho - mer, I've heard it said be - fore ____ But I

ain't gon - na hear it said ___ no more.

Additional lyrics

2. Now, there's a certain thing
   That I learned from my friend, Mouse
   A fella who always blushes
   And that is that ev'ryone
   Must always flush out his house
   If he don't expect to be
   Goin' 'round housing flushes.
   Open the door, Homer,
   I've heard it said before.
   Open the door, Homer,
   I've heard it said before
   But I ain't gonna hear it said no more.

3. "Take care of all your memories"
   Said my friend, Mick
   "For you cannot relive them
   And remember when you're out there
   Tryin' to heal the sick
   That you must always
   First forgive them."
   Open the door, Homer,
   I've heard it said before.
   Open the door, Homer,
   I've heard it said before
   But I ain't gonna hear it said no more.

Outlaw Blues

Words and Music by Bob Dylan

Bright, in 4

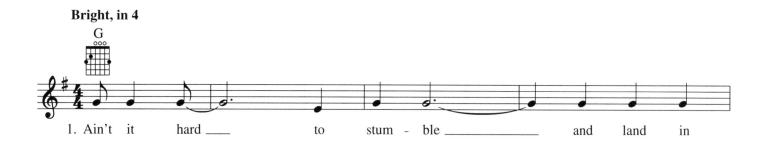

1. Ain't it hard ____ to stum - ble _____ and land in

some fun - ny la - goon? Ain't it hard_

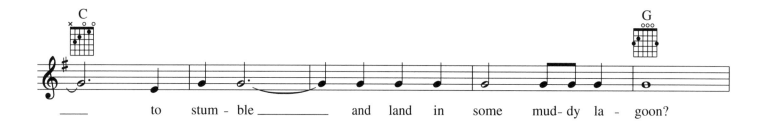

____ to stum - ble _____ and land in some mud - dy la - goon?

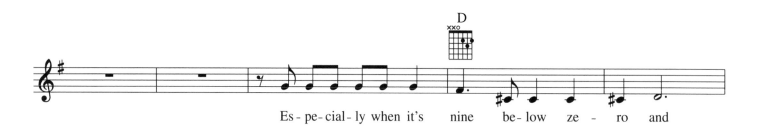

Es - pe - cial - ly when it's nine be - low ze - ro and

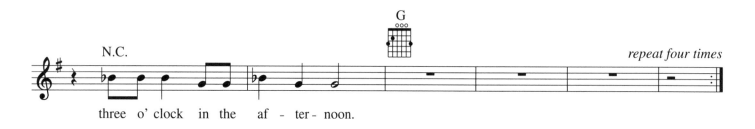

three o' clock in the af - ter - noon.

repeat four times

Additional lyrics

2. Ain't gonna hang no picture,
   Ain't gonna hang no picture frame.
   Ain't gonna hang no picture,
   Ain't gonna hang no picture frame.
   Well, I might look like Robert Ford
   But I feel just like a Jesse James.

3. Well, I wish I was on some
   Australian mountain range.
   Oh, I wish I was on some
   Australian mountain range.
   I got no reason to be there, but I
   Imagine it would be some kind of change.

4. I got my dark sunglasses,
   I got for good luck my black tooth.
   I got my dark sunglasses,
   I'm carryin' for good luck my black tooth.
   Don't ask me nothin' about nothin',
   I just might tell you the truth.

5. I got a woman in Jackson,
   I ain't gonna say her name.
   I got a woman in Jackson,
   I ain't gonna say her name.
   She's a brown-skin woman,
   But I love her just the same.

Oxford Town

Words and Music by Bob Dylan

Bright

1. Ox - ford Town, Ox - ford Town Ev - 'ry - bod - y's got their heads bowed down The

sun don't shine a - bove the ground Ain't a - go - in' down to Ox - ford Town

2. He went down to Ox - ford Town Guns and clubs fol - lowed him down

All be - cause his face was brown Bet - ter get a - way from Ox - ford Town

3. Ox - ford Town a - round the bend He come in - to the door, he could-n't get in

All be - cause of the col - or of his skin What do you think_ a - bout that, my frien'?

Paths of Victory

Words and Music by Bob Dylan

Additional lyrics

Refrain

2. I walked down by the river,
   I turned my head up high.
   I saw that silver linin'
   That was hangin' in the sky.

Refrain

3. The evenin' dusk was rollin',
   I was walking down the track.
   There was a one-way wind a-blowin'
   And it was blowin' at my back.

Refrain

4. The gravel road is bumpy,
   It's a hard road to ride,
   But there's a clearer road a-waitin'
   With the cinders on the side.

Refrain

5. That evening train was rollin',
   The hummin' of its wheels,
   My eyes they saw a better day
   As I looked across the fields.

Refrain

6. The trail is dusty,
   The road it might be rough,
   But the good road is a-waitin'
   And boys it ain't far off.

Refrain

Peggy Day

Words and Music by Bob Dylan

Percy's Song

Words and Music by Bob Dylan

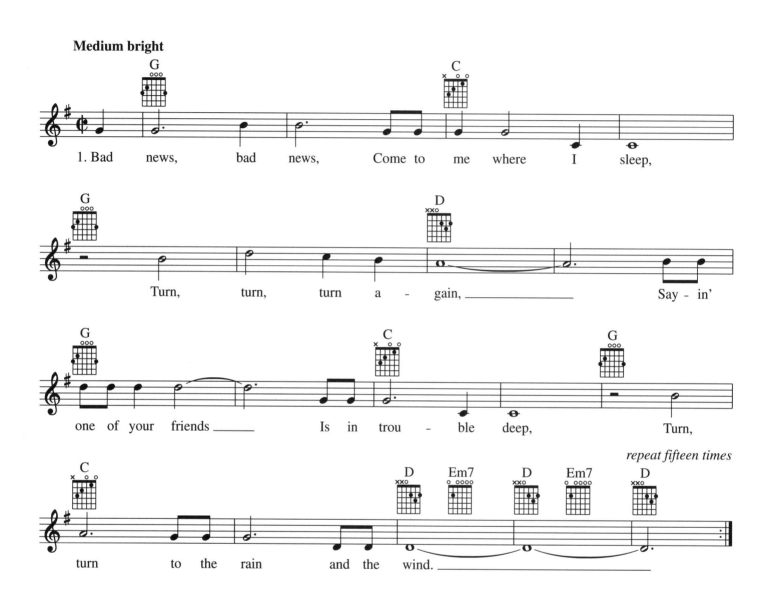

Medium bright

1. Bad news, bad news, Come to me where I sleep,

Turn, turn, turn a - gain, _____ Say - in'

one of your friends _____ Is in trou - ble deep, Turn,

repeat fifteen times

turn to the rain and the wind. _____

Additional lyrics

2. Tell me the trouble,
   Tell once to my ear,
   Turn, turn, turn again.
   Joliet prison
   And ninety-nine years,
   Turn, turn to the rain
   And the wind.

3. Oh what's the charge
   Of how this came to be,
   Turn, turn, turn again.
   Manslaughter
   In the highest of degree,
   Turn, turn to the rain
   And the wind.

4. I sat down and wrote
   The best words I could write,
   Turn, turn, turn again.
   Explaining to the judge
   I'd be there on Wednesday night,
   Turn, turn to the rain
   And the wind.

5. Without a reply,
   I left by the moon,
   Turn, turn, turn again.
   And was in his chambers
   By the next afternoon,
   Turn, turn to the rain
   And the wind.

6. Could ya tell me the facts?
   I said without fear,
   Turn, turn, turn again.
   That a friend of mine
   Would get ninety-nine years,
   Turn, turn to the rain
   And the wind.

7. A crash on the highway
   Flew the car to a field,
   Turn, turn, turn again.
   There was four persons killed
   And he was at the wheel,
   Turn, turn to the rain
   And the wind.

8. But I knew him as good
   As I'm knowin' myself,
   Turn, turn, turn again.
   And he wouldn't harm a life
   That belonged to someone else,
   Turn, turn to the rain
   And the wind.

9. The judge spoke
   Out of the side of his mouth,
   Turn, turn, turn again.
   Sayin', "The witness who saw,
   He left little doubt,"
   Turn, turn to the rain
   And the wind.

10. That may be true,
    He's got a sentence to serve,
    Turn, turn, turn again.
    But ninety-nine years,
    He just don't deserve,
    Turn, turn to the rain
    And the wind.

11. Too late, too late,
    For his case it is sealed,
    Turn, turn, turn again.
    His sentence is passed
    And it cannot be repealed,
    Turn, turn to the rain
    And the wind.

12. But he ain't no criminal
    And his crime it is none,
    Turn, turn, turn again.
    What happened to him
    Could happen to anyone,
    Turn, turn to the rain
    And the wind.

13. And at that the judge jerked forward
    And his face it did freeze,
    Turn, turn, turn again.
    Sayin', "Could you kindly leave
    My office now, please,"
    Turn, turn to the rain
    And the wind.

14. Well his eyes looked funny
    And I stood up so slow,
    Turn, turn, turn again.
    With no other choice
    Except for to go,
    Turn, turn to the rain
    And the wind.

15. I walked down the hallway
    And I heard his door slam,
    Turn, turn, turn again.
    I walked down the courthouse stairs
    And I did not understand,
    Turn, turn to the rain
    And the wind.

16. And I played my guitar
    Through the night to the day,
    Turn, turn, turn again.
    And the only tune
    My guitar could play
    Was, "Oh the Cruel Rain
    And the Wind."

Playboys and Playgirls

Words and Music by Bob Dylan

Moderately

1. Oh, ye play-boys and play-girls ain't a-gon-na run my world, __

Ain't a-gon-na run my world, __ Ain't a-gon-na run my world. __ Ye

play-boys and play-girls Ain't a-gon-na run my world, __ Not now or

1.-6.

no oth-er time. _____

7.

2. You _____

Additional lyrics

2. You fallout shelter sellers
   Can't get in my door,
   Can't get in my door,
   Can't get in my door.
   You fallout shelter sellers
   Can't get in my door,
   Not now or no other time.

3. Your Jim Crow ground
   Can't turn me around,
   Can't turn me around,
   Can't turn me around.
   Your Jim Crow ground
   Can't turn me around,
   Not now or no other time.

4. The laughter in the lynch mob
   Ain't a-gonna do no more,
   Ain't a-gonna do no more,
   Ain't a-gonna do no more.
   The laughter in the lynch mob
   Ain't a-gonna do no more,
   Not now or no other time.

5. You insane tongues of war talk
   Ain't a-gonna guide my road,
   Ain't a-gonna guide my road,
   Ain't a-gonna guide my road.
   You insane tongues of war talk
   Ain't a-gonna guide my road,
   Not now or no other time.

6. You red baiters and race haters
   Ain't a-gonna hang around here,
   Ain't a-gonna hang around here,
   Ain't a-gonna hang around here.
   You red baiters and race haters,
   Ain't a-gonna hang around here,
   Not now or no other time.

7. Ye playboys and playgirls
   Ain't a-gonna own my world,
   Ain't a-gonna own my world,
   Ain't a-gonna own my world.
   Ye playboys and playgirls,
   Ain't a-gonna own my world,
   Not now or no other time.

Please, Mrs. Henry

Words and Music by Bob Dylan

Additional lyrics

2. Well, I'm groanin' in a hallway
   Pretty soon I'll be mad
   Please, Missus Henry, won't you
   Take me to your dad?
   I can drink like a fish
   I can crawl like a snake
   I can bite like a turkey
   I can slam like a drake
   Please, Missus Henry, Missus Henry, please!
   Please, Missus Henry, Missus Henry, please!
   I'm down on my knees
   An' I ain't got a dime

3. Now, don't crowd me, lady
   Or I'll fill up your shoe
   I'm a sweet bourbon daddy
   An' tonight I am blue
   I'm a thousand years old
   And I'm a generous bomb
   I'm T-boned and punctured
   But I'm known to be calm
   Please, Missus Henry, Missus Henry, please!
   Please, Missus Henry, Missus Henry, please!
   I'm down on my knees
   An' I ain't got a dime

4. Now, I'm startin' to drain
   My stool's gonna squeak
   If I walk too much farther
   My crane's gonna leak
   Look, Missus Henry
   There's only so much I can do
   Why don't you look my way
   An' pump me a few?
   Please, Missus Henry, Missus Henry, please!
   Please, Missus Henry, Missus Henry, please!
   I'm down on my knees
   An' I ain't got a dime.

Pledging My Time

Words and Music by Bob Dylan

Slow blues, with a 12/8 feel

1. Well, ear- ly in the morn-

in' / ba - by? / stuff - y,
'Til late at night,____ / I'll take you where you wan - na go. / I can hard - ly breathe.____
I got a poi - son / And if it don't work / Ev - 'ry - bod- y's gone but

head - ache,____ / out,_____ / me and you__
But I feel all right.___ / You'll be the first to know.__ / And I can't be the last to leave.__
I'm pledg- ing my / I'm pledg- ing my / I'm pledg- ing my

time_____ / time_____ / time_____
to you,_____ / to you,_____ / to you,_____
Hop - in' you'll come through, too.__ / Hop - in' you'll come through, too.__ / Hop - in' you'll come through, too.__

Political World

Words and Music by Bob Dylan

Brightly, with a driving beat (in 4)

1. We live in a po-lit-i-cal world, __ Love don't have an-y place. __ We're liv-ing in times where men __ com-mit crimes And crime __ __ don't have a face. __

2. We live in a po-lit-i-cal world, __ I-ci-cles hang-ing down, __ Wed-ding bells ring and an - gels sing, __ Clouds __ cov-er up the ground. __

3. We live in a po-lit-i-cal world, __

Wis-dom is thrown in-to jail, __   It rots in a cell, is mis-guid – ed as hell Leav-ing

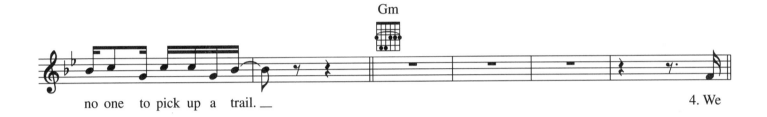

Gm

no one to pick up a trail. __   4. We

G

live in a po-lit-i-cal world __   Where mer-cy walks the plank, __

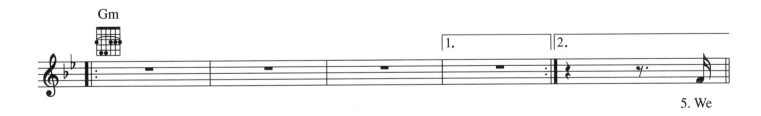

Life is in mir-rors,   death dis-ap-pears Up the steps in-to the near-est bank. __

Gm

1.   2.

5. We

G

live in a po-lit-i-cal world __   Where cour-age is a thing of the past, __

Hous-es are haunt-ed, chil-dren are un-want-ed, The next day could be your last.___ 6. We

live in a po-lit-i-cal world,___ The one we can see and can feel___ But there's

no one to check,___ it's all a stacked deck, We all know for sure that it's real.___

Gm

G

7. We live in a po-lit-i-cal world, ___ In the

cit-ies of lone-some fear,___ Lit-tle by lit-tle you turn in the mid-dle But you're

nev-er sure why you're here. ___ 8. We live in a po-lit-i-cal world ___

Un-der the mi-cro-scope,___ You can trav-el an-y-where and hang___ your-self there, You

Gm

al-ways got more than e-nough rope. 9. We

live in a po-lit-i-cal world,__ Turn-ing and a-thrash-ing a-bout,__ As

soon as you're a-wake, you're trained__ to take__ What looks like the eas-y way out.__

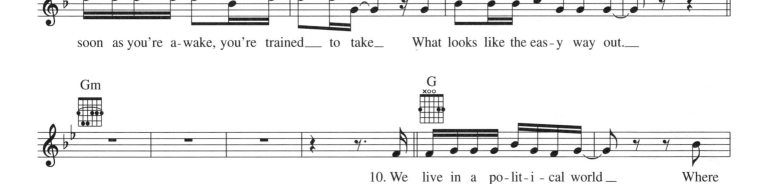

10. We live in a po-lit-i-cal world__ Where

peace is not wel-come at all,__ It's turned a-way from the door__ to wan-der some more__ Or

put up a-gainst the wall. __ 11. We live in a po-lit-i-cal world, __ Ev-ery-

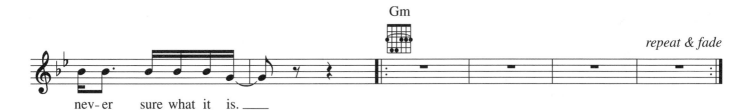

thing is hers__ or his,__ Climb in-to the frame and shout__ God's name But you're

repeat & fade

nev-er sure what it is. ____

Positively 4th Street

Words and Music by Bob Dylan

Medium tempo

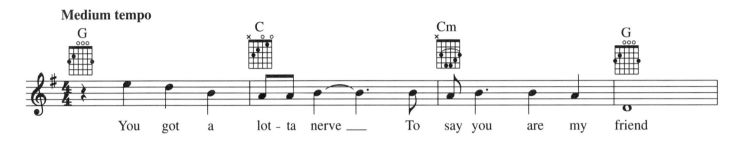

You got a lot-ta nerve ___ To say you are my friend

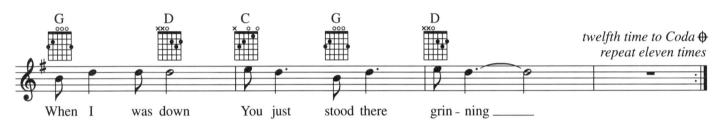

twelfth time to Coda
repeat eleven times

When I was down You just stood there grin - ning ___

✠ *Coda*

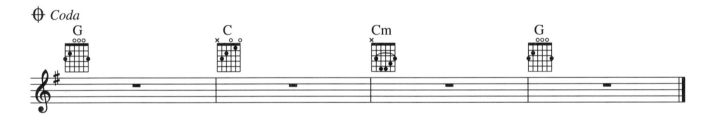

Additional lyrics

2. You got a lotta nerve
   To say you gotta helping hand to lend
   You just want to be on
   The side that's winning

3. You say I let you down
   You know it's not like that
   If you're so hurt
   Why then don't you show it

4. You say you lost your faith
   But that's not where it's at
   You had no faith to lose
   And you know it

5. I know the reason
   That you talk behind my back
   I used to be among the crowd
   You're in with

6. Do you take me for such a fool
   To think I'd make contact
   With the one who tries to hide
   What he don't know to begin with

7. You see me on the street
   You always act surprised
   You say, "How are you?" "Good luck"
   But you don't mean it

8. When you know as well as me
   You'd rather see me paralyzed
   Why don't you just come out once
   And scream it

9. No, I do not feel that good
   When I see the heartbreaks you embrace
   If I was a master thief
   Perhaps I'd rob them

10. And now I know you're dissatisfied
     With your position and your place
     Don't you understand
     It's not my problem

11. I wish that for just one time
     You could stand inside my shoes
     And just for that one moment
     I could be you

12. Yes, I wish that for just one time
     You could stand inside my shoes
     You'd know what a drag it is
     To see you

Precious Angel

Words and Music by Bob Dylan

Additional lyrics

2. My so-called friends have fallen under a spell.
   They look me squarely in the eye and they say, "All is well."
   Can they imagine the darkness that will fall from on high
   When men will beg God to kill them and they won't be able to die?

   Sister, lemme tell you about a vision I saw.
   You were drawing water for your husband, you were suffering under the law.
   You were telling him about Buddha, you were telling him about Mohammed in the same breath.
   You never mentioned one time the Man who came and died a criminal's death.

   Chorus

3. Precious angel, you believe me when I say
   What God has given to us no man can take away.
   We are covered in blood, girl, you know our forefathers were slaves.
   Let us hope they've found mercy in their bone-filled graves.

   You're the queen of my flesh, girl, you're my woman, you're my delight,
   You're the lamp of my soul, girl, and you touch up the night.
   But there's violence in the eyes, girl, so let us not be enticed
   On the way out of Egypt, through Ethiopia, to the judgment hall of Christ.

   Chorus

Precious Memories

Traditional, arranged by Bob Dylan

Moderately

1. As I trav - el _____ down life's path - way, _____
2. Pre - cious fa - ther, _____ lov - ing moth - er, _____

Know not what the years may hold.
Glide a - cross the lone - ly years.

As I pon - der, _____ hopes grow fond - er. _____
And old homes scenes _____ of my child - hood _____

Pre - cious mem - o - ries flood my ___ soul.
In fond mem - o - ry ap - pears. _____

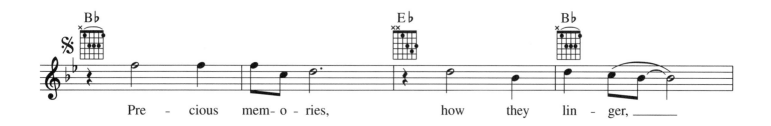

Pre - cious mem- o - ries, how they lin - ger, ____

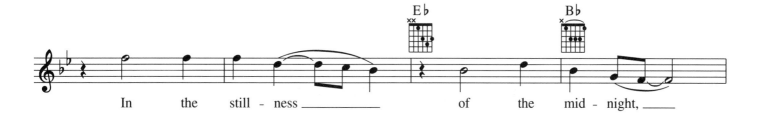

How they __ ev - er flood my soul. _____

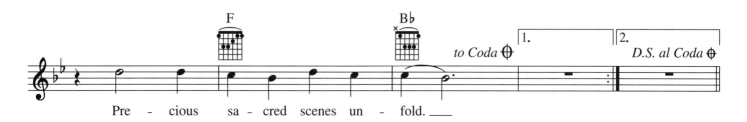

In the still - ness _____ of the mid - night, ____

Pre - cious sa - cred scenes un - fold. ___

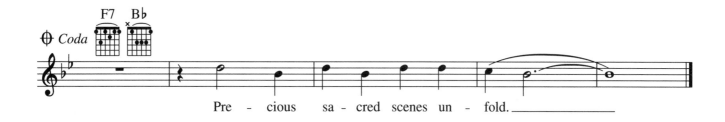

Pre - cious sa - cred scenes un - fold. _____

Pressing On

Words and Music by Bob Dylan

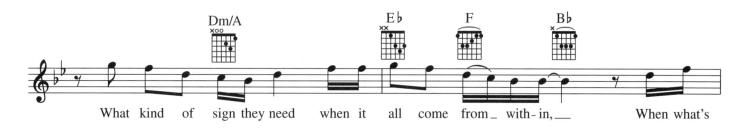

What kind of sign they need when it all come from_ with- in,__ When what's

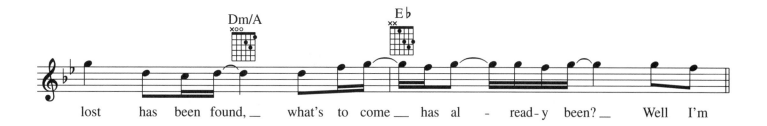

lost has been found, _ what's to come _ has al - read- y been? _ Well I'm

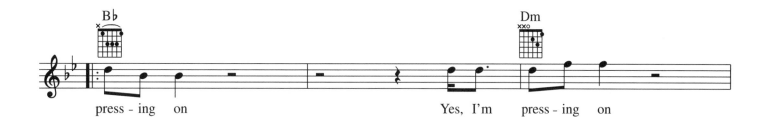

press - ing on   Yes, I'm press - ing on

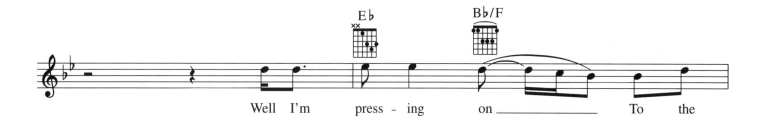

Well I'm press - ing on _____ To the

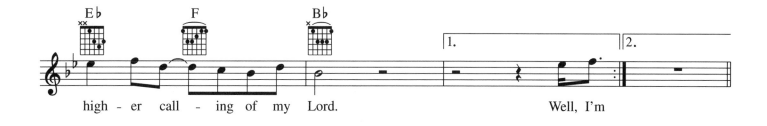

high - er call - ing of my Lord.   Well, I'm

Shake the dust _ off of your feet, _ don't look back. _

Noth - ing __ now can hold you down, __ noth-ing that __ you lack. __

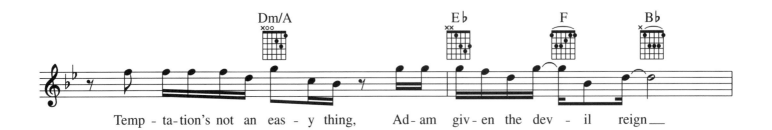

Temp - ta-tion's not an eas - y thing, Ad- am giv- en the dev - il reign __

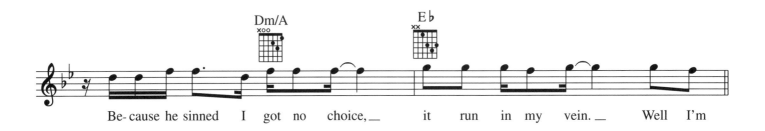

Be- cause he sinned I got no choice, __ it run in my vein. __ Well I'm

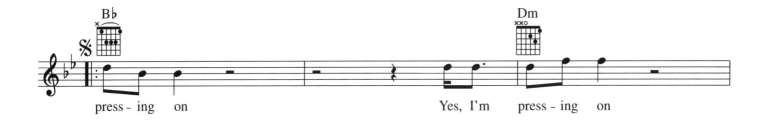

press - ing on Yes, I'm press - ing on

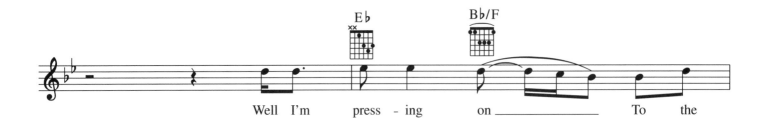

Well I'm press - ing on __ To the

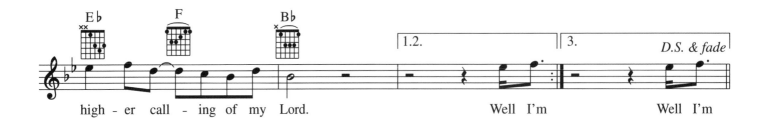

high - er call - ing of my Lord. Well I'm Well I'm

1.2.   3.   D.S. & fade

Tomorrow Is a Long Time

Words and Music by Bob Dylan

* ad lib quasi recitative

Property of Jesus

Words and Music by Bob Dylan

Additional lyrics

3. When the whip that's keeping you in line doesn't make him jump,
   Say he's hard-of-hearin', say that he's a chump.
   Say he's out of step with reality as you try to test his nerve
   Because he doesn't pay no tribute to the king that you serve.

   Chorus

4. Say that he's a loser 'cause he got no common sense
   Because he don't increase his worth at someone else's expense.
   Because he's not afraid of trying, 'cause he don't look at you and smile,
   'Cause he doesn't tell you jokes or fairy tales, say he's got no style.

   Chorus

5. You can laugh at salvation, you can play Olympic games,
   You think that when you rest at last you'll go back from where you came.
   But you've picked up quite a story and you've changed since the womb.
   What happened to the real you, you've been captured but by whom?

   Chorus

Too Much of Nothing

Words and Music by Bob Dylan

Moderately slow

Now, too much of noth-ing can make a man feel ill at ease.
Too much of noth-ing can make a man a-buse a king.
Too much of noth-ing can turn a man in-to a liar,
He can

One man's tem-per might rise__ While an-oth-er man's tem-per might freeze.
walk the streets and boast like most But he would-n't know a thing.
cause one man to sleep on nails And an-oth-er man to eat fire.
In the
Now, it's
Ev-'ry

day of con-fes-sion __ we can-not mock-a soul.__ Oh, when there's too much of noth-ing,
all been done be-fore, It's all been writ-ten in the book,__ But when there's too much of noth-ing,
bod-y's do-in' some-thin'__ I heard it in a dream. But when there's too much of noth-ing, It just

no one has con-trol.
No-bod-y should look.
makes a fel-la mean.

Say hel-lo to Val-e-rie__ Say hel-lo to Viv-i-an__

1.2.   **3.**

Send them all my sal-a-ry__ on the wa-ters of ob-liv-i-on.   liv-i-on.

Queen Jane Approximately

Words and Music by Bob Dylan

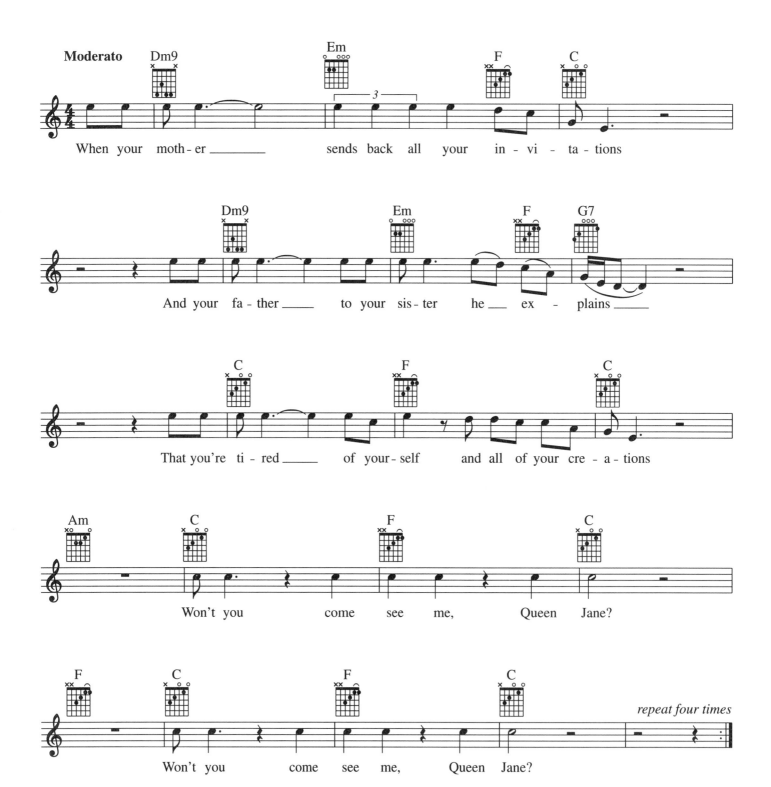

When your moth- er _____ sends back all your in - vi - ta - tions

And your fa - ther _____ to your sis - ter he __ ex - plains _____

That you're ti - red _____ of your- self and all of your cre - a - tions

Won't you come see me, Queen Jane?

repeat four times

Won't you come see me, Queen Jane?

Additional lyrics

2. Now when all of the flower ladies want back what they have lent you
   And the smell of their roses does not remain
   And all of your children start to resent you
   Won't you come see me, Queen Jane?
   Won't you come see me, Queen Jane?

3. Now when all the clowns that you have commissioned
   Have died in battle or in vain
   And you're sick of all this repetition
   Won't you come see me, Queen Jane?
   Won't you come see me, Queen Jane?

4. When all of your advisers heave their plastic
   At your feet to convince you of your pain
   Trying to prove that your conclusions should be more drastic
   Won't you come see me, Queen Jane?
   Won't you come see me, Queen Jane?

5. Now when all the bandits that you turned your other cheek to
   All lay down their bandanas and complain
   And you want somebody you don't have to speak to
   Won't you come see me, Queen Jane?
   Won't you come see me, Queen Jane?

Quinn the Eskimo
(The Mighty Quinn)

Words and Music by Bob Dylan

Moderately slow, with a steady beat

Come all with-out, come all with-in, You'll not see noth-in' like the

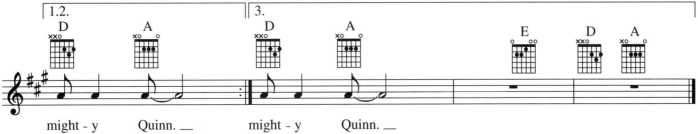

might-y Quinn. ___ might-y Quinn. ___

Additional lyrics

2. I like to do just like the rest, I like my sugar sweet,
But guarding fumes and making haste,
It ain't my cup of meat.
Ev'rybody's 'neath the trees,
Feeding pigeons on a limb
But when Quinn the Eskimo gets here,
All the pigeons gonna run to him.
Come all without, come all within,
You'll not see nothing like the mighty Quinn.

3. A cat's meow and a cow's moo, I can recite 'em all,
Just tell me where it hurts yuh, honey,
And I'll tell you who to call.
Nobody can get no sleep,
There's someone on ev'ryone's toes
But when Quinn the Eskimo gets here,
Ev'rybody's gonna wanna doze.
Come all without, come all within,
You'll not see nothing like the mighty Quinn.

Quit Your Low Down Ways

Words and Music by Bob Dylan

2. Well, you can run __
3. Well, you can run __
4. And you can hitch __
5. Oh, you can read __

Additional lyrics

2. Well, you can run down to the White House,
   You can gaze at the Capitol Dome, pretty mama,
   You can pound on the President's gate
   But you oughta know by now it's gonna be too late.

Refrain

3. Well, you can run down to the desert,
   Throw yourself on the burning sand.
   You can raise up your right hand, pretty mama,
   But you better understand you done lost your one good man.

Refrain

4. And you can hitchhike on the highway,
   You can stand all alone by the side of the road.
   You can try to flag a ride back home, pretty mama,
   But you can't ride in my car no more.

Refrain

5. Oh, you can read out your Bible,
   You can fall down on your knees, pretty mama,
   And pray to the Lord
   But it ain't gonna do no good.

Refrain

Ragged & Dirty

Traditional, arranged by Bob Dylan

Moderate blues

Capo on second fret

1. Lord, I'm broke, I'm __ hun - gry, __ rag - ged and dir - ty __ too, __

Broke __ and hun - gry, __ rag - ged and dir - ty __ too. __

__ If I clean __ up, sweet mom - ma, can I

stay all __ night with you? _____

Additional lyrics

2. Lord, I went to my window, babe, I couldn't see through my blinds,
   Went to my window, babe, I couldn't see through my blinds.
   Heard my best friend a-comin' and I thought I heard my baby cry.

3. Lord, if I can't come in here, baby, then just let me sit down in your door,
   If I can't come in here, baby, then just let me sit down in your door.
   And I would leave so soon that your man won't never know.

4. How can I live here, baby, Lord, and feel at ease?
   How can I live here, baby, Lord, and feel at ease?
   Well, that woman I got, man, she does just what she feels.

5. Lord, you shouldn't mistreat me, baby, because I'm young and wild,
   Shouldn't mistreat me, baby, because I'm young and wild.
   You must always remember, baby, you was once a child.

6. 'Cause I'm leaving in the morning, if I have to ride the blinds,
   Leaving in the morning, if I have to ride the blinds.
   Well, I been mistreated and I swear I don't mind dyin'.

Rainy Day Women #12 & 35

Words and Music by Bob Dylan

Additional lyrics

2. Well, they'll stone ya when you're walkin' 'long the street.
   They'll stone ya when you're tryin' to keep your seat.
   They'll stone ya when you're walkin' on the floor.
   They'll stone ya when you're walkin' to the door.
   But I would not feel so all alone,
   Everybody must get stoned.

3. They'll stone ya when you're at the breakfast table.
   They'll stone ya when you are young and able.
   They'll stone ya when you're tryin' to make a buck.
   They'll stone ya and then they'll say, "good luck."
   Tell ya what, I would not feel so all alone,
   Everybody must get stoned.

4. Well, they'll stone you and say that it's the end.
   Then they'll stone you and then they'll come back again.
   They'll stone you when you're riding in your car.
   They'll stone you when you're playing your guitar.
   Yes, but I would not feel so all alone,
   Everybody must get stoned.

5. Well, they'll stone you when you walk all alone.
   They'll stone you when you are walking home.
   They'll stone you and then say you are brave.
   They'll stone you when you are set down in your grave.
   But I would not feel so all alone,
   Everybody must get stoned.

Restless Farewell

Words and Music by Bob Dylan

Additional lyrics

2. Oh ev'ry girl that ever I've touched,
   I did not do it harmfully.
   And ev'ry girl that ever I've hurt,
   I did not do it knowin'ly.
   But to remain as friends and make amends
   You need the time and stay behind.
   And since my feet are now fast
   And point away from the past,
   I'll bid farewell and be down the line.

3. Oh ev'ry foe that ever I faced,
   The cause was there before we came.
   And ev'ry cause that ever I fought,
   I fought it full without regret or shame.
   But the dark does die
   As the curtain is drawn and somebody's eyes
   Must meet the dawn.
   And if I see the day
   I'd only have to stay,
   So I'll bid farewell in the night and be gone.

4. Oh, ev'ry thought that's strung a knot in my mind,
   I might go insane if it couldn't be sprung.
   But it's not to stand naked under unknowin' eyes,
   It's for myself and my friends my stories are sung.
   But the time ain't tall,
   Yet on time you depend and no word is possessed
   By no special friend.
   And though the line is cut,
   It ain't quite the end,
   I'll just bid farewell till we meet again.

5. Oh a false clock tries to tick out my time
   To disgrace, distract, and bother me.
   And the dirt of gossip blows into my face,
   And the dust of rumors covers me.
   But if the arrow is straight
   And the point is slick,
   It can pierce through dust no matter how thick.
   So I'll make my stand
   And remain as I am
   And bid farewell and not give a damn.

Ring Them Bells

Words and Music by Bob Dylan

Rita May

Words and Music by Bob Dylan and Jacques Levy

Ri - ta May, Ri - ta May, You got your bod-y in the way.
May, How'd you ev - er get that way?
May, Lay - ing in a stack of hay,

You're so damn ___ non - cha - lant But it's your mind that I want.
When do you ev - er see the light? Don't you ev - er feel a fright?
Do you re - mem- ber where you been? What's that cra - zy place you're in?

You got me huff - in' and a - puff - in', Next to you I feel like noth - in', Ri - ta
You got me burn - in' and I'm turn - in' But I know I must be learn - in', Ri - ta
I'm gon - na have to go to col - lege 'Cause you are the book of know - ledge, Ri - ta

May. Ri - ta May, Ri - ta
May. All my friends have told me if I

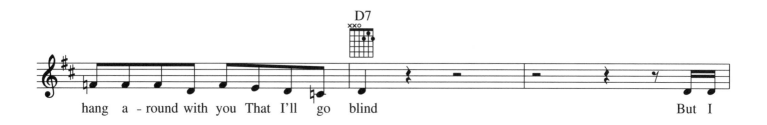

hang a - round with you That I'll go blind

know that when you hold me That there real - ly must be some-thin' on your mind._____

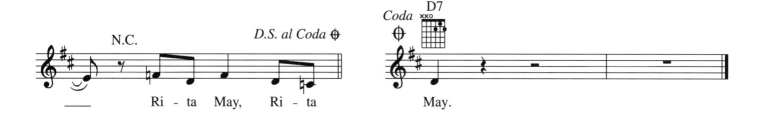

N.C.   *D.S. al Coda*   *Coda*

____ Ri - ta May, Ri - ta   May.

But I

Rocks and Gravel

Words and Music by Bob Dylan

Romance in Durango

Words and Music by Bob Dylan and Jacques Levy

1. Hot chil - i pep - pers in the blis - ter - ing sun ____

Dust on my face ____ and my cape, ____

Me and Mag - da - le - na on ____ the run ____

I think this time we shall es - cape. ____

559

Additional lyrics

2. Past the Aztec ruins and the ghosts of our people
   Hoofbeats like castanets on stone.
   At night I dream of bells in the village steeple
   Then I see the bloody face of Ramon.

   Was it me that shot him down in the cantina
   Was it my hand that held the gun?
   Come, let us fly, my Magdalena
   The dogs are barking and what's done is done.

   Chorus

3. At the corrida we'll sit in the shade
   And watch the young torero stand alone.
   We'll drink tequila where our grandfathers stayed
   When they rode with Villa into Torreon.

   Then the padre will recite the prayers of old
   In the little church this side of town.
   I will wear new boots and an earring of gold
   You'll shine with diamonds in your wedding gown.

   The way is long but the end is near
   Already the fiesta has begun.
   The face of God will appear
   With His serpent eyes of obsidian.

   Chorus

4. Was that the thunder that I heard?
   My head is vibrating, I feel a sharp pain.
   Come sit by me, don't say a word
   Oh, can it be that I am slain?

   Quick, Magdalena, take my gun
   Look up in the hills, that flash of light.
   Aim well my little one
   We may not make it through the night.

   Chorus

True Love Tends to Forget

Words and Music by Bob Dylan

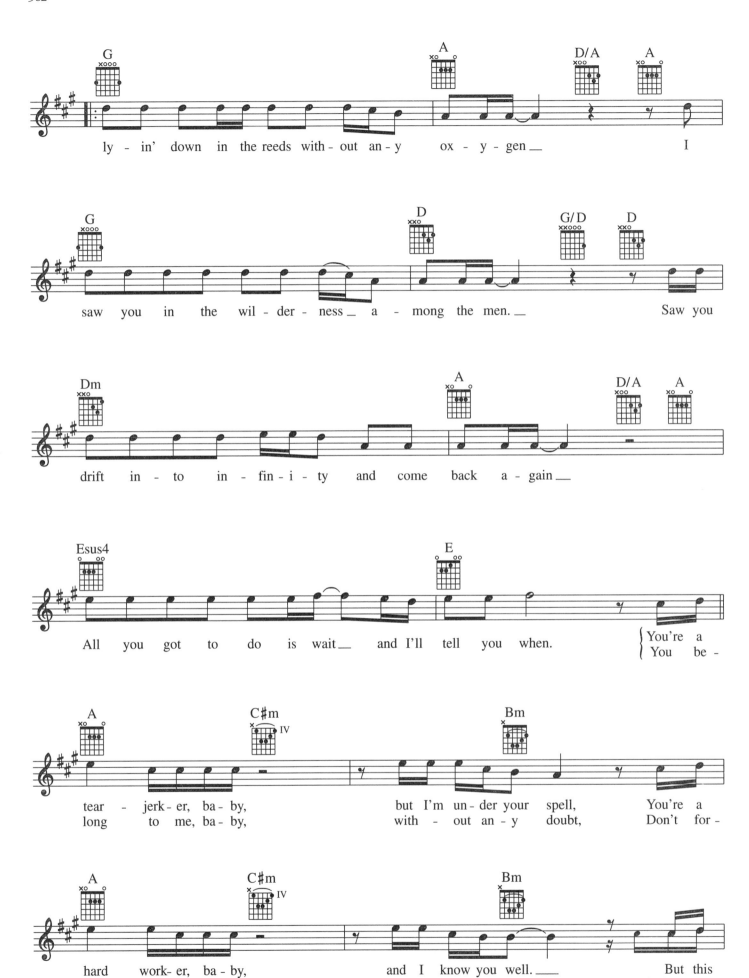

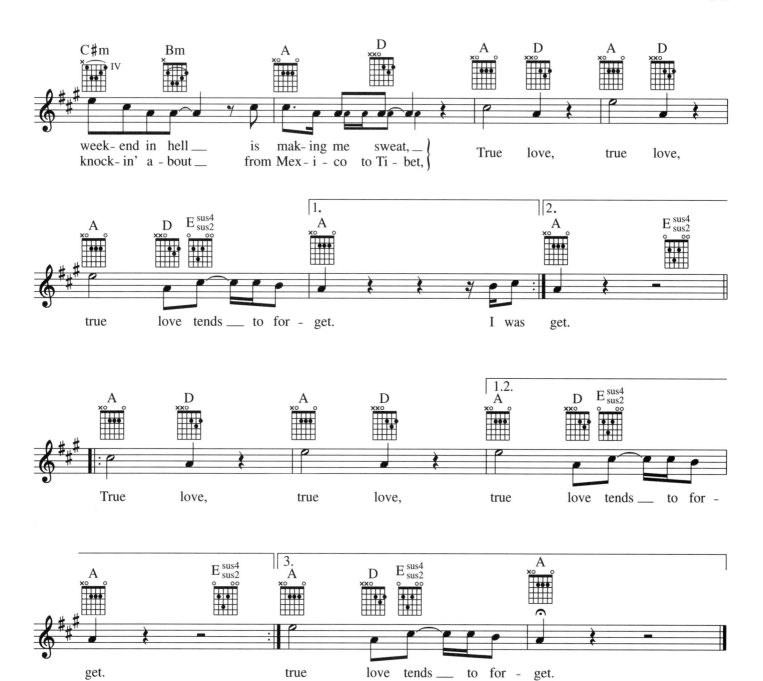

Sad-Eyed Lady of the Lowlands

Words and Music by Bob Dylan

Additional lyrics

2. With your sheets like metal and your belt like lace,
   And your deck of cards missing the jack and the ace,
   And your basement clothes and your hollow face,
   Who among them can think he could outguess you?
   With your silhouette when the sunlight dims
   Into your eyes where the moonlight swims,
   And your match-book songs and your gypsy hymns,
   Who among them would try to impress you?

Chorus

3. The kings of Tyrus with their convict list
   Are waiting in line for their geranium kiss,
   And you wouldn't know it would happen like this,
   But who among them really wants just to kiss you?
   With your childhood flames on your midnight rug,
   And your Spanish manners and your mother's drugs,
   And your cowboy mouth and your curfew plugs,
   Who among them do you think could resist you?

Chorus

4. Oh, the farmers and the businessmen, they all did decide
   To show you the dead angels that they used to hide.
   But why did they pick you to sympathize with their side?
   Oh, how could they ever mistake you?
   They wished you'd accepted the blame for the farm,
   But with the sea at your feet and the phony false alarm,
   And with the child of a hoodlum wrapped up in your arms,
   How could they ever, ever persuade you?

Chorus

5. With your sheet-metal memory of Cannery Row,
   And your magazine-husband who one day just had to go,
   And your gentleness now, which you just can't help but show,
   Who among them do you think would employ you?
   Now you stand with your thief, you're on his parole
   With your holy medallion which your fingertips fold,
   And your saintlike face and your ghostlike soul,
   Oh, who among them do you think could destroy you

Chorus

Watching the River Flow

Words and Music by Bob Dylan

Moderate blues

What's the mat- ter with me, ___ I don't have
Wish I was back in the cit - y ___ In- stead of this

much to say, ___ With the
old bank of sand, ___

Day- light sneak- in' through the win- dow And I'm still in this all
sun beat- ing down o- ver the chim- ney tops __ And the one I love __ so close at

night ca - fé. Walk- in' to and fro __ be- neath the
hand. If I had wings __ and I could

moon Out to where the trucks are ___ roll- 'in slow,
fly, I know where I would go.

Sara

Words and Music by Bob Dylan

1. I laid on a dune,__ I looked at the sky, When the chil-dren were ba-bies and played on the beach. You came up be-hind me, I saw you go by, You were al-ways so close and still with-in reach. Sa - ra,_____ Sa - ra, What-ev-er made you want to change your mind? Sa - ra,_____ Sa - ra, So eas-y to look at, so hard to de-fine.

2. I can

Additional lyrics

2. I can still see them playin' with their pails in the sand,
They run to the water their buckets to fill.
I can still see the shells fallin' out of their hands
As they follow each other back up the hill.

    Sara, Sara,
    Sweet virgin angel, sweet love of my life,
    Sara, Sara,
    Radiant jewel, mystical wife.

3. Sleepin' in the woods by a fire in the night,
Drinkin' white rum in a Portugal bar,
Them playin' leapfrog and hearin' about Snow White,
You in the marketplace in Savanna-la-Mar.

    Sara, Sara,
    It's all so clear, I could never forget,
    Sara, Sara,
    Lovin' you is the one thing I'll never regret.

4. I can still hear the sounds of those Methodist bells,
I'd taken the cure and had just gotten through,
Stayin' up for days in the Chelsea Hotel,
Writin' "Sad-Eyed Lady of the Lowlands" for you.

    Sara, Sara,
    Wherever we travel we're never apart.
    Sara, oh Sara,
    Beautiful lady, so dear to my heart.

5. How did I meet you? I don't know.
A messenger sent me in a tropical storm.
You were there in the winter, moonlight on the snow
And on Lily Pond Lane when the weather was warm.

    Sara, oh Sara,
    Scorpio Sphinx in a calico dress,
    Sara, Sara,
    You must forgive me my unworthiness.

6. Now the beach is deserted except for some kelp
And a piece of an old ship that lies on the shore.
You always responded when I needed your help,
You gimme a map and a key to your door.

    Sara, oh Sara,
    Glamorous nymph with an arrow and bow,
    Sara, oh Sara,
    Don't ever leave me, don't ever go.

Saved

Words and Music by Bob Dylan and Tim Drummond

Saved, _ Saved, _ And I'm

so glad. _ Yes, I'm so glad, _

I'm so glad, _ So glad, _

I want to thank You, Lord, I just want to

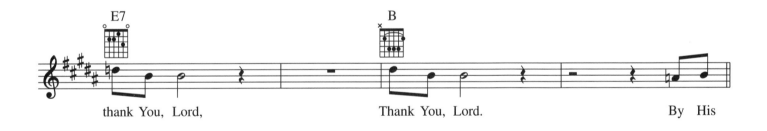

thank You, Lord, Thank You, Lord. By His

truth I can be up - right, By His strength I do en - dure, _ By His

pow - er I've _ been lift - ed, In His love I am se - cure. _ He

bought me with a price, __ Freed __ me from the pit, __ Full of

emp - ti - ness __ and wrath And the fire that burns in it. I've been

saved __ By the blood of the lamb, __

Saved __ By the blood of the lamb, __

Saved, __ Saved, __ And I'm

so glad. __ Yes, I'm so glad, __ I'm

so glad, __ So glad, __ I want to

Saving Grace

Words and Music by Bob Dylan

Moderately, with expression

1. If You find it in Your heart, can I be for - giv - en? _____

Guess I owe You some kind of a - pol - o - gy.

I've es - caped death so man - y times, I know I'm on - ly liv - ing _____

By the sav - ing grace ___ that's o - ver me.

2. By this time I'd - a thought I would be sleep - ing

In a pine box for all e - ter - ni - ty.

Additional lyrics

4. Well, the devil's shining light, it can be most blinding,
   But to search for love, that ain't no more than vanity.
   As I look around this world all that I'm finding
   Is the saving grace that's over me.

5. The wicked know no peace and you just can't fake it,
   There's only one road and it leads to Calvary.
   It gets discouraging at times, but I know I'll make it
   By the saving grace that's over me.

Went to See the Gypsy
Words and Music by Bob Dylan

Moderately fast

Went to see the gyp - sy, Stay - in' in a big ho - tel.

He smiled when he saw me com - ing, And he said, "Well, __ well, __ well."

His room was dark and crowd - ed,

Lights were low __ and dim. "How are you?" __ he said __

__ to me, __ I said __ it back to him. __

I went down to the lob - by __ To make a small __

Seeing the Real You at Last

Words and Music by Bob Dylan

Additional lyrics

2. Well, didn't I risk my neck for you,
   Didn't I take chances?
   Didn't I rise above it all for you,
   The most unfortunate circumstances?

   Well, I have had some rotten nights,
   Didn't think that they would pass.
   I'm just thankful and grateful
   To be seeing the real you at last.

3. I'm hungry and I'm irritable
   And I'm tired of this bag of tricks.
   At one time there was nothing wrong with me
   That you could not fix.

   Well, I sailed through the storm
   Strapped to the mast,
   But the time has come
   And I'm seeing the real you at last.

4. When I met you, baby,
   You didn't show no visible scars.
   You could ride like Annie Oakley,
   You could shoot like Belle Starr.

   Well, I don't mind a reasonable amount of trouble,
   Trouble always comes to pass
   But all I care about now
   Is that I'm seeing the real you at last.

5. Well, I'm gonna quit this baby talk now,
   I guess I should have known.
   I got troubles, I think maybe you got troubles,
   I think maybe we'd better leave each other alone.

   Whatever you gonna do,
   Please do it fast.
   I'm still trying to get used to
   Seeing the real you at last.

Series of Dreams

Words and Music by Bob Dylan

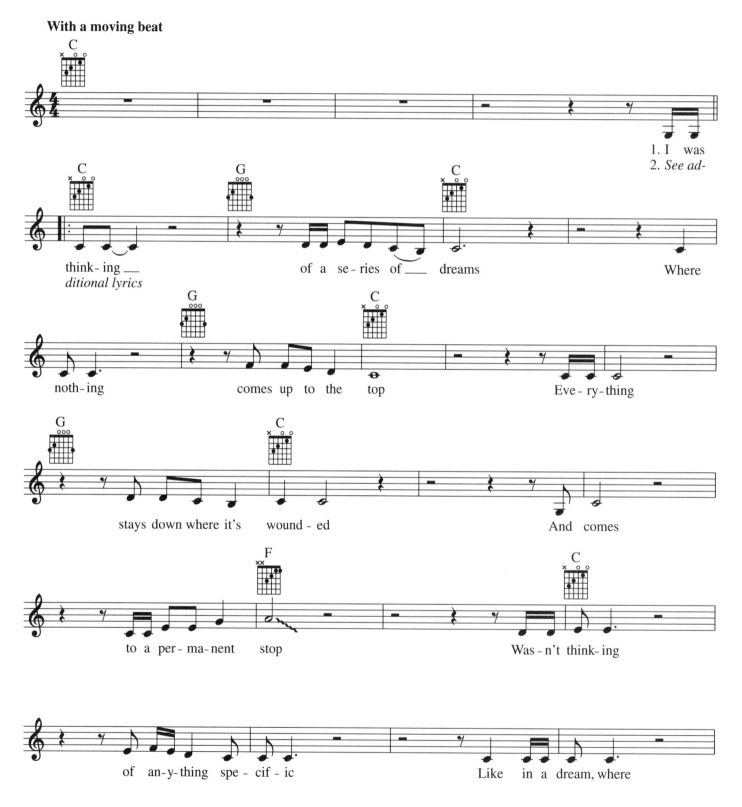

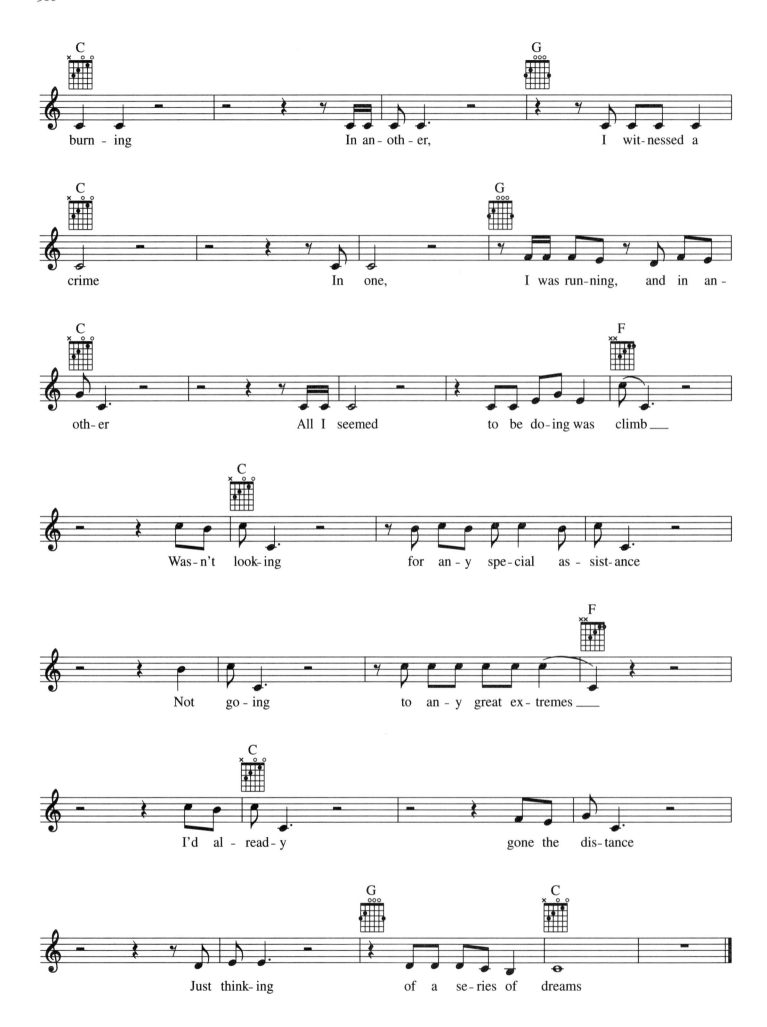

Additional lyrics

2. Thinking of a series of dreams
   Where the time and the tempo fly
   And there's no exit in any direction
   'Cept the one that you can't see with your eyes
   Wasn't making any great connection
   Wasn't falling for any intricate scheme
   Nothing that would pass inspection
   Just thinking of a series of dreams

Seven Curses

Words and Music by Bob Dylan

Slowly and sadly

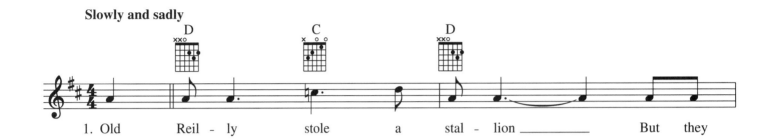

1. Old Reil - ly stole a stal - lion _____ But they

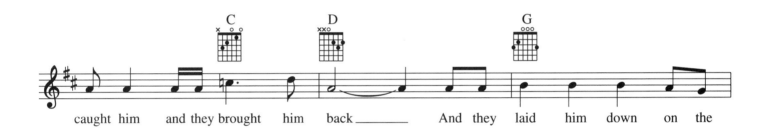

caught him and they brought him back_____ And they laid him down on the

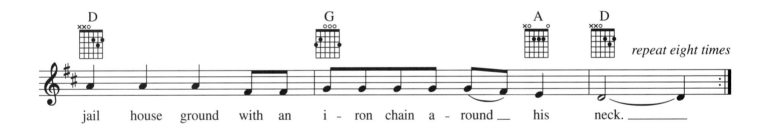

repeat eight times

jail house ground with an i - ron chain a - round ___ his neck._____

Additional lyrics

2. Old Reilly's daughter got a message
That her father was goin' to hang.
She rode by night and came by morning
With gold and silver in her hand.

3. When the judge he saw Reilly's daughter
His old eyes deepened in his head,
Sayin', "Gold will never free your father,
The price, my dear, is you instead."

4. "Oh I'm as good as dead," cried Reilly,
"It's only you that he does crave
And my skin will surely crawl if he touches you at all.
Get on your horse and ride away."

5. "Oh father you will surely die
If I don't take the chance to try
And pay the price and not take your advice.
For that reason I will have to stay."

6. The gallows shadows shook the evening,
In the night a hound dog bayed,
In the night the grounds were groanin',
In the night the price was paid.

7. The next mornin' she had awoken
To know that the judge had never spoken.
She saw that hangin' branch a-bendin',
She saw her father's body broken.

8. These be seven curses on a judge so cruel:
   That one doctor will not save him,
   That two healers will not heal him,
   That three eyes will not see him.

9. That four ears will not hear him,
   That five walls will not hide him,
   That six diggers will not bury him
   And that seven deaths shall never kill him.

She Belongs to Me

Words and Music by Bob Dylan

Moderato

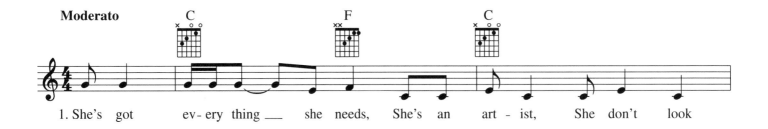

1. She's got ev - ery thing __ she needs, She's an art - ist, She don't look

back. She's got ev- ery thing __ she needs, She's an

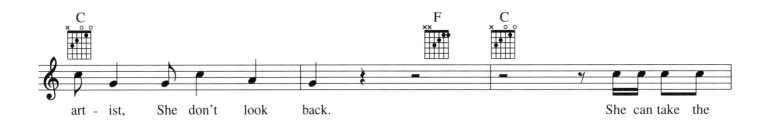

art - ist, She don't look back. She can take the

repeat four times

dark out of the night-time And __ paint the day - time black.

Additional lyrics

2. You will start out standing
   Proud to steal her anything she sees.
   You will start out standing
   Proud to steal her anything she sees.
   But you will wind up peeking through her keyhole
   Down upon your knees.

3. She never stumbles,
   She's got no place to fall.
   She never stumbles,
   She's got no place to fall.
   She's nobody's child,
   The Law can't touch her at all.

4. She wears an Egyptian ring
   That sparkles before she speaks.
   She wears an Egyptian ring
   That sparkles before she speaks.
   She's a hypnotist collector,
   You are a walking antique.

5. Bow down to her on Sunday,
   Salute her when her birthday comes.
   Bow down to her on Sunday,
   Salute her when her birthday comes.
   For Halloween give her a trumpet
   And for Christmas, buy her a drum.

She's Your Lover Now

Words and Music by Bob Dylan

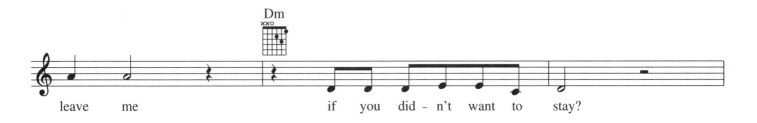

leave me   if you did – n't want to stay?

Why'd you have to treat me so bad? Did it have to be that

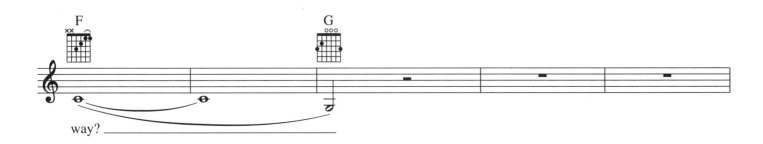

way? _____

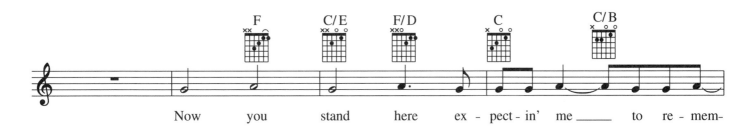

Now you stand here ex - pect - in' me _____ to re - mem-

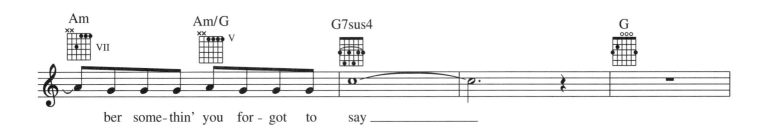

ber some - thin' you for - got to say _____

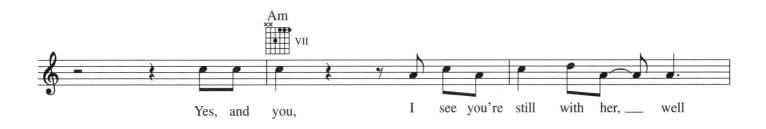

Yes, and you,   I see you're still with her, ___ well

That's fine 'cause she's com - in' on so strange,

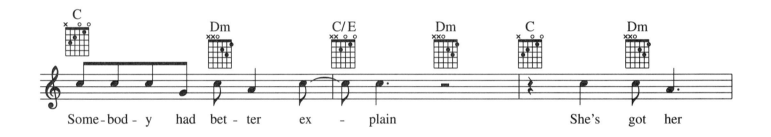

can't you tell?

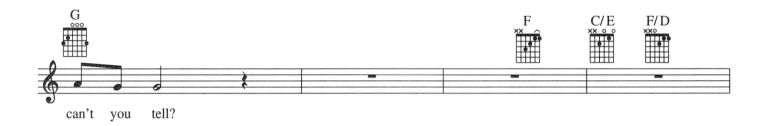

Some - bod - y had bet - ter ex - plain   She's got her

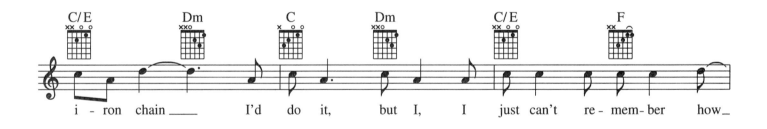

i - ron chain ____   I'd do it, but I, I just can't re - mem - ber how__

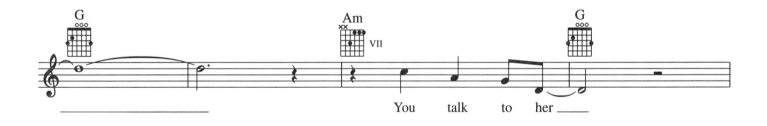

_____   You talk to her ____

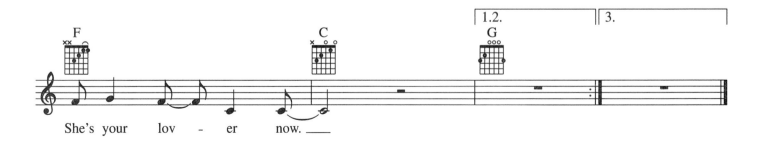

She's your lov - er now. ____

Additional lyrics

2. I already assumed
   That we're in the felony room
   But I ain't a judge, you don't have to be nice to me
   But please tell that
   To your friend in the cowboy hat
   You know he keeps on sayin' ev'rythin' twice to me
   You know I was straight with you
   You know I've never tried to change you in any way
   You know if you didn't want to be with me
   That you could . . . didn't have to stay.
   Now you stand here sayin' you forgive and forget. Honey, what can I say?
   Yes, you, you just sit around and ask for ashtrays, can't you reach?
   I see you kiss her on the cheek ev'rytime she gives a speech
   With her picture books of the pyramid
   And her postcards of Billy the Kid
   (Why must everybody bow?)
   You better talk to her 'bout it
   You're her lover now.

3. Oh, ev'rybody that cares
   Is goin' up the castle stairs
   But I'm not up in your castle, honey
   It's true, I just can't recall
   San Francisco at all
   I can't even remember El Paso, uh, honey
   You never had to be faithful
   I didn't want you to grieve
   Oh, why was it so hard for you
   If you didn't want to be with me, just to leave?
   Now you stand here while your finger's goin' up my sleeve
   An' you, just what do you do anyway? Ain't there nothin' you can say?
   She'll be standin' on the bar soon
   With a fish head an' a harpoon
   An' a fake beard plastered on her brow
   You'd better do somethin' quick
   She's your lover now.

Shenandoah

Traditional, arranged by Bob Dylan

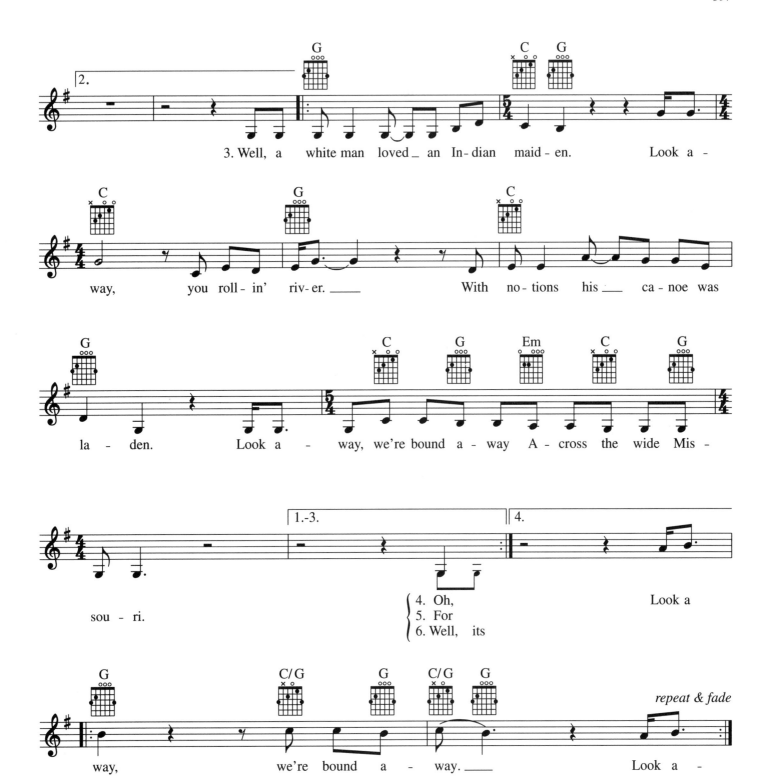

Additional lyrics

4. Oh, Shenandoah, I love your daughter.
   Look away, you rollin' river.
   It was for her I'd cross the water.
   Look away, we're bound away
   Across the wide Missouri.

5. For seven long years I courted Sally.
   Look away, you rollin' river.
   Seven more years I longed to have her.
   Look away, we're bound away
   Across the wide Missouri.

6. Well, it's fare-thee-well, my dear,
   I'm bound to leave you.
   Look away, you rollin' river.
   Shenandoah, I will not deceive you.
   Look away, we're bound away
   Across the wide Missouri.

What Good Am I?

Words and Music by Bob Dylan

Shot of Love

Words and Music by Bob Dylan

Additional lyrics

3. I don't need no alibi when I'm spending time with you.
   I've heard all of them rumors and you have heard 'em too.
   Don't show me no picture show or give me no book to read,
   It don't satisfy the hurt inside nor the habit that it feeds.

   I need a shot of love, I need a shot of love.

4. Why would I want to take your life?
   You've only murdered my father, raped his wife,
   Tattooed my babies with a poison pen,
   Mocked my God, humiliated my friends.

   I need a shot of love, I need a shot of love.

5. Don't wanna be with nobody tonight
   Veronica not around nowhere, Mavis just ain't right.
   There's a man that hates me and he's swift, smooth and near,
   Am I supposed to set back and wait until he's here?

   I need a shot of love, I need a shot of love.

6. What makes the wind wanna blow tonight?
   Don't even feel like crossing the street and my car ain't actin' right.
   Called home, everybody seemed to have moved away.
   My conscience is beginning to bother me today.

   I need a shot of love, I need a shot of love.

   I need a shot of love, I need a shot of love.
   If you're a doctor, I need a shot of love.

Simple Twist of Fate

Words and Music by Bob Dylan

1. They sat to-geth-er in the park As the eve-ning sky grew dark, She looked at him and he felt a spark tin-gle to his bones. 'Twas then he felt a-lone and wished that he'd gone straight And watched out for a sim-ple twist of fate. They walked a-long by the old ca-nal A lit-tle con-fused, I re-

Additional lyrics

2. A saxophone someplace far off played
   As she was walkin' by the arcade.
   As the light bust through a beat-up shade where he was wakin' up,
   She dropped a coin into the cup of a blind man at the gate
   And forgot about a simple twist of fate.

   He woke up, the room was bare
   He didn't see her anywhere.
   He told himself he didn't care, pushed the window open wide,
   Felt an emptiness inside to which he just could not relate
   Brought on by a simple twist of fate.

3. He hears the ticking of the clocks
   And walks along with a parrot that talks,
   Hunts her down by the waterfront docks where the sailers all come in.
   Maybe she'll pick him out again, how long must he wait
   Once more for a simple twist of fate.

   People tell me it's a sin
   To know and feel too much within.
   I still believe she was my twin, but I lost the ring.
   She was born in spring, but I was born too late
   Blame it on a simple twist of fate.

Silent Weekend

Words and Music by Bob Dylan

Si - lent week- end, Oh __ Lord, I ____ sure wish Mon-day would come.__
Si - lent week- end, Man a- live, I'm burn-in' up on my brain.__

She's up - pi - ty, she's roll- in', She's in the groove, she's stroll-ing o - ver
She knows when I'm just teas-in' But it's not like-ly in the sea- son To

the juke box play- in' deaf and dumb. ___ Well, __ I done a whole lot- ta think- in' 'bout a

whole lot of cheat - in', And I, __ may- be I did some just to please.__ But I just

wal- loped a lot- ta piz- za af- ter mak- in' our peace,__ Puts ya down __ on bend- ed knees.__

o - pen up a pas- sen- ger train. __

Sittin' on Top of the World

Traditional, arranged by Bob Dylan

Additional lyrics

3. Now don't come runnin'
   Holdin' up your hand,
   Can get me a woman
   Quick as you can get a man.
   Now she's gone,
   An' I don't worry.
   Lord, I'm sittin' on top of the world.

4. Happen for days,
   Didn't know your name,
   Oh, why should I worry
   Or crave you in vain?
   Now she's gone,
   An' I don't worry.
   Lord, I'm sittin' on top of the world.

5. Went to the station,
   Down in the yard,
   Gonna get me a freight train,
   Work's done got hard.
   Now she's gone,
   An' I don't worry.
   Lord, I'm sittin' on top of the world.

6. The lonesome days,
   They have gone by,
   Why should I beg you?
   You said good-bye.
   Now she's gone,
   An' I don't worry.
   Lord, I'm sittin' on top of the world.

Slow Train

Words and Music by Bob Dylan

Moderately slow blues, with a steady beat

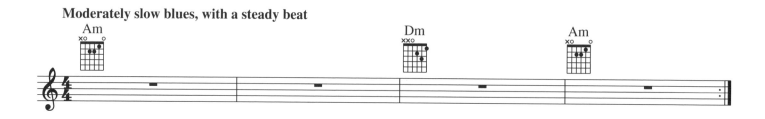

1. Some - times   I   feel so low-down and dis - gust - ed   Can't help but

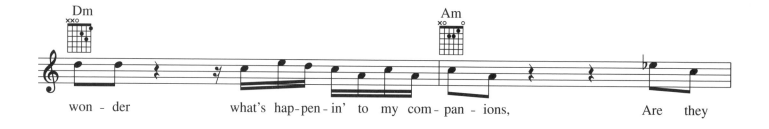

won - der   what's hap-pen - in' to my com - pan - ions,   Are they

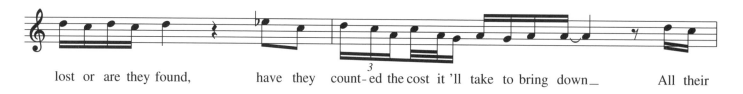

lost or are they found,   have they count - ed the cost it 'll take to bring down_   All their

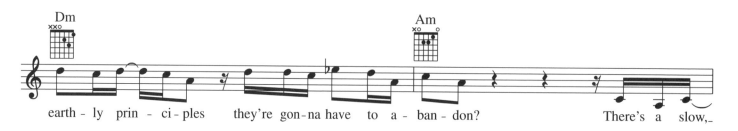

earth - ly prin - ci - ples   they're gon-na have to a - ban - don?   There's a slow,_

Additional lyrics

3. All that foreign oil controlling American soil,
   Look around you, it's just bound to make you embarrassed.
   Sheiks walkin' around like kings, wearing fancy jewels and nose rings,
   Deciding America's future from Amsterdam and to Paris
   And there's a slow, slow train comin' up around the bend.

4. Man's ego is inflated, his laws are outdated, they don't apply no more,
   You can't rely no more to be standin' around waitin'
   In the home of the brave, Jefferson turnin' over in his grave,
   Fools glorifying themselves, trying to manipulate Satan
   And there's a slow, slow train comin' up around the bend.

5. Big-time negotiators, false healers and woman haters,
   Masters of the bluff and masters of the proposition
   But the enemy I see wears a cloak of decency,
   All non-believers and men stealers talkin' in the name of religion
   And there's a slow, slow train comin' up around the bend.

6. People starving and thirsting, grain elevators are bursting
   Oh, you know it costs more to store the food than it do to give it.
   They say lose your inhibitions, follow your own ambitions,
   They talk about a life of brotherly love, show me someone who knows how to live it.
   There's a slow, slow train comin' up around the bend.

7. Well, my baby went to Illinois with some bad-talkin' boy she could destroy
   A real suicide case, but there was nothin' I could do to stop it,
   I don't care about economy, I don't care about astronomy
   But it sure do bother me to see my loved ones turning into puppets,
   There's a slow, slow train comin' up around the bend.

Something There Is About You

Words and Music by Bob Dylan

Moderately bright

1. Some - thing there is a - bout ____ you that
2. Thought I'd shak - en the won - der and the
4. Some - thing there is a - bout ____ you that

strikes a match _ in me ____ Is it the way your bod -
phan - toms of ___ my youth __ Rain - y days on the
moves with style _ and grace _ I was in a whirl-

- y moves or is it the way your hair blows free? ____
Great Lakes, walk- in' the hills of old Du - luth. __
wind, now I'm in some bet - ter place. __

Or is it be - cause you re - mind me
There was me and Dan - ny Lo - pez,
My hand's on the sa - ber and

of some- thing that used _____ to be ____
cold eyes,__ black night and then there was Ruth ____
you've ___ picked up on the ___ ba - ton ____

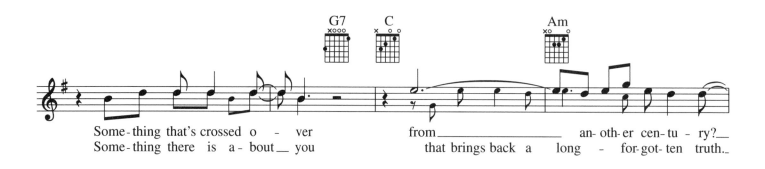

Some- thing that's crossed o - ver from_____ an- oth- er cen- tu - ry?__
Some- thing there is a - bout__ you that brings back a long - for- got- ten truth.__

1.　　　　2.

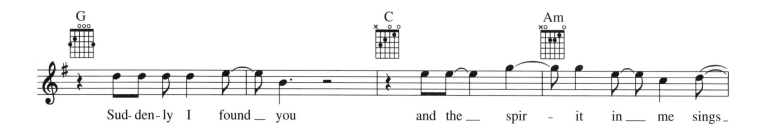

Sud- den- ly I found __ you and the __ spir - it in __ me sings __

Don't have to look no fur - ther,

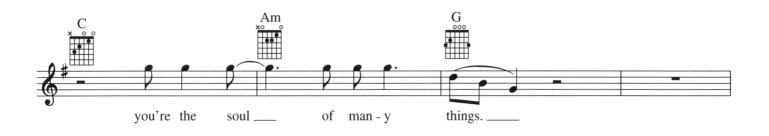

you're the soul ___ of man - y things. ___

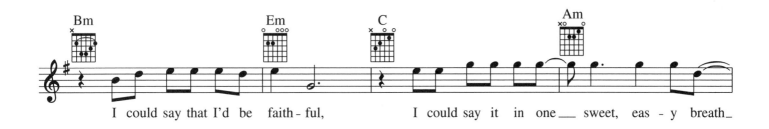

I could say that I'd be faith - ful, I could say it in one ___ sweet, eas - y breath ___

___ But to you that would be cruel - ty

and to me it sure - ly would be death. ___

D.C. al Coda ⊕   ⊕ *Coda*

Some - thin' there is a - bout ___ you ___ that I

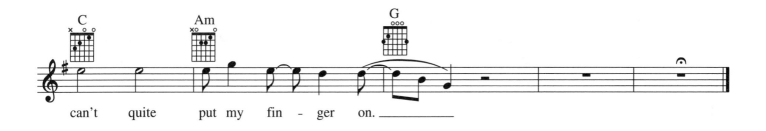

can't quite put my fin - ger on. ___

Solid Rock

Words and Music by Bob Dylan

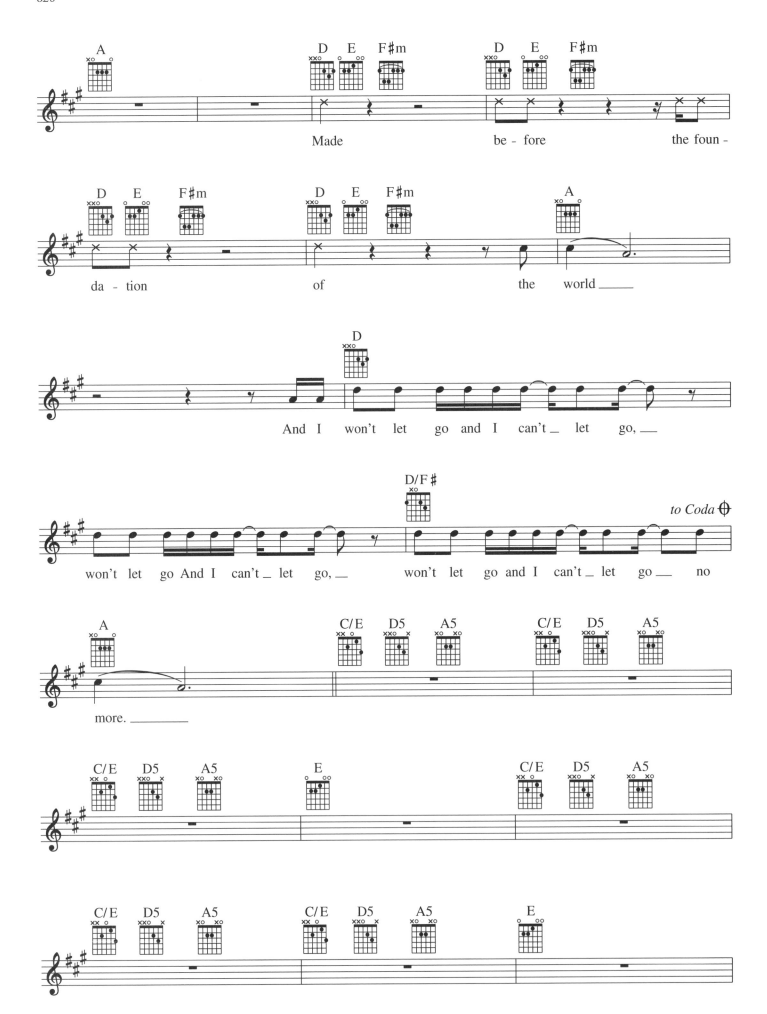

Song to Woody

Words and Music by Bob Dylan

Additional lyrics

2. Hey, hey Woody Guthrie, I wrote you a song
   'Bout a funny ol' world that's a-comin' along.
   Seems sick an' it's hungry, it's tired an' it's torn,
   It looks like it's a-dyin' an' it's hardly been born.

3. Hey, Woody Guthrie, but I know that you know
   All the things that I'm a-sayin' an' a-many times more.
   I'm a-singin' you the song, but I can't sing enough,
   'Cause there's not many men that done the things that you've done.

4. Here's to Cisco an' Sonny an' Leadbelly too,
   An' to all the good people that traveled with you.
   Here's to the hearts and the hands of the men
   That come with the dust and are gone with the wind.

5. I'm a-leavin' tomorrow, but I could leave today,
   Somewhere down the road someday.
   The very last thing that I'd want to do
   Is to say I've been hittin' some hard travelin' too.

Spanish Harlem Incident

Words and Music by Bob Dylan

Moderato

1. Gyp - sy gal, ___ the hands of Har - lem Can - not hold ___ you to its heat. ___ Your tem - pera - ture's ___ too hot for tam - ing, Your flam - ing feet ___ burn up the street. ___ I am home - less, come and take ___ me In - to reach of your rat - tling drums. ___

repeat two times

Let me know, babe, a - bout my for - tune Down a - long my rest - less palms. ___

Additional lyrics

2. Gypsy gal, you got me swallowed.
   I have fallen far beneath
   Your pearly eyes, so fast an' slashing,
   An' your flashing diamond teeth.
   The night is pitch black, come an' make my
   Pale face fit into place, ah, please!
   Let me know, babe, I got to know, babe,
   If it's you my lifelines trace.

3. I been wond'rin' all about me
   Ever since I seen you there.
   On the cliffs of your wildcat charms I'm riding,
   I know I'm 'round you but I don't know where.
   You have slayed me, you have made me,
   I got to laugh halfways off my heels.
   I got to know, babe, will I be touching you
   So I can tell if I'm really real.

Stack A Lee

Traditional, arranged by Bob Dylan

Briskly, in 2

1. Haw - lin Al - ley _____ on a dark and drizz - ly night, ___

Bil - ly Lyons and Stack - A - Lee had ___ one ter - ri - ble fight. All a -

bout _____ that John B. Stet - son hat. _____

Additional lyrics

2. Stack-A-Lee walked to the bar-room, and he called for a glass of beer,
   Turned around to Billy Lyons, said, "What are you doin' here?"
   "Waitin' for a train, please bring my woman home."

3. "Stack-A-Lee, oh Stack-A-Lee, please don't take my life.
   Got three little children and a-weepin', lovin' wife.
   You're a bad man, bad man, Stack-A-Lee."

4. "God bless your children and I'll take care of your wife.
   You stole my John B., now I'm bound to take your life."
   All about that John B. Stetson hat.

5. Stack-A-Lee turned to Billy Lyons and he shot him right through the head,
   Only taking one shot to kill Billy Lyons dead.
   All about that John B. Stetson hat.

6. Sent for the doctor, well the doctor he did come,
   Just pointed out Stack-A-Lee, said, "Now what have you done?
   You're a bad man, bad man, Stack-A-Lee."

7. Six big horses and a rubber-tired hack,
   Taking him to the cemetery, but they failed to bring him back.
   All about that John B. Stetson hat.

8. Hawlin Alley, thought I heard the bulldogs bark.
   It must have been old Stack-A-Lee stumbling in the dark.
   He's a bad man, gonna land him right back in jail.

9. High police walked on to Stack-A-Lee, he was lying fast asleep.
   High police walked on to Stack-A-Lee, and he jumped forty feet.
   He's a bad man, gonna land him right back in jail.

10. Well they got old Stack-A-Lee and they laid him right back in jail.
    Couldn't get a man around to go Stack-A Lee's bail.
    All about that John B. Stetson hat.

11. Stack-A-Lee turned to the jailer, he said, "Jailer, I can't sleep.
    'Round my bedside Billy Lyons began to creep."
    All about that John B. Stetson hat.

Standing in the Doorway
Words and Music by Bob Dylan

know if I saw you,   if I would kiss you or kill you

It prob-'ly would-n't mat-ter to you an-y-how __

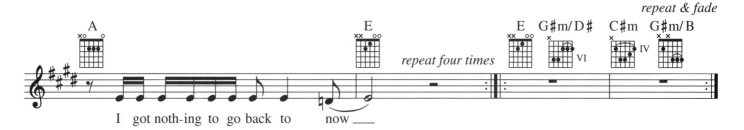

You left me stand-ing   in the door-way, cry-ing

repeat & fade

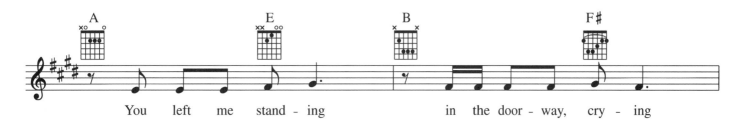

repeat four times

I got noth-ing to go back to   now __

Additional lyrics

2. The light in this place is so bad
   Making me sick in the head
   All the laughter is just making me sad
   The stars have turned cherry red
   I'm strumming on my gay guitar
   Smoking a cheap cigar
   The ghost of our old love has not gone away
   Don't look like it will anytime soon
   You left me standing in the doorway crying
   Under the midnight moon

3. Maybe they'll get me and maybe they won't
   But not tonight and it won't be here
   There are things I could say but I don't
   I know the mercy of God must be near
   I've been riding the midnight train
   Got ice water in my veins
   I would be crazy if I took you back
   It would go up against every rule
   You left me standing in the doorway, crying
   Suffering like a fool

4. When the last rays of daylight go down
   Buddy, you'll roll no more
   I can hear the church bells ringing in the yard
   I wonder who they're ringing for
   I know I can't win
   But my heart just won't give in
   Last night I danced with a stranger
   But she just reminded me you were the one
   You left me standing in the doorway crying
   In the dark land of the sun

5. I'll eat when I'm hungry, drink when I'm dry
   And live my life on the square
   And even if the flesh falls off of my face
   I know someone will be there to care
   It always means so much
   Even the softest touch
   I see nothing to be gained by any explanation
   There are no words that need to be said
   You left me standing in the doorway crying
   Blues wrapped around my head

Step It Up and Go

Traditional, arranged by Bob Dylan

Additional lyrics

3. Front door shut, back door too,
   Blinds pulled down, what' cha gonna do?
   Gotta step it up and go-Yeah, go,
   Can't stand pat, swear you gotta step it up and go.

4. Got a little girl, her name is Ball,
   Give a little bit, she took it all.
   I said step it up and go-Yeah, man,
   Can't stand pat, swear you gotta step it up and go.

5. Me an' my baby walkin' down the street,
   Tellin' everybody 'bout the chief of police.
   Gotta step it up and go-Yeah, go,
   Can't stand pat, swear you gotta step it up and go.

6. Tell my woman I'll see her at home,
   Ain't no lovin' since she been gone.
   Gotta step it up and go-Yeah, go,
   Can't stand pat, swear you gotta step it up and go.

7. Well, I'll sing this verse, ain't gonna sing no more,
   Hear my gal call me and I got to go.
   Step it up and go-Yeah, man,
   Can't stand pat, swear you gotta step it up and go.

Stuck Inside of Mobile
with the Memphis Blues Again

Words and Music by Bob Dylan

Chorus

Oh, Ma-ma, _____ can this real - ly be _____ the end, _____ To be stuck_

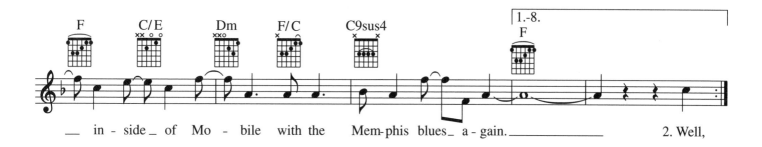

_ in - side _ of Mo - bile with the Mem-phis blues_ a - gain. _____ 2. Well,

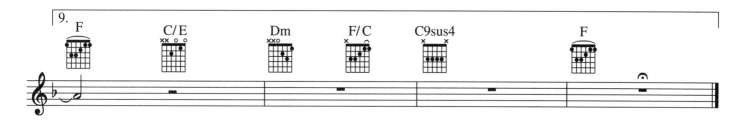

Additional lyrics

2. Well, Shakespeare, he's in the alley
   With his pointed shoes and his bells,
   Speaking to some French girl,
   Who says she knows me well.
   And I would send a message
   To find out if she's talked,
   But the post office has been stolen
   And the mailbox is locked.

   Chorus

3. Mona tried to tell me
   To stay away from the train line.
   She said that all the railroad men
   Just drink up your blood like wine.
   An' I said, "Oh, I didn't know that,
   But then again, there's only one I've met
   An' he just smoked my eyelids
   An' punched my cigarette."

   Chorus

4. Grandpa died last week
   And now he's buried in the rocks,
   But everybody still talks about
   How badly they were shocked.
   But me, I expected it to happen,
   I knew he'd lost control
   When he built a fire on Main Street
   And shot it full of holes.

   Chorus

5. Now the senator came down here
   Showing ev'ryone his gun,
   Handing out free tickets
   To the wedding of his son.
   An' me, I nearly got busted
   An' wouldn't it be my luck
   To get caught without a ticket
   And be discovered beneath a truck.

   Chorus

6. Now the preacher looked so baffled
When I asked him why he dressed
With twenty pounds of headlines
Stapled to his chest.
But he cursed me when I proved it to him,
Then I whispered, "Not even you can hide.
You see, you're just like me,
I hope you're satisfied."

Chorus

7. Now the rainman gave me two cures,
Then he said, "Jump right in."
The one was Texas medicine,
The other was just railroad gin.
An' like a fool I mixed them
An' it strangled up my mind,
An' now people just get uglier
An' I have no sense of time.

Chorus

8. When Ruthie says come see her
In her honky-tonk lagoon,
Where I can watch her waltz for free
'Neath her Panamanian moon.
An' I say, "Aw come on now,
You must know about my debutante."
An' she says, "Your debutante just knows what you need
But I know what you want."

Chorus

9. Now the bricks lay on Grand Street
Where the neon madmen climb.
They all fall there so perfectly,
It all seems so well timed.
An' here I sit so patiently
Waiting to find out what price
You have to pay to get out of
Going through all these things twice.

Chorus

Sweetheart Like You

Words and Music by Bob Dylan

Slowly, with a beat

1. Well, the pres-sure's down, the boss ain't here,_ He gone North,_ he ain't a-

round, _ They say that van-i-ty got the best of him But he sure_

left af-ter sun-down._ By the way, that's a cute hat, And that smile's_

____ so hard to re-sist But what's a sweet-heart like you do-

in' in a dump like this?_ 2. You know, I 3. You know, a

Bridge I

You know you can make a name for your-self, You can hear them tires_ squeal,

636

Additional lyrics

2. You know, I once knew a woman who looked like you,
   She wanted a whole man, not just a half,
   She used to call me sweet daddy when I was only a child,
   You kind of remind me of her when you laugh.
   In order to deal in this game, got to make the queen disappear,
   It's done with a flick of the wrist.
   What's a sweetheart like you doin' in a dump like this?

3. You know, a woman like you should be at home,
   That's where you belong,
   Watching out for someone who loves you true
   Who would never do you wrong.
   Just how much abuse will you be able to take?
   Well, there's no way to tell by that first kiss.
   What's a sweetheart like you doin' in a dump like this?

   Bridge 1:
   You know you can make a name for yourself,
   You can hear them tires squeal,
   You can be known as the most beautiful woman
   Who ever crawled across cut glass to make a deal.

4. You know, news of you has come down the line
   Even before ya came in the door.
   They say in your father's house, there's many mansions
   Each one of them got a fireproof floor.
   Snap out of it, baby, people are jealous of you,
   They smile to your face, but behind your back they hiss.
   What's a sweetheart like you doin' in a dump like this?

   Bridge 2:
   Got to be an important person to be in here, honey,
   Got to have done some evil deed,
   Got to have your own harem when you come in the door,
   Got to play your harp until your lips bleed.

5. They say that patriotism is the last refuge
   To which a scoundrel clings.
   Steal a little and they throw you in jail,
   Steal a lot and they make you king.
   There's only one step down from here, baby,
   It's called the land of permanent bliss.
   What's a sweetheart like you doin' in a dump like this?

Subterranean Homesick Blues

Words and Music by Bob Dylan

Additional lyrics

2. Maggie comes fleet foot
   Face full of black soot
   Talkin' that the heat put
   Plants in the bed but
   The phone's tapped anyway
   Maggie says that many say
   They must bust in early May
   Orders from the D. A.
   Look out kid
   Don't matter what you did
   Walk on your tip toes
   Don't try "No Doz"
   Better stay away from those
   That carry around a fire hose
   Keep a clean nose
   Watch the plain clothes
   You don't need a weather man
   To know which way the wind blows

3. Get sick, get well
   Hang around a ink well
   Ring bell, hard to tell
   If anything is goin' to sell
   Try hard, get barred
   Get back, write braille
   Get jailed, jump bail
   Join the army, if you fail
   Look out kid
   You're gonna get hit
   But users, cheaters
   Six-time losers
   Hang around the theaters
   Girl by the whirlpool
   Lookin' for a new fool
   Don't follow leaders
   Watch the parkin' meters

4. Ah get born, keep warm
   Short pants, romance, learn to dance
   Get dressed, get blessed
   Try to be a success
   Please her, please him, buy gifts
   Don't steal, don't lift
   Twenty years of schoolin'
   And they put you on the day shift
   Look out kid
   They keep it all hid
   Better jump down a manhole
   Light yourself a candle
   Don't wear sandals
   Try to avoid the scandals
   Don't wanna be a bum
   You better chew gum
   The pump don't work
   'Cause the vandals took the handles

T.V. Talkin' Song

Words and Music by Bob Dylan

With a moving funky beat

1. One time in Lon - don I'd gone out for a walk, Past a place called Hyde Park where peo - ple talk 'Bout all kinds of dif - f'rent gods, _ they have their point of view _ To an - y - one pass - ing by, _ that's who _ they're talk - ing to. _ 2. There was some - one on a plat - form talk - ing to the folks _ A - bout the T. _ _ V. _ god _ and all the pain that it in - vokes. _ "It's

too bright a light," he said, __ "for an-y-bod-y's eyes, __

If you've nev-er seen __ one, it's a bless-ing in dis-guise."__

Interlude (Instrumental ad lib.)

Instrumental ad lib.   repeat & fade

Additional lyrics

3. I moved in closer, got up on my toes,
   Two men in front of me were coming to blows
   The man was saying something 'bout children when they're young
   Being sacrificed to it while lullabies are being sung.

4. "The news of the day is on all the time,
   All the latest gossip, all the latest rhyme,
   Your mind is your temple, keep it beautiful and free,
   Don't let an egg get laid in it by something you can't see."

5. "Pray for peace!" he said, you could feel it in the crowd.
   My thoughts began to wander. His voice was ringing loud,
   "It will destroy your family, your happy home is gone
   No one can protect you from it once you turn it on."

6. "It will led you into some strange pursuits,
   Lead you to the land of forbidden fruits.
   It will scramble up your head and drag your brain about,
   Sometimes you gotta do like Elvis did and shoot the damn thing out."

7. "It's all been designed," he said, "To make you lose your mind,
   And when you go back to find it, there's nothing there to find."
   "Everytime you look at it, your situation's worse,
   If you feel it grabbing out for you, send for the nurse."

8. The crowd began to riot and they grabbed hold of the man,
   There was pushing, there was shoving and everybody ran.
   The T.V. crew was there to film it, they jumped right over me,
   Later on that evening, I watched it on T.V.

Talkin' World War III Blues

Words and Music by Bob Dylan

Additional lyrics

2. I said, "Hold it, Doc, a World War passed through my brain."
   He said, "Nurse, get your pad, this boy's insane,"
   He grabbed my arm, I said "Ouch!"
   As I landed on the psychiatric couch,
   He said, "Tell me about it."

3. Well, the whole thing started at 3 o'clock fast,
   It was all over by quarter past.
   I was down in the sewer with some little lover
   When I peeked out from a manhole cover
   Wondering who turned the lights on.

4. Well, I got up and walked around
   And up and down the lonesome town.
   I stood a-wondering which way to go,
   I lit a cigarette on a parking meter
   And walked on down the road.
   It was a normal day.

5. Well, I rung the fallout shelter bell
   And I leaned my head and I gave a yell,
   "Give me a string bean, I'm a hungry man."
   A shotgun fired and away I ran.
   I don't blame them too much though,
   I know I look funny.

6. Down at the corner by a hot-dog stand
   I seen a man, I said, "Howdy friend,
   I guess there's just us two."
   He screamed a bit and away he flew.
   Thought I was a Communist.

7. Well, I spied a girl and before she could leave,
   "Let's go and play Adam and Eve."
   I took her by the hand and my heart it was thumpin'
   When she said, "Hey man, you crazy or sumpin',
   You see what happened last time they started."

8. Well, I seen a Cadillac window uptown
   And there was nobody aroun'
   I got into the driver's seat
   And I drove 42nd Street
   In my Cadillac.
   Good car to drive after a war.

9. Well, I remember seein' some ad,
   So I turned on my Conelrad.
   But I didn't pay my Con Ed bill,
   So the radio didn't work so well.
   Turned on my record player-
   It was Rock-A-Day, Johnny singin',
   "Tell Your Ma, Tell Your Pa,
   Our Loves Are Gonna Grow Ooh-wah, Ooh-wah."

10. I was feelin' kinda lonesome and blue,
    I needed somebody to talk to.
    So I called up the operator of time
    Just to hear a voice of some kind.
    "When you hear the beep
    It will be three o'clock,"
    She said that for over an hour
    And I hung it up.

11. Well, the doctor interrupted me just about then,
    Sayin, "Hey I've been havin' the same old dreams,
    But mine was a little different you see.
    I dreamt that the only person left after the war was me.
    I didn't see you around."

12. Well, now time passed and now it seems
    Everybody's having them dreams.
    Everybody sees themselves walkin' around with no one else.
    Half of the people can be part right all of the time,
    Some of the people can be all right part of the time.
    I think Abraham Lincoln said that.
    "I'll let you be in my dreams if I can be in yours,"
    I said that.

Tangled Up in Blue

Words and Music by Bob Dylan

Moderately, in 2

1. Ear - ly one morn - in' the sun was shin - in', I was lay - in' in bed ____

____ Won - d'rin' if ____ she'd changed at all ____ If her hair ____ was still

red. Her folks, they said our lives ____ to - geth - er

Sure was gon - na be rough ____ They nev - er did like ____ Ma - ma's

home - made dress, ____ Pa - pa's bank - book was - n't big e - nough. And

Additional lyrics

2. She was married when we first met
Soon to be divorced
I helped her out of a jam, I guess,
But I used a little too much force.
We drove that car as far as we could
Abandoned it out West
Split up on a dark sad night
Both agreeing it was best.
She turned around to look at me
As I was walkin' away
I heard her say over my shoulder,
"We'll meet again someday on the avenue,"
Tangled up in blue.

3. I had a job in the great north woods
Working as a cook for a spell
But I never did like it all that much
And one day the ax just fell.
So I drifted down to New Orleans
Where I happened to be employed
Workin' for a while on a fishin' boat
Right outside of Delacroix.
But all the while I was alone
The past was close behind,
I seen a lot of women
But she never escaped my mind, and I just grew
Tangled up in blue.

4. She was workin' in a topless place
   And I stopped in for a beer,
   I just kept lookin' at the side of her face
   In the spotlight so clear.
   And later on as the crowd thinned out
   I's just about to do the same,
   She was standing there in back of my chair
   Said to me, "Don't I know your name?"
   I muttered somethin' underneath my breath,
   She studied the lines on my face.
   I must admit I felt a little uneasy
   When she bent down to tie the laces of my shoe,
   Tangled up in blue.

5. She lit a burner on the stove and offered me a pipe
   "I thought you'd never say hello," she said
   "You look like the silent type."
   Then she opened up a book of poems
   And handed it to me
   Written by an Italian poet
   From the thirteenth century.
   And every one of them words rang true
   And glowed like burnin' coal
   Pourin' off of every page
   Like it was written in my soul from me to you,
   Tangled up in blue.

6. I lived with them on Montague Street
   In a basement down the stairs,
   There was music in the cafés at night
   And revolution in the air.
   Then he started into dealing with slaves
   And something inside of him died.
   She had to sell everything she owned
   And froze up inside.
   And when finally the bottom fell out
   I became withdrawn,
   The only thing I knew how to do
   Was to keep on keepin' on like a bird that flew,
   Tangled up in blue.

7. So now I'm goin' back again,
   I got to get to her somehow.
   All the people we used to know
   They're an illusion to me now.
   Some are mathematicians
   Some are carpenter's wives.
   Don't know how it all got started,
   I don't know what they're doin' with their lives.
   But me, I'm still on the road
   Headin' for another joint
   We always did feel the same,
   We just saw it from a different point of view,
   Tangled up in blue.

Tell Me, Momma

Words and Music by Bob Dylan

Additional lyrics

2. Hey, John, come and get me some candy goods
   Shucks, it sure feels like it's in the woods
   Spend some time on your January trips
   You got tombstone moose up and your brave-yard whips
   If you're anxious to find out when your friendship's gonna end
   Come on, baby, I'm your friend!
   And I know that you know that I know that you show
   Something is tearing up your mind.

   Chorus

3. Ohh, we bone the editor, can't get read
   But his painted sled, instead it's a bed
   Yes, I see you on your window ledge
   But I can't tell just how far away you are from the edge
   And, anyway, you're just gonna make people jump and roar
   Whatcha wanna go and do that for?
   For I know that you know that I know that you know
   Something is tearing up your mind.

   Chorus

Tears of Rage

Words and Music by Bob Dylan and Richard Manuel

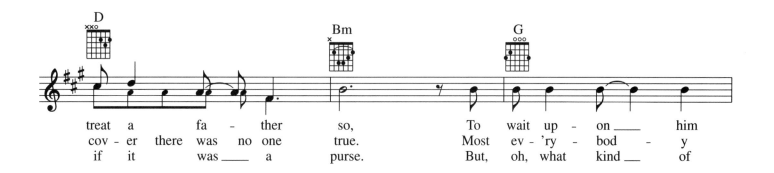

treat a fa - ther so,
cov - er there was no one true.
if it was ____ a purse.

To wait up - on ____ him
Most ev - 'ry - bod - y
But, oh, what kind ____ of

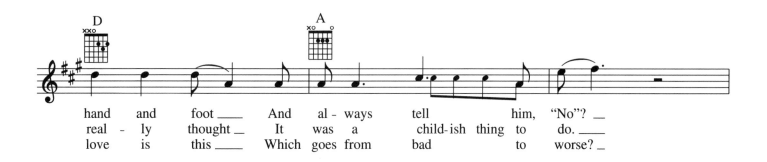

hand and foot ____ And al - ways tell him, "No"? __
real - ly thought __ It was a child-ish thing to do. ____
love is this ____ Which goes from bad to worse? __

Tears of rage, tears of grief, ___ Why must I al - ways
Tears of rage, tears of grief, ___ Must I al - ways
Tears of rage, tears of grief, ___ Must I al - ways

be the thief? Come to me now, _ you know We're so a - lone
be the thief? Come to me now, _ you know We're so ____ low
be the thief? Come to me now, _ you know We're so ____ low

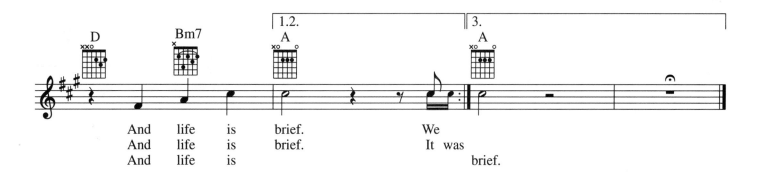

And life is brief. We
And life is brief. It was
And life is brief.

Tell Me That It Isn't True

Words and Music by Bob Dylan

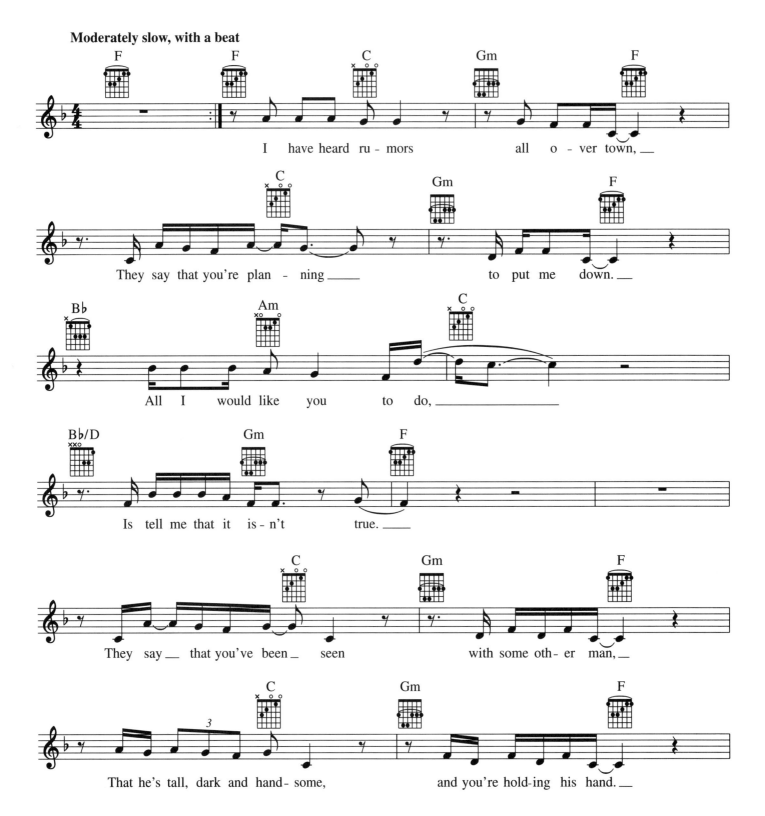

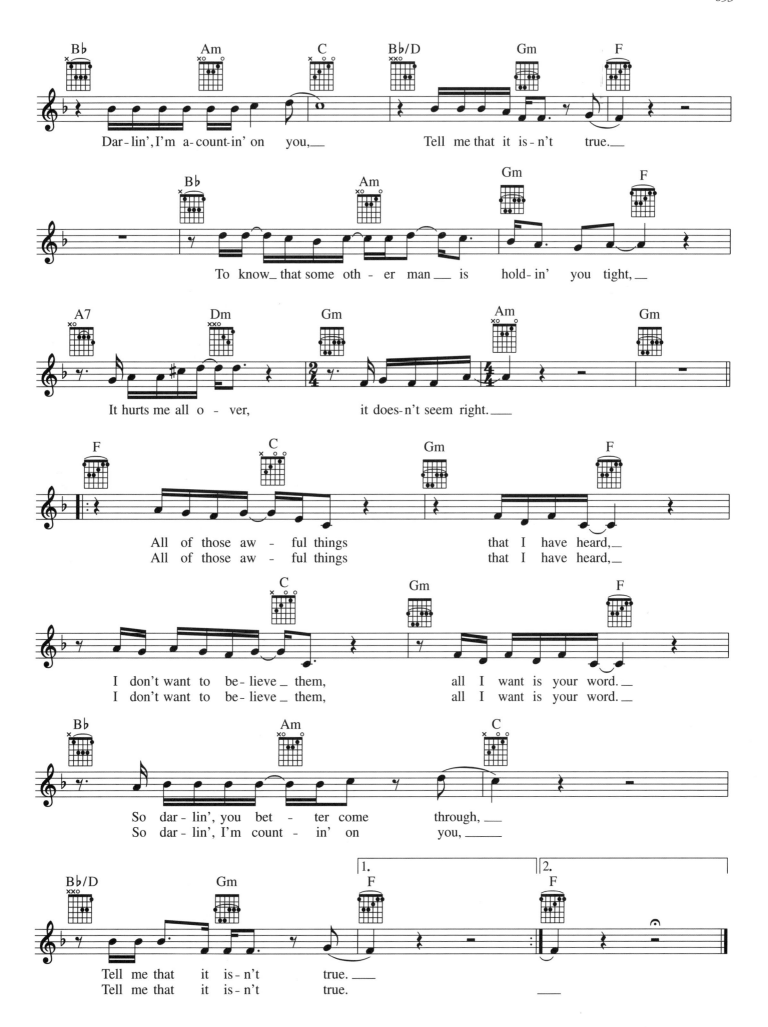

Temporary Like Achilles

Words and Music by Bob Dylan

Moderately slow, with a feeling of $\frac{12}{8}$

1. Stand - ing on your win - dow, hon - ey, Yes, I've __ been here be - fore.__
2. Kneel - ing 'neath your ceil - ing, Yes, I guess I'll __ be here for a while.__

rush in - to your hall - way, Lean a - gainst your vel - vet door.

chil - les is in your al - ley - way, He don't want __ me here, He does brag.__

__
__
__
__

Feel - ing so __ harm - less, __ I'm

I'm tryin' to read your por - trait, _ but, I'm

I watch up - on your scor - pion __ Who

He's point - ing to the sky And he's

look - ing at your sec - ond __ door. __

help - less, like a rich man's _ child. __

crawls a - cross your cir - cus floor. __

hun - gry, like a man in __ drag. __

How come __ you __ don't __ send me no _____ re - gards? _____

How come __ you __ send __ some - one out _____ to have me _____ barred?__

Just what __ do __ you __ think _____ you have to _____ guard?__

How come __ you get some - one like him _____ to be your _____ guard?__

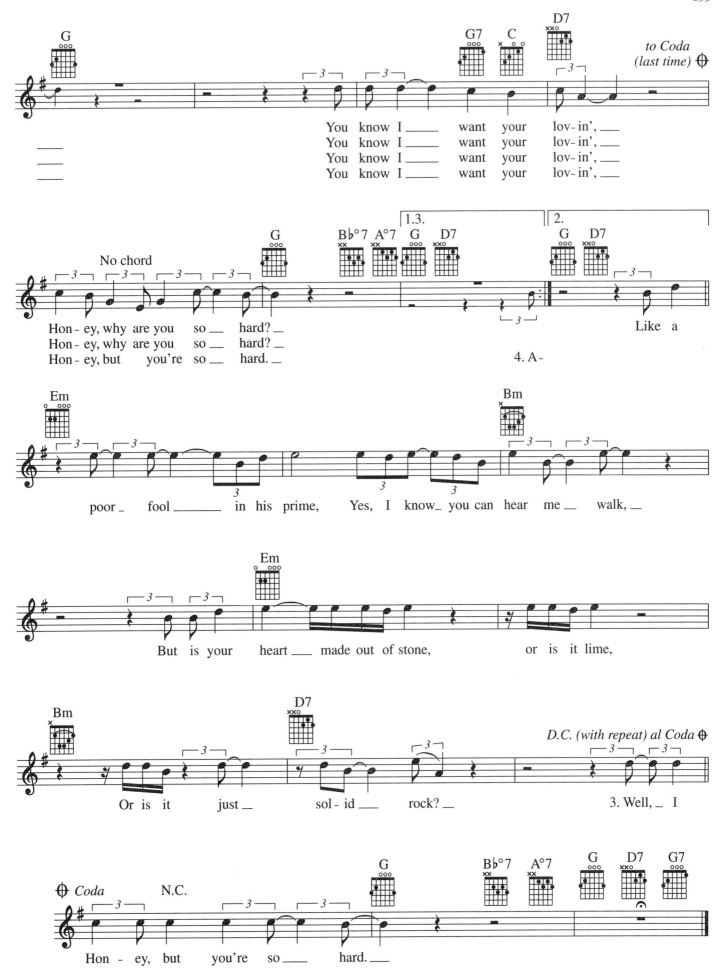

Things Have Changed

Words and Music by Bob Dylan

A wor-ried man with a wor-ried mind No one in front of me and

noth-ing be-hind __ There's a wom-an on my lap __ and she's drink-ing cham -

pagne __ Got white skin, got as - sas-sin's eyes __

I'm look-ing up in-to the sap-phire tint-ed skies __ I'm well __ dressed,

wait-ing on the last train __ Stand-ing on the gal-lows with my __

head ___ in a noose ___ An - y

min - ute now I'm ex - pect - ing all hell _____ to break loose

Peo - ple are cra - zy and times ___ are strange I'm

locked in tight, ___ I'm out of range I used to care, but

things have changed ___

1.-3. 4.

Additional lyrics

2. This place ain't doing me any good
   I'm in the wrong town, I should be in Hollywood
   Just for a second there I thought I saw something move
   Gonna take dancing lessons do the jitterbug rag
   Ain't no shortcuts, gonna dress in drag
   Only a fool in here would think he's got anything to prove

Bridge #2:
Lot of water under the bridge, Lot of other stuff too
Don't get up gentlemen, I'm only passing through

Chorus

3. I've been walking forty miles of bad road
   If the bible is right, the world will explode
   I've been trying to get as far away from myself as I can
   Some things are too hot to touch
   The human mind can only stand so much
   You can't win with a losing hand

Bridge #3:
Feel like falling in love with the first woman I meet
Putting her in a wheel barrow and wheeling her down the street

Chorus

4. I hurt easy, I just don't show it
   You can hurt someone and not even know it
   The next sixty seconds could be like an eternity
   Gonna get low down, gonna fly high
   All the truth in the world adds up to one big lie
   I'm in love with a woman who don't even appeal to me

Bridge #4:
Mr. Jinx and Miss Lucy, they jumped in the lake
I'm not that eager to make a mistake

Chorus

Tight Connection to My Heart
(*Has Anybody Seen My Love?*)

Words and Music by Bob Dylan

Additional lyrics

2. You want to talk to me,
   Go ahead and talk.
   Whatever you got to say to me
   Won't come as any shock.
   I must be guilty of something,
   You just whisper it into my ear.
   Madame Butterfly
   She lulled me to sleep,
   In a town without pity
   Where the water runs deep.
   She said, "Be easy, baby,
   There ain't nothin' worth stealin' in here."

   You're the one I've been looking for,
   You're the one that's got the key.
   But I can't figure out whether I'm too good for you
   Or you're too good for me.

   Chorus

3. Well, they're not showing any lights tonight
   And there's no moon.
   There's just a hot-blooded singer
   Singing "Memphis in June,"
   While they're beatin' the devil out of a guy
   Who's wearing a powder-blue wig.
   Later he'll be shot
   For resisting arrest,
   I can still hear his voice crying
   In the wilderness.
   What looks large from a distance,
   Close up ain't never that big.

   Never could learn to drink that blood
   And call it wine,
   Never could learn to hold you, love,
   And call you mine.

This Wheel's on Fire

Words and Music by Bob Dylan and Rick Danko

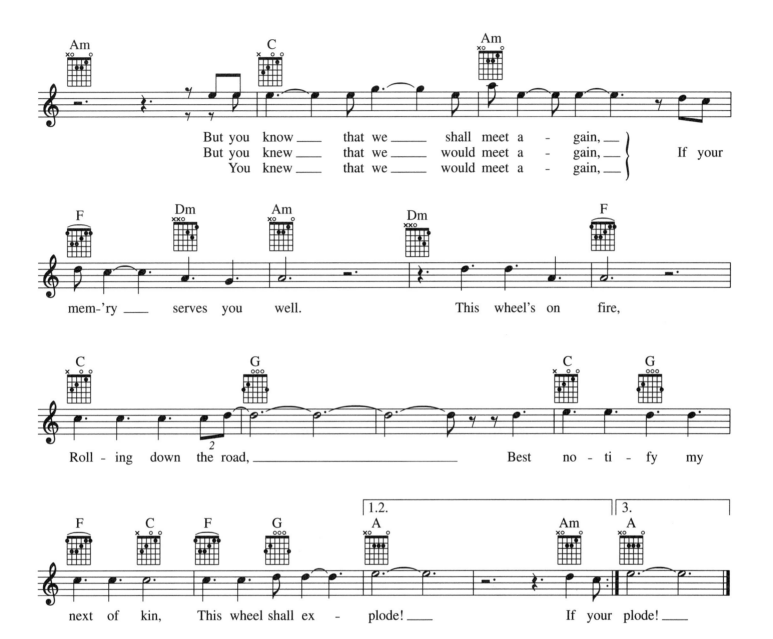

But you know ___ that we ___ shall meet a - gain, ___
But you knew ___ that we ___ would meet a - gain, ___
You knew ___ that we ___ would meet a - gain, ___ } If your

mem-'ry ___ serves you well. This wheel's on fire,

Roll - ing down the road, _____ Best no - ti - fy my

next of kin, This wheel shall ex - plode! ___ If your plode! ___

Three Angels

Words and Music by Bob Dylan

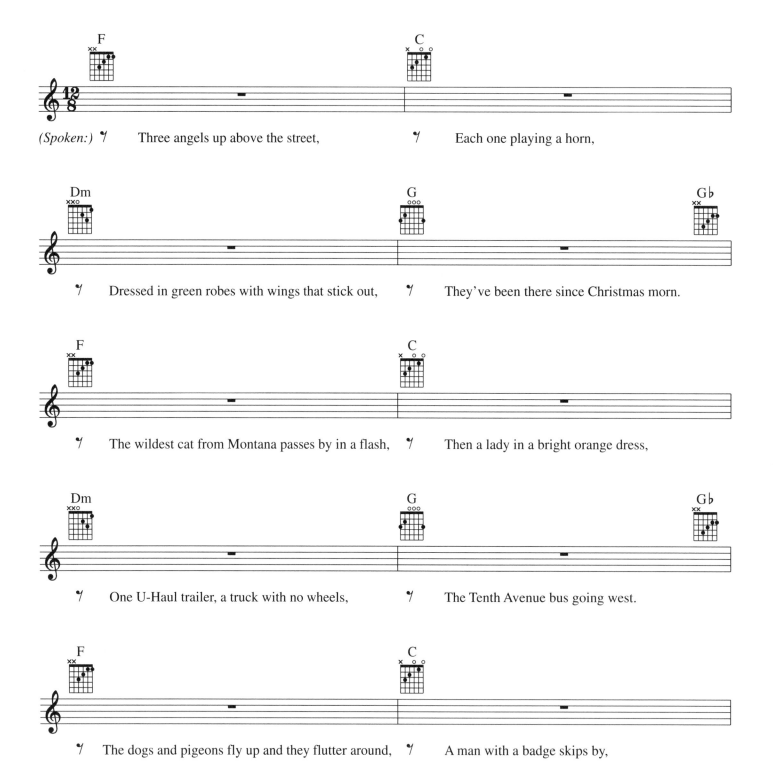

(Spoken:) Three angels up above the street,   Each one playing a horn,

Dressed in green robes with wings that stick out,   They've been there since Christmas morn.

The wildest cat from Montana passes by in a flash,   Then a lady in a bright orange dress,

One U-Haul trailer, a truck with no wheels,   The Tenth Avenue bus going west.

The dogs and pigeons fly up and they flutter around,   A man with a badge skips by,

Dm	G	G♭

𝄽   Three fellas crawlin' on their way back to work,   𝄽   Nobody stops to ask why.

F	C

𝄽   The bakery truck stops outside of that fence   𝄽   Where the angels stand high on their poles,

Dm	G	G♭

𝄽   The driver peeks out, trying to find one face   𝄽   In this concrete world full of souls.

F	C

𝄽   The angels play on their horns all day,   𝄽   The whole earth in progression seems to pass by.

Dm	A♭	B♭ C

𝄽   But does anyone hear the music they play,   𝄽   Does anyone even try?   𝄽

'Til I Fell in Love with You

Words and Music by Bob Dylan

Noth-ing can heal me now, but your

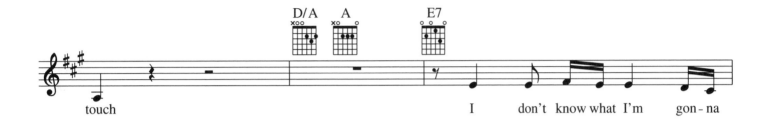

touch I don't know what I'm gon-na

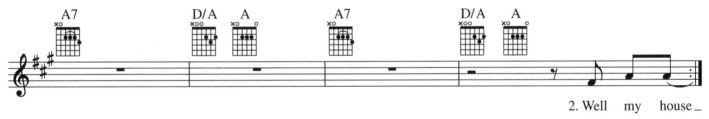

do I was all right 'til I _____ fell in love with you

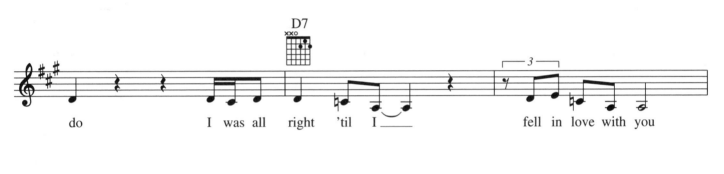

2. Well my house _

Additional lyrics

2. Well my house is on fire; burning to the sky
   I thought it would rain but the clouds passed by
   Now I feel like I'm coming to the end of my way
   But I know God is my shield and he won't lead me astray
   Still I don't know what I'm gonna do
   I was all right 'til I fell in love with you

3. Boys in the street beginning to play
   Girls like birds flying away
   When I'm gone you will remember my name
   I'm gonna win my way to wealth and fame
   I don't know what I'm gonna do
   I was all right 'til I fell in love with you

4. Junk is piling up; taking up space
   My eyes feel like they're falling off my face
   Sweat falling down, I'm staring at the floor
   I'm thinking about that girl who won't be back no more
   I don't know what I'm gonna do
   I was all right 'til I fell in love with you

5. Well I'm tired of talking; I'm tired of trying to explain
   My attempts to please you were all in vain
   Tomorrow night before the sun goes down
   If I'm still among the living, I'll be Dixie bound
   I just don't know what I'm gonna do
   I was all right 'til I fell in love with you.

6. *Instrumental*

The Times They Are A-Changin'

Words and Music by Bob Dylan

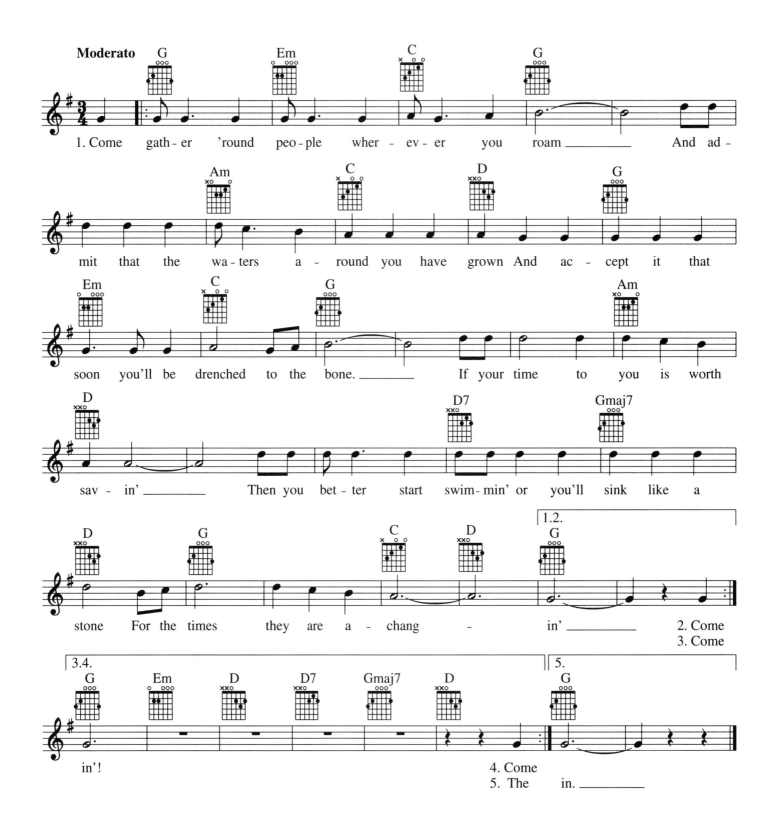

Additional lyrics

2. Come writers and critics
   Who prophesize with your pen
   And keep your eyes wide
   The chance won't come again
   And don't speak too soon
   For the wheel's still in spin
   And there's no tellin' who
   That it's namin'.
   For the loser now
   Will be later to win
   For the times they are a-changin'.

3. Come senators, congressmen
   Please heed the call
   Don't stand in the doorway
   Don't block up the hall
   For he that gets hurt
   Will be he who has stalled
   There's a battle outside
   And it is ragin'.
   It'll soon shake your windows
   And rattle your walls
   For the times they are a-changin'.

4. Come mothers and fathers
   Throughout the land
   And don't criticize
   What you can't understand
   Your sons and your daughters
   Are beyond your command
   Your old road is
   Rapidly agin'.
   Please get out of the new one
   If you can't lend your hand
   For the times they are a-changin'.

5. The line it is drawn
   The curse it is cast
   The slow one now
   Will later be fast
   As the present now
   Will later be past
   The order is
   Rapidly fadin'.
   And the first one now
   Will later be last
   For the times they are a-changin'.

To Be Alone with You

Words and Music by Bob Dylan

To Ramona

Words and Music by Bob Dylan

Additional lyrics

2. Your cracked country lips,
   I still wish to kiss,
   As to be under the strength of your skin.
   Your magnetic movements
   Still capture the minutes I'm in.
   But it grieves my heart, love,
   To see you tryin' to be a part of
   A world that just don't exist.
   It's all just a dream, babe,
   A vacuum, a scheme, babe,
   That sucks you into feelin' like this.

3. I can see that your head
   Has been twisted and fed
   By worthless foam from the mouth.
   I can tell you are torn
   Between stayin' and returnin'
   On back to the South.
   You've been fooled into thinking
   That the finishin' end is at hand.
   Yet there's no one to beat you,
   No one t' defeat you,
   'Cept the thoughts of yourself feeling bad.

4. I've heard you say many times
   That you're better 'n no one
   And no one is better 'n you.
   If you really believe that,
   You know you got
   Nothing to win and nothing to lose.
   From fixtures and forces and friends,
   Your sorrow does stem,
   That hype you and type you,
   Making you feel
   That you must be exactly like them.

5. I'd forever talk to you,
   But soon my words,
   They would turn into a meaningless ring.
   For deep in my heart
   I know there is no help I can bring.
   Everything passes,
   Everything changes,
   Just do what you think you should do.
   And someday maybe,
   Who knows, baby,
   I'll come and be cryin' to you.

Tombstone Blues

Words and Music by Bob Dylan

Very bright in 2

Verse

1. The sweet pret-ty things are in bed now of course The
2.-6. *See additional lyrics*

cit-y fa-thers they're try-ing to en-dorse _____ The

re-in-car-na-tion of Paul Re-vere's horse But the

town has no need to be nerv-ous _____

The ghost of Belle Starr she hands down her wits To

Jez-e-bel and nun she vi-o-lent-ly knits _____ A

Additional lyrics

2. The hysterical bride in the penny arcade
   Screaming she moans, "I've just been made"
   Then sends out for the doctor who pulls down the shade
   Says, "My advice is to not let the boys in"

   Now the medicine man comes and he shuffles inside
   He walks with a swagger and he says to the bride
   "Stop all this weeping, swallow your pride
   You will not die, it's not poison"

   Chorus

3. Well, John the Baptist after torturing a thief
   Looks up at his hero the Commander-in-Chief
   Saying, "Tell me great hero, but please make it brief
   Is there a hole for me to get sick in?"

   The Commander-in-Chief answers him while chasing a fly
   Saying, "Death to all those who would whimper and cry"
   And dropping a bar bell he points to the sky
   Saving, "The sun's not yellow it's chicken"

   Chorus

4. The king of the Philistines his soldiers to save
   Put jawbones on their tombstones and flatters their graves
   Puts the pied pipers in prison and fattens the slaves
   Then sends them out to the jungle

   Gypsy Davey with a blowtorch he burns out their camps
   With his faithful slave Pedro behind him he tramps
   With a fantastic collection of stamps
   To win friends and influence his uncle

   Chorus

5. The geometry of innocence flesh on the bone
   Causes Galileo's math book to get thrown
   At Delilah who sits worthlessly alone
   But the tears on her cheeks are from laughter

   Now I wish I could give Brother Bill his great thrill
   I would set him in chains at the top of the hill
   Then send out for some pillars and Cecil B. DeMille
   He could die happily ever after

   Chorus

6. Where Ma Raney and Beethoven once unwrapped their bed roll
   Tuba players now rehearse around the flagpole
   And the National Bank at a profit sells road maps for the soul
   To the old folks home and the college

   Now I wish I could write you a melody so plain
   That could hold you dear lady from going insane
   That could ease you and cool you and cease the pain
   Of your useless and pointless knowledge

   Chorus

Tonight I'll Be Staying Here with You

Words and Music by Bob Dylan

Moderately slow, with a beat

Throw my tick- et out the win – dow,

Throw my suit - case out there, too, ___ Throw my

trou - bles out the door, I don't need them an - y more 'Cause to -

night I'll be stay - ing here with you.

I should have left this town ___ this morn- ing But it was more than I could

do. Oh, your love comes on so strong And I've

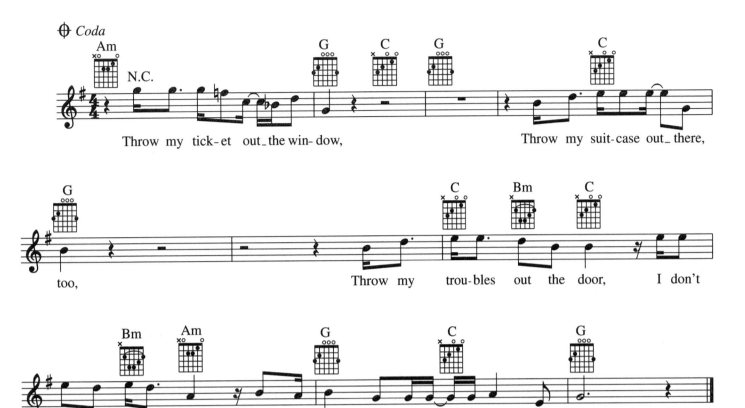

Coda

Throw my tick- et out the win- dow, Throw my suit-case out there,

too, Throw my trou-bles out the door, I don't

need them an- y more 'Cause to- night I'll be stay - ing here with you.

Tough Mama

Words and Music by Bob Dylan

Additional lyrics

2. Dark Beauty
   Won't you move it on over and make some room?
   It's my duty to bring you down to the field where the flowers bloom.
   Ashes in the furnace, dust on the rise,
   You came through it all the way, flyin' through the skies.
   Dark Beauty
   With that long night's journey in your eyes.

3. Sweet Goddess
   Born of a blinding light and a changing wind,
   Now, don't be modest, you know who you are and where you've been.
   Jack the Cowboy went up north
   He's buried in your past.
   The Lone Wolf went out drinking
   That was over pretty fast.
   Sweet Goddess
   Your perfect stranger's comin' in at last.

4. Silver Angel
   With the badge of the lonesome road sewed in your sleeve,
   I'd be grateful if this golden ring you would receive.
   Today on the countryside it was a-hotter than a crotch,
   I stood alone upon the ridge and all I did was watch.
   Sweet Goddess
   It must be time to carve another notch.

5. I'm crestfallen
   The world of illusion is at my door,
   I ain't a-haulin' any of my lambs to the marketplace anymore.
   The prison walls are crumblin', there is no end in sight,
   I've gained some recognition but I lost my appetite.
   Dark Beauty
   Meet me at the border late tonight.

Trouble

Words and Music by Bob Dylan

side of the world, __ you'll find trou-ble there. _____

C   **D**   **Am**

Rev-o-lu - tion e-ven ain't no so-lu-tion for trou-ble. __

Chorus

Trou - ble,   Trou - ble,   trou - ble,

to Coda ⊕ |1. |2.   *D.S. al Coda* ⊕

trou - ble,   Noth-in' but   trou - ble.

⊕ *Coda* |1.

|2.

Trou - ble,   Trou - ble,

repeat & fade

trou-ble,   trou-ble,   trou-ble,   Noth-in' but   trou-ble.

Additional lyrics

3. Drought and starvation, packaging of the soul,
   Persecution, execution, governments out of control.
   You can see the writing on the wall inviting trouble.

   Chorus

4. Put your ear to the train tracks, put your ear to the ground,
   You ever feel like you're never alone even when there's nobody else around?
   Since the beginning of the universe man's been cursed by trouble.

   Chorus

5. Nightclubs of the broken-hearted, stadiums of the damned,
   Legislature, perverted nature, doors that are rudely slammed.
   Look into infinity, all you see is trouble.

   Chorus

Trust Yourself

Words and Music by Bob Dylan

Moderately

A7

Trust your-self, _

Trust your-self to do the things that on-ly
Trust your-self to know the way that will prove true

you know best. _ Trust your-self, _   Trust your-self to do what's right and not be
in the end. _ Trust your-self, _   Trust your-self to find the path where there is

sec-ond-guessed. _   Don't trust me _ to show _ you beau-ty _   When
no if and when. _   Don't trust me _ to show _ you the truth _   When the

beau-ty may on - ly turn to rust. _   If you need some-bod-y you can
truth may on-ly be ash-es and dust. _   If you want some-bod-y you can

trust,   trust your - self. ____   Trust your - self,_
trust,   trust your - self. _

_   Well, you're on ____ your own, _   you

al - ways were, _   In a land _ of wolves _ and thieves. _   Don't

put your hope _ in un - god - ly man _ Or be a slave to what some-bod - y else be -

lieves. _   (Oh, _) trust your - self ____   And you won't _

_ be dis - ap - point - ed when vain peo - ple let you down. Trust your - self   And

look not for an - swers where no an - swers can be found.   Don't trust me to show you love _

_____ When my love may be on-ly lust. _____ If you

want some-bod-y you can trust, trust your-self. _____

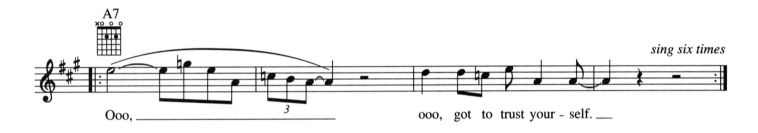

sing six times

Ooo, _____ ooo, got to trust your-self. _____

repeat & fade

Trust your-self. _____ Trust your-self. _____

Tryin' to Get to Heaven

Words and Music by Bob Dylan

Moderately

1. The air is get-ting hot-ter _____
3.-6. *See additional lyrics*

There's a rum-bl-ing in the skies___ I've been wad-ing through the high___

mud-dy wat-er With the heat ris - ing in my eyes

Ev - ery day your mem-o - ry grows dim - mer

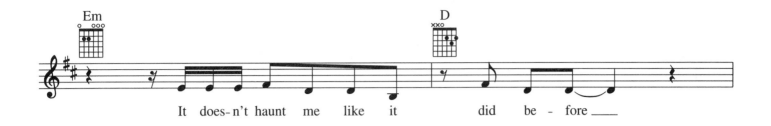

It does-n't haunt me like it did be - fore ___

I've been walk - ing through the mid - dle of no - where ___

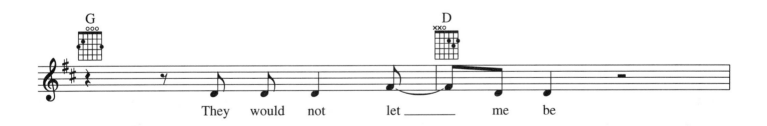

Trying to get ___ to heaven ___ be - fore ___ they close ___ the door

2. When I was in Mis - sour - i

They would not let ___ me be

I had to leave there in a hur - ry

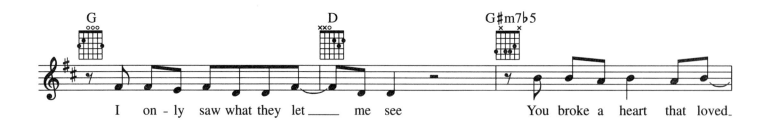

I on-ly saw what they let _____ me see   You broke a heart that loved_

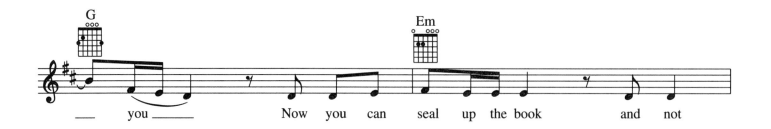

_____ you _____   Now you can seal up the book   and not

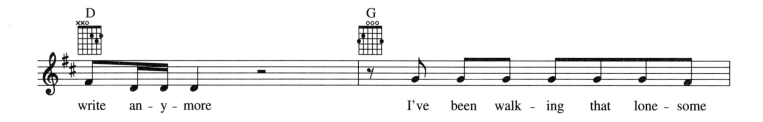

write an-y-more   I've been walk-ing that lone-some

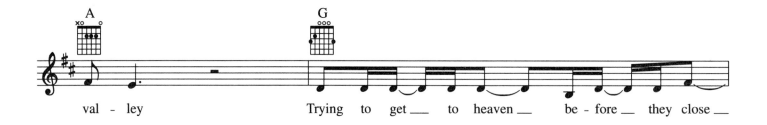

val-ley   Trying to get _ to heaven _ be-fore _ they close _

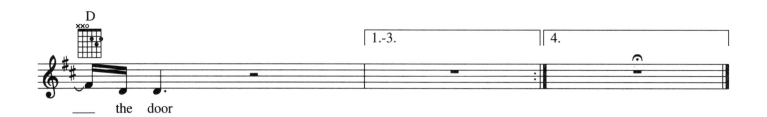

_ the door

Additional lyrics

3. People on the platforms
   Waiting for the trains
   I can hear their hearts a-beatin'
   Like pendulums swinging on chains
   When you think that you lost everything
   You find out you can always lose a little more
   I'm just going down the road feeling bad
   Trying to get to heaven before they close the door

4. *Instrumental*

5. I'm going down the river
   Down to New Orleans
   They tell me everything is gonna be all right
   But I don't know what "all right" even means
   I was riding in a buggy with Miss Mary-Jane
   Miss Mary-Jane got a house in Baltimore
   I been all around the world, boys
   Now I'm trying to get to heaven before they close the door

6. Gonna sleep down in the parlor
   And relive my dreams
   I'll close my eyes and I wonder
   If everything is as hollow as it seems
   Some trains don't pull no gamblers
   No midnight ramblers, like they did before
   I been to Sugar Town, I shook the sugar down
   Now I'm trying to get to heaven before they close the door

Two Soldiers

Traditional, arranged by Bob Dylan

Waltz tempo

1. He was just a blue - eyed Bos - ton boy, _____ His voice was

low with pain. _____ "I'll do your bid - ding, com - rade

mine, _____ If I ride back a - gain. _____

___ But if you ride back ___ and I am left, You'll do as much ___ for

me. _____ Moth- er, you know, must hear the news, _____

_____ So write to her ten - der - ly. _____

Additional lyrics

2. "She's waiting at home like a patient saint,
   Her fond face pale with woe.
   Her heart will be broken when I am gone,
   I'll see her soon, I know."
   Just then the order came to charge,
   For an instance hand touched hand.
   They said, "Aye," and away they rode,
   That brave and devoted band.

3. Straight was the track to the top of the hill,
   The rebels they shot and shelled,
   Plowed furrows of death through the toiling ranks,
   And guarded them as they fell.
   There soon came a horrible dying yell
   From heights that they could not gain,
   And those whom doom and death had spared
   Rode slowly back again.

4. But among the dead that were left on the hill
   Was the boy with the curly hair.
   The tall dark man who rode by his side
   Lay dead beside him there.
   There's no one to write to the blue-eyed girl
   The words that her lover had said.
   Momma, you know, awaits the news,
   And she'll only know he's dead.

Ugliest Girl in the World

Words and Music by Bob Dylan and Robert Hunter

Medium rock

1. Well, the

wom-an that I love she got a hook in her nose   Her eye - brows meet, she wears
2. If I ev- er lose her I will go___ in-sane   I go half cra - zy when she

sec-ond hand clothes   She speaks with a stut- ter and she walks with a hop   I
calls_ my name When she says, "ba - ba ba-ba ba - by, I l - l - love you"   There ain't

don't know why I love her but I just can't stop   You know _ I ___ love her
noth-ing in the world that I would-n't do

Chorus

Yeah I love her   I'm in love with the

Additional lyrics

3. The woman that I love she got two flat feet
   Her knees knock together walking down the street
   She cracks her knuckles and she snores in bed
   She ain't much to look at but like I said

   Chorus

4. I don't mean to say that she got nothing goin'
   She got a weird sense of humor that's all her own
   When I get low she sets me on my feet
   Got a five inch smile but her breath is sweet

   Chorus

5. The woman that I love she a got a prizefighter nose
   Cauliflower ears and a run in her hose
   She speaks with a stutter and she walks with a hop
   I don't know why I love her but I just can't stop

Unbelievable

Words and Music by Bob Dylan

Moderately bright, with a driving shuffle beat (♪♩ = ♩.♪)

It's un - be -

liev - a - ble, it's strange but true, _____ It's in - con -

ceiv - a - ble it could hap - pen to you. ___

You go north __ and you __ go south __ Just like bait __ in the

fish - 's mouth. __ Ya must be liv - in' in the shad- ow of some kind of e - vil star. __

It's un - be - liev - a - ble it would get this far.

Interlude

It's un - de - ni - a - ble what they'd have you to think,

It's in - de - scrib - a - ble it can drive you to drink.

They said it was the land of milk

and hon - ey, Now they say it's the land of mon - ey.

Who - ev - er thought they could ev - er make that stick.

It's un-be-liev-a-ble you can get this rich this quick.

Funky instrumental (ad lib.)

Ev-ery head __ is so dig-ni-fied, __ Ev-ery moon __ is so

sanc-ti-fied, Ev-ery urge is so sat-is-fied __ as

long as you're __ with me. _____ All the sil-ver,

all the gold, __ All the sweet-hearts you can hold __ That don't __

__ come back with sto-ries un-told, are hang-ing on __ a tree. __

Additional lyrics

Bridge #2:
Once there was a man who had no eyes,
Every lady in the land told him lies,
He stood beneath the silver skies and his heart began to bleed.
Every brain is civilized,
Every nerve is analyzed,
Everything is criticized when you are in need.

It's unbelievable, it's fancy-free,
So interchangeable, so delightful to see.
Turn your back, wash your hands,
There's always someone who understands
It don't matter no more what you got to say
It's unbelievable it would go down this way.

Under the Red Sky

Words and Music by Bob Dylan

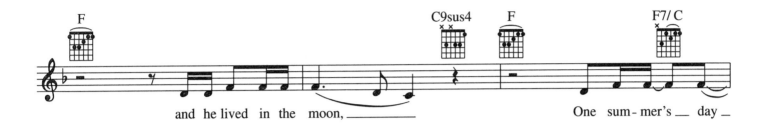

and he lived in the moon, _____ One sum-mer's __ day __

_____ he came pass-ing by. __ There

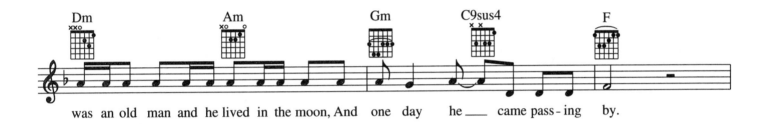

was an old man and he lived in the moon, And one day he __ came pass-ing by.

Bridge

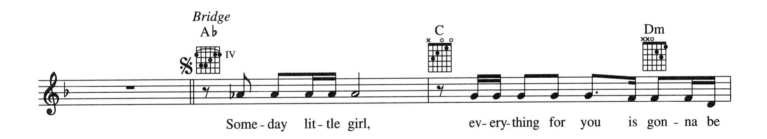

Some-day lit-tle girl, ev-ery-thing for you is gon-na be

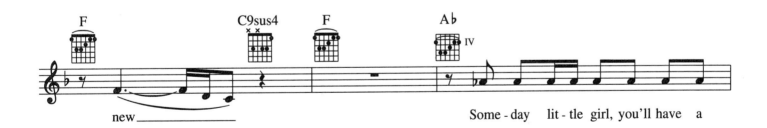

new_____ Some-day lit-tle girl, you'll have a

dia-mond as big as your shoe _____ Let the wind blow low,

let the wind blow — high.   One

day   the lit - tle boy   and the lit - tle girl   were both   baked   in   a   pie._____

Let the wind blow low, and the wind blow high. One

day   the lit - tle boy   and lit - tle girl   were both baked in a   pie.

second time: fade

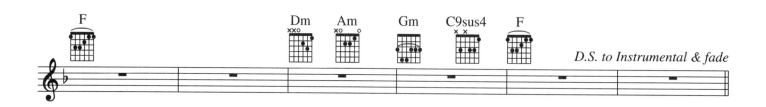

Additional lyrics

Bridge #2:
This is the key to the kingdom and this is the town
This is the blind horse that leads you around

Let the bird sing, let the bird fly,
One day the man in the moon went home and the river went dry.
Let the bird sing, let the bird fly,
The man in the moon went home and the river went dry.

Under Your Spell

Words and Music by Bob Dylan and Carole Bayer Sager

Moderately slow

1. Some-thin' a-bout you that I can't shake,__ Don't know how much more__ of this I can take, __ Ba - by, I'm un-der your spell. __

I was knocked out and load-ed in the na-ked night. When my last dream ex-plod-ed, I no-ticed your light. Ba - by, oh__

__ what a sto-ry I could tell.

Ev-ery-where you go it's e-

Additional lyrics

2. It's been nice seeing you, you read me like a book
   If you ever want to reach me, you know where to look
   Baby, I'll be at the same hotel.

   I'd like to help you but I'm in a bit of a jam,
   I'll call you tomorrow if there's phones where I am.
   Baby, caught between heaven and hell.

3. But I will be back, I will survive,
   You'll never get rid of me as long as you're alive.
   Baby, can't you tell.

   Well it's four in the morning by the sound of the birds,
   I'm starin' at your picture, I'm hearin' your words.
   Baby, they ring in my head like a bell.

   Bridge:
   Everywhere you go it's enough to break hearts
   Someone always gets hurt, a fire always starts.
   You were too hot to handle, you were breaking every vow.
   I trusted you baby, you can trust me now.

4. Turn back baby, wipe your eye,
   Don't think I'm leaving you here without a kiss goodbye.
   Baby, is there anything left to tell?

   I'll see you later when I'm not so out of my head,
   Maybe next time I'll let the dead bury the dead.
   Baby, what more can I tell?

   Coda:
   Well the desert is hot, the mountain is cursed,
   Pray that I don't die of thirst.
   Baby, two feet from the well.

Union Sundown

Words and Music by Bob Dylan

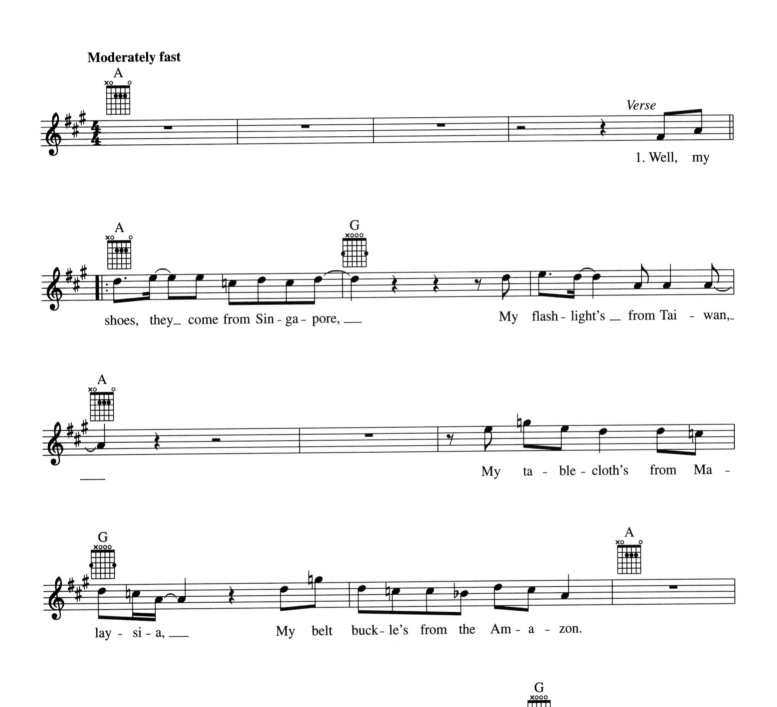

Moderately fast

Verse

1. Well, my

shoes, they_ come from Sin - ga - pore, ___   My flash - light's _ from Tai - wan,_

___   My ta - ble - cloth's from Ma -

lay - si - a, ___   My belt buck - le's from the Am - a - zon.

You know, this shirt I wear comes from the Phil - ip - pines   And the car   I

Additional lyrics

2. Well, this silk dress is from Hong Kong
   And the pearls are from Japan.
   Well, the dog collar's from India
   And the flower pot's from Pakistan.
   All the furniture, it says "Made in Brazil"
   Where a woman, she slaved for sure
   Bringin' home thirty cents a day to a family of twelve,
   You know, that's a lot of money to her.

   Chorus

3. Well, you know, lots of people complainin' that there is no work.
   I say, "Why you say that for
   When nothin' you got is U.S.-made?"
   They don't make nothin' here no more,
   You know, capitalism is above the law.
   It say, "It don't count 'less it sells."
   When it costs too much to build it at home
   You just build it cheaper someplace else.

   Chorus

4. Well, the job that you used to have,
   They gave it to somebody down in El Salvador.
   The unions are big business, friend,
   And they're goin' out like a dinosaur.
   They used to grow food in Kansas
   Now they want to grow it on the moon and eat it raw.
   I can see the day coming when even your home garden
   Is gonna be against the law.

   Chorus

5. Democracy don't rule the world,
   You'd better get that in your head.
   This world is ruled by violence
   But I guess that's better left unsaid.
   From Broadway to the Milky Way,
   That's a lot of territory indeed
   And a man's gonna do what he has to do
   When he's got a hungry mouth to feed.

   Chorus

Up to Me

Words and Music by Bob Dylan

Additional lyrics

2. If I'd thought about it I never would've done it, I guess I would've let it slide,
   If I'd lived my life by what others were thinkin', the heart inside me would've died.
   I was just too stubborn to ever be governed by enforced insanity,
   Someone had to reach for the risin' star,
   I guess it was up to me.

3. Oh, the Union Central is pullin' out and the orchids are in bloom,
   I've only got me one good shirt left and it smells of stale perfume.
   In fourteen months I've only smiled once and I didn't do it consciously,
   Somebody's got to find your trail,
   I guess it must be up to me.

4. It was like a revelation when you betrayed me with your touch,
   I'd just about convinced myself that nothin' had changed that much.
   The old Rounder in the iron mask slipped me the master key,
   Somebody had to unlock your heart,
   He said it was up to me.

5. Well, I watched you slowly disappear down into the officers' club,
   I would've followed you in the door but I didn't have a ticket stub.
   So I waited all night 'til the break of day, hopin' one of us could get free,
   When the dawn came over the river bridge,
   I knew it was up to me.

6. Oh, the only decent thing I did when I worked as a postal clerk
   Was to haul your picture down off the wall near the cage where I used to work.
   Was I a fool or not to try to protect your identity?
   You looked a little burned out, my friend,
   I thought it might be up to me.

7. Well, I met somebody face to face and I had to remove my hat,
   She's everything I need and love but I can't be swayed by that.
   It frightens me, the awful truth of how sweet life can be,
   But she ain't a-gonna make me move,
   I guess it must be up to me.

8. We heard the Sermon on the Mount and I knew it was too complex,
   It didn't amount to anything more than what the broken glass reflects.
   When you bite off more than you can chew you pay the penalty,
   Somebody's got to tell the tale,
   I guess it must be up to me.

9. Well, Dupree came in pimpin' tonight to the Thunderbird Cafe,
   Crystal wanted to talk to him, I had to look the other way.
   Well, I just can't rest without you, love, I need your company,
   But you ain't a-gonna cross the line,
   I guess it must be up to me.

10. There's a note left in the bottle, you can give it to Estelle,
    She's the one you been wond'rin' about, but there's really nothin' much to tell.
    We both heard voices for a while, now the rest is history,
    Somebody's got to cry some tears,
    I guess it must be up to me.

11. So go on, boys, and play your hands, life is a pantomime,
    The ringleaders from the county seat say you don't have all that much time.
    And the girl with me behind the shades, she ain't my property,
    One of us has got to hit the road,
    I guess it must be up to me.

12. And if we never meet again, baby, remember me,
    How my lone guitar played sweet for you that old-time melody.
    And the harmonica around my neck, I blew it for you, free,
    No one else could play that tune,
    You know it was up to me.

Visions of Johanna

Words and Music by Bob Dylan

Walkin' Down the Line

Words and Music by Bob Dylan

Wallflower

Words and Music by Bob Dylan

Moderate country waltz

won - d'rin' what's go - in' on. ___
you're gon - na be mine one of these days, Mine a - lone. _

Wall - flow'r, wall - flow'r, Won't you dance with me? The
Wall - flow'r, wall - flow'r, Take a chance on me.

night will soon be gone.
Please let me ride you home.

Walls of Red Wing

Words and Music by Bob Dylan

Additional lyrics

2. From the dirty old mess hall
   You march to the brick wall,
   Too weary to talk
   And too tired to sing.
   Oh, it's all afternoon
   You remember your home town,
   Inside the walls,
   The walls of Red Wing.

3. Oh, the gates are cast iron
   And the walls are barbed wire.
   Stay far from the fence
   With the 'lectricity sting.
   And it's keep down your head
   And stay in your number,
   Inside the walls,
   The walls of Red Wing.

4. Oh, it's fare thee well
   To the deep hollow dungeon,
   Farewell to the boardwalk
   That takes you to the screen.
   And farewell to the minutes
   They threaten you with it,
   Inside the walls,
   The walls of Red Wing.

5. It's many a guard
   That stands around smilin',
   Holdin' his club
   Like he was a king.
   Hopin' to get you
   Behind a wood pilin',
   Inside the walls,
   The walls of Red Wing.

6. The night aimed shadows
   Through the crossbar windows,
   And the wind punched hard
   To make the wall-siding sing.
   It's many a night
   I pretended to be a-sleepin',
   Inside the walls,
   The walls of Red Wing.

7. As the rain rattled heavy
   On the bunk-house shingles,
   And the sounds in the night,
   They made my ears ring.
   'Til the keys of the guards
   Clicked the tune of the morning,
   Inside the walls,
   The walls of Red Wing.

8. Oh, some of us'll end up
   In St. Cloud Prison,
   And some of us'll wind up
   To be lawyers and things,
   And some of us'll stand up
   To meet you on your crossroads,
   From inside the walls,
   The walls of Red Wing.

Wanted Man

Words and Music by Bob Dylan

Additional lyrics

2. I might be in Colorado or Georgia by the sea,
   Working for some man who may not know at all who I might be.
   If you ever see me comin' and if you know who I am,
   Don't you breathe it to nobody 'cause you know I'm on the lam.

3. Wanted man by Lucy Watson, wanted man by Jeannie Brown,
   Wanted man by Nellie Johnson, wanted man in this next town.
   But I've had all that I've wanted of a lot of things I had
   And a lot more than I needed of some things that turned out bad.

4. I got sidetracked in El Paso, stopped to get myself a map,
   Went the wrong way into Juarez with Juanita on my lap.
   Then I went to sleep in Shreveport, woke up in Abilene
   Wonderin' why the hell I'm wanted at some town halfway between.

5. Wanted man in Albuquerque, wanted man in Syracuse,
   Wanted man in Tallahassee, wanted man in Baton Rouge,
   There's somebody set to grab me anywhere that I might be
   And wherever you might look tonight, you might get a glimpse of me.

6. Wanted man in California, wanted man in Buffalo,
   Wanted man in Kansas City, wanted man in Ohio,
   Wanted man in Mississippi, wanted man in old Cheyenne,
   Wherever you might look tonight, you might see this wanted man.

Watered-Down Love

Words and Music by Bob Dylan

Additional lyrics

3. Love that's pure won't lead you astray,
   Won't hold you back, won't mess up your day,
   Won't pervert you, corrupt you with stupid wishes,
   It don't make you envious, it don't make you suspicious.

   Chorus

4. Love that's pure ain't no accident,
   Always on time, is always content,
   An eternal flame, quietly burning,
   Never needs to be proud, restlessly yearning.

   Chorus

We Better Talk This Over

Words and Music by Bob Dylan

Moderately

1. I think ___ we bet-ter talk ___ this o-ver

May-be when we both_get so-ber You'll un-der-stand I'm on-ly a man Doin' the best that I can. ___

This sit-u-a-tion can on-ly get rough-er.

Why _____ should we need-less-ly suf-fer? Let's call it a day, ___ go our own dif-f'rent ways Be-fore we de-cay.

Additional lyrics

2. I feel displaced, I got a low-down feeling
    You been two-faced, you been double-dealing.
    I took a chance, got caught in the trance
    Of a downhill dance.

    Oh, child, why you wanna hurt me?
    I'm exiled, you can't convert me.
    I'm lost in the haze of your delicate ways
    With both eyes glazed.

    You don't have to yearn for love, you don't have to be alone,
    Somewheres in this universe there's a place that you can call home.

3. I guess I'll be leaving tomorrow
    If I have to beg, steal or borrow.
    It'd be great to cross paths in a day and a half
    Look at each other and laugh.

    But I don't think it's liable to happen
    Like the sound of one hand clappin'.
    The vows that we kept are now broken and swept
    'Neath the bed where we slept.

    Don't think of me and fantasize on what we never had,
    Be grateful for what we've shared together and be glad.

    Why should we go on watching each other through a telescope?
    Eventually we'll hang ourselves on all this tangled rope.

    Oh, babe, time for a new transition
    I wish I was a magician.
    I would wave a wand and tie back the bond
    That we've both gone beyond.

Wedding Song

Words and Music by Bob Dylan

Additional lyrics

2. Ever since you walked right in, the circle's been complete,
   I've said goodbye to haunted rooms and faces in the street,
   To the courtyard of the jester which is hidden from the sun,
   I love you more than ever and I haven't yet begun.

3. You breathed on me and made my life a richer one to live,
   When I was deep in poverty you taught me how to give,
   Dried the tears up from my dreams and pulled me from the hole,
   Quenched my thirst and satisfied the burning in my soul.

4. You gave me babies one, two, three, what is more, you saved my life,
   Eye for eye and tooth for tooth, your love cuts like a knife,
   My thoughts of you don't ever rest, they'd kill me if I lie,
   I'd sacrifice the world for you and watch my senses die.

5. The tune that is yours and mine to play upon this earth,
   We'll play it out the best we know, whatever it is worth,
   What's lost is lost, we can't regain what went down in the flood,
   But happiness to me is you and I love you more than blood.

6. It's never been my duty to remake the world at large,
   Nor is it my intention to sound a battle charge,
   'Cause I love you more than all of that with a love that doesn't bend,
   And if there is eternity I'd love you there again.

7. Oh, can't you see that you were born to stand by my side
   And I was born to be with you, you were born to be my bride,
   You're the other half of what I am, you're the missing piece
   And I love you more than ever with that love that doesn't cease.

8. You turn the tide on me each day and teach my eyes to see,
   Just bein' next to you is a natural thing for me
   And I could never let you go, no matter what goes on,
   'Cause I love you more than ever now that the past is gone.

What Can I Do for You?

Words and Music by Bob Dylan

Filled up a hun – ger that had al – ways been de – nied,

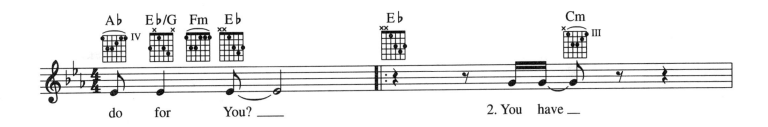

O- pened up a door no man can shut and You o-pened it up so wide And You've

cho - sen me to be a - mong the few. What can I

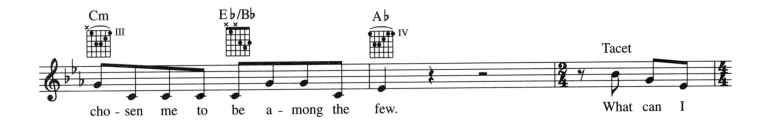

do for You? _____ 2. You have _____

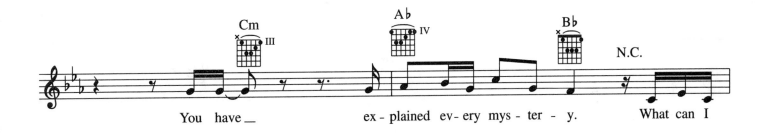

laid down Your life for me. What can I do for You? _____

You have _____ ex - plained ev - ery mys - ter - y. What can I

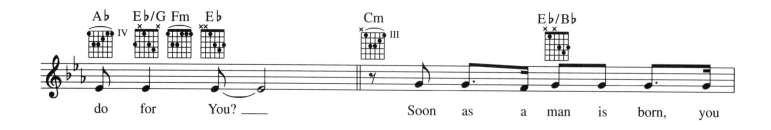

do   for   You? ___   Soon   as   a   man   is   born,   you

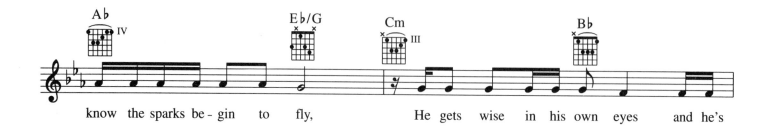

know   the sparks be - gin   to   fly,   He   gets   wise   in   his   own   eyes   and   he's

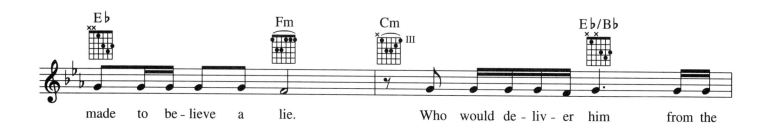

made   to   be - lieve   a   lie.   Who   would   de - liv - er   him   from   the

death he's   bound   to   die?   Well,   You've   done   it   all and there's   no more an-y-one   can   pre-tend   to

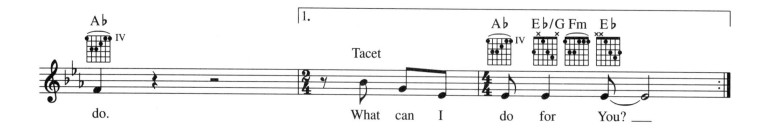

do.   What   can   I   do   for   You? ___

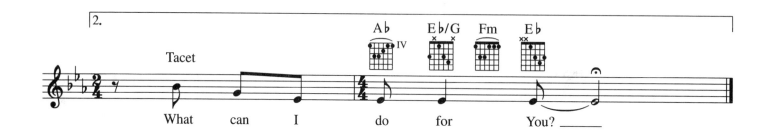

What   can   I   do   for   You? _____

Additional lyrics

3. You have given all there is to give.
   What can I do for You?
   You have given me life to live.
   How can I live for You?

   I know all about poison, I know all about fiery darts,
   I don't care how rough the road is, show me where it starts,
   Whatever pleases You, tell it to my heart.
   Well, I don't deserve it but I sure did make it through.
   What can I do for You?

What Was It You Wanted?

Words and Music by Bob Dylan

Slow, with a steady beat

What was it you want-ed?

Tell me a-gain so I'll know. __ What's hap-pen-ing in there,

What's go-ing on in your show. __ What was it you want-ed,

Could you say it a-gain?__ I'll be back in a min-ute

You can get it to-geth-er by then.

What was it you want-ed You can tell me, I'm back,__

We can start it all o-ver Get it back __ on the track,__

Whatcha Gonna Do

Words and Music by Bob Dylan

Additional lyrics

2. Tell me what you're gonna do
When the devil calls your cards.
Tell me what you're gonna do
When the devil calls your cards.
Tell me what you're gonna do
When the devil calls your cards.
O Lord, O Lord,
What shall you do?

3. Tell me what you're gonna do
When your water turns to wine.
Tell me what you're gonna do
When your water turns to wine.
Tell me what you're gonna do
When your water turns to wine.
O Lord, O Lord,
What should you do?

4. Tell me what you're gonna do
When you can't play God no more.
Tell me what you're gonna do
When you can't play God no more.
Tell me what you're gonna do
When you can't play God no more.
O Lord, O Lord,
What shall you do?

5. Tell me what you're gonna do
When the shadow comes creepin' in your room.
Tell me what you're gonna do
When the shadow comes creepin' in your room.
Tell me what you're gonna do
When the shadow comes creepin' in your room.
O Lord, O Lord,
What should you do?

When He Returns

Words and Music by Bob Dylan

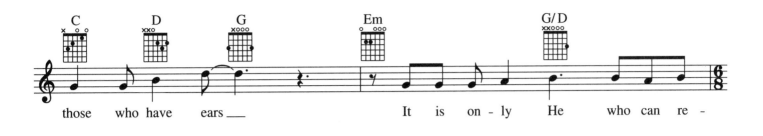

those who have ears ___ It is on-ly He who can re -

duce ___ me to tears. Don't ___ you cry and

don't ___ you die and ___ don't you burn ___

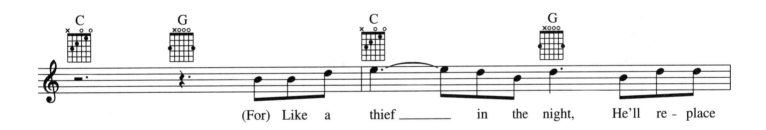

(For) Like a thief ___ in the night, He'll re-place

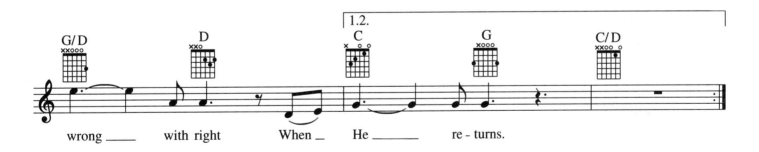

1.2.

wrong ___ with right When __ He ___ re-turns.

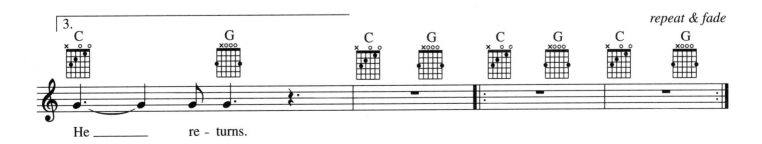

3.

repeat & fade

He ___ re-turns.

Additional lyrics

2. Truth is an arrow and the gate is narrow that it passes through,
   He unleashed His power at an unknown hour that no one knew.
   How long can I listen to the lies of prejudice?
   How long can I stay drunk on fear out in the wilderness?
   Can I cast it aside, all this loyalty and this pride?
   Will I ever learn that there'll be no peace, that the war won't cease
   Until He returns?

3. Surrender your crown on this blood-stained ground, take off your mask,
   He sees your deeds, He knows your needs even before you ask.
   How long can you falsify and deny what is real?
   How long can you hate yourself for the weakness you conceal?
   Of every earthly plan that be known to man, He is unconcerned,
   He's got plans of His own to set up His throne
   When He returns.

When the Night Comes Falling from the Sky

Words and Music by Bob Dylan

Additional lyrics

2. I can see through your walls and I know you're hurting,
   Sorrow covers you up like a cape.
   Only yesterday I know that you've been flirting
   With disaster that you managed to escape.

   I can't provide for you no easy answers,
   Who are you that I should have to lie?
   You'll know all about it, love,
   It'll fit you like a glove
   When the night comes falling from the sky.

3. I can hear your trembling heart beat like a river,
   You must have been protecting someone last time I called.
   I've never asked you for nothing you couldn't deliver,
   I've never asked you to set yourself up for a fall.

   I saw thousands who could have overcome the darkness,
   For the love of a lousy buck, I've watched them die.
   Stick around, baby, we're not through,
   Don't look for me, I'll see you
   When the night comes falling from the sky.

4. In your teardrops, I can see my own reflection,
   It was on the northern border of Texas where I crossed the line.
   I don't want to be a fool starving for affection,
   I don't want to drown in someone else's wine.

   For all eternity I think I will remember
   That icy wind that's howling in your eye.
   You will seek me and you'll find me
   In the wasteland of your mind
   When the night comes falling from the sky.

5. Well, I sent you my feelings in a letter
   But you were gambling for support,
   This time tomorrow I'll know you better
   When my memory is not so short.

   This time I'm asking for freedom,
   Freedom from a world which you deny.
   And you'll give it to me now,
   I'll take it anyhow
   When the night comes falling from the sky.

When I Paint My Masterpiece

Words and Music by Bob Dylan

Moderately slow

Oh, the streets of Rome are filled with rub- ble,___ An- cient foot-
hours I've spent___ in- side the Col- i- se- um,___ Dodg- ing li-
Rome and land- ed in Brus- sels,___ On a plane_

prints _____ are ev- ery- where. _ You can
ons _____ and wast- in' time. __ Oh, those
_ ride so bump- y that I al- most cried. __

al- most think_____ that you're see - in' dou- ble_____ On a
might- y kings of the jun- gle, I could hard- ly stand to see 'em, ___ Yes, it
Cler- gy- men in un- i- form and young girls pull- in' mus- cles,___ Ev- ery-

cold, dark night __ on the Span- ish Stairs. _____
sure has been __ a long, hard climb. _____
one was there to greet me when I stepped in - side. _____

Got to hur- ry on back_____ to my ho- tel room, Where I've
Train wheels run- nin' through the back of my mem- o- ry,_____ When I
News- pa - per- men eat- ing can- dy_____

When the Ship Comes In

Words and Music by Bob Dylan

Medium bright

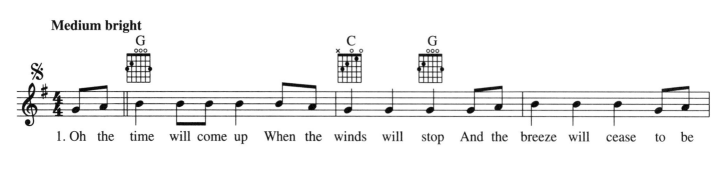

1. Oh the time will come up When the winds will stop And the breeze will cease to be

breath-in'. _____ Like the still-ness in the wind 'Fore the hur-ri-cane be-gins, The

ho-ur when the ship comes in. Oh the seas will split And the ship will hit And the

sands on the shore-line will be shak-ing. _____ Then the tide will sound And the

D.S. three times ℅

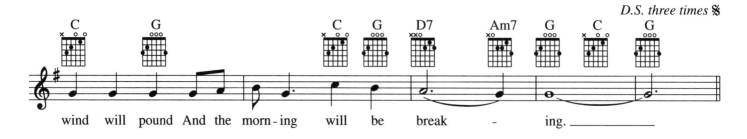

wind will pound And the morn-ing will be break - ing. _____

Additional lyrics

2. Oh the fishes will laugh
   As they swim out of the path
   And the seagulls they'll be smiling.
   And the rocks on the sand
   Will proudly stand,
   The hour that the ship comes in.

   And the words that are used
   For to get the ship confused
   Will not be understood as they're spoken.
   For the chains of the sea
   Will have busted in the night
   And will be buried at the bottom of the ocean.

3. A song will lift
   As the mainsail shifts
   And the boat drifts on to the shoreline.
   And the sun will respect
   Every face on the deck,
   The hour that the ship comes in.

   Then the sands will roll
   Out a carpet of gold
   For your weary toes to be a-touchin'.
   And the ship's wise men
   Will remind you once again
   That the whole wide world is watchin'.

4. Oh the foes will rise
   With the sleep still in their eyes
   And they'll jerk from their beds and think they're dreamin'.
   But they'll pinch themselves and squeal
   And know that it's for real,
   The hour when the ship comes in.

   Then they'll raise their hands,
   Sayin' we'll meet all your demands,
   But we'll shout from the bow your days are numbered.
   And like Pharaoh's tribe,
   They'll be drownded in the tide,
   And like Goliath, they'll be conquered.

When You Gonna Wake Up?

Words and Music by Bob Dylan

Moderately

Verse

1. God don't make prom - is - es that He don't keep. ___

You got some big dreams, ba - by, but in or - der to dream you got - ta still be a -

sleep.

Chorus

When you gon - na wake up,

when you gon - na wake up

When you gon - na wake up

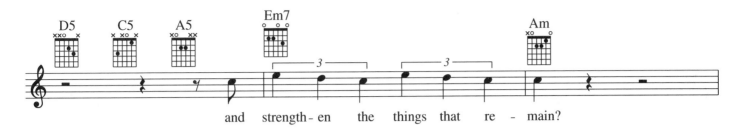

and strength-en the things that re - main?

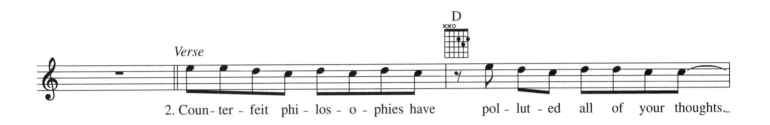

Verse

2. Coun-ter-feit phi-los-o-phies have pol-lut-ed all of your thoughts.

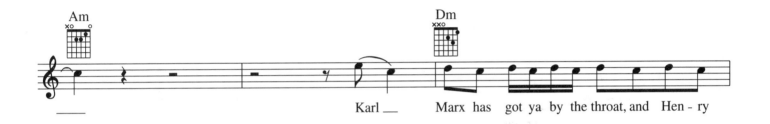

Karl __ Marx has got ya by the throat, and Hen-ry

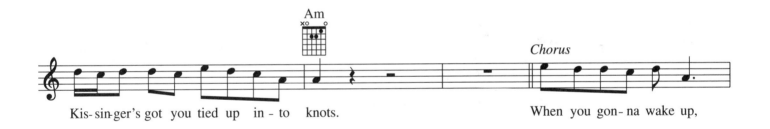

Chorus

Kis-sin-ger's got you tied up in-to knots. When you gon-na wake up,

when you gon - na wake up

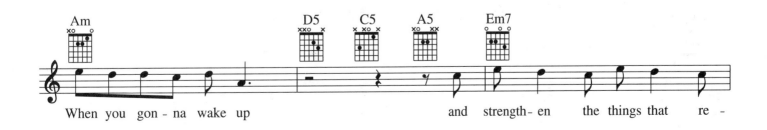

When you gon - na wake up and strength-en the things that re -

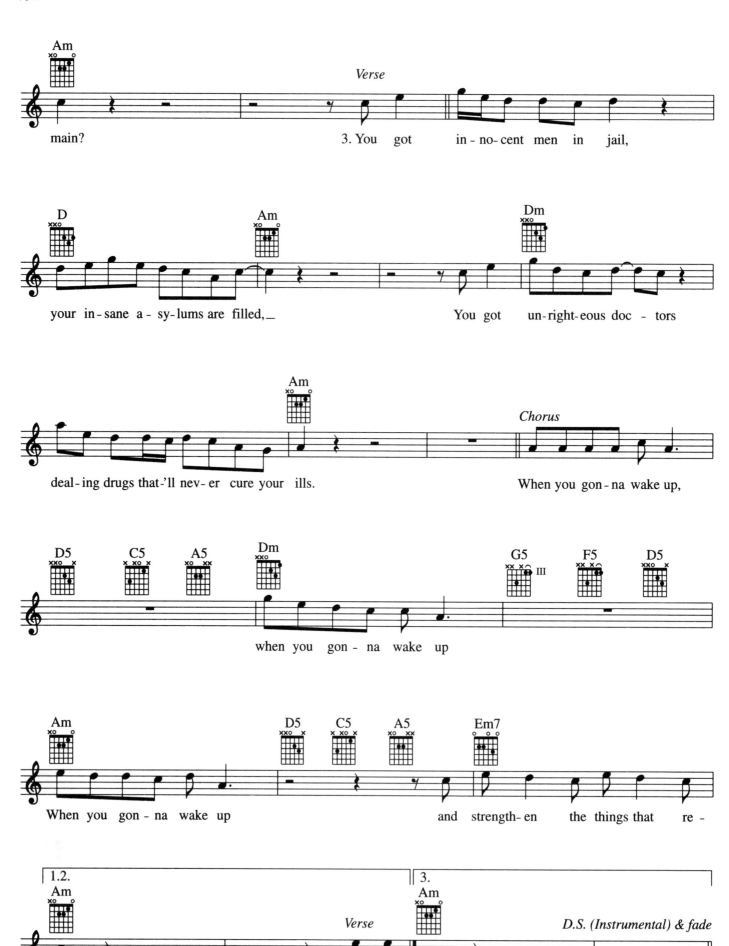

Additional lyrics

4. You got men who can't hold their peace and women who can't control their tongues,
   The rich seduce the poor and the old are seduced by the young.

   Chorus

5. Adulterers in churches and pornography in the schools,
   You got gangsters in power and lawbreakers making rules.

   Chorus

6. Spiritual advisors and gurus to guide your every move,
   Instant inner peace and every step you take has got to be approved.

   Chorus

7. Do you ever wonder just what God requires?
   You think He's just an errand boy to satisfy your wandering desires.

   Chorus

8. You can't take it with you and you know that it's too worthless to be sold,
   They tell you, "Time is money" as if your life was worth its weight in gold.

   Chorus

9. There's a Man up on a cross and He's been crucified.
   Do you have any idea why or for who He died?

   Chorus

Where Are You Tonight?

Words and Music by Bob Dylan

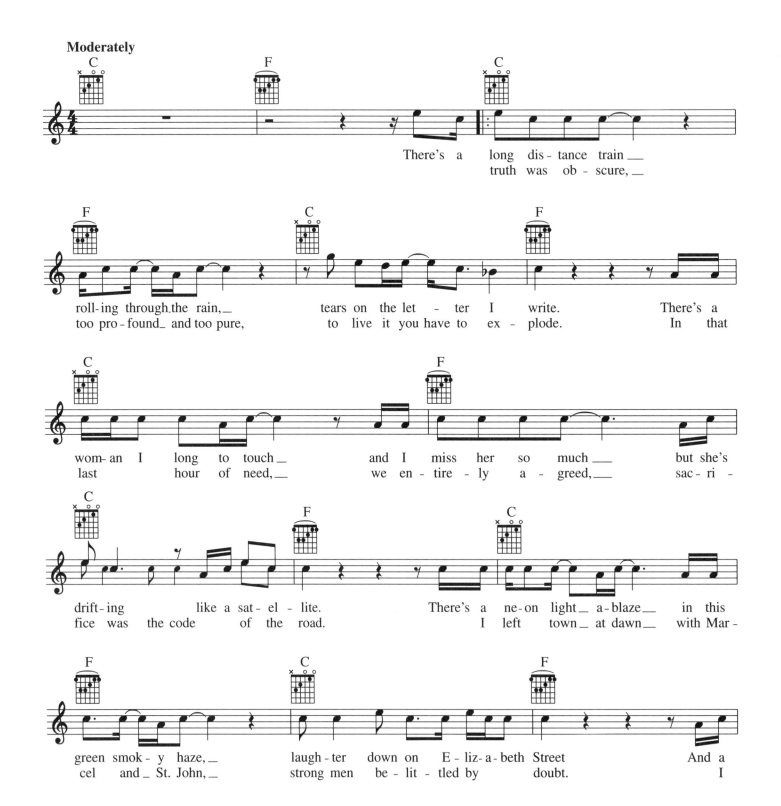

Moderately

There's a long dis- tance train __
truth was ob - scure, __

roll- ing through. the rain, __
too pro - found __ and too pure,

tears on the let - ter I write.
to live it you have to ex - plode.

There's a
In that

wom- an I long to touch __
last hour of need, __

and I miss her so much __
we en - tire - ly a - greed, __

but she's
sac - ri -

drift- ing like a sat- el - lite.
fice was the code of the road.

There's a ne- on light __ a- blaze __ in this
I left town __ at dawn __ with Mar -

green smok- y haze, __
cel and __ St. John, __

laugh- ter down on E - liz- a- beth Street
strong men be - lit - tled by doubt.

And a
I

nick- els and dimes, ___ the guy ___ you were lov - in' ___ could-n't stay
dark side of this room and a path - way that leads up ___ to the

clean. It felt out - a place, ___ my foot in his ___ face, ___ but he should-a stayed ___
stars. If you don't be-lieve there's a price ___ for this sweet par-a - dise, ___ re- mind ___

1.
___ where his mon - ey was ___ green. ___
___ me to show you the ___ scars. ___

2.
D.S. al Coda

I ___ There's a

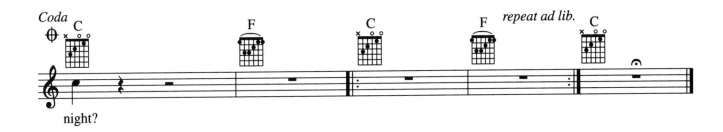

Coda   *repeat ad lib.*

night?

Where Teardrops Fall

Words and Music by Bob Dylan

Who Killed Davey Moore?

Words and Music by Bob Dylan

Additional lyrics

Refrain

2. "Not us," says the angry crowd,
   Whose screams filled the arena loud.
   "It's too bad he died that night
   But we just like to see a fight.
   We didn't mean for him t' meet his death,
   We just meant to see some sweat,
   There ain't nothing wrong in that.
   It wasn't us that made him fall.
   No, you can't blame us at all."

Refrain

3. "Not me," says his manager,
   Puffing on a big cigar.
   "It's hard to say, it's hard to tell,
   I always thought that he was well.
   It's too bad for his wife an' kids he's dead,
   But if he was sick, he should've said.
   It wasn't me that made him fall.
   No, you can't blame me at all."

Refrain

4. "Not me," says the gambling man,
   With his ticket stub still in his hand.
   "It wasn't me that knocked him down,
   My hands never touched him none.
   I didn't commit no ugly sin,
   Anyway, I put money on him to win.
   It wasn't me that made him fall.
   No, you can't blame me at all."

Refrain

5. "Not me," says the boxing writer,
   Pounding print on his old typewriter,
   Sayin', "Boxing ain't to blame,
   There's just as much danger in a football game."
   Sayin', "Fist fighting is here to stay,
   It's just the old American way.
   It wasn't me that made him fall.
   No, you can't blame me at all."

Refrain

6. "Not me," says the man whose fists
   Laid him low in a cloud of mist,
   Who came here from Cuba's door
   Where boxing ain't allowed no more.
   "I hit him, yes, it's true,
   But that's what I am paid to do.
   Don't say 'murder,' don't say 'kill.'
   It was destiny, it was God's will."

Refrain

The Wicked Messenger

Words and Music by Bob Dylan

1. There was a wick - ed mes - sen - ger ___ From E - li he did come, With a mind that mul - ti - plied ___ The small - est mat - ter. When ques - tioned who had sent for him, He an - swered with his thumb, For his tongue it could not speak, but on - ly flat - ter. ___

2. He
3. Oh, the

Additional lyrics

2. He stayed behind the assembly hall,
   It was there he made his bed,
   Oftentimes he could be seen returning.
   Until one day he just appeared
   With a note in his hand which read,
   "The soles of my feet, I swear they're burning."

3. Oh, the leaves began to fallin'
   And the seas began to part,
   And the people that confronted him were many.
   And he was told but these few words,
   Which opened up his heart,
   "If ye cannot bring good news, then don't bring any."

Winterlude

Words and Music by Bob Dylan

Bright waltz

1. Win - ter - lude, Win - ter - lude, oh _____ dar - lin', _____

_____ Win - ter - lude by the road to - night. _____ To -

night there will be no quar - rel - in', _____ Ev - 'ry -

thing is gon - na be al - right. _____ Oh, I

see by the an - gel be - side me _____ That love has a

rea - son _____ to shine. _____ You're that one I _____ a - dore, come

o - ver here and give me more, Then Win - ter - lude, this dude thinks you're

1.2.

fine. _____

2. Win - ter -

3.

grand. _____

Additional lyrics

2. Winterlude, Winterlude, my little apple,
   Winterlude by the corn in the field,
   Winterlude, let's go down to the chapel,
   Then come back and cook up a meal.
   Well, come out when the skating rink glistens
   By the sun, near the old crossroads sign.
   The snow is so cold, but our love can be bold,
   Winterlude, don't be rude, please be mine.

3. Winterlude, Winterlude, my little daisy,
   Winterlude by the telephone wire,
   Winterlude, it's makin' me lazy,
   Come on, sit by the logs in the fire.
   The moonlight reflects from the window
   Where the snowflakes, they cover the sand.
   Come out tonight, ev'rything will be tight,
   Winterlude, this dude thinks you're grand.

With God on Our Side

Words and Music by Bob Dylan

Additional lyrics

2. Oh the history books tell it
They tell it so well
The cavalries charged
The Indians fell
The cavalries charged
The Indians died
Oh the country was young
With God on its side.

3. Oh the Spanish-American
War had its day
And the Civil War too
Was soon laid away
And the names of the heroes
I's made to memorize
With guns in their hands
And God on their side.

4. Oh the First World War, boys
It closed out its fate
The reason for fighting
I never got straight
But I learned to accept it
Accept it with pride
For you don't count the dead
When God's on your side.

5. When the Second World War
Came to an end
We forgave the Germans
And we were friends
Though they murdered six million
In the ovens they fried
The Germans now too
Have God on their side.

6. I've learned to hate Russians
All through my whole life
If another war starts
It's them we must fight
To hate them and fear them
To run and to hide
And accept it all bravely
With God on my side.

7. But now we got weapons
Of the chemical dust
If fire them we're forced to
Then fire them we must
One push of the button
And a shot the world wide
And you never ask questions
When God's on your side.

8. In a many dark hour
I've been thinkin' about this
That Jesus Christ
Was betrayed by a kiss
But I can't think for you
You'll have to decide
Whether Judas Iscariot
Had God on his side.

9. So now as I'm leavin'
I'm weary as Hell
The confusion I'm feelin'
Ain't no tongue can tell
The words fill my head
And fall to the floor
If God's on our side
He'll stop the next war.

World Gone Wrong

Traditional, arranged by Bob Dylan

wrong. _____ I can't be good no more, _____ once like I did be - fore. _____ I can't be good, ba - by, ____ Ho - ney, be - cause the world's _ gone ____ wrong. _____

Additional lyrics

3. I told you, baby, right to your head,
   If I didn't leave you I would have to kill you dead.
   I can't be good no more, once like I did before.
   I can't be good, baby,
   Honey, because the world's gone wrong.

4. I tried to be loving and treat you kind,
   But it seems like you never right, you got no loyal mind.
   I can't be good no more, once like I did before.
   I can't be good, baby,
   Honey, because the world's gone wrong.

5. If you have a woman and she don't treat you kind,
   Praise the Good Lord to get her out of your mind.
   I can't be good no more, once like I did before.
   I can't be good, baby,
   Honey, because the world's gone wrong.

6. Said, when you been good now, can't do no more,
   Just tell her kindly, "There is the front door."
   I can't be good no more, once like I did before.
   I can't be good, baby,
   Honey, because the world's gone wrong.

7. Pack up my suitcase, give me my hat,
   No use to ask me, baby, 'cause I'll never be back.
   I can't be good no more, once like I did before.
   I can't be good, baby,
   Honey, because the world's gone wrong.

Yea! Heavy and a Bottle of Bread

Words and Music by Bob Dylan

Slowly, with a beat

(Spoken:) Well, the comic book and me, just us, we caught the bus. The

poor little chauffeur, though, she was back in bed On the very next day, with a nose full

of pus. (Sung:) Yea! Heav - y and a bot - tle of bread

Yea! Heav - y and a bot-tle of bread Yea! Heav - y and a

bot - tle of bread (Spoken:) It's a one track town, just brown, and a breeze, too,

Pack up the meat, sweet, we're headin' out For Wichita in a pile of fruit.

You Ain't Goin' Nowhere

Words and Music by Bob Dylan

Moderately

1. Clouds so   swift ___   Rain won't   lift ___   Gate won't   close ___
2. I   don't   care ___   How man - y   let - ters they   sent ___   Morn - ing   came ___   and
3. Buy   me a   flute ___   And   a   gun that   shoots ___   Tail - gates ___   and

Rail - ings   froze ___   Get your   mind ___   off win - ter   time ___
morn - ing   went ___   Pick up your   mon - ey   And   pack up your   tent ___
sub - sti - tutes ___   Strap your - self ___   To   the   tree   with   roots ___

You ain't   goin' ___   no - where ___
You ain't   goin' ___   no - where ___   }   Whoo - ee! ___   Ride   me high ___   To -
You ain't   goin' ___   no - where ___

mor - row's the   day   My   bride's gon - na   come   Oh,   oh, ___   Are   we gon - na   fly

Down in the eas-y chair! __ __ 4. Gen-ghis Khan, __ He

could not keep__ All his kings__ Sup-plied with sleep __ We'll climb that hill__ no

mat-ter how steep __ When we get up to it. ___ ___

You Angel You

Words and Music by Bob Dylan

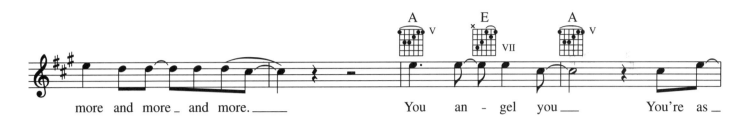

more and more _ and more. _____ You an - gel you __ You're as _

__ fine as __ can __ be. __ The way you smile _ like a sweet ba - by child, _ It just

falls all o - ver me. ___ You   gim - me more _ And more _

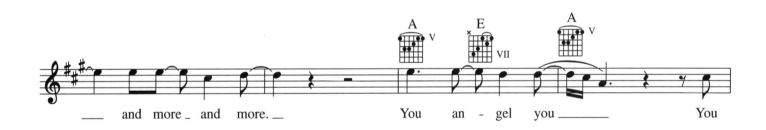

___ and more _ and more. _ You an - gel you _____ You

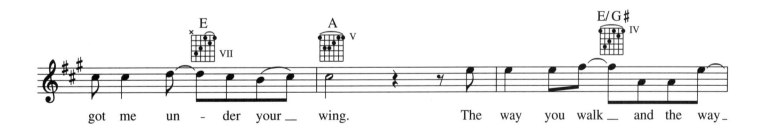

got me un - der your _ wing. The way you walk _ and the way _

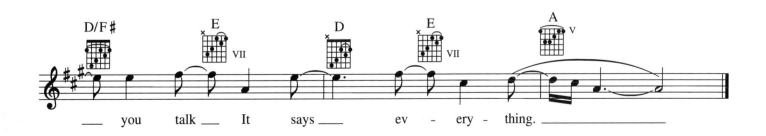

___ you talk __ It says ___ ev - ery - thing. _____

You're a Big Girl Now
Words and Music by Bob Dylan

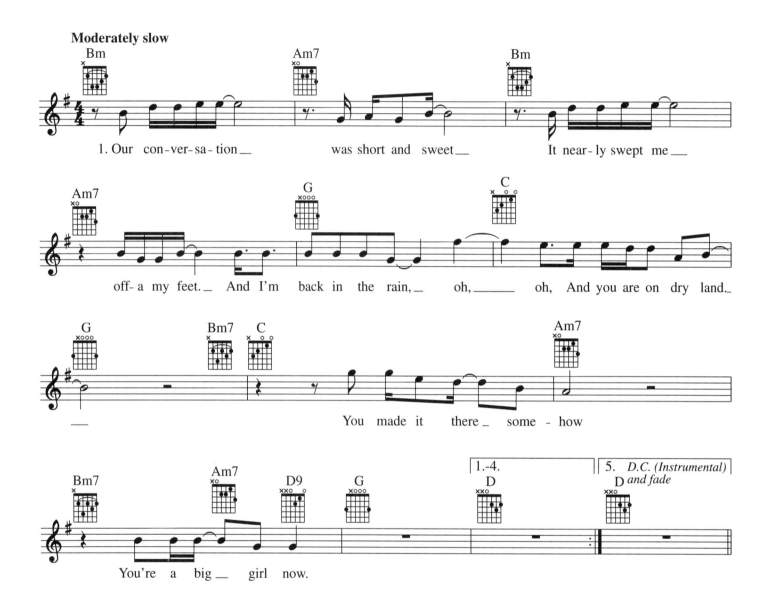

Moderately slow

1. Our con-ver-sa-tion __ was short and sweet __ It near-ly swept me __ off- a my feet. __ And I'm back in the rain, __ oh, _____ oh, And you are on dry land. __

__ You made it there __ some - how

You're a big __ girl now.

1.-4.

5. *D.C. (Instrumental) and fade*

Additional lyrics

2. Bird on the horizon, sittin' on a fence,
   He's singin' his song for me at his own expense.
   And I'm just like that bird, oh, oh,
   Singin' just for you.
   I hope that you can hear,
   Hear me singin' through these tears.

3. Time is a jet plane, it moves too fast
   Oh, but what a shame if all we've shared can't last.
   I can change, I swear, oh, oh,
   See what you can do.
   I can make it through,
   You can make it too.

4. Love is so simple, to quote a phrase,
   You've known it all the time, I'm learnin' it these days.
   Oh, I know where I can find you, oh, oh,
   In somebody's room.
   It's a price I have to pay
   You're a big girl all the way.

5. A change in the weather is known to be extreme
   But what's the sense of changing horses in midstream?
   I'm going out of my mind, oh, oh,
   With a pain that stops and starts
   Like a corkscrew to my heart
   Ever since we've been apart.

You're Gonna Make Me Lonesome When You Go

Words and Music by Bob Dylan

1. I've seen love go by my door It's never been this close before Never been so easy or so slow. Been shooting in the dark too long When somethin's not right it's wrong Yer gonna make me lonesome when you go.

2. Dragon clouds so high above I've only known careless love, It's always hit me from below. This time around it's more correct Right on target, so direct, Yer gonna make me lonesome when you go.

3. Purple clover, Queen Anne lace, Crimson hair across your face, You could make me cry if you don't know. Can't remember what I was thinkin' of You might be spoilin' me too much, love, Yer gonna make me wonder what I'm doin', Flowers on the hillside, bloomin' crazy, Yer gonna make me wonder what I'm doin', go.

You're Gonna Quit Me

Traditional, arranged by Bob Dylan

Additional lyrics

3. You're gonna quit me, baby,
   Put me outta doors, Lawd, Lawd.

Instrumental

4. Six months on the chain gang,
   Believe me, it ain't no fun, Lawd, Lawd.

5. Day you quit me, baby,
   That's the day you die, Lawd, Lawd.

6. Jailhouse ain't no plaything,
   Believe me, ain't no lie, Lawd, Lawd.

7. Day you quit me, baby,
   That's the day you die, Lawd, Lawd.

Instrumental

Wiggle Wiggle

Words and Music by Bob Dylan

Additional lyrics

Bridge #2:
Wiggle 'til you're high, wiggle 'til you're higher,
Wiggle 'til you vomit fire,
Wiggle 'til it whispers, wiggle 'til it hums,
Wiggle 'til it answers, wiggle 'til it comes.

Wiggle, wiggle, wiggle like satin and silk,
Wiggle, wiggle, wiggle like pail of milk,
Wiggle, wiggle, wiggle, rattle and shake,
Wiggle like a big fat snake.